Classical Antiquity and Medieval Ireland

Bloomsbury Studies in Classical Reception

Bloomsbury Studies in Classical Reception presents scholarly monographs offering new and innovative research and debate to students and scholars in the reception of Classical Studies. Each volume will explore the appropriation, reconceptualization and recontextualization of various aspects of the Graeco-Roman world and its culture, looking at the impact of the ancient world on modernity. Research will also cover reception within antiquity, the theory and practice of translation, and reception theory.

Classical Antiquity and Medieval Ireland

An Anthology of Medieval Irish Texts and Interpretations

Edited by Michael Clarke, Erich Poppe and
Isabelle Torrance

BLOOMSBURY ACADEMIC
LONDON • NEW YORK • OXFORD • NEW DELHI • SYDNEY

BLOOMSBURY ACADEMIC
Bloomsbury Publishing Plc, 50 Bedford Square, London, WC1B 3DP, UK
Bloomsbury Publishing Inc, 1359 Broadway, 12th Floor, New York, NY 10018, USA
Bloomsbury Publishing Ireland, 29 Earlsfort Terrace, Dublin 2, D02 AY28, Ireland

BLOOMSBURY, BLOOMSBURY ACADEMIC and the Diana logo are
trademarks of Bloomsbury Publishing Plc

First published in Great Britain 2024
Paperback edition published 2026

Cover design: Terry Woodley
Cover image: Detail from a manuscript of Boethius' *Consolation of Philosophy* written in an Irish hand
about 1140 CE, possibly at Glendalough. © Firenze, Biblioteca Laurenziana, MS Plut. 78. 19, fol. 4r,
reproduced by permission of the Biblioteca Laurenziana, Firenze

A catalogue record for this book is available from the British Library.

Library of Congress Cataloging-in-Publication Data
Names: Clarke, Michael (Michael J.), editor. | Poppe, Erich, editor. | Torrance, Isabelle C., editor.
Title: Classical antiquity and medieval Ireland : an anthology of medieval Irish texts and interpretations /
edited by Michael James Clarke, Erich Poppe and Isabelle Torrance.
Description: London ; New York : Bloomsbury Academic, 2024. |
Series: Bloomsbury studies in classical reception | Includes bibliographical references and index. |
Introduction and essays in English; work extracts in English, translated from the originl middle Irish.
Identifiers: LCCN 2023053561 (print) | LCCN 2023053562 (ebook) | ISBN 9781350333277 (hardback) |
ISBN 9781350333314 (paperback) | ISBN 9781350333284 (pdf) | ISBN 9781350333291 (ebook)
Subjects: LCSH: Irish literature–Middle Irish, 1100–1550–Classical influences. |
Irish literature–Middle Irish, 1100–1550–Texts. | Literature, Medieval–History and criticism.
Classification: LCC PB1322 .C48 2024 (print) | LCC PB1322 (ebook) |
DDC 891.6/209—dc23/eng/20240129
LC record available at https://lccn.loc.gov/2023053561
LC ebook record available at https://lccn.loc.gov/2023053562

ISBN: HB: 978-1-3503-3327-7
         PB: 978-1-3503-3331-4
         ePDF: 978-1-3503-3328-4
         eBook: 978-1-3503-3329-1

Series: Bloomsbury Studies in Classical Reception

Typeset by RefineCatch Limited, Bungay, Suffolk

To find out more about our authors and books visit www.bloomsbury.com
and sign up for our newsletters.

Contents

Illustrations

Contributors

Elizabeth Boyle is Lecturer in the Department of Early Irish at the National University of Ireland, Maynooth, where she was Head of Department from 2015–2020. She is interested in the intellectual, religious and cultural history of pre-modern Ireland and has published widely on these topics. Recent books include *History and Salvation in Medieval Ireland* (2021) and *Book of Uí Mhaine* (2023, edited with Ruairí Ó hUiginn). She is co-organizer of the medieval Irish manuscripts conferences hosted by the Royal Irish Academy.

Mariamne M. Briggs completed her PhD in Celtic Studies in 2019 at the University of Edinburgh. Her research interest is in the reception of classical epics in medieval Irish literature, particularly in the Middle Irish translation of Statius' epic *Thebaid,* and the scholia which circulated with it in the Middle Ages. She is currently developing work exploring the depiction of women in the Middle Irish *Thebaid*. Her research on 'Removing the Muses: Responses to Statian Subjectivity in the Middle Irish *Thebaid*' was published in *Crossing Borders in the Insular Middle Ages* (2019).

John Carey was educated at Harvard University, where he was subsequently appointed Associate Professor of Celtic Languages and Literatures. Thereafter he held research fellowships at the Warburg Institute (University of London), the Institute of Irish Studies (Queen's University Belfast) and the School of Celtic Studies (Dublin Institute for Advanced Studies); he is now Professor of Early and Medieval Irish at University College Cork. His books include *King of Mysteries: Early Irish Religious Writings* (1998, 2000), *A Single Ray of the Sun: Religious Speculation in Early Ireland* (1999, 2011), *Ireland and the Grail* (2007), *In Tenga Bithnua: The Ever-New Tongue* (2010), *The Mythological Cycle of Medieval Irish Literature* (2018) and *Magic, Metallurgy and Imagination in Medieval Ireland: Three Studies* (2019). He is a member of the Royal Irish Academy.

Michael Clarke is Established Professor of Classics at the University of Galway. His research ranges from classical and ancient epic to medieval Irish texts, on which he has published widely. Books include *Flesh and Spirit in the Songs of Homer* (1999), *Achilles Beside Gilgamesh* (2019) and *Medieval Multilingual Manuscripts: Case Studies from Ireland to Japan*, edited with Máire Ní Mhaonaigh (2022). His principal research target is the Third Recension of *Togail Troí*, which remains largely unpublished, along with wider work on heroic epic, language change and manuscript studies.

Robert Crampton is an independent scholar and a leading expert on the little-studied *Fingal Chlainne Tanntail* 'The Kin-Slaying of the Family of Tantalus', which was the subject of his PhD at the Department of Anglo-Saxon, Norse and Celtic, Cambridge University (2010), supervised by Máire Ní Mhaonaigh. He has also published on the uses of exaggeration in *Merugud Uilixis meic Leirtis* and *Fingal Chlainne Tanntail* in Ralph O'Connor (ed.) *Classical Literature and Learning in Medieval Irish Narrative* (2014).

Gregory R. Darwin is Senior Lecturer in Irish in the department of English at Uppsala University, where he teaches courses on medieval and modern Irish language and literature. Originally from Toronto, Canada, he earned a PhD in Celtic Languages and Literatures from Harvard University in 2019 and has previously held positions at Université de Bretagne Occidentale and Aarhus University. His research interests include the folklore of Ireland and Gaelic Scotland, migratory legends of the supernatural, popular magical belief, medieval and modern Irish-language poetry, and classical reception in early modern Ireland, and he has published a number of articles on these topics. Currently, he is in the process of preparing his first monograph, on marriage between humans and beings from the sea in Gaelic and Nordic tradition.

Brigid Ehrmantraut completed her PhD in the Department of Anglo-Saxon, Norse and Celtic at the University of Cambridge. Her first monograph *Classical Myth in Medieval Ireland* (2025) focused on the reception of classical mythology in medieval Ireland between the tenth and twelfth centuries, situating the adaptation and translation of classical epic within a medieval Christian worldview. Her research interests include classical reception, the languages and literatures of medieval Britain and Ireland, and intellectual history. She is currently Associate Lecturer in Latin and in the History of the British Isles, c. 1100–1500 at the University of St Andrews.

Nicolai Egjar Engesland is currently (2025–2027) a Taighde Éireann – Research Ireland Government of Ireland Postdoctoral Fellow (GOIPD/2025/1365) in the Department of Early and Medieval Irish, University College Cork. He is preparing a critical edition and translation of the 'Lower Connacht Recension' of *Auraicept na nÉces* under the mentorship of Kevin Murray. The edition will build on the monoptic editions he prepared under Research Council of Norway grant no. 324 602. Engesland's primary research interests include the history of linguistic thought in medieval Ireland and Iceland, as well as the history of Old West Norse as elucidated by Irish sources. He has taught Old Irish for Roinn na Gaeilge, University of Galway (2022–2023), and is the academic consultant for Celtic languages and onomastics for *Store norske leksikon* (2021–).

Barbara Hillers is Associate Professor in Folklore at Indiana University, Bloomington; previously she taught at the Edinburgh University, Harvard, and, most recently, at University College Dublin. She has co-edited two books, *Child's Children: Ballad Study and Its Legacies* (2012) and *Charms, Charmers and Charming in Ireland: From the Medieval to the Modern* (2020). Many of her publications on oral narrative and song investigate medieval and modern continuities and the interplay between the oral and the written in Gaelic tradition. She has written a number of articles on the *Wandering of Ulysses* (*Merugud Uilixis*) and on other aspects of the Irish classical adaptations.

Peadar Mac Gabhann (Peter Smith) is Reader in Irish at Ulster University. His broad-ranging research interest include the Irish manuscript tradition, medieval Irish learning, medieval Irish poetry, Early Modern Irish prose and verse (1200-1650), eighteenth-century Ulster poetry, the Irish folk song tradition in Irish and in English, Modern Irish dialectology and Irish historiography. Significant publications on the genre and poetics of medieval Irish historical verse include 'Eochaid Úa Flainn's Éitset Áes Ecna Aíbind and Medieval Irish Poetics' in *Adapting Texts and Styles in a Celtic Context* (2016), 'An Edition of Tigernmas mac Follaig aird' in *Clerics, Kings and Vikings* (2015), 'A eolcha Érenn airde: a medieval poem on the pre-Christian kings of Ireland' (*Zeitschrift für celtische Philologie*, 2013) and *Politics and Land in Early Ireland* (2013). He is currently preparing a critical edition of Flann Mainistrech's poem *Flaithius Rómán ríge glonn* (which features in this volume).

Brent Miles works principally in the areas of medieval Celtic languages and literatures, with strong secondary interests in Anglo- and Hiberno-Latin and classical literature in the medieval curriculum. He has published very widely in these areas, including *Heroic Saga and Classical Epic in Medieval Ireland* (2011) and *Don Tres Troí: The Middle Irish History of the Third Troy* (2020). He has held teaching posts in Ireland and Poland, and currently teaches Medieval and Celtic Studies at the University of Toronto.

Máire Ní Mhaonaigh is Professor of Celtic and Medieval Studies at the University of Cambridge and a Fellow of St John's College. She has published widely on medieval Irish literature and history, as well as on early Irish, British and Scandinavian connections and medieval Ireland's place in a wider European world. She is involved with a number of major research projects, including the electronic Dictionary of medieval Irish (www.dil.ie), and currently leads work on medieval Irish *dindshenchas* (literature of place). In 2023, she was elected an Honorary Member of the Royal Irish Academy in recognition of her outstanding contribution to scholarship.

Maio Nagashima is a PhD candidate in the Department of Anglo-Saxon, Norse and Celtic at the University of Cambridge. He completed his MA in Classics at the University of Tokyo in 2018 and his BA in English at Tokyo University of Foreign Studies in 2015. His chief interests lie in the European intellectual milieu in which medieval Irish adaptations of classical texts were produced. His doctoral research explores the manuscript tradition of *In Cath Catharda*, the late twelfth- or early thirteenth-century Irish adaptation of Lucan's *Bellum Civile*, and the influence of the contemporaneous exegesis on the production and transmission of the vernacular Irish version.

Ralph O'Connor is Professor in the Literature and Culture of Britain, Ireland and Iceland at the University of Aberdeen, where he teaches in the departments of Gaelic, History and English. His research concerns narratives of the distant past in medieval Gaelic literature, medieval and early modern Norse-Icelandic sagas, and modern science. Among other books, he is the author of *The Earth on Show: Fossils and the Poetics of Popular Science, 1802–1856* (2007) and *The Destruction of Da Derga's Hostel: Kingship and Narrative Artistry in a Mediaeval Irish Saga* (2013), and the editor of *Classical Literature and Learning in Medieval Irish Narrative* (2014). He is currently completing a book comparing the concept of the saga in medieval Gaelic and Norse-Icelandic narrative traditions.

Cillian O'Hogan is Assistant Professor at the Centre for Medieval Studies, University of Toronto. His research interests are late antique and medieval Latin poetry, history of the book, translation in the Middle Ages (especially Greek-Latin and Latin-Irish), and the transmission and reception of classical and late antique literature in the Middle Ages. Publications include the monograph *Prudentius and the Landscapes of Late Antiquity* (2016), as well as articles and book chapters on a number of classical, late antique and medieval texts and manuscripts. He is currently completing a book on Latin poetry from 300 to 1000 CE and his next project is a large-scale study of the transmission and reception of Prudentius in the Middle Ages.

Erich Poppe was Professor of Celtic Languages and Literatures at the University of Marburg (Germany) until his retirement in spring 2017. His main scholarly interests are strategies of translation and textual transfer in medieval Ireland and Wales, the impact of translations on their target languages and cultures, medieval Irish literary theory, Middle and Early Modern Welsh syntax and style, and the history of Celtic Studies. He has published on the Irish versions of Virgil's *Aeneid* and of Lucan's *Bellum Civile*, on the fifteenth-century translations associated with Uilliam Mac an Leagha, and on Irish texts about Arthur and Charlemagne. He currently conducts research on the language of medieval Welsh translations from Latin transmitted in the fourteenth-century 'Book of the Anchorite' and on Early Modern Welsh translations within the Priority Programme 'Early Modern Translation Cultures (1450–1800)' of the German Research Foundation.

Marie-Luise Theuerkauf is a Research Associate in the Department of Celtic Languages and Literatures at Harvard University. A graduate of University College Cork, she has held research positions at the Dublin Institute for Advanced Studies, Trinity College Dublin, and the University of Cambridge. Her research focuses on classical reception in medieval Irish literature and on Irish origin legends. Her first monograph, Dindshenchas Érenn, was published by University College Cork in 2023.

Isabelle Torrance is Professor of Classical Reception at the Department of English, Aarhus University, and Director of the Centre for Irish Studies. She is Principal Investigator of the ERC project 'Classical Influences and Irish Culture' (grant no. 818366). She has published numerous articles and seven books on classical literature and its reception, most recently the co-edited volume *Classics and Irish Politics, 1916–2016* (2020).

Patrick Wadden is Professor of History at Belmont Abbey College, North Carolina. Since completing his doctoral studies at the University of Oxford in 2012, he has published widely on the history and learned culture of early medieval Ireland and Britain. Medieval history writing is one of his primary research interests. He is the co-editor, with Lindy Brady, of *Origin Legends in Early Medieval Western Europe* (2022).

Cameron Wachowich is Teaching Associate in Modern Irish at the Department of Anglo-Saxon, Norse and Celtic in the University of Cambridge. He completed a PhD at the Centre for Medieval Studies in the University of Toronto in 2024. His doctoral dissertation focused on the transmission and reception of Orosius' *Historiae adversus Paganos* in Ireland, Britain and the wider Insular world. He also holds a BA (Hons) from the University of Toronto in Celtic Studies and MAs from the Universities of Galway and Toronto in Old and Middle Irish and Medieval Studies respectively. He has published on Irish classical reception, the reception of Arthurian literature in Irish bardic poetry, as well as the enigmatic word *ormesta*. His interests include medieval literature both Latin and vernacular, historical linguistics and textual criticism.

Daniel James Watson is Bergin Fellow at the Dublin Institute for Advanced Studies. He works primarily on the history of philosophy and theology, with a focus on early medieval Ireland. He is currently editing an epitome of Eriugena's *Periphyseon* found in Oxford, Bodleian Library MS Auct. F. 3.15, which was composed in Ireland during the twelfth century. He is also co-editing the volume *Irish Platonisms*, forthcoming with Bloomsbury, which traces the history of Platonic influences on Irish authors, and writing a monograph on early medieval Irish vernacular philosophy. Recent publications include peer reviewed articles on Mongán mac Fiachnai (*Celtica*, 2020), on the prologue to *Senchas Már* (*Dionysius*, 2018), and on Proclus' commentary on Plato's *Republic* (*International Journal of the Platonic Tradition*, 2017).

Acknowledgements

This volume is the result of a seedling planted in the project 'Classical Influences and Irish Culture', funded by the European Research Council (grant no. 818366) and hosted at the Centre for Irish Studies, Aarhus University, Denmark (2019–25). The project recognized the medieval period as a significant phase of Irish classicism and created a dedicated post-doctoral position in this area (taken up by contributor Daniel Watson), but the scale and scope of medieval Irish engagements with classical antiquity had been vastly underestimated. This became clear through a series of inspiring encounters and conversations driven by collegiality and curiosity, a fortuitous result of our ERC project seminars being forced online by the Covid-19 pandemic. Of the regular work-in-progress seminars run by the ERC project from 2019 to 2022, those with medieval content were the best attended, with close to fifty attendees at a peak. Virtually all of the contributors to this volume had either shared their own work through this platform or given their expert feedback on the work of others as seminar participants before the volume was conceived. Our network came to encompass scholars at all career stages from across Europe, North America and even reaching Japan.

The volume itself has arisen from a workshop-style conference held at Aarhus University in late August 2022, which was generously supported by a Carlsberg Foundation Conference Grant (CF21-0694) and attended by over one hundred participants thanks to hybrid facilities. Conceptually, the conference was a testing ground for pre-agreed contributions to this anthology, whose format is the result of Michael Clarke's vision for opening up the field in line with the overall goals of the ERC project. A further visionary move by Michael was recruiting a senior Celticist to our side, and we were both delighted when Erich Poppe agreed, with characteristic generosity and good will, to expand his responsibilities from contributor to co-editor. Armed with three editors in different fields – a Classicist with long involvement in medieval Irish studies (Clarke), a senior Celticist and mentor to many of the other contributors (Poppe) and a Classical Reception Studies scholar (Torrance) – we hoped that we would have all our bases covered. In the face of the overwhelming quantity of relevant texts, it is safe to say that we have, of course, not been able to cover all bases. A major challenge of this volume has been to select an array of excerpts from the most important texts that allow for a mostly brief but representative sample of material, along with explication, yet are substantial enough to give a flavour of the style and function of the works. We might have included more synchronistic poetry, for instance, perhaps some verse sections from the Irish *Sex Aetates Mundi* 'Six Ages of the World', or added further excerpts from the important and little-studied *Scéla Alaxandair* 'The Saga of Alexander'. No doubt there are other desiderata. At the same time, we must acknowledge, with extreme gratitude, the generosity of all the scholars who have contributed to this book, each with particular expertise in their specific texts and together producing a work of scholarship that is far more than the sum of its parts. With precious little if any time for such commitments, all of our invited contributors have delivered their chapters with scholarly rigour, extraordinary good will and an open-mindedness that has made the editorial process a rare pleasure.

To Alice Wright at Bloomsbury we owe a significant debt of gratitude for her willingness to produce our volume in the Studies in Classical Reception series, regardless of its atypical content and format in the context of that series; we hope our volume will generate further analyses of medieval literature as Classical Reception. To Lily MacMahon and Zoe Osman, who took over from Alice, we are also indebted for their patience and professionalism. The Open Access publication costs for this book have been covered by the European Research Council (grant no. 818366). It is a great pleasure to acknowledge that support.

Isabelle Torrance (Aarhus, Sankt Hans 2023)

A Guide to Editorial Practices for Middle Irish Texts

Michael Clarke

The principal language of the texts in this anthology is Middle Irish, the Celtic variety that flourished in Ireland and much of Scotland in the period stretching (roughly) from 900 to 1200 CE. Most of our texts are from the later end of that range. Only occasionally do we print Old Irish from before *c.* 900 (see Ch. 23), while in Ch. 22 in particular we include material in Early Modern Irish, which is roughly coeval with Middle English.

The terms 'Middle' and 'Irish' need a little explanation. The name by which the medieval speech-community called themselves was *Goídil*, 'Gaels', and hence the clearest technical label for the language is *Goidelic* or 'Gaelic'. In Scotland, 'Gaelic' continues to be used routinely for all stages of the language, and 'Gaels' for its speakers. In Ireland and elsewhere, however, the term 'Irish' is nearly always preferred – a choice originally made in the late nineteenth century, associated with the Gaelic League's campaign to restore it as the national speech of the country. Throughout its history in the island, however, the language has always co-existed and interacted with others, notably Latin, Norse, French and English in different ways and in different periods. 'Middle', too, is a slippery word, because there are no decisive break-points in the history of the language. The manuscript evidence is usually ambiguous, and forms conventionally associated with different phases of development are seen alongside each other, even within a single sentence. Scribes were poised between passive copying, systematic modernization and the adoption of an archaizing traditional register or *Kunstsprache*. This affects the practices followed by the editor of any text, because there is no room for standardization of the kind familiar (for example) in editions of classical Greek, Latin, Old English, or Old Norse literature.

The published editions

The Middle Irish literary achievement was barely known before the late Victorian age, when an astonishing burst of activity by scholars of the 'heroic age' – Whitley

Stokes, Kuno Meyer, George Calder and others – led to the production of editions and translations that often remain authoritative. Because of the sheer urgency of their project, those scholars worked hastily, with no lexicon, reference grammar or set of editorial norms for guidance. For all their brilliance, the early published editions are often unreliable in detail and inconsistent with each other in terms of editorial technique. Despite the gradual appearance of new editions prepared to modern scholarly standards, in many cases the works of the heroic age remain the sole authority, while some of the texts have still not been fully published at all.

In preparing the selections for this book, each text called for its own editorial strategy. In some cases the contributor has been able to draw on an edition that they themselves have published previously. In others, we have worked directly from the manuscript evidence, sometimes presenting a transcription from a single witness rather than collating them all. Often the most practicable course has been to reproduce unchanged the text published by another scholar, sometimes a recent predecessor but more often Stokes or one of his contemporaries. Again, sometimes we present an 'interim edition' updated from the published version in light of a preliminary reassessment of the manuscript, but likely to be superseded once a fuller study of the text has been made. In each case the subtitle of the extract indicates the strategy adopted; and the range of policies seen there is a reminder of the sheer scale of the practical philological work that remains to be done.

The translations

Similar principles apply to the facing translations. Subtitles clarify whether we are printing our own original work, the work of peers and predecessors, or a reproduction or revision of an earlier publication. Many of the earlier scholars, notably Stokes, used 'Wardour Street English', named after a London street formerly notorious for the trade in fake antiques (Fowler 1906: 122; the term was originally used of the false archaisms in William Morris's translations from ancient and medieval heroic literature). Waves become *billows*, body-armour is a *corslet* and *cunning folk* means sorcerers; syntax and sentence structure tend towards the obscure. Often these old translations have been re-used, updated, or replaced according to what seemed most useful and most practicable. Where we ourselves have translated directly from the sources, what we offer here is often an interim version, reflecting the emerging but incomplete state of knowledge in the field.

Treatment of manuscripts

The medieval Irish scribe is seldom a mere copyist; more often he is *fer léiginn* 'the man of learning', and his work may well represent creative scholarship rather than passive transmission (see further Johnston 2013, especially pp. 99–101). This, coupled with the absence of standardization in the literary language itself, tends nowadays to encourage very close fidelity to the minutiae of the manuscript data. Modern editions reproduce the transmitted spellings, and carefully *italicize* wherever words and parts of words have been expanded from scribal contractions. Stokes and his contemporaries were much more likely to standardize spellings and to expand contractions silently, and they often did so inconsistently from one case to another. Here again, our individual strategies vary according to the nature of each textual challenge. In many cases, expanded contractions have been printed without italicization, especially in cases where we have adapted from an earlier publication, or with poetry in which the strict count of syllables and the rules of metrical ornamentation act as a control on variation. Stricter practices are often on display where our contributor has followed modern norms while editing afresh from a manuscript.

Palaeographical challenges

Many of the manuscripts that preserve our texts are beautiful artefacts, and their scribal conventions are astonishingly regular and consistent over many hundreds of years of text-production, both with Irish and with Latin. However, the long and shifting history of Irish pronunciation and orthography presents countless challenges. For the purposes of this book, it is particularly noteworthy that the manuscripts vary widely in the extent to which they give a graphic indication of the three key types of sound-mutation in the language. These are (a) the mutation of consonantal sounds by lenition (informally known as 'aspiration', Modern Irish *séimhiú*), (b) nasalization ('eclipsis', *urú*), which is effectively the voicing of unvoiced consonants and the nasalization of voiced, and (c) the prefixing of aspiration (*h-*) to word-initial vowels. These mutations are pervasive, playing a major role in case-grammar and syntax, and their use has shifted through time and through dialect variation. The tendency to lenite and eventually simplify consonantal sounds or clusters of sounds, especially in medial and final position, has spread progressively over time, driven by changing orthographic conventions as much as by the living realities of pronunciation. Such features are marked only sporadically in the manuscripts, and this variability continues in published editions. As a general rule, where manuscripts mark lenition they do so with a raised dot over the letter (*punctum delens*), while editions represent this with a following *h*, just as in standard Modern Irish spelling. Nasalization is usually represented by inserting the voiced equivalent where the base consonant is voiceless, and inserting a nasal where the base consonant is voiced: thus *c, t, b, d* change respectively to *gc, dt, mb, nd*, and in pronunciation the first (eclipsing) consonant is the dominant one. Very often, however, the manuscripts do not show the expected mutations, and it is left to the reader to supply them in pronunciation; conversely, the mutated sound may be shown on its own, so that the identity of the underlying one must be inferred by the listener or reader.

Contractions

Gaelic script is characterized by a profusion of conventional signs (Latin *notae*, Irish *noda*), many of them originating in the set of *notae Tironianae* traditionally ascribed to Cicero's secretary Tiro. Interpreting these signs can be tricky, as with the following common examples:

Nod	Latin	Irish	meaning-values	sound-values
⁊	*et*	*ocus*	'and'	*et, ed, eth, edh, ocus*
ꝼ̄	*sed*	*acht*	'but'	*acht, sed, sedh, set, sett*
.⁊.	*id est*	*edhón*	'that is …', 'namely …'	*edon, edhon, idhon*

In a given instance, the first of these signs could be read as Latin *et*, or as Irish *ocus*, or as a language-neutral symbol of co-ordination, like the mathematical symbol '+'. Alternatively, it might be a purely phonetic unit, representing the sound-shapes seen in the word *et* or the word *ocus*. This principle applies in the same way to all such signs. For example, although *.i.* is usually a logical connective introducing an example or explanation of the point made immediately beforehand, similar to modern 'i.e …', it can also stand for a pure sound. The sequence *laim.i.*, ostensibly 'hand, therefore …', on at least one occasion needs to be sounded out as *laimedon* – none other than *Laomedon*, king of Troy (in *Scéla Alaxandair*, Book of Ballymote; see Peters 1967: 102, line 2). Alongside major symbols like these, letters are variegated by more minor *noda*, forming a range of straight and curved lines and strokes representing the sounds that follow (or occasionally precede) the letter in question.

To gain an initial sense of how the system works, readers may find it useful to begin by examining the text, mostly in Latin, from the *Annals of Tigernach* (Ch. 3), and comparing the visible configuration in the script of the sole surviving manuscript (Figure 1). Patrick Wadden has here silently expanded the contractions, in the course of producing an edition that serves as an updated revision of that published by Whitley Stokes in 1895. Turning to a text edited in the modern manner by one of our contributors, compare Barbara Hillers' edition of *Merugud Uilixis* (Ch. 18), which sets out to represent precisely the manuscript data of the Book of Ballymote (Figure 6), italicizing all expansions and adjustments. Each of our contributors' editorial practices are located somewhere on the scale of variation represented by these two examples.

The Irish verb

Special challenges are raised by the complexity of the Irish verb-system and its changes over time. In Old Irish, the paradigm of a given verb is liable to include a bewildering variety of surface forms. Much of the variation is triggered by shifts in the tonal centre of the word, usually due to the presence of preverbal particles (*no, ro, do* etc) marking tense or mood, or to the addition of prefixes to form compound verbs with new meanings of their own. Many paradigms also include suppletive stems originally unconnected to the main stem of the verb in question. Additionally, pronominal elements representing the direct object of the verb are inserted ('infixed') between preverbal particle and stem. In Middle Irish and beyond, this system becomes progressively simplified, often seeing the replacement of old forms by means of a new verb-stem built on the basis of the verbal noun, which had served as a quasi-infinitive in the Old Irish paradigm of the verb in question. Infixed pronouns gradually become obsolete, supplanted by independent pronouns placed after the verb as in the modern language. Nonetheless many remnants of the old system persist, especially in the most basic-level verbs, where they abound as virtual fossils; and some of these remnants survive to this day in the conjugational patterns of the 'irregular verbs' of modern Irish. The verb-systems of the texts in this book include examples from all stages of this history of development.

For dealing with the verb, modern editors have a variety of conventions for representing the link between a preverbal element and the main stem: sometimes a raised dot or *punctum* (˙) is used, sometimes the editor inserts a hyphen, and sometimes the preverbal particle is printed as if joined to the stem with no indication of a separation between the two. This diversity is maintained in the range of text selections printed here.

Using this anthology

Each text extract presented in this book is the result of a negotiation based on the art of the possible, balancing practicability with respect for the manuscript data. The list of editorial symbols below shows the resources most commonly used to indicate editors' adjustments to the raw data of their manuscripts. We have deployed these symbols only to the extent that seemed useful in each instance, and they tend to appear especially fully where the contributor has worked directly from a single manuscript. Elsewhere, where there was little or no doubt about the expansion of a contracted spelling, italics have often been silently omitted; and where an already-published edition has been followed directly, the practices of its original editor have normally been repeated (often in a simplified form).

Further reading

For the lexical data of the medieval Irish language in all its stages, the electronic *Dictionary of the Irish Language* (*eDIL*, www.dil.ie) is the standard resource. McCone (2005: 12–19) gives a convenient brief introduction to spelling and pronunciation. Stifter (2006) provides an excellent philological introduction to the Old Irish language, keyed generally to its earliest attested stages; the same author's survey essay (2009) is invaluable when used alongside it for correlating the details with the overview. For Middle Irish, the standard survey by Breatnach (2006) can be supplemented by McCone (2005: 173–218).

There are two traditional routes to fluency in Middle Irish. The first depends upon first acquiring a basic grounding in Old Irish. With that basis, one can then adapt inductively by working through a learner-oriented edition of a Middle Irish text. Ideal for this purpose is Kenneth Jackson's edition of *Aislinge Meic Con Glinne* 'The Vision of Mac Con Glinne' (1990), which includes an invaluable language guide (73–140) that draws the reader from Old Irish norms to those of his text. The same scholar's edition of *Cath Maighe Léna* 'The Battle of Mag Léna' (1938), with full vocabulary listings, draws the reader further towards the norms of the later period. Alternatively, the learner who has Modern Irish can model Middle Irish practices by 'splitting the difference' between Old and Modern, perhaps using as a reference point the lightly archaizing style of the early seventeenth-century historian Geoffrey Keating in his monumental history of Ireland, *Foras Feasa ar Éirinn* (Comyn and Dinneen 1902–14).

Neither of the above methods is perfect. To immerse oneself directly in the texts on which this book is based, the best resource to begin with will probably be Calder's edition of *Imtheachta Aeniasa* 'The Wanderings of Aeneas' (also known as 'The Irish *Aeneid*', Calder 1907), whose spellings usually respond well to searches in *eDIL*. It is an added bonus that the reader accustomed to Virgil will be well equipped to see the medieval scholar-author's compositional strategy in action. The vocabulary list in Calder's edition of *Togail na Tebe* 'The Siege of Thebes' (Calder 1922) is invaluable for lexical study. For the manuscripts themselves, the Irish Script on Screen website (https://www.isos.dias.ie/) can be explored with the aid of the invaluable collection of manuscript contractions and other symbols assembled by the Van Hamel Foundation for Celtic Studies under the title *Tionscadal na Nod* (https://codecs.vanhamel.nl/Show:Tionscadal_na_Nod).

Principal symbols used in the presentation of manuscript data

ḟ, ṡ, etc	The dot over the letter (Latin *punctum delens*) indicates that the consonant is reduced by lenition (Modern Irish *séimhiú*).
á, é, í etc	The vowel is marked with an accent, usually visible in the manuscript(s).
ā, ē, ī etc	The editor has supplied the indication of a long vowel.
italics	An abbreviation (Latin *nota*, Irish *nod*) has been expanded by the editor.
[ ]	There is a gap (lacuna) in the manuscript(s).
[text]	The editor has supplied text to fill a lacuna.
< text >	The editor has supplied material omitted by the scribe.
(text)	The words in brackets are a marginal gloss/scholion in the manuscript.

Where additional symbols have been used, or any different convention followed, this is explained in the individual contribution. In all cases, punctuation and capitalization have been added or standardized by the editor. In the translations, proper names have been standardized to the usual English form, except in cases of doubt over the identification, where the manuscript spelling is retained.

Part One

Introduction

1

The Culture of the Book and Classical Learning in the Gaelic Middle Ages

Michael Clarke and Máire Ní Mhaonaigh

The texts presented in this book form part of the vast range of composition, re-composition, and manuscript transmission that characterized Gaelic learning in the Middle Ages. The origins of the earliest work in our anthology, *Auraicept na nÉces* 'The Scholars' Primer', stretch back into the Old Irish period, perhaps as far as the eighth or ninth century (Ch. 23), and there are elements of continuity, as well as diversity, from then down to the late fifteenth century, which saw the composition of the latest text presented here, *Stair Ercuil ocus a Bás* 'The Life and Death of Hercules', probably from a printed book in English that was itself derived from a Burgundian narrative in French (see below, and Ch. 22). These pole texts, and the range of narratives on the chronological spectrum in between, reflect an established book culture that was dynamic and varied, responding to changing social and political circumstances, as well as participating in currents of scholarship and creativity seen across Europe right through the period.

The ultimate origins of the textual communities of medieval Ireland are bound up with the coming of Christianity in the fifth century. In Ireland, as everywhere else in Europe beyond the limits of the Roman Empire, Christianity brought with it the authority of texts in a learned language, represented in this case by the prestige status of the Latin-language codex. From the beginning, however, the relationship between conversion and literacy was not a simple one of cause and effect (Edwards and Ní Mhaonaigh 2017: 5–8), and there was a level of literacy (albeit limited) in Ireland even before Christianization took root (Johnston 2013: 11–13). Nonetheless, it was in the early Christian period that the Roman alphabet and the codex format were adopted, and thereafter – how early remains unclear – highly sophisticated approaches in the art of biblical interpretation were applied in Irish monastic schools (Stansbury 2016), involving codification in the form of commentaries and exegetical glossing (Moran and Whitman 2022). This science extended to the study of grammatical texts as well, including the extraordinary corpus of glosses in mixed Latin and Old Irish on one of the principal surviving manuscripts of Priscian's treatise on the Latin language (Hofman 1988, Moran 2012, Moran 2015); and Latin glosses to Virgil in Continental transmission show signs of significant contributions by scholars whose first language was Old Irish.[1]

Throughout Europe, the recurring pattern is that in each region (at different times) Christian textuality went on to stimulate the production and transmission of a new literature in the vernacular language of the converted (cf. Mortensen 2018 on the wider European context). In the case of medieval Ireland, this meant that Latin book-learning became the springboard for new modes of text-production in Old Irish. In one crucial respect, however, the Irish response to the embrace of ecclesiastical book-culture was unusual: the recording and canonization of literature in the indigenous language took place soon after the conversion period, and Old Irish was being treated as a learned book-language in its own right before many neighbouring vernaculars. Only in the case of Old English is there evidence for limited vernacular writing also from the seventh century (see Godden 2012, 586–8); the question of the date of the earliest British poetry remains contested (see Lewis 2022, 59–63). The rich evidence from Ireland represents the work of a learned elite, involving both clerics and the protégés of secular nobility and kings (Johnston 2013: 14–23).

The sense of an enmeshed dialogue between the ecclesiastical and the secular, and between Irish-language subtlety and Latinate erudition, continues as a theme into the Middle Irish period and beyond. Texts often represent their lore and science as the result of a negotiation between secular and ecclesiastical spheres of power. As early as the Old Irish period, the Prologue to the great legal compilation *Senchas Már* (its name translates roughly as 'The Great Knowledge') dramatizes a meeting under the newly-converted king Lóegaire between the clerics of the new dispensation, led by St Patrick, and the scholars of the indigenous old order, at which they negotiate a balanced relationship between the old law of unguided pagan humanity (*recht aicnid* 'law of nature'), and the divinely-sanctioned Law of the Christian Church (Carey 1994a, Wadden 2016b). Within the Middle Irish corpus there is a similar narrative frame for *Dindshenchas Érenn*, 'Knowledge of Ireland's Notable Places' (see Chs 27 and 28). At the opening it is explained that the *Dindshenchas* originated at an assembly involving a king of Tara, a bishop of Armagh (in other words, St Patrick's successor), and the poets and people of Ireland. Pre-eminent among them was the sage or scholarly master (*suí*) Fintan mac Bóchra, whose preternatural lifespan enabled him to recount all the origin-tales of Ireland's toponyms from the island's first settlement down to the text's narrative present (Stokes 1894–95: 1894, 277–8). Fintan mac Bóchra was a survivor of the Flood and was kin to Noah (Bondarenko 2012); his biblical associations construct a framework of global significance around the often minutely detailed local traditions that he is said to recount. Later in this book we will see him again in a different context, called upon to apply his primeval knowledge to fixing the boundaries of the centre of royal and even numinous power over the island (Ch. 29). A similar pattern of continuity is at play in the celebrated work from the beginning of the thirteenth century and thus the very end of the Middle Irish period, *Acallam na Senórach,* traditionally known in English as 'The Colloquy of the Ancients' but perhaps more naturally rendered 'The Elders in Conversation'. Its tales about the warriors of Finn mac Cumaill, supposedly describing events of the later third century CE, are communicated to Patrick and his followers by a spectral revenant from the ancient times of the warrior-bands (*fíanna*) themselves. Patrick interrupts the flow of the tales to ask his guardian angels whether it is proper for their religious duties to be interrupted in this way, but the angels reassure him that it is right for the tales to be preserved and 'written on poets' tablets in refined language, so that the hearing of them will provide entertainment for the lords and commons of later times' (tr. Dooley and Roe 1999: 12; see Stokes 1900a: 9, lines 297–302, with Murray 2017: 33).

In all this, the evocation of the remote past of Ireland serves to explain and make intelligible the realities of the present. A marked characteristic of medieval Irish literature is what Frank O'Connor famously called 'the backward look':[2] what was presented as older knowledge and tradition about Ireland and its people, mediated in the texts by the authority of scholar or *literatus* (Old Irish *senchaid,* 'historian', related to *senchas* 'lore, knowledge') and often framed by the fictive agency of a supernatural revenant like Fintan or Patrick in the examples mentioned above (Nagy 1997: 1–22 and *passim*). Less familiar in modern reception is the *outward look,* the medieval Irish scholars' effort to transmit, extend, and recreate in their own language the knowledge and traditions of the world as a whole, with Graeco-Roman antiquity located close to its centre, alongside the master narrative of salvation history (Ní Mhaonaigh 2001, Boyle 2021).

In itself, there is nothing unique about medieval Gaelic interest in the past of the famous peoples of Mediterranean Europe. The same themes can be seen looming large in the historiographical projects of any of the new nations of Europe in the period, from the Carolingian realms to the rise of the courtly library in the France of the Valois (Spiegel 2002: 84-7), but the Irish version is unusual. Here as elsewhere in Christendom the fundamental reference source was the Chronicle of Eusebius-Jerome, which arranged the linear history of each ancient people – Assyrians, Hebrews, Romans, Athenians and so on – in parallel columns, formulated by time-reckoning since Abraham and the first holder of 'world-kingship', Ninus son of Belus of the Assyrians (Burgess 2002, Burgess and Kulikowski 2013, Boyle 2021: 118–50). What is striking about the Irish scholars in the 'long eleventh century' is the care with which they coordinated the placing of the real or mythical events of the Irish past within the same scheme, almost as if the history of Ireland and its kingship lists were being assembled in a new column added to the Chronicle (O'Sullivan 2021, Clarke 2023). In this project the peoples of biblical and Graeco-Roman tradition – effectively, those within the historical horizons defined by Jerusalem, Athens, Troy and Rome – served to define and contextualize the history of the people of what might be perceived as a remote island in the western Ocean. Irish history and identity found meaning in this global context, and in that sense the literature was profoundly cosmopolitan (Ní Mhaonaigh 2017b and 2023). The chronicles and historical poetry exhibited in the first part of this book are witnesses to this (Chs 3, 4 and 5).

Early documentary sources for medieval Irish intellectual life are dominated by just three monumental manuscripts. The first, *Lebor na hUidre* 'The Book of the Dun Cow' (*c.* 1100) bears witness to the themes described above at the simplest level of layout. Its sequence of texts was planned so that *Sex Aetates Mundi* 'Six Ages of the World', the theologically-informed account of world history from Creation to the Incarnation and thus to the dominion of the Romans in the Sixth Age, was juxtaposed with the account of the origins of the Irish in *Lebor Gabála Érenn* 'The Book of Invasions of Ireland', although *Lebor Gabála* no longer survives in the manuscript's current form (Ní Mhaonaigh 2017b: 61–3). The next-earliest extant codex, MS Rawlinson B502 in the Bodleian Library, Oxford, exhibits the same theme through translation as well as parallelism. The most ambitious work preserved in it is the extraordinary poetic sequence *Saltair na Rann* 'The Psalter of the Quatrains', which crystallizes the narrative sweep of salvation history from Creation to the Last Judgement in the precise metrical forms of Irish syllabic verse. The third codex, the so-called 'Book of Leinster' (Dublin, TCD MS 1339, *c.* 1150–1200), represents an emerging canon of medieval Irish literature in prose and verse, again beginning with *Lebor Gabála* and later including two thematically intertwined monuments of heroic narrative. On the one hand, we have *Táin Bó Cúailnge* 'The Cattle-Raid of Cooley', the central narrative of the deeds of the Ulster warriors about the time of

Augustus (cf. Ch. 3). On the other hand, it also includes the earliest surviving manuscript copy of *Togail Troí* 'The Siege of Troy', which narrates the Trojan War (see Chs 6–10). As we will see in detail later in this book, the two texts were understood fundamentally in historical terms, and the stylistic register and imaginative repertoire of the two sagas move towards something like a generic unity (Miles 2011 and Ch. 7 in this volume; cf. O'Connor 2013: 228–49).

A cluster of other surviving manuscripts come from the later fourteenth and fifteenth centuries, and the more ambitious among them serve as virtual encyclopedias of Irish and international world-knowledge. The classic example is the Book of Ballymote (Dublin, RIA MS 23 P 12) of *c.* 1390 CE. It begins with a much expanded and elaborated version of *Sex Aetates Mundi*, and it preserves copies of many of the antiquity-sagas that dominate the present book. The manuscript's focus on historiography, and the balance between outward-looking and Ireland-centred concerns, are key to its interpretation (Ní Mhaonaigh 2018). Its scribes transmitted and often reshaped material from much earlier manuscripts (Ó hUiginn 2018b: 204–8). Inheriting a highly developed scribal culture shaped by its bilingual (Latin-Irish) milieu, these scribes remained drawn to the past to create textual monuments of relevance that spoke to contemporary concerns.

From the late fourteenth century onward, more and more manuscripts enter the record. For our concerns in the present book, none is more significant than Dublin, RIA MS D.iv.2, alias the Book of Kilcormac (sadly preserved only with large gaps), which contains the longest and most ambitious set of Irish antiquity-sagas to survive. Closely related to it is the late fifteenth-century manuscript now divided into two parts as Dublin, King's Inns MS 12 and MS 13, with copies of several of the same texts in versions closely related to D.iv.2. These three manuscripts together form the principal repository for the central body of texts in which Graeco-Roman antiquity is evoked in the Middle Irish language, and their shared witness is central to this book (see esp. Chs 9–10, 12–20).

Internal evidence within the manuscripts provides precious clues to their origins and makers. A marginal note in the Book of Ballymote records that the most prolific of its three scribes, Maghnus Ó Duibhgeannáin, completed his version of *Togail Troí*, the canonical Irish narrative of the siege of Troy, in the house of his teacher (*oide*), Domhnall Mac Aodhagáin; another places the writing of the first section in the house of a secular lord, Tomaltach Mac Donnchaidh (Ó hUiginn 2018b: 192, 202–4). Such comments provide glimpses of evolving aspects of Gaelic book culture: specifically, the increasing tendency for manuscript production to take place in secular noble houses rather than religious communities, and the concentration of scribal activity in successive generations of well-established learned families like those of Ó Duibhgeannáin and Mac Aodhagáin.

Monastic houses of the type in which eleventh- and twelfth-century manuscripts were compiled had undergone significant changes in the context of developments in church organization, which also saw the introduction of new religious orders to Ireland from the twelfth century onward (Flanagan 2010). Nonetheless, in the later Middle Ages the dynamics of book-production continued to be driven by ecclesiastical and lay concerns alongside each other (Ó Macháin 2018: 228–30). The two spheres cannot be separated, a fact exemplified by such scribes as Ádhamh Ó Cianáin. A pupil of Seán Ó Dubhagáin, whose own family was renowned for historical learning, Ádhamh was the scribe of Dublin, National Library of Ireland, MS G2–3, which includes genealogies, law texts and verse. He died in 1373 as a canon of the abbey of Lisgoole, Co. Fermanagh (Ó Muraíle 2005: 397–8).

Scholars poised between ecclesiastical and secular worlds are also prominent in earlier periods. Cormac mac Cuilennáin, associated with the ninth-century glossary bearing his name, *Sanas Cormaic* 'Cormac's Glossary', as well as other works, was both king and bishop of Cashel (Ní Mhaonaigh 2011). Royal courts and religious centres had a shared interest in all branches of learning, and book-culture served the common needs of various overlapping elite groups requiring tokens of social status – lofty ancestry, authority over the landscape, continuity with heroic ideals of the past, and (not least) high cultural knowledge as an end in itself. As the evidence of the Irish antiquity-sagas indicates, Latin literature had come to serve local dynastic politics by the eleventh century; the classical and the contemporary became enmeshed. In the broadest typological terms, this is parallel to the situation in England and across Europe as a whole, where the myth of Trojan origins in its quasi-historical sense served as a paradigm of authenticity, while the validation of kingship and empire in Virgilian epic provided a framework for modern rulers and their court poets to articulate their own ambitions (Ingledew 1994: 666–76, Tyler 2012). The interdependence between ecclesiastical and secular power, as well as the pivotal place of the Troy–Rome nexus in worldly and salvation history alike, ensured that both religious and lay leaders were invested in narrative sequences that provided 'the clothing for vital ideas, alive, powerful, and at work transforming the society that produced them via the medium of literature' (Jaeger 1994: 327). Readers of the texts in this anthology will encounter (for example) the analogies drawn between a series of Trojan and pre-Christian Irish warriors in the twelfth-century poem *Clann*

Ollaman uaisle Emna ('The noblemen of Emain Macha are the descendants of Ollam', see Ch. 24), and the sustained correlation between the heroism of Murchad who died in the battle of Clontarf in 1014 and that of Hector, in the twelfth-century literary biography of Murchad's father, Brian Boru (Clarke and Ní Mhaonaigh 2020: 479–87, and Ch. 25 in this volume). Such correlations bear witness to the level of historiographical literacy that the scholar-authors applied to weaving Irish and classical strands into the fabric of an image of the remote past.

Languages in contact

The fabric in question was of various linguistic hues. Medieval Irish learning was fundamentally multilingual, and this principle should inform our approach even to texts in which only one language is realized on the surface. For the twelfth-century period that saw the making of the three monumental codices outlined above, perhaps the most eloquent witness to this point is in the Laurentian Library in Florence, and reproduced on the cover of this book. This manuscript of Boethius' *Consolation of Philosophy* carries one of the most elaborate sets of marginal glosses known from any copy of Boethius of its time, with the text and marginalia all in Gaelic script, and it has been shown to have originated at the monastic scriptorium at Glendalough (Firenze, Biblioteca Laurenziana, MS Pluteus 78.19; Ó Néill 2005). The fact that so few classical Latin manuscripts survive within Ireland itself is best seen as an accidental result of time, dampness, and the political and religious vicissitudes of later ages (Sharpe 2010, Ó Corráin 2011–12). The Middle Irish antiquity-sagas derived from poetic sources reflect tenacious engagement with the details of the Latin texts underlying them, often using scholia for additional detail and paying close attention to the precise rendering of technical and critical vocabulary (for examples see O'Hogan 2014, and Ch. 16 in this volume; Clarke and Ní Mhaonaigh 2020: 485–7; Clarke 2021). Other manuscripts attest to the continuing interest in Latin in other ways, including the early fifteenth-century codex, Dublin, Royal Irish Academy MS 23 P 16, *An Leabhar Breac* 'The Speckled Book', which contains bilingual Latin-Irish homiletic and theological texts (see e.g. Miles 2014) as well as preserving much earlier religious poetry and prose in both languages, often copiously glossed.

In the Middle Irish period, literary borrowing and intertextual influence crossed linguistic boundaries in both directions. This is neatly illustrated by the pairing between two texts concerning the 'Wonders of Ireland', one a Latin poem *De mirabilibus Hibernie* and the other a prose composition in Irish, *Do ingantaib Érenn* (Boyle 2014). In the period after the invasion and settlement, beginning in 1169, the sense of a multilingual market-place starts to involve the new elites as well. For example, indigenous sources for the national Apostle St Patrick fed the creation of the *Life of Patrick* by Jocelin of Furness towards the end of the twelfth century, composed at the request of the Anglo-Norman warlord and Chief Justiciar John de Courcy (Flanagan 2013). The Conquest added further linguistic complexity by strengthening the position of Old French and ultimately Middle English as languages of social authority and creativity. A narrative account of the Conquest itself, commonly known as the Song of Dermot and the Earl, but to which a recent editor has accorded the title *La geste des engleis en Yrlande* 'The Deeds of the English in Ireland' (Mullally 2002), was composed in Ireland in Old French octosyllabic couplets around the last decade of the twelfth century. Its composition points to the existence of an established French learned community already at this early date (Busby 2017). As English succeeded French as the language of the new elites and the ecclesiastics who ministered to them, it eventually became possible for mainstream chivalric literature – such as Arthurian narratives – to be rendered into Irish and shaped in turn by the linguistic repertoire of the antiquity-sagas. In this collection the latest text represented, *Stair Ercuil ocus a Bás* 'The History of Hercules and his Death' (Quin 1939, and Ch. 22 in this volume), shows Uilliam Mac an Leagha putting Early Modern Irish clothing on a Burgundian pseudohistory of the 1460s, Raoul Le Fèvre's *Recoeil des histoires de Troyes* 'Compendium of the Histories of Troy'. As Darwin explains (Ch. 22), internal evidence suggests that Uilliam was working from the English-language version printed in Bruges by William Caxton in the 1470s.

Uilliam Mac an Leagha represents the continuing vitality of Irish learned culture in the late fifteenth century. His *Stair Ercuil* sits in the manuscript Dublin, TCD, MS 1298 among heroic narratives on indigenous subjects as well as Irish renderings of Middle English romances, *Sir Bevis of Hampton* and *Sir Guy of Warwick* (Byrne 2016, cf. Poppe 2005). Bound in with these (probably at the time the book was first compiled) was another set of texts including a copy of the most ambitious of the antiquity sagas, *In Cath Catharda*, the Irish rendering of Lucan's *Civil War* (see Chs 14–16). Here, on the cusp of the international era of print, we see the juxtaposition in a single manuscript of a range of texts that represent a flow of knowledge and narrative traditions that brought together the literary, historical and mythological horizons of Gaelic Ireland and the wider world of European antiquity. Making sense of that unity on its own terms presents a continuing challenge, as well as an opportunity to be guided toward seeing European antiquity in new and unexpected ways.

Notes

1   The key corpora are the so-called *Scholia Bernensia* ('Bern Scholia') on Virgil's *Eclogues* and *Georgics* (Hagen 1867, Ziolkowski and Putnam 2008: 674–96), preserved in Bern, Burgerbibliothek, MS 172 (on which see also Clarke 2021), along with the *Brevis Expositio* and *Explanatio in Bocolica* discussed in Ch. 8 of this volume. On the possible Irish authorship and/or transmission of elements (or more) of these and other scholia see Miles 2011: 15–50, Lambert 1986.
2   O'Connor 1967, *passim*. See Nagy 1997: xiv.

2

The Irish Antiquity-Sagas in Context

Ralph O'Connor

Most of the texts in this book are assigned by modern scholarship to a broad category of prose narrative known as the saga, an originally Old Norse term whose meaning overlaps with its Irish cognate *scél*.[1] In a medieval Irish context – or rather medieval Gaelic, since the Irish-speaking and Irish-writing world included much of Scotland in the Middle Ages – the saga embraced a wide range of styles and formats. The earliest surviving Gaelic sagas were probably composed in the eighth century, the latest some time in the nineteenth. Medieval sagas include short anecdotes and huge epics, pithy summary and elaborately ornamented descriptive runs, quickfire backchat and ritualized dialogues in verse. Like their Norse-Icelandic counterparts, sagas often included verse, but only a few examples can really be described as prosimetrum. With the other kinds of vernacular narrative represented in this book (synthetic national history, historical verse, place-lore, annalistic chronicle) they shared a basic purpose of telling history, although they were written with a degree of invention, expansion and embellishment associated today with fiction rather than history. They were marked by a preference for prose combined with a sometimes highly dramatic focus on individual events.[2]

Sagas shared these features with orally composed legends and folktales. Indeed, many sagas themselves seem designed for reading aloud, and knowledge of a wide range of sagas was held in law-texts to be the prerogative of the highest-status court poets, an elite group who are portrayed in those law-texts as delivering their knowledge in speech rather than in writing even though many of them were literate (Johnston 2013; Breatnach 1987: 159). In this context, oral storytelling surely informed saga-writing, but in ways to which we no longer have direct access. It is unlikely that any written saga is a straight transcription of an oral tale: the surviving saga texts were composed, not 'written down'. Until the decades around 1200, this activity took place in monasteries. Later, when

Gregorian church reform de-secularized the monasteries, sagas and other literary texts were written by members of hereditary learned orders serving Irish and Scottish noble families, including (later) those of Anglo-Norman descent who had become absorbed into the indigenous cultural order by the fourteenth century. Throughout the Middle Ages, those who composed and reworked sagas drew on every aspect of their literary environments: not just the popular and learned oral lore that surrounded them, but also written texts, including Latin ones (not least the Bible, in both periods).

This fusion of literary contexts is particularly striking in the antiquity-sagas. Here subject matter taken from Latin book-learning is recast in Irish prose. The source texts include epic poems and commentaries on them (Virgil's *Aeneid*, Lucan's *Civil War*, Statius' *Thebaid*), but also works of Latin prose about Alexander and the Trojan War (Miles 2011: 51–94; O'Connor 2014b). These are translations only in the very broad medieval sense; it is easier for us to conceptualize them as reworkings or adaptations. Their authors sometimes rendered the source text closely, but often departed radically from it in wording, structure and meaning to achieve their purposes. In this corpus the boundary between translation and original composition becomes very blurred (see esp. Ch. 13 in this volume).[3]

In the surviving mnemonic lists that purport to describe the narratives known (and recited) by court poets or *filid*, some of these sagas of classical antiquity are included alongside sagas of the Gaelic past (Mac Cana 1980: 52–5, 84). So, alongside a saga about alleged first-century Irish history like *Togail Bruidne Da Derga* ('The Destruction of Da Derga's Hostel'), we find the Irish history of the Trojan War, *Togail Troí* ('The Siege of Troy'), also included in the tale-lists and preserved in manuscripts alongside other sagas. *Togail Troí* is the best-known of the Irish antiquity-sagas, adapting the *De Excidio Troiae Historia* 'History of the Destruction of Troy' attributed to Dares Phrygius (Meister 1873). It retells that bald account with all the narrative resources at the author's disposal, learnt from the study of Latin rhetoric and epic poetry and from hearing and reading other Irish sagas (Myrick 1993; Mac Gearailt 2000/1; Clarke 2009; Miles 2011; Chs 6, 7, 8, 9 and 10 in this volume).

Togail Troí was much studied, copied and rewritten. Like several other antiquity-sagas, it was very influential in the development of vernacular Irish saga style more generally, as can be seen from later Middle Irish reworkings of core Gael-oriented sagas such as *Táin Bó Cúailnge* (The Cattle-Raid of Cooley). On the relative proportions of Gaelic and classical aesthetics at work in Irish sagas, scholarly debate continues, in part because it is so difficult to disentangle one from the other in practice (Miles 2011; Clarke 2006, 2021; essays in O'Connor 2014a). From its beginnings, and especially in the richly productive Middle Irish period (*c.* 900–1200), the surviving literary tradition is as steeped in Latinity and Christian theology as it is in vernacular learning, orality and the values of secular society. Indigenous and classical frames of reference are intimately interwoven. Individual sagas (antiquity-sagas included) differ in how much voice they give to one or the other priority, but they are two sides of a single coin.

Decolonizing Gaelic literature again?

Among Celticists, the balance between indigenous and Latin elements in medieval Irish literature has been the subject of passionate debate. There is an inescapable colonial context here which deserves considering alongside wider reception histories of Latinity as a tool of cultural and political imperialism. Given the long history of British rule over Gaelic cultures, the Gaels have generally been seen as the victims rather than the agents of colonialism, so consideration of colonial issues in their literature is usually limited to the English and later British element from the Norman invasion onwards. In this sense, scholars and champions of medieval Gaelic literature have arguably decolonized it twice in the past century. First, in the Gaelic Revival and the aftermath of Ireland's achievement of political independence, Ireland's cultural independence from the United Kingdom was promoted by underscoring the distinctive, ancient and imaginatively rich cultural inheritance that was felt to set it apart, in certain respects, from the rest of western Europe (an attitude sometimes labelled 'nativism' by its critics). Second, in the post-war period and especially since the 1980s, a revisionist movement sought to show that those who handled that inheritance in the Middle Ages did so actively, participating in mainstream Latin European intellectual currents rather than dreaming at the 'Celtic fringe' (Johnston 2013: 16–22). That movement was reacting, in part, against the passivity that they felt to be implicit in the racial stereotype of the 'visionary Celt', an image which had energized the Gaelic Revival in early twentieth-century Ireland and Scotland. Both approaches represent different ways of putting the early Gaels on the international cultural map. They each focus on one side of the coin just mentioned; they are not mutually exclusive, despite sparking many disputes.

The more recent movement, which has generated renewed interest in the Irish antiquity-sagas, positions the Gaels' Latinity as a badge of their cultural centrality and agency. This dynamic upends the usual postcolonial associations of Latin as an unwelcome external force foisted upon unwilling indigenous peoples. Another way of expunging colonial associations from medieval Gaels' engagement with classical culture is to consider the Roman imperial backdrop. Unlike most of medieval Europe, Ireland and (what would become) Gaelic Scotland had never fallen under Roman control, despite the ambitions of Agricola and Septimius Severus in northern Scotland and the abundant evidence of culture-contact with Rome (Freeman 2001: 20–32; cf. Johnston 2013: 1–26 for some implications). The key parallel here is with Iceland, where vernacular Norse saga-writing also developed in comparable ways from the twelfth century onwards to embrace, and be fertilized by, prose adaptations of the Latin classics in a land uncolonized by Rome (Würth 1998, Poppe 2009). Gaelic and Norse-Icelandic engagement with the Latin classics thus took root and flourished independently of a Roman colonial past, and also well before the advent of larger *imperia* presided over by Anglo-Norman rulers and the expansionist Norwegian monarchy.

It might be assumed, then, that medieval Gaelic literature needs no further decolonization. However, Gaelic engagement with the classics was not exempt from the colonialist and elitist assumptions visible in the work of other medieval European writers. This is important to acknowledge if we are to appreciate the antiquity-sagas in their own context. There are several aspects to consider. First, the concept of 'indigeneity' as used in social sciences today does not map onto the medieval Gaelic self-image. Like most European nations, the Gaels saw themselves as conquering colonists. Scottish Gaels celebrated their forebears as Irish immigrants who had colonized Scotland in the relatively recent past. The central grand narrative of Irish legendary history, *Lebor Gabála Érenn* or 'The Book of Invasions of Ireland', celebrates the Irish, too, as inheritors of a glorious conquest carried out by their ancestors in ancient times against the island's previous occupants, who had themselves wrested it from their predecessors (Carey 2005).

Second, while my mention of oral storytelling above might seem to suggest that medieval Gaelic narrative belonged to 'the people' rather than only to the elites associated with a classical education in modern times, literacy (especially in Latin) was a method of promoting elitism and segregation in access to learning, both before and after the centre of gravity of literary production shifted from monasteries to noble households. There were no medieval hedge schools; attendance at ecclesiastical schools was very expensive. The producers of medieval Gaelic literature were unapologetically elitist. When the twelfth-century Irish historical poet Gilla in Choimded Ua Cormaic warned fellow scholars that incorporating lower-born individuals and serfs (*dáerchlann, mogaid*) into genealogies was tantamount to falsification (*míscríbend*, 'mis-writing'), he voiced a commonplace aristocratic equation between the moral and social high ground (Ó Cróinín 2005: 184; for wider context see the historical poetry in Chs 4 and 5 of this volume). The very lists of oral stories mentioned above situate their tellers at the top of a social hierarchy. With a few carnivalesque exceptions, ordinary people play only bit-parts in this web of story. The outlook of the surviving literature is aristocratic. If any of its contents were built around stories that could have been shared by ordinary people at the time (as can be seen in *Merugud Uilixis*, Ch. 18 in this volume), these were recast to serve a hierarchical ideology. Isabelle Torrance reminds us (Ch. 31) that much medieval Gaelic literature was written to be performed and heard in spaces where it could potentially reach a wider social spectrum; but if so, this was typically a means of disseminating elitist ideology, not diluting it. As Elva Johnston has put it (2013: 175), the literature 'impressed an elitist discourse on the rest of society'. This is only to be expected of a culture in which churches as well as kingdoms were run by and for members of the same noble dynasties, while the majority of the population (in the early Middle Ages at least) was not even free.

Third, literacy across the Gaelic world was the product of Christianization, again imposed by a tiny elite (Johnston 2013: 13–23). Lack of direct evidence spares us the details, and the cultural dynamics were complex; but it is impossible to avoid colonial overtones when we imagine how literacy would have spread. Even those who trumpeted the Church triumphant in the person of St Patrick sometimes imagined how it might have felt for the custodians of the old order. In the late seventh-century Hiberno-Latin *Life of St Patrick* attributed to Muirchú, a pagan king's two druids prophesy the great change in strikingly colonial terms (Bieler 1979: 74–7):

> [they] prophesied frequently that a foreign way of life was about to come to them, a kingdom, as it were, with an unheard-of and burdensome teaching, brought from afar over the seas, enjoined by few, received by many; it would be honoured by all, would overthrow kingdoms, kill the kings who offered resistance, seduce the crowds, destroy all their gods, banish all the works of their craft, and reign for ever.

The general sense of disquiet is amplified by what follows, a Latin rendering of an Irish poem allegedly prophesying St Patrick himself. This poem defamiliarizes the missionary by showing him as he might have struck a pagan: a blasphemer with bizarre paraphernalia, 'with his stick bent in the head' (his staff or sceptre) preaching 'from his house with a hole in its head' (a church with bell-tower). Patrick's coming is celebrated, not criticized, for evoking such disquiet among the pagans, just as *Lebor Gabála* extols the Gaels' colonial conquests in the distant past. If Latin literacy became 'indigenous' to medieval Ireland, it was only indigenous for a small elite who adopted it as part of a massive culture-change that they imposed on the rest of the population: 'enjoined by few, received by many'.

Finally, the authority of the classical tradition gave some literate Gaels the kind of 'cultural cringe' often associated with colonized societies. Johnston (2013: 33) again sums up the identity issues at stake: 'Irish scholars were ever eager to show that they were part of a greater intellectual world. They were aware of their relatively recent and lowly entrance on to the stage of salvation history.' They saw the history of the ancient Mediterranean and Near East as prestigious, not only because of its connection with salvation history but also because it concerned the centre of the world, to which Ireland and Gaelic Scotland existed as a margin. Like other non-Roman writers around the edges of the old empire, the Gaels grafted their own history onto that prestigious domain, whether by genealogical descent or by analogy (Poppe and Schlüter 2011, Clarke 2015). They engaged with the classical tradition to show that their culture measured up to a classical yardstick, that medieval Gaels mattered, and that Ireland was part of Europe rather than off the edge of the map (Oschema 2017). Appropriation of classical literary techniques in vernacular literature may be seen in a similar way. The whole business is founded on a pre-existing assumption of the superior prestige of the classical tradition. That assumption suffuses medieval and modern European classicism; it is encoded within the very word 'classics'. Medieval Ireland was no exception.

Once we drop anachronistic expectations that the Gaels were exempt from the colonialist, elitist and imperialist ideologies pervading the rest of medieval Europe, we may better appreciate the genuinely distinctive aspects of Irish classicism, and how Gaels made the classics their own. Here it is not enough to stop at a diagnosis of 'cultural imperialism'. Everything depends on what writers *did* with the prestigious texts they adapted. Should we point the finger at the Ukrainian poet Ivan Kotliarevsky for cultural imperialism when, in 1798, he launched the modern Ukrainian literary tradition by writing his riotous Cossack parody of Virgil's *Aeneid*, upending key Virgilian themes to criticize Russian imperial ambition and the complicity of Ukrainian landowners (Pavlyshyn 1985)? To say so would be to miss the point: the unquestioned status of the classics was the very ground on which Kotliarevsky's work made its subversive impact.

Medieval Irish literature, despite its rich comic vein, offers nothing quite like Kotliarevsky's *Eneida* in its reworkings of classical texts. But a comparable cultural and linguistic self-confidence can be seen in the long project of comparison, synchronism and emulation between Gaelic periphery and classical centre. The case of the bilingual sacred anthology *Liber Hymnorum* 'Book of Hymns' shows just how far this confidence in the Irish language and idioms could be pushed (Clarke 2022a). The antiquity-sagas fit firmly into this context, adapting classical texts into an already vibrant and sophisticated vernacular idiom, sometimes even aiming to outdo their sources' own handling of classical rhetoric and epic poetics. *Togail Troí* is a case in point (Miles 2011: 95–144), and the present volume highlights diverse aspects of the Irish antiquity-sagas' stylistic repertoire.

Learning and literature in the antiquity-sagas

The best-known Irish antiquity-sagas are the four monumental texts about the central wars of classical antiquity: *Togail Troí* 'The Siege of Troy', *Imtheachta Aeniasa* 'The Wanderings of Aeneas' (from Virgil's *Aeneid*), *In Cath Catharda* 'The Civil War' (from Lucan's *De Bello Civili*) and *Togail na Tebe* 'The Siege of Thebes' (from Statius's *Thebaid*). The last three retell Latin epics, and all four are written in ostentatiously epic style. Their main claim to fame outside Celtic studies lies in their being some of the earliest vernacular reworkings of their classical source-texts in existence, part of a movement that significantly predates the three mid-twelfth-century French *romans d'antiquité* (O'Connor 2014b: 4–5, 9–10). The latter were written in rhymed couplets and approach their subject-matter in a way quite different from their Irish counterparts, while nonetheless participating in the same broad project of telling and explaining history. And as this book illustrates, the epic mode of the longer Irish antiquity-sagas is only part of a diverse spectrum of styles, techniques and priorities seen in the corpus as a whole. The antiquity-sagas also include several intriguing and little-known shorter texts, several of which are translated here in full. Unbound by metrical constraints, saga style in the Gaelic world (as in the West Norse world) embodied a wide range of styles, high and low. Heightened narrative, description and utterance can swerve without warning into laconic summary or enumeration; in some shorter sagas the latter mode dominates entirely. Works which might appear, on the surface, to lack artistry may have other, less flamboyant, but equally real aspirations.

Confident aesthetic judgement upon the antiquity-sagas may, therefore, need to await a clearer sense of the full range of forms and techniques available to medieval Gaelic saga-writers, and authors generally. We have no surviving early Irish tracts about how to compose prose narratives (an absence also seen in the Norse-Icelandic context), so we have to feel our way and give our texts the benefit of the many doubts that cloud this whole area. Only a minority of even the more famous sagas have been treated to full-scale literary analysis; whole swathes of Gaelic narrative are only beginning to be seen as consciously composed texts rather than artless compilations, such as the place-lore known as *dindshenchas* and even the annalistic chronicles so often used by historians (Ní Mhaonaigh 2023, and cf. Chs 3, 4, 27 and 28 in this volume). This anthology offers a chance to view the narrative strategies of the antiquity-sagas in close-up. Future research may be better placed to set each work as a whole within the larger saga corpus and the wider generic ecosystem of medieval Gaelic literature.

Until then, it is worth avoiding the common habit of dividing the antiquity-sagas (as we divide other kinds of sagas) between what we think of as 'literary' and non-literary texts: those which seem to be designed to move or entertain, and those we suspect were composed simply to set down information. Of course, in ancient times as well, many of the source-texts of our antiquity-sagas were themselves pigeonholed by commentators on one or other side of a perceived division between history and poetry. Everyone knew (then) that Dares Phrygius was a historian, but classical verse epic had a more ambivalent status both before and after Christianization. Were Virgil, Statius and Lucan primarily poets or historians? Different commentators had different answers, and some made brave attempts to see them as both poets and historians (Cullhed 2017).

As for the Irish retellings of these verse epics, it has become increasingly clear since the 1990s that recasting them in Irish prose pulled them generically further into the world of history (Poppe 1995, 2009; Clarke 2009). The same gravitational pull towards history-writing is seen in the Icelandic antiquity-sagas (Würth 1998). Adaptation into 'saga' form accentuates the historical frame of reference. In keeping with the fundamentally historical, information-led orientation of the antiquity-sagas is their frequent use of commentaries, scholia and other scholastic resources, sometimes to supplement what is in a poetic source, sometimes to replace it completely (cf. Clarke 2014c). Our understanding of this aspect of antiquity-saga composition has been transformed in the past two decades by several contributors to the present volume.[4] Sometimes commentary-material provides a saga's entire content, as with the tales of the 'third Troy', Harmonia's necklace, and the Minotaur (Miles 2007, 2020; Hillers 1999b; see also Chs 10, 12 and 20 in this volume). The longer antiquity-sagas also made extensive use of the commentary tradition as a source of information and linkages with other narratives. Servius' commentary on the *Aeneid* was fundamental to the writing and subsequent reworking of *Togail Troí* (Miles 2011). The composition of *In Cath Catharda* 'The Civil War' involved frequent recourse to late-antique and early medieval interpretations and explications of Lucan's text in scholia and commentaries, including some that were also used in the twelfth-century Icelandic adaptation of Sallust and Lucan, *Rómverja sögur* (The Sagas of the Romans; O'Hogan 2014, Poppe 2016a, b; Nagashima 2021; cf. Ch. 16 in this volume).

This historical frame of reference is mirrored in these texts' cyclic arrangements in historiographically oriented manuscripts like the Book of Ballymote, produced in fourteenth-century Ireland (Poppe 2009: 270–1, 279–81; Ní Mhaonaigh 2022). In this connection, it would be fascinating to know more about the extent to which stylistic and structural differences between (for example) the numerous recensions of *Togail Troí*, distributed between several different Irish manuscripts, were shaped by (or somehow related to) these manuscripts' different purposes and principles of selection, as has been suggested for some of their Icelandic counterparts (Würth 1998, 2006; Poppe 2009: 268–76). The manuscript held in Dublin's Royal Irish Academy as MS D.iv.2, with its eclectic collection of short and long antiquity-sagas in otherwise unknown recensions, would make an excellent case-study along these lines. But it is telling that the second recension of *Togail Troí*, a work which was clearly designed to perform and dramatize history as well as record it, was included in two manuscripts for which a primarily historical or scholarly purpose has been uncovered, namely the Book of Leinster and the Book of Ballymote (Schlüter 2010, Poppe 2009). Here, then, is another reminder that history-writing in medieval Europe (not just on the Celtic fringe) could include performative, artful, entertaining and rhetorically embellished narrative (Taranu and O'Connor 2022). Not all history-writing was intended for performance, or composed to be entertaining, but a historical purpose in itself implied no lessening of artistic ambition. Narrative was a medium of information, and the repertoire of rhetorical techniques in which that information was presented gave it meaning and authority as a carrier of cultural memory (see Poppe 2014a).

The same applies on a smaller scale to *Merugud Uilixis* 'The Wandering of Ulysses', where the part that retells bits of Homer's *Odyssey* in condensed and strikingly divergent form turns out to be the result, not of a lack of Latin learning as some had suspected, but of skilful recasting of a previously unidentified Latin source. Michael Clarke has shown that the first part of this antiquity-saga is a dramatized reworking of part of a dry scholastic summary of the relevant narrative called *Excidium Troie* 'The Destruction of Troy' (Clarke 2020). It recapitulates in microcosm the achievement of *Togail Troí* in elevating its laconic source to epic status via an ambitious combination of classical and home-grown narrative techniques. What makes the *Merugud* unusual as an antiquity-saga is that the story's climax, as Ulysses finally arrives home, is built around an international folktale, presumably part of the environment of oral storytelling in which the author lived (Hillers 2014; cf. Ch. 18 in this volume). If we bring these perspectives together, *Merugud Uilixis* shows us how intimately interwoven were the worlds of oral narrative and Latin learning in medieval Ireland, and how the same author could move seamlessly between these two worlds in order to retell one of the greatest stories of the classical tradition in a distinctively Irish manner. Nor was this folkloric component, or the saga's narrative verve, felt to disqualify it from use as a historical account. In the fourteenth century it was included as a sequel to *Togail Troí* in the historiographically oriented Book of Ballymote.

In this wonderful saga, the noisy dichotomies between nativist and anti-nativist, oral and literary, historical and literary conceptions of medieval Gaelic textual culture dissolve into thin air. And if there was anything like a cultural cringe at play in medieval Gaelic attitudes towards the classics, *Merugud Uilixis*, perhaps more than any other saga, shows how gracefully this could be sidestepped. In the antiquity-sagas, medieval Gaels took full ownership of the classical tradition to instruct and delight their elite audiences. This volume now offers a taste of that experience to a wider readership.[5]

Notes

1　On the semantics of *scél* and 'saga', see O'Connor 2023 and 2024, forthcoming.

2　The best single-volume account of medieval Gaelic sagas is Ó Cathasaigh 2014. On Irish history-writing generally, see Ní Mhaonaigh 2018. On sagas as a form of imaginative history-writing, see Poppe 2014a, b and O'Connor 2022.

3　Such blurring is widespread in medieval vernacular writing. Geoffrey Chaucer and Nordic romance adaptations provide helpful points of comparison (Ellis 2019, Bampi 2017).

4　Classical commentaries, and related scholarly tools such as glossaries and *florilegia*, have also been shown to have played an important role in the mediation of classical subject-matter or rhetorical devices in other branches of medieval Gaelic literature: see, in particular, Clarke 2014b and Clarke 2014c.

5　I am very grateful to the editors of this volume and the conference participants for their helpful feedback on earlier versions of this chapter.

Part Two

Chronology and Correlation

3

The Irish World Chronicle in the First Fragment of the *Annals of Tigernach*

Patrick Wadden

The text is preserved in Oxford, Bodleian Library, MS Rawlinson B502, which can be viewed online at http://image.ox.ac.uk/show?collection=bodleian&manuscript=msrawlb502.

The extract presented here is an interim edition revised from Stokes 1895: 403–7, in light of the manuscript, with contractions silently expanded. The glosses, which in the manuscript are placed between the lines as well as sometimes in the margins, are here printed within round brackets. In the manuscript, the letter 'K' for 'Kalends' notionally represents a single year, and the sequence 'KKK . . .' stands for a series of years within which no special events have been noted.

Text: From Caesar to Herod

[f. 9v a] (Incipit regnum Romanorum, quod permanebit usque in finem saeculi.)

K. Tertio anno regni Cleopatrae Iulius Cessar (qui Cleopatram uiolauit) primus Romanorum singulare obtenuit imperium, a quo Romanorum princepes Cessares apellati sunt.

Mochta mac Murchorad regnauit in Emain annis iii.

K. Cessar a cesso utero matris dictus est.

K. Cassius (.i. dux Románus) Iudea capta templum Hierusalem spoliauit.

K. Euchu mac Dare regnauit in Emain annis .iii.

(Orosius) Cessar, postquam orbem domuit ⁊ Pompeum uícit, Romam redit: ibi, dum rei puplicae statum contra exempla maiorum clementer instaurat, auctoribus Bruto ⁊ Cassio, conscio etiam plurimo senatu, post .iiii. annos ⁊ .ui. menses monarchiae suae, in cúria .xx. ⁊ iii. uulneribus a suis confosus interit. In coniuratione contra eum fuisse amplius quam .lx. conscios ferunt. Duo, scilicet, Brúti ⁊ Gaius Cassius aliiqui quam plurimi. Cuius corpus in Foro fragmentís tribunalium ac subselliorum crematum est. Ab hinc imperatores.

(iiimdccclxui.) K. Anno ab Urbe condita .d.ccx. interfecto Iulio Cessare Octouianus, qui testamento Iulii Cessaris auunculi sui et hereditatem ⁊ nomen asumpserat, quique postea rerum potitus Augustus est dictus, regnauit annis quinquaginti sex ⁊ mensibus .ui. ⁊ diebus xii, quorum .xu. uiuente Cleopatra quadragenti uero ⁊ unum postea uixit annos. A quo Augusti reges Rómanorum apellati sunt.

Qui statim ordinatus .u. bella ciuilia gessit, Mutinense (.i. ciuitas), Pilipense (ciuitas), Perusinum (ciuitas), Siculum (insola), Actiacum (ciuitas): e quibus duo, hoc est, primum ac nouisimum aduersus Marcum Antonium, secundum aduersums Brútum et Cassium, tertium aduersus Lucium Antonium, quartum [fol. 9v b] aduersus Sextum Pompeum (Gnei) Pompei filium confécit.

KK. Echu Sálbude mac Loch regnauit in Emain annis .iii.

Translation by the author

(Here begins of the kingdom of the Romans, which will continue until the end of the world.)

K. In the third year of Cleopatra's reign, Julius Caesar (who raped Cleopatra), was the first to attain sole rule of the Romans. Roman rulers are called 'Caesars' after him.

Mochta son of Murchorad reigned for three years in Emain.

K. Caesar was named for having been cut from his mother's womb.

K. Judea having been captured, Cassius (i.e. a Roman military leader) sacked the Temple of Jerusalem.

K. Eochu son of Dáre reigned in Emain for three years.

(Orosius:) Caesar, after he conquered the world and defeated Pompey, returned to Rome. There, while he was restoring the condition of the republic benignly, though contrary to the precedent of his forefathers, he died after four years and six months of his reign, having been stabbed twenty-three times by his friends in the curia, at the direction of Brutus and Cassius but with the knowledge of most of the senate. They report that there were more than sixty in the conspiracy against him: that is, the two Brutuses and Gaius Cassius, and many others. His body was cremated in the Forum over fragments of tribunal platforms and benches. From this point there were emperors.

(3966)[1] K. In the 710th year since the foundation of Rome, Julius Caesar having been killed, Octavian, according to the will of his uncle Julius Caesar, became his heir and assumed his name. Having obtained power over public affairs, he was called Augustus. He reigned for fifty-six years, six months and twelve days, of which Cleopatra was living for fifteen, and he lived forty-one years afterwards. It is from him that kings of the Roman are called 'Augustuses'.

As soon as he was had been appointed, he waged five civil wars, those of Mutina[2] (i.e. a city), Philippi (a city), Perusia (a city), Sicily (an island), and Actium (a city). Of these, he fought two – that is, the first and the last – against Mark Antony, the second he fought against Brutus and Cassius, the third against Lucius Antonius, the fourth against Sextus Pompeius, the son of Gnaeus Pompeius.

KK Eochu Sálbuide son of Loch reigned in Emain for three years.

KKK. Fergus mac Leti, qui conflixit contra bestiam hi Loch Rudraige ⁊ ibi demersus est, regnauit in Emain annis .xii.

KKKKK. (Natiuitas Conculainn maic Soaltaim.) Undecimo anno Augusti, deficiente in Iudea pontificatu, Herodes, nihil ad eam pertinens, utpote Antipatri Ascolonitae et Cipriadis (.i. matris) Arabicae filius, postquam occidit Hircanum pontificem, a Romanis suscepit imperium Iudeorum, quod tenuit annis xxxui. Qui ne ignobilis forte et a Iudeorum semine argueretur extraneus, combussit libros omnes quibus nobilitas gentis Iudeae in templo reseruabatur asscripta.

Hác ténus qui uocabantur Lagidiae in Aegipto regnauerunt .i. annis .ccxcu.

Insuper etiam ut sobolem suam regio illorum generi Herodes commisceret, proiecta Doside femina Hierusolmitana, quam priuatus acceperat uxorem, ⁊ nato ex ea filio Antipatro sociat sibi Miriamnem filiam Alanxandri, neptem Aristoboli fratris Hircani, qui ante eum rexerat Iudeos. Haec .u. ei filios genuit, quorum duos, Alaxandrum ⁊ Aristobolum, ipse necauit in Samaria.

Nec mora etiam, post matrem illorum qua nihil carius nouerat, peremit. E quibus Aristobulus Herodem ex Beronice susceperat filium quem in Actibus Apostulorum ab angelo percussum legimus.

KKKK. Marcus Antonius Niger uictus ab Augusto in Ala(xa)ndria sese propria manu interfecit, ⁊ Cleopatra uxor eius serpentis morsu in sinistra tacta examinata est.

Hóc anno cepit regnare in (†) Emain Conchobor mac Nessa, qui regnauit annis .lx.

Ro rannad hÉriu íarsin hi cóic, íar n-árcain [fol. 10r a] Conare Móir maic Etarsceóil hi mBrudin Dá Dergga, etir Conchobur mac Nessa ocus Coirpre Nia Fer ⁊ Tigernach Tétbannach ⁊ Dedad mac Sin ⁊ Ailill mac Mágag. (Isin tsechtmad bliadain iar ndith Conairi ro gab Lugaid Reoderg rígi.)

KKKKKKKKKKKKKK. (†) Maria mater Domini nata est.

KKKK. (Slógad tána bó Cualngi.) Uirgilius Maro in Brundissi .lii. aetatis suae anno mortus est. Cuius ossa in Necapoli humata sunt, hóc epitaphio, quod ipse ante mortem suam dictauerat, tumulo eius superposito:

KKK Fergus son of Léte, who fought against a beast in Loch Rudraige and was submerged there, reigned in Emain for twelve years.

KKKKK (The birth of Cú Chulainn son of Súaltam) In the eleventh year of Augustus, the rule of the priests came to an end in Judea. Herod, who did not belong to it [i.e. Judea], since he was the son of Antipater of Ascalon and Cypros (i.e. his mother) of Arabia, later killed the high-priest Hyrcanus. He received rule over the Jews from the Romans, and held it for thirty-six years. This man, lest it be proven that he was of ignoble ancestry and foreign to the Jewish stock, burnt all the books preserved in the Temple in which the nobility of the people of Judaea was preserved in writing.

As far as this, those called the Lagids reigned in Egypt for 295 years.

Furthermore Herod, in order to blend his line with their royal stock, having cast aside Dosis, a woman of Jerusalem whom he had married as a private person, and with whom he had a son, Antipater, took to himself Mariamne, the daughter of Alexander and granddaughter of Aristobolus brother of Hyrcanus, who had ruled over the Jews before him. She bore him five sons, two of whom – Alexander and Aristobolus – he himself killed in Samaria.

Not long afterwards, he also slew their mother, though nothing was more beloved to him. Of these sons, Aristobolus had a son, Herod, with Berenice. We read in the Acts of the Apostles that this son was struck down by an angel.

KKKK Marcus Antonius Niger, having been defeated by Augustus, killed himself by his own hand in Alexandria, and Cleopatra his wife was killed after being touched by a snake's bite on her left hand.

In this year, Conchobar son of Nes began to reign in (†)[3] Emain; he reigned for sixty years.

Subsequently, Ireland was divided into five – after the destruction of Conare Mór son of Etarscél in Dá Derga's Hostel – between Conchobar son of Nes and Coirpre Nia Fer and Tigernach Tétbannach and Dedad son of Sen and Ailill son of Mága. (In the seventh year after the death of Conare, Lugaid Reoderg assumed the kingship.)

KKKKKKKKKKKKKK. (†) Mary mother of the Lord was born.

KKKK. (The hosting of the cattle-raid of Cooley). Vergilius Maro died in Brindisi, in the fifty-second year of his life. His bones were buried in Naples, and this epitaph, which he himself had composed before his death, was placed on his tomb:

Mantua me genuit, Calubri rapuere, tenet nunc Parthinope

cecini pascua (.i. Bucolica), rura (.i. Georgica), duces (.i. librum Aenedae).

KKKKKKK. Finit quinta aetas mundi continens annos .d.lxxxix. Incipit sexta mundi aetas ab Incarnatione Christi usque ad diem iudicii. Beda boat breuiter sequentia haec:

Sexta mundi aetas nulla generatione uel sirie temporum certa, sed ut aetas decrepita ipsa totius saeculi morte consumenda.

Cétna bliadain tossaich ógtathcuir is hí sein in bliadain ria gen Crist. Bliadain tanaisse immorro de nóidécdu hi ro genair.

(iiimdcccclii) K. Ab initio mundi .umcxc iuxta .lxx. Interpretes. Secundum uero Ebreicam ueritatem .iiimdcccclii. Ab Urbe uero condita anno .dcclii. Anno quoque imperii Cessaris Augusti .xlii. Anno secundo decinouenalis ⁊ uii. feria Iesus Christus Filius Dei sextam mundi aetatem suo aduentu consecrauit.

Beda ait: Anno Cessaris Augusti .xlii. A morte uero Cleopatrae ⁊ Antoníi quando ⁊ Aegiptus in prouinciam uersa est anno .xxuii. Olimpiadis centissimae .lxxxxiii. anno tertio. Ab Urbe autem condita anno .dcclii .i. eo anno quo compresis cunctarum per orbem terrae gentium motibus firmissimam uerissimamque pacem ordinatione [fol. 10r b] Dei Cessar compossuit, Iesus Christus Filius Dei sextam mundi aetatem consecrauit aduentu .i.

(†) K. Mors Con Chulaind fortissimi herois Scottorum la Lugaid mac Trí Con (.i. ri Muman) ⁊ la Ercc mac Coirpri Níad Fir (.i. ri Temrach) ⁊ la trí maccu Calattin de Chonnachtaib. (Mors Emiri uxoris Conculaind.) Uii. mbliadna a áes intan rogab gaisced, .xuii. mbliadna dano a aes intan mbói indegaid Tána bó Cúailge, xxuii. bliadna immorro a aes intan atbath.

(Mors Eirc maic Corpri rig Temrach ⁊ Lugdach maic Con Roi la Conall Cernach, ⁊ inriud cethri coiced n-Erenn la secht Maini o Ultaib.)

Kii. Kiii. Ku. Kui. Anno imperii Augusti .xluii. Herodes moritur.

Mantua produced me, the Calabrians snatched me away, Naples now holds me. I sang of pastures (i.e. the Bucolics), of the countryside (i.e. the Georgics) and leaders (i.e. the Book of the Aeneid)

KKKKKKK. Here ends the fifth age of the world, containing 589 years. Here begins the sixth age of the world, from the Incarnation of Christ until the Day of Judgment. Bede briefly declares what follows:

The sixth age of the world has no fixed generation or succession of times, but like senility, this age will be consumed by the death of the whole world.

The first year of the beginning of the new Great Cycle, that is the year before Christ's birth. It was, however, the second year of the decennoval in which he was born.

(3952) K. From the beginning of the world, 5190 [years], according to the Seventy Translators; but 3952 according to the Hebrew Truth. From the foundation of Rome, verily, 752. It was also in the forty-second year of the rule of Caesar Augustus; in the second year of the decennoval and [a year beginning on] the seventh feria – Jesus Christ the Son of God consecrated the sixth age of the world by His coming.

Bede says: In the forty-second year of Caesar Augustus, and the twenty-seventh year since the death of Cleopatra and Antony, when Egypt was converted into a [Roman] province, in the third year of the one hundred and ninety third Olympiad, in the seven hundred and fifty-second year since the foundation of Rome, i.e. in the year in which the movements of all peoples were restrained throughout the world and, by God's decree, Caesar established the firmest and truest peace: Jesus Christ the Son of God consecrated the sixth age of the world by His coming.

(†) The death of Cú Chulainn, bravest hero of the Gaels, by Lugaid son of Trí Coin (i.e. king of Munster) and by Erc son of Coirpre Nía Fer (i.e. king of Tara) and by the three sons of Calatin of the Connachta. (The death of Emer, Cú Chulainn's wife.) He was seven years of age when he took up arms; seventeen years of age, moreover, at the time of the Cattle raid of Cooley; twenty-seven years of age, indeed, when he died.

(The death of Erc son of Coirpre king of Tara, and Lugaid son of Cú Roí by Conall Cernach, and the invasion of four provinces of Ireland by the seven Maines of the Ulaid).

Kii. Kiii. Ku. Kui. Herod died in the forty-seventh year of the rule of Augustus.

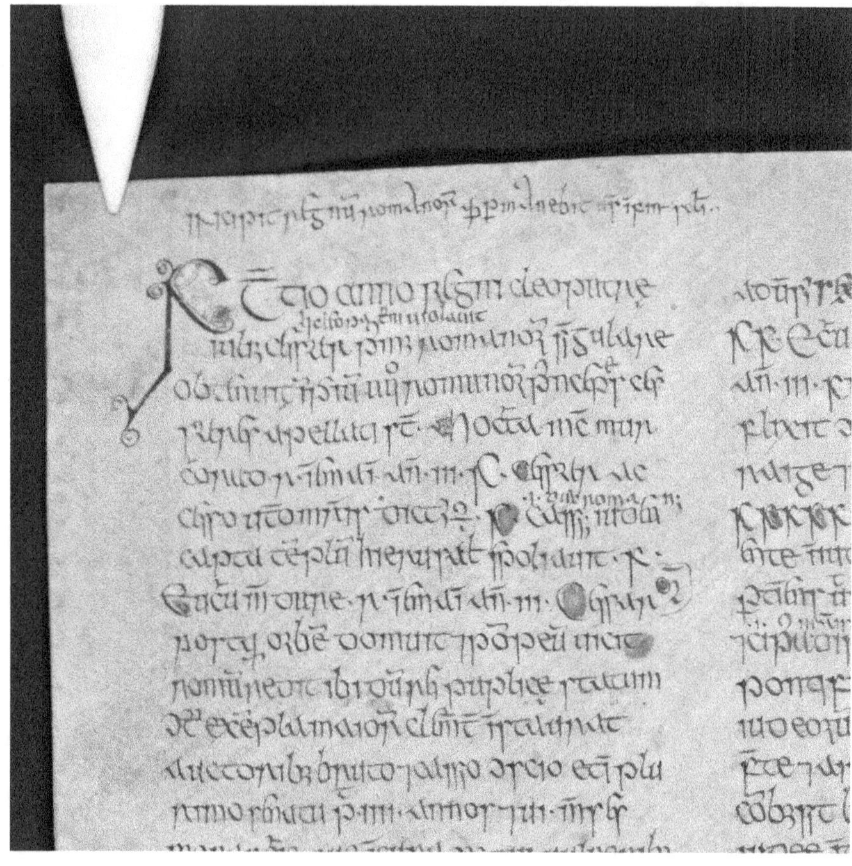

Figure 1 Oxford, Bodleian Library MS Rawlinson B502, fol. 9v, detail: from the First Fragment of the *Annals of Tigernach*. Image copyright Bodleian Libraries, Oxford. Reproduced under a Creative Commons licence by courtesy of Bodleian Online.

Essay: Global and local history in the Irish World Chronicle

This extract is taken from an annalistic text extant in an eleventh- or twelfth-century manuscript – one of two originally distinct manuscripts now combined as Oxford, Bodleian Library, MS Rawlinson B502 (Ó Cuív 2001–3: 1.162–66, 181–82). It was previously edited (and partially translated) by Whitley Stokes as the 'First Fragment' of the *Annals of Tigernach*. The annals of that name were probably written in the monastery of Clonmacnoise late in the eleventh century, though their other surviving fragments are preserved in manuscripts of significantly later date. The First Fragment represents the most extensive of three surviving versions of a text commonly known as the Irish World Chronicle, other versions of which are found at the beginning of the *Annals of Inisfallen* and *Annals of Boyle* (Mac Airt 1944: 1–45; Freeman 1924–27: 1924. 302–17). The title was coined by O'Rahilly (1957: 235–59). The Irish World Chronicle was probably initially compiled in Clonmacnoise in the late tenth or the early eleventh century (Dumville 1977). It has attracted relatively little scholarly attention in the past, though that is rapidly changing.[4]

The Irish World Chronicle is an account of the history of the world, as the world was known and understood in medieval Western Europe. It is laid out in the form of annals in all three surviving versions, though this format is awkward as individual entries often cover more than a single year. Eoin MacNeill (1914: 41–5) argued this was the result of a rather clumsy conversion of the text from its original form. It almost certainly began with Creation, though the version preserved in Rawlinson B502 is fragmentary and opens in the time of the biblical prophets Hosea, Amos, Isaiah, and Jonah – roughly the eighth century BCE. Precisely when the Irish World Chronicle ends is open to debate – probably in the fifth or sixth century – though our fragment breaks off in the middle of the second century CE, in the reign of the emperor Antoninus Pius. During the centuries it covers, it reports major historical events of antiquity. These include the succession of kings of the great kingdoms of the ancient world – the Romans, Persians, and Macedonians, but also the Hebrews, Egyptians, Lydians and Assyrians – as well as information pertaining to the histories of these kingdoms and the deaths (and occasionally the births) of significant political and cultural figures. For early Irish historians, it seems, 'classical' antiquity was viewed as part of a broader landscape of the past, rather than as a discrete unit.

Gradually at first, but with increasing volume and frequency over time, these records of the history of the ancient world become interspersed with reports of events from Ireland's distant past, including (in our extract) the famous cattle-raid of Cooley – *táin bó Cúailgne*, the story of which is related in the Old Irish saga of the same name – and the births and deaths of persons who played important roles in those events, including the warrior identified as the bravest hero among the Gaels (*Scotti*), Cú Chulainn, and the flawed king of Ulster, Conchobar mac Nessa. The cattle-raid supposedly occurred in Ireland around the time of the life, death, and resurrection of Jesus. This was before the coming of literacy to Ireland, so these events were not recorded in any contemporary source. Nonetheless, here as in other medieval Irish scholarship, they are treated as historical, on a par with the civil wars of the Romans and the births and deaths of emperors, philosophers and poets of the ancient world (Toner 2000).

It is the case that most of the 'international' or 'global' material is in Latin, whereas Irish events are frequently recorded in the vernacular. But the distinction is not consistent; there are plenty of records relating to the Irish in Latin and there are records of non-Irish events in the vernacular. It is possible that the choice of language was determined to some extent by the compiler's source materials, though more work must be done before any firm conclusions can be drawn. The precise nature and identity of the sources for Irish history is unclear; many of the Irish events reported here are dealt with at greater length in extant narrative texts, but the relationship between our text and these needs further study. With regards to the 'international' events and the different chronological frameworks within which they are reported (the succession of world kingdoms and the six ages of the world), on the other hand, it is clear that the compiler's major sources were Jerome's translation of the *Chronicon* of Eusebius of Caesarea, Bede's *Chronica Maiora* (= *De Temporum Ratione* 'On the Reckoning of Time' 66–71) and the *Histories against the Pagans* of Orosius (Arnaud-Lindet 1990–1, tr. Fear 2010). Other sources named in the text include the historical works of the first-century Romano-Jewish historian Flavius Josephus and the third-century Christian historian Julius Africanus, though references to these were in some or all cases copied directly from Bede and other intermediary sources and do not amount to independent witnesses (MacNeill 1914: 36, 52–3). I suspect the compiler had access to fewer sources than has previously been stated.

It is also apparent that the Irish World Chronicle expanded over time as new material was added from different sources and the text 'corrected' through comparison with other authorities. This much is clear from the current shape of the collection of items in the fragment, a collection which, as MacNeill pointed out (1914: 45, 49), is '*in a condition of active growth*, thickly stuck over with interlinear and marginal accretions'; some of the additions are corrections, while others arose 'from an effort to develop the text'. MacNeill was highly critical of the fact that this feature of the text is not readily apparent in Stokes' edition. As can be seen in the extract above, these glosses and other scholia provide the names of sources, additional dating information, and further details about both international and Irish history. R. I. Best (1914) identified the hand responsible for writing many of them – including the record of Cú Chulainn's birth and several others in the extract above – as that of the scribe designated 'Hand H', who made important modifications to *Lebor na hUidre*, the first great surviving manuscript of vernacular material, written in Clonmacnoise in the early twelfth century (cf. Oskamp 1972: 68, and contributions to Ó hUiginn 2015).

Although the compiler (and revisers) of our work did not, in the vast majority of cases, engage directly with early Greek or Roman sources, they patently did not think of themselves as divorced from the world of classical antiquity about which they wrote. In fact, they seem to have thought of themselves as belonging to an intellectual tradition rooted in Greece and Rome, as well as Old Testament Israel. See, for instance, the record of the birth of Sallust, where he is described as 'the first historiographer' (*primus … historiagraphus*; Stokes 1895: 402). This information was derived from Isidore of Seville's *Chronica Maiora*, most likely via Bede's *De Temporibus*, and there is no evidence that the compiler had access to any of Sallust's works.[5] Nonetheless, the reference is enlightening. In an entry corresponding to the year 641 CE, the *Annals of Tigernach* (third fragment) report the death of Domnall mac Áeda, king of Ireland. The annalist implies that there was a degree of uncertainty about who succeeded to the kingship, referring to the opinion of 'some historiographers' (*quidam … historiagraphi*) that four men held the kingship jointly thereafter (Stokes 1896b: 186). These historiographers are Irish, rather than Roman. Their concern was with the succession of Irish kings, not with the internal or external conflicts of the late Roman republic. Yet, from his choice of words, we may deduce that the annalist saw them as pursuing the same intellectual discipline as Sallust and other historians of antiquity.

An interlinear gloss on the 641 annal supports this argument. This gloss, which is appended only to the first part of the word *historiagraphi*, reads .i. *stair* ('that is, *stair*').[6] *Stair*, the vernacular Irish term for history, is derived from the Latin *historia*, and was likewise used to refer to what were believed to be accurate accounts of past events (Poppe 2008; Poppe 2014a: 139–40). In light of the context of its appearance in the *Annals of Tigernach*, we may understand *stair* as a reference to vernacular historical writing, the kind of thing written by the Irish *historiagraphi* cited in the main text. The word *historia* appears with some frequency referring to books of the Old Testament (once each for the books of

Judith, Esther, and First Maccabees, following Jerome and Bede in each case), as well as the works of Herodotus, Flavius Josephus, and Julius Africanus (Stokes 1895: 386, 388, 390, 400n). It appears, therefore, that medieval Irish historians perceived an equivalence between the Irish vernacular tradition of historical writing – *stair* – and that of antiquity, including the works of Greek, Roman, Hebrew, and early Christian historians.

The relationship between classical *historia* and medieval Irish *stair* extended to matters of content and style. Effectively, medieval Irish scholars were influenced in their depiction of Ireland's past by the conventions of the genre as they inherited them. As noted above, the text before us displays a keen interest in the succession of kings in the great kingdoms of antiquity, a feature and framework derived ultimately from Eusebius (see MacNeill 1914 for further discussion). It is hardly surprising, therefore, that the first thread of Irish history to be woven into this rich historical tapestry is a record of the succession to the kingship of Emain Macha, the ancient capital of Ulster (five reigns are recorded in the extract above). Before the reign of the first of these kings, the text states, *omnia monimenta Scottorum usque Cimbáed incerta errant,* 'All the records of the Gaels are uncertain prior to [the reign of] Cimbáed' (Stokes 1895: 394). In parallel with the other peoples whose histories were also reported in the text, it made sense to begin Irish history with a record of the succession of kings. Moreover, when the record of Irish affairs begins to flesh out, its shape also suggests that received accounts of the history of antiquity were influential models. We may take as an example the account of the reign of Cormac mac Airt as king of Ireland. The beginning of Cormac's reign reads as a catalogue of battles against rival Irish dynasties and kings (Stokes 1896a: 12–13). This has echoes of the account of the events during the establishment of the Roman Empire. The reign of Octavian/Augustus, as depicted in the extract above, was likewise initiated by a series of battles against rivals.

The authors and compilers of our text engaged with classical antiquity not as a distinct historical epoch but as part of a broadly inclusive view of the history of the world as they knew it. This view was inherited from early Christian historians, including Eusebius, Orosius, and Isidore. These late antique sources also provided most of the information about world history available to the compiler of the Irish World Chronicle, so that we may say that his engagement with the ancient history of the Graeco-Roman world was indirect, mediated through sources mostly concerned with salvation history. Nonetheless, the compiler saw himself and other medieval Irish historians as practitioners of a discipline whose roots lay among both the Greeks and Romans, as well as the authors of the historical books of the Old Testament.

Notes

1   This is one of a series of marginal notes indicating the number of years from the Creation to the date in question.

2   There is a brief interlinear gloss above the name of each of the five battles listed. The clearest in meaning is that over *Siculum*, correctly identifying this adjective as referring to an island (*insola*). Of the others, the first reads *.i.c.* and the other three consist of the letter *c* only. The *.i.* must stand for *idán, edán, edón*, earlier *ed ón*, 'that is', from Latin *id est* (see above, p. xxiv). *Mutinense, Pilipense, Perusinum* and *Actiacum* are all adjectives derived from the names of towns, so it seems likely that *ciuitas* 'town, city' is the correct expansion for each *c*. (Stokes, however, expanded each *c* as *campus* 'plain'. This is unlikely, especially because it was well known in the period that Actium was a naval battle.) I am grateful to Michael Clarke for his assistance here and elsewhere.

3   This is the first of a series of crosses entered into the margin. Most are associated with references to Christian figures, but further study of their significance is required.

4   Máire Ní Mhaonaigh's 2019 Kelleher Lecture (2023) provides a vital reappraisal of the text and will hopefully spark further interest and study. I am very grateful to Prof. Ní Mhaonaigh for allowing me to read the text of her lecture prior to its publication.

5   Isidore, *Chronica Maiora* 225, Mommsen 1894: 452; Bede *De Temporibus* (*On Times*) 21, Jones 1975–80: 3.607–8, Kendall and Wallis 2010: 124–5.

6   Oxford, Bodleian Library MS Rawlinson B488, fol. 10r b, l. 4. There is a punctum between *historia* and *graphi*, suggesting the scribe understood it as a compound and attached the gloss only to the first element. The manuscript can be viewed online at https://digital.bodleian.ox.ac.uk/objects/2bebcdbb-ef7a-4985-bd16-4e9a8d897919/ . Stokes 1896b: 186 read the gloss as *sdair*, which is an acceptable variant spelling.

4

Gilla Cóemáin's *Annálad anall uile* 'All the annals heretofore …'

Peadar Mac Gabhann

The following extract presents the opening and closing quatrains of the poem, based on my edition and translation in Smith 2007: 188–203 for which I hold the copyright; the full poem may be found there, along with detailed notes on the chronological calculations and correlations.

Dates added on the right-hand side: AM = Anno mundi, year of the world since Creation; AAbr =Anno Abraham, year since Abraham; all other dates are CE.

Text: Opening and closing sequences of the poem

Gilla Cóemáin cecinit:

1.   Annálad anall uile
     ó thús betha barrbuide
     aisnéidfet-sa sunda sain
     cosin n-aimsir ndédenaig.

2.   Sé blíadna coícat, gním nglan,
     míle ar sé cétaib blíadan
     rímim, ar is rús cen ail,
     co Dílind ó Thús Domain.

3.   Dá cét a dó nóchat nár
     ó Dílind co hAbrahám;
     ó Abrám noí cét, ní scíth,
     cethracha a dó co Dauíd.

4.   Ó Dauíd co Brait, ní bréc,
     sechtó a trí cethri chét;
     ó Brait co Críst, caín a blá,
     a noí cóic cét ochtmoga.

5.   Trí míle blíadan, ní bréc,
     dá blíadain coícat noí cét
     co gein Meic Maire tall tair
     anall ó Thosach Domain.

6.   A dó sechtmogat, séol nglan,
     acht is ar míle blíadan
     ó Gein Críst co blíadain mbáin
     sechtmaide uate Enáir.

7.   A cethair fichet, fír dam,
     ocus cóic míle blíadan
     cosin mblíadain-se, is blad brass,
     ór delbad domun drechmas.

8.   Dá cét mblíadan cosin mbúaid
     co Mesc Túir noíthig Nebrúaid
     ó Dílind acht deich mblíadna
     is derb duit cía nos ríagla.

9.   A dó sescat, sáer in bríg,
     ó Mesc in Túir co flaith Nín;
     dá blíadain fichet ó shain
     co Abraám cosin n-athair.

Translation

Gilla Cóemáin chanted:

All the annals heretofore
from the beginning of the yellow-topped world
I will relate herein
until the most recent times.

Fifty-six years – a pure deed –
one thousand and six hundred years,
I compute – for it is a great knowledge without blemish –
until the Flood from the Beginning of the World.   **AM 1656**

Two hundred and two and noble ninety
from the Flood till Abraham;   **AM 1948**
from Abraham nine hundred – it is no repose –
[and] forty-two till David.   **AM2890**

From David until the Captivity – it is no falsehood –
four hundred and seventy-three;   **AM 3363**
from the Captivity until Christ – fair his cry –
five hundred and eighty-nine.   **AM 3952**

Three thousand years – it is no falsehood –
fifty-two years [and] nine hundred
until the Birth of the Son of Mary yonder in the East,
since the Beginning of the World.   **AM 3952**

Seventy-two years – a pure course –
save that it is in addition to a thousand years
from the Birth of Christ until this year [inclusively]
on feria seven of January.   **AD 1072**

Twenty-four – it is true for me –   **AM 5024**
and five thousand years
until this year – it is a vigorous fame –
since the beautiful-surfaced world was moulded.

Two hundred years until the victory,
to the Confusion of Nimrod's famed Tower   **AM 1466**
from the Flood, save ten years,   **AM 1656**
it will be certain for you, even if you check them.

Sixty-two – noble the virtue –
from the Confusion of the Tower until Ninus' reign;
twenty-two years from then   **AM 1528**
until Abraham, until the father.   **AM 1550**

10. Sesca blíadan cen nach mbrón
    ó Abrám co Partholón;
    día ragaib in n-inis find
    trí chét blíadan íar nDílind.

11. Ó gein Abrám, éol dam sain,
    co tarmthecht Mara Romair
    cóic blíadna cóic cét co cert
    día ro báded slúag Égept.

12. 'sind amsir-sin, rádit raind,
    ro toglad tíar Tor Conaind,
    ocus luid Srú sair for fecht
    dochum na Scithía a hÉgept.

13. Medón flatha Ascathías sain
    tarmthecht Mara rúaid Romair
    dá cét blíadain dara éis
    dered flatha Lampadéis.[1]

14. Hi flaith Lampadéis, léir blad,
    ruc Uesogés in slúagad
    ocus tánic slúag as lía
    'na degaid asin Scithía.

15. Isind amsir-sin ane
    tosach neirt na Cíchloscthe;
    'sind amsir-sin, cid ord bind,
    trebsat Fir Bolgg i nHérind.

16. Ochtmoga blíadan día és
    ba rí in talman Tutanés;
    is 'na ré ro gabsat tair
    Gáedil isna Gáethlaigib.

17. 'sind amsir-sin, cí at-ber,
    ro gníd Cath Maige Tured;
    'sind amsir-sin, cen goí ngá,
    ro toglad Troí Troíanna.

18. Thenías ba hé ainm ind ríg
    boí i comaimsir do Dau-íd;
    is and luid i n-úir in rí
    i n-aimsir dúir Darcelli.

19. Darcellus ba flaith na fond
    dar thríall Solom a thempoll;
    i mmedón flatha ind fhir fhind
    táncatar Gáedil Hérind.

Sixty years without any sorrow
from Abraham until Partholón;   **AM 1610**
when he took the fair island
[it was] three hundred years after the Flood.   **AM 1956**

From the birth of Abraham – that is known to me –
until the crossing of the Red Sea
five years [and] five hundred exactly   **AAbr 505**
[from] when the army of Egypt was drowned.

In that time – quatrains say –
the Tower of Conann was sacked in the West,
and Srú went eastwards on an expedition
to Scythia from Egypt.

That [was] the middle of the reign of Ascatades,   **AAbr 498–537**
the crossing of the blood-stained Red Sea;   **AAbr 505**
two hundred years after it
[was] the end of Lamparés' reign.

In Lamparés' reign – clear the renown –   **AAbr 690–719**
Vesozes carried out the hosting
and an army which was more numerous came
after him out of Scythia.

In that period, then,
the beginning of the Amazons' domination;   *c.* **AAbr 810**
in that time – though it be a melodious sequence –
the Fir Bolg dwelt in Ireland.

Eighty years after it
Tautanes was king of the world;   **AAbr 811–842**
it is in his era that
the Goídil settled in the Maeotic Marshes in the East.

[It is] in that period then – though I may say it –
[that] the battle of Mag Tuired was fought;
[it is] in that period – without false deception –
[that] Trojan Troy was sacked.   **AAbr 835**

Thineus was the name of the king   **AAbr 883–912**
who was contemporaneous with David;   **AAbr 941–980**
it is then that the king went into the soil,
in the austere time of Dercylus.   **AAbr 913–952**

Dercylus was lord of the territories   **AAbr 913–952**
when Solomon strove [to build] his temple;   **AAbr 984**
[it was] in the middle of the fair man's reign   **AAbr 981–1020**
that the Goídil reached Ireland.

20. Astiagés abb cen fhell
    dar airged Ierusalem;
    tiugfhlaith Med, maith ra molad,
    i comfhlaithis Nabcodon.

21. Darcellus, Solom na sleg
    comaimser is Mic Míled;
    cóic cét acht fiche día n-és
    Nabcodon Astiagés.

22. Sírna rí Temra na tor
    i comfhlaithis Nabcodon;
    and-sin fechta, fáth ngaile,
    cath Móna truim Trógaide.

23. Trícha trí chét ó shain 'lle
    co tús flatha Úgaine;
    deired flatha Pers, blad nglicc,
    tossach flatha meic Pilip.

24. Sesca trí chét mblíadan mbil
    ó fhlaith aird Alaxandair
    cor génair Mac maith Maire
    ocus ó fhlaith Úgaine.

Quatrains 25–33 continue aligning the pre-Christian history of Ireland with events from world history until the death of Christ; quatrains 34–58 move forward through Irish history from the arrival of Saint Patrick until the time of composition around the year 1072. Only the concluding quatrains are printed here; for the full edition and translation see Smith 2007.

53. Cethri blíadna ó shen i-lle
    cor chuired cath na Craíbe
    ó chath na Craíbe 's a deich
    co bás Bríain meic Cennétich.

54. Noí mblíadna íar mbás Bríaïn
    éc meic Domnaill' na díaid;
    a dó cethrachat, céim nglan,
    ó shain bás Dondchaid Muman.

55. Dá blíadain, ní bréc, i nglíaid
    ó éc Dondchada meic Bríain,
    cath Saxan, séol co nglaine,
    i torchair rí Lochlainne.

Astyages [was] lord without treachery   **AAbr 1419–1456**
when Jerusalem was plundered;   **AAbr 1426**
the last lord of the Medes – well was he praised –
[was] in contemporary sovereignty with Nabuchodonosor.   **d. AAbr 1445**

Dercylus [and] Solomon of the lances [were]   **AAbr 981-1020**
the contemporaries of the Sons of Míl;
five hundred years save twenty after them
[were] Nabuchodonosor [and] Astyages.   **AAbr 1419–1456**

Sírna, the king of Tara of the Towers, [was]
in contemporary sovereignty with Nabuchodonosor;   **d. AAbr 1445**
[it is] then [that] was fought – a cause of valour –
the battle of grievous Móin Trógaide.

Three hundred and thirty [years] thenceforth
until the beginning of the reign of Úgaine;
the end of the sovereignty of the Persians, shrewd renown,
[and] the beginning of the reign of Philip's son.   **AAbr 1681**

Three hundred and sixty fortunate years
from the distinguished reign of Alexander   **AM 1681–1692**
until the goodly Son of Mary was born
and from [the time of] the reign of Úgaine.

Four years thenceforth
until the battle of the Cráeb was engaged   1004
from the battle of the Cráeb and ten
until the death of Brían son of Cennétech.   1014

Nine years after the death of Brían
the death of the son of Domnall after it;   1022
forty-two – a pure step –
thence until the death of Donnchad of Munster.   1064

Two years – it is no falsehood – in battle
from the death of Donnchad son of Brían
the battle of the Saxons – a pure course –   1066
in which fell the king of Norway.

56. Cóic blíadna ó shen i-lle
    cosin mblíadain-se i táimne
    sechtmad úathaid, slicht sádal,
    for Enáir ra hannálad.
    Annálad.

57. A dó secht ndeich ar míle
    ó gein Críst, cía chomríme,
    cosin mblíadain-seo, cí at-ber,
    i torchair Díarmait dúrgen.

58. A Chríst, a grían os cach gurt,
    airchis dom'anmain im' churp,
    nírop sheng do thairbirt dam,
    bud irdairc lem th'annálad.
    Annálad.

Five years thenceforth   **1072**
until this present year in which we are
the seventh feria – an easy division –
upon January was recorded.
Annals.

Two [and] seven tens plus a thousand   **1072**
from the birth of Christ – howsoever you may compute [it] –
until this year – though I may say it –
in which resolute Díarmait fell.

O Christ, O sun over every field,
have compassion on my soul in my body,
may your giving to me be not restricted,
let your annals be famous because of me.
Annals.

Essay: The poetry of historical synchronisms

Annálad anall uile ('All the annals heretofore') belongs to the genre of historical poetry and the sub-genre of synchronistic poetry (see Smith 2002 for working definitions of these terms). F. J. E. Raby (1934: 259–60) evokes the wider European context from which Irish historical poetry emerged, citing such examples as the monumental *Annales de gestis Caroli magni imperatoris libri quinque* ('Annals of the Deeds of the Emperor Charles the Great in Five Books'), composed about 890 CE on the basis of pre-existing prose histories, which stands as one of the earliest known versifications of annalistic material from Continental Europe. Around the same time, Irish literature also first saw the emergence of long historical poems, a genre that would be practised throughout the Middle Irish period (for an early example of the genre see O'Brien 1955). While we have a large corpus of these poems, few of them bring together synchronisms and computations in a single work in the way that *Annálad anall uile* does.

The poem is written in a loose version of the syllabic metre called *deibide*; a more complex variety of the same metre is to be seen in Flann Mainistrech's poem presented in Chapter 5. Internal historical evidence dates the composition to no later than 1072, and possibly to as early as 1066, the date of the Battle of Stamford Bridge at which occurred the death of King Harald Hardradi of Norway (quatrain 55). The only indication of authorship is found in the Book of Leinster, which records the ascription 'Gilla coemain cecinit', 'Gilla Cóemáin sang [this]' (*Gill-coemaī .cc̄.*; see Best et al. 1954–83: 3.496, line 15407). Gilla Cóemáin composed four other historical poems: *Ériu ard inis na rríg* ('Noble Ireland, island of the kings'), 151 quatrains on the pre-Christian kings of Ireland (Smith 2007: 100–61); *At-tá sund forba fessa* ('Herein is the apex of knowledge'), 37 quatrains on the Christian kings until the death of Brían Bórama 'Brian Boru' (Smith 2007: 170–87); *Tigernmas mac Follaig aird* ('Tigernmas son of noble Follach'), 14 quatrains on Tigernmas, an eminent pre-Christian king of Ireland (Smith 2015); and *Góedel Glas ó tát Goídil* ('Góedel Glas whence the Irish'), 40 quatrains on the transmigration of the Irish from North Africa via the Black Sea, the Mediterranean and the Iberian Peninsula to Ireland (Lehmacher 1921; I am currently preparing a new edition of this poem). He is also credited with having translated from Latin into Irish the *Historia Brittonum*, a tenth-century account of the origins and ancestry of the peoples of Britain (Van Hamel 1932, xii, xxvi, 1).

In *Annálad*, quatrains 1–33 place the history of pre-Christian Ireland in its international context by synchronizing the dates of the reigns of Irish kings, and important Irish events, with reigns and events from Assyria, Israel, the Medes'

Empire, Persia and Macedonia (see Smith 2007: 188–211). Quatrain 33 marks Christ's age at the time of the Crucifixion, while quatrains 34–58 record the intervals of time between the deaths of various kings and significant battles from the arrival of St Patrick in 432 until the death in 1072 of Díarmait mac Maíl na mBó, King of Ireland 'with opposition' (Smith 2007: 200–11). These later quatrains occasionally synchronize events in Christian Ireland with events occurring elsewhere such as the death of Pope Gregory the Great in AD 604 (line 37d).

The overall chronological structure of the pre-Christian section is based on the framework of world history that was laid down by Eusebius of Caeserea (260/265–339) in Greek and mediated through Latin by his translators, including Jerome (*c.* 342/347–420) and Rufinus of Aquileia (*c.* 345–411; Schöne 1900; Grafton and Williams 2006). The first six quatrains of *Annálad* employ Bede's systematization of the Six Ages of the World.[2] The remainder of the pre-Christian section incorporates dates from Jerome's translation of the *Chronicle* of Eusebius.[3] Supplementary information comes from other texts including the *Historiae adversus Paganos* 'Histories against the Pagans' of Orosius (*c.* 380–416). Quatrain 14, for example, which mentions Vesozes, draws on Orosius 1.14, para 1.3. Quatrains 34–48 derive their information from a hitherto unidentified version of the post-Patrician Irish Annals that may have been associated with Clonmacnoise (Smith 2007: 88; Smith 2002: 339).

It is impossible to distinguish with any degree of certainty the instances in which the poet has drawn directly from the Latin writers, as opposed to those in which materials from Roman authors have come via compilations made by earlier Irish scholars (see further Smith 2002: 333, with Smith 2007: 88). It is possible that he took much or all that he required for quatrains 1–33 from the 'pre-Patrician' section of the Irish annals, whose chronology owes much to Rufinus of Aquileia (McCarthy 2008). He may have used an epitome of the chronological 'highlights' of the annals, similar to that preserved in fragmentary form in the so-called 'Laud Synchronisms' (Meyer 1913). The ultimate exemplar could in fact have been a Latin text of Eusebian materials based on the Greek original that has come down to us via the Armenian translation of the *Chronicle* (Karst 1911). Such a text might have functioned as a kind of 'timeline' that enabled historical authors to quickly cross-check regnal years and dates.

The author is a historian who could versify the record of the past with relative ease. It could be argued, however, that he lacked a robust sense of the poetic aesthetic. *Annálad* exhibits a comparatively low level of metrical ornamentation, with few examples of internal rhyme in the lines *c* and *d* of each quatrain (Smith 2007: 260). Internal rhyme in the first couplet of each quatrain (admittedly not a formal requirement of *deibide*) is similarly a rarity. Had our author's obituary survived in the annals, he might have merited the epithet *suí senchusa* 'scholar of history', but not that of *suí filidechta* 'scholar of poetics'.[4] Nonetheless, the poem does much to show how history should be recorded and cultivated. By embedding significant meaning within chevilles – ornamental phrases at the ends of lines – and choosing words that hark back to his subject matter, the writer conveys his message with powerful effect. Chevilles in medieval Irish poetry have been conventionally perceived as bland, meaningless phrases whose function was to fulfil the syllable-count of any given line; the reality, however, is more complex.

Constant references to the marking of time illustrate that the provision of a chronological framework for the historical narrative was fundamental to the work of medieval Irish historians. Hence the word *aimser* – (a) 'point of time'; (b) 'period of time'; (c) 'age, period, epoch' – occurs repeatedly (lines 1d, 12a, 15a, 17a, 17c, 18d), with the related *comaimser* – (a) 'contemporaneity'; (b) 'synchronism' (18b, 21b). In the same semantic field is *ré* 'period, lapse of time' (16c).[5] From a different semantic field, but related in the context of this poem, are the words *flaith* 'lordship, sovereignty, rule' (13a, 14a, 19c, 24b) and *comfhlaithius* 'joint, equal sovereignty; contemporaneous sovereignty' (20d, 22b). Such allusions provide fundamental reference-points in the construction of the chronology. *Annálad* is defined as (a) ' the act of keeping annals; annal, record' and (b) 'computation'. The term connotes not only the end-product, 'the historical record', but the sustained elaboration of that artefact. Fundamental also to this act of historical record-keeping and historical elaboration is reciting or *recounting* the events of history in sequence to an informed audience. Hence we see the verb *aisnéidfetsa* 'I will recount' (1c), from the verb *as-indét* 'declares, tells, relates (about)', with the cognate verbal noun *aisndís* 'recounting'.

All-pervasive in this poem is the view that historical scholarship should be founded on systematic methods, the most fundamental of which was the computation of dates. The keyword is *rím*: (a) 'the act of counting, enumerating'; (b) 'telling, relating'. Thus, the author declares: *rímim, ar is rús cen ail*, 'I compute – for it is a great knowledge without blemish' (2c). The word *ríagal* – 'rule, authority, measure' – conveys the notion of an accepted chronology of events, a historical 'time-line': *is réil in ríagail* 'the rule is clear' (46b). The related verb *ríaglaid* ('regulates, orders, arranges') appears in *is derb duit cia nos ríagla* – 'it is certain for you, even if you check them' (8d). Images of the poet casting his eye down a timeline are suggested by nominal chevilles like *séol nglan* 'a pure course' (6a), *cid ord bind* 'though it be a melodious sequence' (15c), *céim nglan* 'a pure leap' (39c), *séol co nglaine* 'a pure course' (55c).

Precise computation is vital. The computation of specific time-lapses dominates many quatrains (see e.g. quatrains 2–13; 16; 21; 23–48; and 50–7). Again, one must cross-check one's own historical account against those of other authors: *is derb duit, cía nos ríagla* 'it is certain for you, even if you check them' (8d), *rádit raind* 'quatrains say' (12a). Compare *cía chure ris nach cinte* 'even if you set it against something certain' (35b), *'sin blíadain sin rádit raind* 'in that year stanzas mention' (36c). This brings certainty: *derb lib* 'be you certain' (31c), *derb dait* 'you may be certain' (34a), *derbaig* 'verify [it]' (42a). Vital too is the guarantee of the veracity of the narrative and its rejection of falsehood: *ní bréc* 'it is no lie' (4a, 5a), *fír dam* 'it is true for me' (i.e. 'I am correct', 7a), *cen goí ngá* 'without false deception' (17c), *ní himmarbréc* 'It is no deception' (43b). History as an instrument for perpetuating the memories of the great personages of the past is seen in the frequent use of the words *blad*, 'fame, renown', *blá*, 'shout, cry': *caín a blá* 'fair his cry [fame]' (4c), *is blad brass* 'it is a vigorous fame' (7c), *léir blad* 'clear the renown' (14a), *blad nglicc* 'a shrewd renown' (23c), *borb a blad* 'fierce his fame' (26c); see also *ní blad bán* 'it is no pure renown' (44a). Colour is added by the linking of specific qualities to individuals with alliteration: Conn Cétchathach is *crúad* 'hard, severe' (28a), Colum Cille is *céolach* 'melodious' (46d), and Flaithbertach is *fíal* 'generous' (49b).

At the heart of the medieval Irish historians' work was a fascination with the measurement of time, a concern rooted in their predecessors' preoccupation with the field of computistics as early as the sixth and seventh centuries CE (see Warntjes 2011). By applying a chronological framework to a pre-Patrician Irish past constructed on the basis of synchronizing Irish events and reigns with widely accepted dates in 'world history', Irish historians firmly grounded post-Patrician Irish historiography on pillars of scholarship which exuded authority, authenticity and veracity. Embodiment of that material in verse form granted it canonical status and made it easily transmissible in a classroom setting.

Glimpses of the poem's chronological methods can be found, perhaps ironically, in synchronisms that turn out to be problematic or erroneous. Quatrains 23–4 synchronize the beginning of the reign of Alexander the Great, after the slaying of Darius of Persia, with the beginning of the reign of the Irish king Úgaine Mór, and calculate 360 years from Alexander and Úgaine to the birth of Christ. However, since Alexander's twelve-year reign ended according to the same reckoning in 321 BCE (*recte* 323), the figures are irreconcileable. At points like this we see the challenge of reconciling Irish dynastic records with Eusebian chronology, especially in relation to the Incarnation and (by extension) the *anno domini* dating of the poet's own time, which he fixes so precisely in quatrains 55–57: five years after the battle of Stamford Bridge, and in the year of the death of Díarmait mac Maíl na mBó. In the present example it is probably significant that the traditions about the dating of Úgaine Mór found in other sources, including the *Lebor Gabála*, are themselves fluctuating and uncertain.

Behind Gilla Cóemáin's work is a protracted process involving the coordination of varying approaches to the measurement of time, as well as the interweaving of the literary strand of the tradition with that of historical calculation. An early stage in this process involved the incorporation of earlier Irish narrative materials into the Eusebian framework, with *scéla*, 'prose narratives', treated as a constituent element of *senchas* 'historical knowledge'. So it comes about, for example, that the mythological battle of Mag Tuired, between the Fomoiri and the Túatha Dé Danann, is synchronized with the sack of Troy (quatrain 17). The fall of Troy resonates with the Irish past here in a way comparable in spirit to that seen in the later poem *Clann Ollaman uaisle Emna* ('The noblemen of Emain Macha are the descendants of Ollam'), discussed by Michael Clarke in Chapter 24 of this volume. As more and more information of this sort was subsumed into the annals, many of the pivotal events (including, for example, the arrival of the Goídil in Ireland) were thrown out of sequence and thus into disharmony with related events. Considered in another light, as more information from the *scélshenchas* (learned narrative) strand of the tradition was incorporated into the annals, there was a greater 'computistic' imperative to push the arrival of the Goídil backward in time. In opposition to the 'computistic' imperative stood the literary imperative. Given the clash between the competing interests of literary parallelism and computistic synchronization, it is no wonder that some of the synchronisms in *Annálad anall uile* are problematic. Nevertheless, *Annálad anall uile* provides us with great insights into the worldview and methods of the medieval Irish historian, into the aesthetics of literary computation, and into both the place of ancient history within such works and the influence of late antique historiography on their content and structure.

Notes

1   This mistake for *Lamparés*, genitive *Lamparéis*, is found in all extant witnesses to the manuscript tradition; see Smith 2007: 192–3, 237–8.

2   See 'Gruppe 1b: Bedasches Schema' in Tristram 1985: 37–42, with Bede at *De Temporum Ratione* 66.1 (Jones 1975–80: 2.463, translated at Wallis 1999: 157); and compare the 'Synchronisms from the Book of Ballymote' (Synchronisms B), Mac Carthy 1892: 239–40.

3   The standard edition is Helm 1913. In Smith 2007 I give detailed notes arising from a comparative study of *Annálad anall uile* and various other texts including the *Chronicle.*

4   The terms *suí filidechta* and *suí senchusa* occur frequently in the annalistic obits. *Suí* is defined as I (a) 'man of learning, scholar, wise man, sage', (b) more specifically 'head of a monastic or poetic school', and II 'expert, master'; see *eDIL* s.v. *suí.* The same dictionary defines *filidecht* (s.v.) as the 'art, office or practice of the *fili*; poetry'; more precise terminology would include 'poetics' as well as 'versification'.

5   Here and below, the definitions cited are from the online *eDIL*, consulted in October 2022.

Flann Mainistrech's *Flaithius Rómán ríge glonn* 'The sovereignty of the Romans was a kingship of feats of prowess'

Peadar Mac Gabhann

The four manuscripts that transmit the series of 'Poems on World Kingship' divide into two groups (for details and notation see below, p. 72). Recension 1 is transmitted in manuscripts D and L¹ and Recension 2 in manuscripts M and L². Where there is a variation between the readings preserved in the two recensions, I have preferred the evidence of Recension 1 in the belief that it represents the earliest extant version of the poem. Within Recension 1, D is usually, but not invariably, the more faithful witness to the Middle Irish grammar and spelling of the original. Recension 2 includes additional verses, omissions and simplifications of language and grammar, but occasionally preserves original features that are obscured in the manuscripts of Recension 1. To summarize, therefore: the readings of D are preferred in the first instance; where they are flawed, or where D contains a gap, then L¹ is followed. Where the Recension 1 manuscripts are both demonstrably faulty, the readings of the Recension 2 manuscripts, M and L², have been adopted.

For the purposes of this anthology, the language of the poem has been lightly standardized in accordance with modern ediitorial practice. Early Modern Irish features, introduced during transmission, have been silently removed, and inclusion of a full apparatus of variants has been postponed pending the presentation of a critical edition.

Evidence exists to demonstrate that Flann's poems continued to be refined and corrected in the later secular schools, long after the original composition. According to Roman tradition, Julius Caesar was stabbed 23 times before he succumbed to a loss of blood. Here are the manuscript data for Flann's line 5d:

*tri*a *cet*hri *crech*taib .xxx.[at] D.	'through four wounds and thirty'
*tri*a .íííí. *crech*taib *tri*chat L[1].	'through four wounds and thirty'
o *tri* crectaibh *cer*t .xxx.it M.	'from three wounds and exactly thirty'
o *tri* crec*h*t certfhicheat L[2].	'from three wounds and exactly twenty'.

In this instance, L[2] restores what the scribe believes to have been the correct reading. Was twenty-four in Flann's original, but later mistakenly rendered as thirty-four, or did Flann's original contain the incorrect figure? Either way, the evidence suggests that the scribe of L[2] or its exemplar adjusted the poem in the interests of exact historical precision.

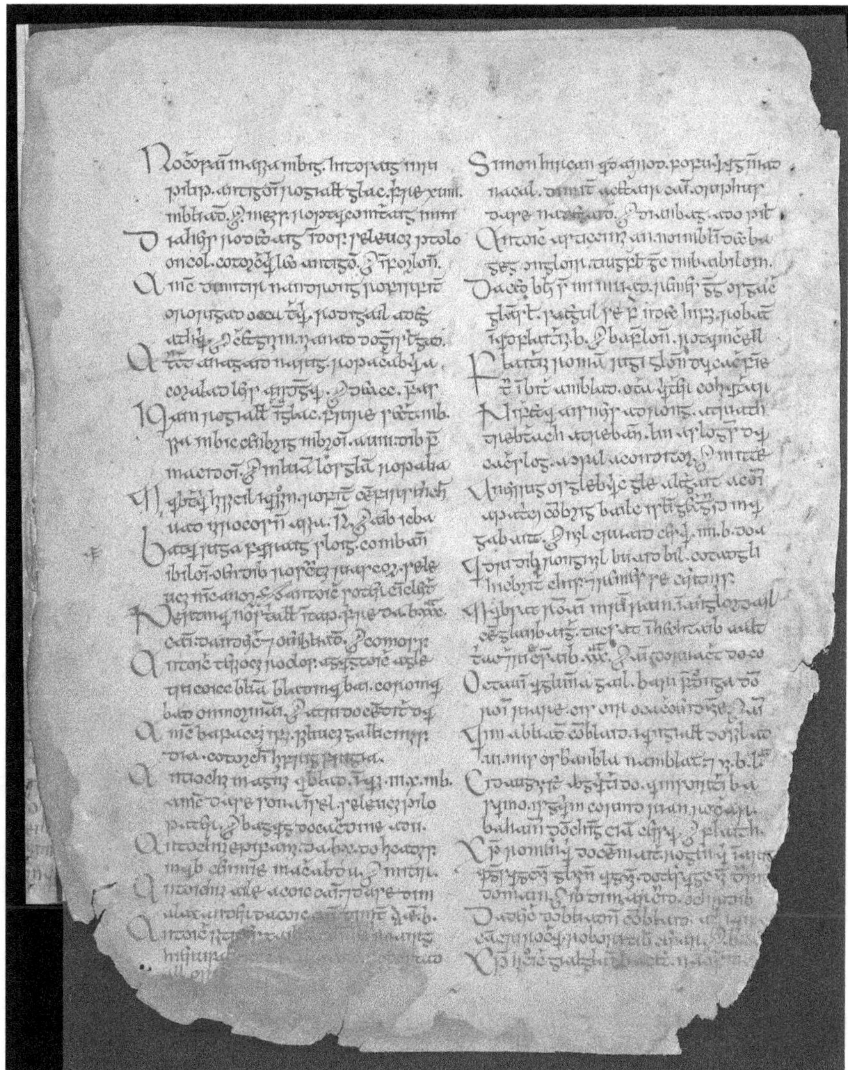

Figure 2 Dublin, Royal Irish Academy MS D.iv.3, fol. 38v: Flann Mainistrech on the kingship of the Romans. Image from ISOS reproduced by kind permission of the Royal Irish Academy.

Text: Opening and closing sections of the poem

Edited by the author from the manuscripts (D, fol. 38vb9 ff.; L¹, fol. 12vb20 ff.; M, fol. 46ra64 ff.; L², fol. 29v5 ff.). In the translation, additions necessary for making sense in English are enclosed in [square brackets]. Dates are given in the margins, with BC *and* AD *(=*BCE*,* CE*) to clarify the more ancient year-numbers.*

1a   Flaithius Rómán ríge glonn,
1b   dar cach fine ba forlonn;
1c   ro tairmchell trá in bith a mblad,
1d   óthá Airther co hÍarthar.

2a   Ní fhétar aisnéis a drong,
2b   a tríath trebthach, a trebonn,
2c   lín a slóg-som dar cach slóg,
2d   a consal, a conditór.

3a   A n-éirig ós glébáirc glé:
3b   a légáit, a coimitte,
3c   a patrice co mbríg bailc,
3d   is lín cach gráid mar gabait.

4a   Airdrí díb ro ngiúil búaid bil
4b   co taidlí Iúil crúaid Cesair;
4c   ceithre blíadna dó hic brith chís
4d   ocus reimes sé certmís.

5a   Marbsat Rómáin in ríg ráin
5b   ina nglórdáil cen glanbáig;
5c   tucsat i n-échtaib a alt,
5d   tría cheithre créchtaib tríchat.

6a   Ochtauin ar glunna gail,
6b   ba rí for drunga domain;
6c   do-rúacht dó co Róim ría ré
6d   cís óir ó cach óenduine.

7a   Áirem a blíadan co mblaid
7b   íar ngíallad do shíl Adaim;
7c   sé mís ós bríanbla na mblat
7d   ocus sé blíadna coícat.

8a   Cid 'Auguist' do-gairthe dó
8b   arin soirthe ba sármó,
8c   is gairm de rind rían ro char,
8d   ba hainm don ching cían 'Cesar'.

Translation by the author

The sovereignty of the Romans [was] a kingship of feats of prowess,
more than any other race were they superior in strength;
indeed, their renown went around the world,
from the East to the West.

Impossible is the enumeration of her peoples,
of their lords of husbandmen, of their tribunes,
and of the full extent of their armies beyond those of every other army,
of their consuls, of their founders.

Their emergence above the lustrous ship of the radiant ones:
their legates, their attendants,
their patricians with resolute authority,
and the number of each grade as they exist.

[They chose] a high-king from among them to whom good victory adhered
until hardy Julius Caesar passed [lit. passes] along;
four years for him levying taxes
and a reign of six months exactly.

The Romans killed the very splendid king
in their glorious assembly without a clean contest;
they put his body among the slain
by means of thirty-four wounds.   [44 BCE]

Octavian on account of feats of valour,
he was king over the peoples of the world;
there came to him in Rome during his era
a tax in gold from every single person.

The reckoning of his years of renown   [44 BCE – 14 CE]
after submission by the descendants of Adam;
six months [presiding] over the hilly plain of the strong ones
and six years [and] fifty.

Though it was 'Augustus' that he was called
on account of his nobility which was great and desirable,
– it is a title, by dint of the powers, which he loved –
'Caesar' was the name of the warrior of yore.

9a   Críst ro ménair de cach maith,
9b   ro génair ina rigfhlaith
9c   ar gresargain gluinn ar guin
9d   do thesargain druing domuin.

10a   Dá deich de blíadnaib co mblaid
10b   a trí íarmaib d'imarcraid;
10c   ó chridib cach crí ra char,
10d   robo rí Tibir Cesar.

11a   Críst hi croich cíallglain, ba chét,
11b   'na ochtmad blíadain déc
11c   coro chaíntis caíme a cern
11d   no léictís daíne in Ifern.

12a   Flaith ceithre mblíadan nammá
12b   Gaí cíallglan Gallicula;
12c   ní súail cech decair do-rat,
12d   Cluid crúaid a cethair déc.

13a   Do Néir dá n-ocht mblíadan mbalc
13b   tríallad olc is écomnart;
13c   ba leis ría n-écimrim de,
13d   cétingrim na Crístaide.

14a   Ro croch Petar tróg tallad,
14b   ocus Pól do díchennad;
14c   ro loisc Róim im Thibre tnú,
14d   is do-rigne i lechtu.

15a   Luaidis a óenar ó thig
15b   cen chóemnad asin chathraig;
15c   rod marb fo-deisin in fer
15d   ba día geisib in gaisced.

16a   Galua, Pison, dúib adéus
16b   Otho ocus Uetelléus;
16c   cen methgíallna ós cach mud
16d   trí lethblíadna don chethrur.

17a   A trí fo thrí, ba tric tríall,
17b   do Thit is do Uespisían;
17c   nírbu gléo i ngort dar glenn,
17d   léo ro hort Ierusalem.

18a   Óenchét déc míle, mod nglé,
18b   lín ríme rucad heise;
18c   is noí cét ro damnad de
18d   hé lín ro marbad innte.

Christ, who conceived of every good,
was born into his royal sovereignty
against the murderous onslaught of the evil deed that wounds us
for the salvation of the people of the world.

Twice ten of years with renown   [14–37 CE]
three after them in addition;
from the hearts of everybody who loved him,
Tiberius Caesar was king.

Christ [was crucified] on the cross of clear meaning, he was the first,
during his [i.e. Tiberius'] eighteenth year
so that they might regret the amusement of their triumphs
which used to cause people to be hurled into hell.

A reign of four years only   [37–41 CE]
of Gaius Caligula of clear senses;
not insignificant is every difficulty that he brought about,
severe Claudius, fourteen.   [41–54 CE]

By Nero for twice eight of powerful years   [54–68 CE]
were evil and weakness sought after;
by him, before their mortal journey,
[was undertaken] the first persecution of the Christians.

He crucified poor Peter who was taken away,   [*c.* 64–68 CE]
as was Paul for beheading;   [*c.* 64 CE]
he burned Rome around the enflamed Tiber,
and he turned it [Rome] into gravestones.

He set off alone from his house
without protection out of the city;
the man killed himself,
valour was not intrinsic to him.

Galba, Piso, to you will I tell of   [68–69 CE]
Otho and Vitellius;   [69 CE]
without weak submission over every way,
three half-years for the four men.

Thrice three, it was a swift expedition,
for Titus and Vespasian;   [69–79 CE]
– it was no contention in a field across a valley –
by them was Jersualem sacked.   [70 CE]

Eleven hundred thousand – a clear way –
[is the] number that was taken out of it [Jerusalem];
and nine hundred [thousand] from it [Jerusalem] were subdued
that is the number that was killed in it.

19a   Tit cen tréis, tríamain nach tan,
19b   blíadain dar éis a athar;
19c   dá chóic co fáthaib na fíann
19d   dá bráthair do Domitían.

20a   Domitían ós grinnlinn glé,
20b   ro ingrinn na Crístaide;
20c   ba día thréoir úair nárbu thais,
20d   ro lád Éoin fora longais.

21a   Luid i mbás coa muintir mbil
21b   ina chruinntig chomrarcnig;
21c   hé ro marb – ni dalb ad-ius
21d   spato díarb ainm Pertinius

22a   Prap tarraid Nérua cís cain
22b   re ceithre mís for blíadain;
22c   in tan ro díbad co dían
22d   is and ro rígad Troían.

23a   Troían ro tríallad cen éc
23b   fri rémes noí mbliadan déc;
23c   tar findlinn fúair súan-se,
23d   ro ingrim na cristaide.

24a   Ro crochad leis, cíarbu chenn,
24b   Símón ab Ierusalem;
24c   robo dímór dál imba
24d   Símón mac cáid Cléopaä.

25a   Comarba Petair atúaid,
25b   in t-ap ro ecair Antúaig,
25c   Ignatius co ngrád cach glain,
25d   leis ro lád do léomanaib.

26a   Ro píanad leis úair ba geint
26b   in suí cíallglan in Clemeint;
26c   ro hairged leis ap Roma
26d   i mMuir chairrcech Cersona.

27a   Comarba Petair, fó fer,
27b   díarbu ainm Alaxander;
27c   leis ro hort in glanfhíal glan
27d   is Madian in tApstal.

28a   At-bath-som de buinnig bréin
28b   ar ba cuinnid cen chóemchéill;
28c   cíarbo chesgrádach sel sunn,
28d   is Espánach in ifurnn.

Titus without weakness, a wretched person at any time,   [79–81 CE]
a year after his father;
two fives with the skills of soldiers
for his brother, for Domitian.   [81–96 CE]

Domitian over the swift pure water,
he persecuted the Christians;
it was by his cold direction, which was not gentle,
that John was sent into exile.   [*c.* 95 CE]

He went to his death by [the hands of] his own household
in his round house of mutual slaughter;
he who killed him – it is no falsehood that I will relate –
[was] a eunuch named Parthenius.

Unexpectedly did Nerva acquire the fair tax   [96–98 CE]
for a period of four months plus a year;
when he was swiftly extinguished
it is then that Trajan was installed as ruler.

Trajan was guided without a death   [98–117 CE]
for a period of nineteen years;
beyond the fair period, he encountered [the final] slumber,
he persecuted the Christians.

Crucified by him, though he was a leader,
was Simon, the abbot of Jerusalem;   [107 or 117 CE]
there was a great number of them around him,
[namely], Simon, the chaste son of Cleophas.

The Successor of Peter from the North,
the abbot who set in order Antioch,
[was] Ignatius with love of every pure person,
by him [Trajan] was he [Ignatius] thrown to the lions.   [108 CE]

Clement, the scholar of pure meanings,
was tortured by him [Trajan] because he was a gentile;
by him [Trajan] was slain the abbot of Rome
in the rocky sea of Chersonesus.   [99 CE]

The Successor of Peter, a prince of men,
whose name was Alexander;
by him [Trajan] was slain the modestly generous, pure one   [*c.* 115 CE]
and Madianus the Apostle.

He [Trajan] died of foul diarrhoea   [117 CE]
for he was a warrior without appropriate sense;
though he was a beloved spear for a while here,
he is a Spaniard in hell.

29a   Adrían co recht ro ríarad
29b   fri ré trí secht sóerblíadan;
29c   hi feib ro tingill, 'na ré,
29d   ro ingrinn na Crístaide.

30a   Antono Pius cona blaid,
30b   ata-díus dom' degdaltaib;
30c   ro dét a recht a ríagail
30d   ré trí secht is óenblíadain.

31a   Marc Anton, firfháel hi fus,
31b   is Lucius cáem Commodus,
31c   a noí déc dóib i-mmalle
31d   co cóir is co comríge.

32a   Cechtar de as toirthe tlus
32b   do-goirthe dó Augustus;
32c   co sain a-nall, ní clóencusc,
32d   ni baí and acht Óenaugust.

33a   Íar Marc maith, ba flaith i fus,
33b   dá shé ro caith Commodus;
33c   eclas do loit, ba sí a mían,
33d   cora hort la hIúlían

34a   Iúlían brithem, bec a chís,
34b   slithem secc na sé certmís;
34c   ra marb in fénnid co fí
34d   Sēuer hic Drochit Mulbi.

35a   Seuer Affer occa tair
35b   ba cathfher hic Romanchaib;
35c   dá secht mblíadan, ba hí a ré
35d   hic píanad na Crístaide.

36a   Clad Saxan do-rónad leis
36b   do chasnam a chomarbais;
36c   cét míle ro shín a fhat
36d   ocus dá míle tríchat.

37a   Tair hic Cáer Ebróc na n-ech
37b   ósin glanrót glé-rindech,
37c   cen chath, de galar gann gus,
37d   is and at-bath Severus.

38a   Siacht a mac co ngrantóir gá
38b   int Antoin Caracalla
38c   a secht ós blaid borb bil
38d   co torchair tair hic Pairthib.

By means of ordinance was Hadrian guided   [117–138 CE]
for a period of thrice seven of noble years;
just as he had promised, in his era,
he persecuted the Christians.

Antoninus Pius with his renown   [138–161 CE]
I will tell of him to my goodly students;
his law [and] his rule were accepted
for a period of thrice seven and one year.

Marcus Antoninus, a true wolf in this world,   [161–180 CE]
and fair Lucius Commodus,
ninteen for them together
with propriety and with joint kingship.

Which ever of the two whose fruit flourished most
he was titled 'Augustus';
up until then – it was no unjust prohibition –
there was only one Augustus.

After goodly Mark, he was a prince in this world,
twice six did Commodus spend;   [180–192 CE]
to destroy the church – that was his desire –
until he was slain by Julian.

Julian the Judge – petty was his tributary income –   [193 CE]
creepy, sapless one [with a reign] of exactly six months;   [28 Mar. – 2 June]
the champion, Severus, killed him venomously,
at the Milvian Bridge.

Severus the African among them in the East   [193–211 CE]
he was a man of battle among the Romans;
twice seven years, that was his period
engaged in torturing the Christians.

The Saxons' Dyke was made by him
to protect his patrimony;
for one hundred miles did its length extend
and thirty-two miles.

In the East at York of the steeds
above the clean highway of well-defined extremities,
without battle, [but] from a mean, fierce disease,
it is there that Severus died.   [211 CE]

His son came as far as the grey-haired champion of the spears   [198–217 CE]
namely, Antonius Caracalla: [211–217 CE]
for seven [did he preside] over a fierce and evil renown
until he fell in the East among the Parthians.

39a   Ophil Macrin, art co ngus,
39b   's a mac Diadumenianus,
39c   i mblíadain ba torcda tair,
39d   coro horta ó míledaib.

40a   Marcus Antoin, ro-chart crí,
40b   sacart Eliogabali;
40c   a chethair flaithius ind fhir
40d   cora marbsatar mílid.

[Quatrains 41–109 are omitted here.]

110a   Anastais Tánaise Tair
110b   cen támthaise tre blíadain;
110c   oc Necea co ndathgním dois,
110d   ra n-aithríg in tres Téothois.

111a   Téothois, óenblíadain a ré
111b   fo chóemríagail Crístaide;
111c   ós cach cloí chíallna cen chair
111d   noí mblíadna don tres Léomain.

112a   Ón chétblíadain Iúil ros gab
112b   co cétríagail tres Léoman,
112c   fíad cach slúag co ndaithe a ndál
112d   at-cúad flaithe na Rómán.

113a   Co flaith fir ro gab Temraig
113b   do-rúacht annálad amlaid
113c   is Murchada maín co mmud
113d   is Cathail chaím hi Caisiul.

114a   Cach flaith, fáilte ós gargbríg glain,
114b   fris ráite 'Airdrí in Domain'
114c   ó Nín co Léomain na clann
114d   ros rím int éolach óenFhlann

115a   Flann féigbinn ro mben brígbreth,
115b   Fer Léiginn mín Mainistrech,
115c   ro glé tríana gním a guth,
115d   ré cach ríg do réidiugud.

115Aa   Trí chét blíadan brethaib blad
115Ab   is a cethair cethrachat
115Ac   ó Chunn, is mórglic in mod,
115Ad   cen chroinic día réidiugod.
115Ae   Ré[idig].

Opilius Macrinus, a valorous bear,   [**217–218** CE]
and his son, Diadumenianus,
for a year he was boar-like in the East,   [**May–June 218** CE]
until they were slain by soldiers.

Marcus Antoninus – it [Rome] despatched a body –
the priest of Elagabalus;
four years was the reign of that man   [**218–222** CE]
until [his own] soldiers killed him.

Anastasius the Second in the East   [**June 713–late 715** CE]
without weakness through a year;
at Nicaea by the swift action of that sheltering tree,
Theodosius the Third deposed him.

Theodosius, a single year was his reign   [**715–717** CE]
under beloved Christian rule;
over every wise and faultless subjugation
[were there] nine years for Leo the Third.   [**717–741** CE]

From the first year that Julius seized her [Rome]   [**49** BCE]
until the aforementioned reign of Leo the Third,
in the presence of every host with the deftness of their assemblies
the [stories of the] reigns of the Romans were related.

Until the reign of the man who took Tara[1]
annalistic record-keeping came down [to us] thus
and [of the reign] of the honoured and wealthy Murchad   [**d. 727** CE]
and [of the reign] of the beloved Cathal in Caiseal.   [**d. 742** CE]

Every sovereign – a joy over every mettlesome and pure meaning –
who were called 'The High-Kings of the World'
from Ninus until prolific Leo,
the learned one, the peerless Flann, has enumerated them.

Perceptive and harmonious Flann by whom powerful interpretation has been derived,
the mild-mannered teacher of Monasterboice,
has clarified through the working of his voice,
the elucidation of the era of every king.

Three hundred years, with interpretations of the famous deeds [of kings],
and forty-four
from Conn – very ingenious is the methodology –   [**d.** *c.* **150** CE]
[when] lacking a chronicle to arrange them.
Make easy.

116a   Conchobar clann mín na cned
116b   Áed, Gairbith, Díarmait dúrgen
116c   Donnchad, dá Níall, cen sním snéid,
116d   ríg na ré-se co roréid.
         Réidig dam, a Dhé nime.

Conchobar of the mild-mannered, wound-inflicting descendants   [r. 1030–73]
Áed, Gairbith, [and] resolute Díarmait   [r. 1068, d. 1061, r. 1040]

Donnchad, the two Néill,   [d. 1064, d. 1061, d. 1063]

kings of this era [who reign] with great ease.
Make easy for me, O God of Heaven.

Essay: Enumerating the Roman emperors in verse

Réidig dam, a Dé de nim 'Make easy for me, O God of Heaven' (hereafter '*Réidig*') is a long sequence of historical poetry. On thematic grounds, eight subsidiary poems are identifiable within it. The series is attributed to Flann Mainistrech, the lector of Mainistir Buite (Monasterboice), who died in the year 1056.[2] Flann's background has been well documented (Dobbs 1921–4: 149–53). He was a scion of a politically influential family that resided in the southern and central districts of modern-day county Louth; they exercised control over the monastery of Mainistir Buite for several generations.[3]

Réidig's 1272 lines recount the histories of the seven dominant 'kingships of the world' – Assyrians, Medes, Persians, Macedonians, dynasties in Asia Minor after Alexander, Seleucids, and finally Romans – within the chronological framework prescribed by Eusebius (cf. Ch. 4; on the poem's subject matter see Schmidt 2009: 232–5, Clarke 2023). Seán Mac Airt published the poems in sequence during the 1950s (cf. n.1), but had not reached the final poem, on the Romans, before his untimely death in 1959. To understand it, something must be said first about the wider context in which it has come down to us.

Four witnesses to the manuscript tradition allow us to reconstruct the text of Flann's poem. They are: (1) The first of two separate copies in the Book of Lecan (Dublin, Royal Irish Academy MS 23 P 2), early fifteenth century [hereafter L[1]];[4] (2) Royal Irish Academy MS D.iv.3, early sixteenth century [D];[5] (3) the copy in the the Book of Uí Mhaine, late fourteenth century [M];[6] and (4) a second copy found later in the Book of Lecan, early fifteenth century [L[2]].[7] Only M is preceded by an ascription to Flann Mainistrech. In the case of the other witnesses, the attribution to him is based on a signature quatrain, 115. He also refers to himself as the poem's author in line 114d.

Examination of the witnesses indicates that the work has come down to us in two recensions. Recension 1 can be reconstituted from the testimony of L[1] and D, while Recension 2 is represented by M and L[2]. The main difference between the two recensions is that the second includes an attempt, probably by a scholar other than Flann, to fill in the gaps in the original.[8] Thus the Recension 2 witnesses, M and L[2], contain eight quatrains which are absent from those of Recension 1. The extra quatrains are numbered 3A, 5A, 5B, 33A (L[2] only), 63A, 63B, 63C and 116A.

The opening quatrain of the whole series of poems identifies the theme of the poem as being *senchus degríg in domuin* – 'the history of the goodly kings of the world':[9]

> Réidig dam, a Dé de nim   Make easy for me, O God of Heaven
> co héimid a n-innisin   the giving of an account of them with alacrity
> úair naco felgním íar fuin   since it is not a poetic activity [to be engaged in]
>   after sunset:
> senchus degríg in domuin   namely, the history of the goodly kings of the world.

Tuirim – 'the act of enumerating, recounting, relating [in a pre-ordained sequence]' – is identified as the fundamental pillar of the *senchas* in quatrain 2.

> Degríg domain do thuirim   To enumerate the goodly kings of the world
> ní soraid, ní snéidshuilig   is not easy, it is not swiftly manageable,
> do neoch, ro thechta cen olc, for anyone — may he possess it without error —
> meni nerta Nóeb Spirut.   unless the Holy Spirit strengthens him.

The guidance of the Holy Spirit is perceived as being indispensable in the writing of history:

> A Spirut Nóeb i-nnosa,   O Holy Spirit now,
> tidnaic dam áeb éolosa,   bestow upon me an aspect of knowledge,
> corbam finnfhisid cach fhir   so that I may be fair and well-informed of every
>   man,
> día n-innisin na ríg-sin.   for the [purpose of the] enumeration of those kings.

We now proceed to examine the final poem on the Romans, *Flaithius Rómán ríge glonn*. Flann's text in Recension 1 contains 116 quatrains. It opens with a short preface that extols the unparalleled strength of Rome and explains that a detailed treatment of its history is beyond the scope of the work in hand. The historical sequence opens at quatrain 3 with a brief account of the rise of Julius Caesar and his subsequent assassination in quatrains 4 and 5. Recension 2 adds further detail in 5A by referring to the treacherous role of Cassius in this act. Thenceforth we are treated to a digest of the history of Rome that contains two strands: secular imperial Rome and ecclesiastical Christian Rome.

The birth of Christ during the reign of Octavian (reigned 27 BCE – 14 CE), is recorded in quatrain 9. Flann's Christian perspective leads him to focus on two aspects of early Church history: firstly, the succession lists for the bishops of Rome, Jerusalem, and Constantinople; and secondly, the periodic bouts of persecution to which the early church was subjected, with particular focus on the martyrs. It is, however, the history of the secular Roman Empire that provides the backdrop to Flann's depiction of nascent Christianity. Each of the emperors is mentioned in sequence. The duration of the reign is stated. In many instances, the circumstance of death is also given. Minor emperors, whose reigns were short, tend to receive limited attention, typically a mere couplet, while more significant emperors find themselves commemorated in an entire quatrain.

The eventual adoption by the Empire of Christianity, following the baptism of Constantine the Great (Flavius Valerius Constantinus) by Pope Silvester I, is highlighted by a reference in quatrain 76 to that Emperor's convocation of the First Council of Nicea in 325 CE. The matter of Rome continues into the Byzantine period and concludes in quatrain 111 with the ascent to the throne at Constantinople of Leo III, the Isaurian, in 717 CE. An interesting remark in 112c–112d refers to the enumeration *fíad cach slúag* 'in the presence of all peoples' at public assemblies of *flaithe na Rómán* 'the sovereigns of the Romans'. Is this an allusion to a similar custom of reciting the histories of the kings at public assemblies in Ireland?

Quatrain 113 brings us back to Ireland and assigns Flann's sources to the first half of the eighth century with his mention of Murchad mac Fergaile m. Maíle Dúin (d. 741), king of the Cenél nÉogain and Cathal mac Finguine (d. 742), king of Munster. A statement of the *raison d'être* for the poem, a recapitulation of its subject matter and a declaration by Flann of authorship are to be found in quatrains 114 and 115. An approximate date for the composition of the poem is suggested in quatrain 116 by reference to the contemporary reigns of Conchobar ua Máel Shechlainn of the Clann Cholmáin of Mide (reigned 1030–73), Áed mac Néill of the Cenél nÉogain (reigned 1068–83); Gairbith Ua Cathasaig, king of Brega (d. 1061); and Díarmait mac Maíl na mBó of the Laigin (reigned 1040–72). Taken together these dates suggest that Flann composed *Réidig* at some time between 1030, the beginning of the reign of Conchobar úa Máel Shechlainn, and 1056, the year of Flann's death. When the poems were first studied in the early twentieth century (Mac Neill 1910, Thurneysen 1915), it was established that much of the information is ultimately derived from Bede's *Chronica Maiora,* where the sequence likewise ends with Leo III. Beyond that, however, it is uncertain as to which intermediate source was used by Flann, and whether it is more likely to have been in Latin or Irish.

Flann is a remarkably gifted versifier of history. *Réidig* is written in the metre called *deibide* (for examples of this metre see also Chs 4 and 6, and on Irish metrics in general see Knott 1957, Murphy 1961). Below is given a sample quatrain, no. 7, from Flann's poem. End-rhyme is indicated in **bold**; internal rhyme is indicated in *italics*; and alliteration is highlighted by <u>underlining</u>.

Áirem a <u>bl</u>í*adan* co m<u>bl</u>**aid**
í*ar* ng*íallad* do shíl Ad**aim**;

> sé mís ós <u>br</u>íanbla na m<u>bl</u>at
> ocus sé bl*íadna* coíc**at**.

Each verse in *deibide* is comprised of a quatrain whose lines are conventionally assigned the letters *a, b, c,* and *d*. A line consists of seven syllables. There is end-rhyme within each of the couplets in a quatrain: in other words, a rhyme between the final word in line *a* and the final word in line *b*, and one between the final word in *c* and the final word in *d*. These end-words of *b* and *d* should be longer (ideally, one syllable longer) than their counterparts in *a* and *c* respectively. This kind of end-rhyme is called *rinn ocus airdrinn*, literally 'edge and high edge'. Because the Irish language historically put the stress in most major words (nouns, verbs, etc.) on the *first* syllable, it follows that rhyme of the *rinn ocus airdrinn* variety will always be between a stressed and an unstressed syllable. Compare an English rhyme such as *bit: rabbit* or (a looser example) *pickle: icicle*.

In the example displayed above, the final *-aid* of *mblaid* will rhyme with *-aim*, the unstressed second syllable of disyllabic *Adaim*. This example also illustrates the more basic principles of rhyme throughout Irish syllabic poetry. Any given rhyme is founded on a correspondence between two vowels that should be identical in quality. After each of those vowels, the subsequent rhyming consonants need not be identical but should belong to the same consonantal group, according to the traditional system of categorisation in the poet's tradition. In the case of *blaid: Adaim*, for instance, both consonants belong to the group known as *na seacht gconnsuine éadroma*, 'the seven light consonants' (Knott 1957: 5, Murphy 1961: 32).

Additionally, it is typical of Flann's poetic style that he frequently uses internal rhyme, not only in the second couplet (where it was a requirement of the metre), but also in the first couplet (where it was not). This last ornamental feature is rare, for example, in the writing of Gilla Cóemáin discussed in Ch. 4. The reader will note how Flann practises alliteration in three out of the four lines quoted above. A further striking aspect of Flann's poetic endeavour is his use of linking alliteration – *fidrad freccomail* 'letters of joining'– whereby the last word of a quatrain alliterates with the first word of the following quatrain.

Flann's contribution to the genre of historical poetry is unparalleled in its breadth and depth. His mastery of metre is matched only by Eochaid Úa Flainn's supreme command of poetic diction (see Smith 2013). *Réidig dam, a Dé de nim* is an excellent example of the unbridled ambition of medieval Irish historians to explain in Irish the history of the known world, with Roman history to the fore here, in a manner that was both informative and aesthetically attractive.

Notes

1 Fergal mac Maíle Dúin, d. 722 ?

2 Mac Airt 1953–9. The *Annals of Ulster* (Mac Airt and Mac Niocaill 1983) for 1056 reads *Flann Mainistrech, aird-fer leighinn 7 sui senchusa Erenn, in uita eterna requiescit*, 'Flann Mainistrech, pre-eminent Latinist and leading scholar of the history of Ireland, rested in peace' (my translation).

3 John Carey, 'Flann Mainistrech', *Oxford Dictionary of National Biography*, accessed 6 March 2023, https://www.oxforddnb.com/display/10.1093/ref:odnb/9780198614128.001.0001/odnb-9780198614128-e-9672?rskey=vGPXVX& result=1.

4 Dublin, RIA MS 23 P 2, The Book of Lecan, fols 11rb5 –13vb51, scribe Adhamh Ó Cuirnín (fl. 1418).

5 Dublin, RIA MS D. iv.3, fols 36ra2–40vb20, scribe Muirgheas mac Páidín Uí Mhaoil Chonaire (d. 1543).

6 Dublin, RIA MS D.ii.1, The Book of Uí Mhaine, fols 44vb1–47rb5, scribe Adam Cusin (fl. *c.* 1407).

7 Dublin, RIA MS 23 P 2, The Book of Lecan, fols 27va25–30vb6, scribe Gilla Ísu Mac Fir Bisigh (fl. 1418).

8 The style of the stanzas that are found in Recension 2 but not in Recension 1 is often clumsy. They lack the terseness of what I believe to be Flann's original work.

9 The citations that I give here are a normalized version of the text of D.

Part Three

The Trojan War

6

Luid Iasón ina luing lóir 'Jason went in his ample ship'

Michael Clarke

The work is represented by 102 quatrains preserved in a single manuscript, Edinburgh, National Library of Scotland, MS 72.i.19, fol. 2vb 25 ff; it is possible that this is only a portion of a poem that was originally much longer. The standard edition is Mac Eoin 1961. Here I present a new edition and translation of the closing section of what survives, based on my own transcription but drawing extensively on Mac Eoin's work. Accents are as in the manuscript, except that those on diphthongs have been transferred to the first vowel. Note that many of these accent-marks are on vowels that cannot have been pronounced long.

Text: A poetic narrative of the wars of Troy

70

O thanic *in* cairde *cert*,
eirghid na righu re re*cht*
et*ir* atuaidh is aneas,
robo chruaid a comhaidhcheas.

When the proper truce was ended,
the rightful kings arose
from the north and from the south;
hard was their encounter.

71

Coméirgid na catha amach
d*ar* múr mór na hardchat*r*ach,
Echtair Aíntinóir gan scís
is Ænías m*ac* Anachís.

The companies rise up
over the high city's great wall,
Hector, Antenor the tireless,
and Aeneas, Anchises' son.

72

Achil in læch tairbtheach tean*n*,
Aiax, Aghme*m*non ímthean*n*,
tucsat t*r*i catha go cruaidh
risi*n* lo*n*gphort anairtúaidh.

Achilles, the violent tough warrior,
Ajax, full-tough Agamemnon,
fought three battles harshly
against the encampment north-eastwards.

73

Beg nár mhoidh in tal*am* t*r*en
fó chossaibh na laech gan lén,
feochud farrge feírg ré fónd
re gáir na mileadh mor-lond.

Almost did the strong earth break
under the warriors' feet, without sorrow,
boiling of the angry sea against the land
with the shout of those most fierce soldiers.

74

Ro feas ceo cíach *ar in* mhuigh
dá n-allus, dá n-análaib,
ro soillsighit neoill go nea*m*
d'arm is d' éideadh na mileadh.

There was perceived a misty mist on the plain
from their sweat, from their breaths,
the clouds with heaven were lit up
by the soldiers' arms and clothing.

75

Am*al* thorai*n*d b*r*atha bind
no m*ar* maid*m* dían do dílínd
samhail na c*u*radh gcródha
gona cathaib commóra.

Like the thunderclap of sweet Judgement Day
or like the fierce breaking of a flood
was the likeness of the valorous warriors
with their full-great battalions.

[fol. 3ra1]

76

Gid mor glóir na ṅgæth, gidh árd,
ac *t*rascradh ná n-omhnadh n-árd,
sía ra clos os chínd *in* tshluaigh
i*m*mirt na cloidhebh comchruaidh.

Though great the voice of the winds, though hard,
casting down the high tree-trunks,
further was heard above the host
the play of the very harsh swords.

77

O ro gabhad in treas trom
ro hiadhadh i*m* Echt*air* oll,
nír gab allus a dha laimh
noco tairnig do a tiúgh-ár.

Once the heavy combat was begun
it closed around the great Hector:
sweat did not overcome his two hands
until he had achieved great slaughter.

78

Gach ar marb Echtair don tshluagh
o ro ghabh *ar arm* d' ímluadh,
nír fhacaibh duíne dá eis
damadh tualaíng uile-aisneis.

All that Hector killed of the host
ever since he took to wielding arms,
no one left record after him,
even were it possible to recount them all.

79

Áit i *m*bídh Eacht*air* *m*ac Priaím,
bá maidhm *ar* G*r*ecaibh don glíaidh;
i bail nach bídh in læch lán,
ar sluagh na T*r*ae ba tiugh-ár.

In the place where stood Hector, Priam's son,
there was defeat upon the Greeks from the combat;
in the place where the great warrior was not,
upon the host of Troy there was great slaughter.

80

Go n-accus aislingthi oll
m*ar*badh Echtair bá garb glond,
ni thic asi*n* cath amach
Eachtair ard-mor illathach.

Till a great vision was seen,
the killing of Hector, fierce in action,
there came not out from the battle
Hector, great and tall, of many hues.

81

As-be*r*t a d*r*ai fris ín rígh,
'Ceangail, cuidhbhrigh do *m*ac mi*n*d,
læch is fearr tánic a glí,
easbach a dhul *ar* nei*m*fní.'

The sorcerer says to the king,
'Bind and imprison your gentle son,
the best warrior who came to birth,
it were in vain if he came to nothing.'

82

Ge ra fasdóidh Echtair árd,
ge*n* gor ligeadh fon ṅgleó ṅgárg,
da bris a chuidbrigh gan cáin,
do-chuaidh fó muirnd i*n* mór-gháidh.

Though mighty Hector had been bound
so that he could not be released into the harsh struggle,
he broke his bonds, without diminution,
he went under the clamour of great peril.

83

In tan da bhí ac sloidhe *in* tshluaigh,
idir aneas is atuaidh,
tig Aichil in ghaiscidh ghlain
gur co*m*raig dó *is* d' Eachtair.

At the time when he was smiting the host,
both in the south and in the north
Achilles of the shining armour came
so that there was conflict between him and Hector.

84

Do-rad Eachtair forguin feig
tresin slíasait saír d' Achéil;
da-rad Achil a gha glas
trena d*ruim* d' Echtair amhnas.

Hector gave a keen wounding
to Achilles, right through the thigh:
Achilles put his grey spear
through the back of hardy Hector.

85

Ge ra goineadh i*n*a druím,
ge ra thuit ar tal*man* truím,
ni thanic læch dár ghíall gail
bidh chomh chalma re hEchtair.

Though he was wounded in the back,
though he fell on the mighty earth,
there never came a warrior whom valour served
that would be as brave as Hector.

86

Ochtmhogha ríg, dighrais modh,
ro m*ar*b Echt*air* a oenor;
nocho feas don læchraidh laín
gach a dorchair dá dheasláimh.

Eighty kings, unassailable the deed,
did Hector kill on his own;
not known to the great warrior-band
is each one that fell by his right hand.

87

Se mhile ochtmogha óg
ar ocht *cét* mile mor-shlogh
itdorchair i comlond chai*n*
du G*r*ecaib re Troiandaib.

Eighty-six thousand young men
added to eight hundred thousand – the great host
that fell in fair combat
of Greeks against the Trojans.

88

Se mile *ocht*mogha án
ar ocht cét mile mórlán,
is *ed* itorchair *ar* sein
do shluaghaib P*r*iaim lá G*r*ecaibh.

A glorious eighty-six thousand
added to full eight hundred thousand,
is what fell after that time
of the hosts of Priam by the Greeks.

89

Seser ar *fichid*, sé cét,
ba he lín luidh dib i n-ég
ar tocht *ar* in croiceand cóir,
nírbh ea*n*gnamh dim deareoil.

Six added to twenty, and six hundred,
that was the count of those who went to death
in the quest for the perfect skin:
it was no wretched lowly exploit.

[fol. 3rb1]

90

Im Iason ro-siacht *in* port
gu La*m*idhon lan-étrocht
focha*í*nd *t*ren toghla na T*r*ae
'sa c*r*aicend go leb*ar* læ.

When Jason came to the harbour
to full-brilliant Laomedon,
that was the strong cause of the siege of Troy,
and the skin with the long fleece.

91

Samson, Treolus gan tar,
Echtair, Ercoil, Aichil án,
*có*iciur is calma ro b*í*
ar tu*í*nd talman togaidhi.

Samson, Troilus without reproach,
Hector, Hercules, shining Achilles,
were the five bravest men that were
on the surface of the excellent earth.

92

Samail cla*í*nde Pria*í*m, ni brec,
ni f*r*ith *ar* tal*m*an na tréd
da m*a*c dég t*r*i *fichit* fir,
ré gaiscead is ré ger-gnim.

The like of the family of Priam, no lie,
was not found on the earth of the multitudes,
twelve and thrice twenty men
for valour and for sharp deeds.

93

Da-luidh Treólus tren amach
d*ár* e*í*s Echtair isin cath,
ba comeas calmacht *í*ar san
d*á*madh chomais d*ó* is d' Eachtair.

Strong Troilus went out
after Hector into the battle,
their bravery would be judged equal
had his age and Hector's been the same.

94

Samail chuilea*n* milchon mi*n*d
leccair fo *t*redaibh a t*í*r,
ros-bru*í*d, ros-leadair go leath,
do f*á*g curaidh cro-l*í*ndteach.

Like the delicate whelp of a hunting-hound
who is loosed onto thc land against the herds
he crushed them, he hewed them apart,
he left heroes in pools of blood.

95

Samail T*r*eolais gan t*á*r,
ar na G*r*ecaib tug tiugh-*á*r,
torchair leis mor læch gu l*ó*r,
do-rad maidhm ar Aghmemnon.

Such was Troilus without reproach,
who set upon the Greeks much slaughter,
many were the warriors who fell at his hands,
he inflicted a rout upon Agamemnon.

96

Ro ghon Achil go bhá tri,
in læch luchair go luath-lí,
ní bhi ard do sluagh na ṅGrec
ar nár mhaidhm *no* nár mor-ég.

He wounded Achilles three times,
the bright warrior of swift lustre,
there was no-one high in the host of the Greeks
that did not suffer defeat or death.

97

Ro feargaigheadh Achil oll,
ro marb sé Treol*us* trom,
leth-trom in chumlaínd gan clodh,
m*a*c mi*n*d 'sa læch lán-mhór.

Great Achilles was angered,
he killed mighty Troilus:
unequal was the combat, without a match,
the delicate lad and the full-great warrior.

98

Fochaínd éga Achil aírd,
día ros-gon m*a*c Priai*m* p*r*imh-gh*a*irg,
is sí ro gairdigh a llá
íngen Priaim Pulixina.

The cause of the death of tall Achilles,
when the son of Priam prime-fierce[1] killed him:
she who shortened his day
was Priam's daughter, Polyxena.

99

Da ṅdechaidh i comdail chai*n*
co teagh ad*a*rta idhail,
d' ḟeis ré hingi*n* Priai*m* na port,
da-rochair læch na luath-trot.

When he went for the fine assignation
to the house where idols were worshipped
to marry the daughter of Priam of the settlements,
then fell the warrior of the swift combats.

100

Gidh eadh, bá leór do deac*air*,
do cuiredh íad i*n* n-æn-lebaidh,
Echtair, Achil ba garb gus,
maræn *ocus* Treolus.

Nonetheless, it was sufficient wonder,
they were laid in a single bed,
Hector, Achilles fierce in valour,
along with Troilus.

101

Da-rochrad*ar* bónd re bond
Troíandaidh, Grégaigh don ghlond,
o thosach beathaidh, ní brég,
ní tugadh ár a leithéid.

They fell heel alongside heel,
Trojans, Greeks in the battle,
since the beginning of the world, it is no lie,
the like slaughter was never done.

102

Mairg rug in coblach cruaidh cain
sluagh na ṅGréc dá n-i*n*nsaighídh,
ni thernáidh don turus taí
do-rat mor læch a lighi.
Luidh Iaso*n* 'na lui*n*g.

Woe for him who brought the hard far fleet
against the host of the Greeks,
he did not escape from the silent journey
that laid low many a warrior.
Jason went in his ship.

Essay: Dares Phrygius in syllabic verse

Throughout the Middle Ages in Europe, the tradition of the Trojan War revolved around an extraordinary text, of unknown origins, which had first come to the attention of Frankish chroniclers in the Merovingian period, perhaps about 670 CE. This was a Latin translation of the supposed eyewitness account of the war by Dares Phrygius, a minor fighter on the Trojan side. His *De Excidio Troiae Historia* 'History of the Destruction of Troy' (Meister 1873, Frazer 1966, Lelli 2016) probably began as a kind of literary joke, an exercise in re-imagining the war without the fictions that the poets laid upon it. If so, however, we have no record of anyone who understood it in this way, and every medieval reader seems to have taken it as the accurate contemporary record that it pretends to be (Merkle 1996, cf. Ní Mheallaigh 2008). In a world where so many peoples claimed to be descended from the Trojans, Dares' witness was vital for making sense of the origins of nations and of the traditions of military virtue, even the ancient foundations of chivalry, as discussed in the excellent study by Frederic N. Clark (2020).

Precisely because Dares is supposed to be an eyewitness, his Latin prose seems formless and unadorned. Perhaps this made it inevitable that poets would choose to re-adapt it into the elegance of verse. On the Continent, poetic rewritings of this kind were created several times, beginning as part of the revival of Latin verse composition in France from the mid-eleventh century onward. The first example we know of is a work in Latin hexameters from about 1050 CE, the *Anonymi Historia*, which begins by praising Dares' version precisely because its truth is not disturbed by *figmenta poetica*, 'poetic inventions' (Stohlmann 1968, line 1). Many other such experiments in recomposition followed, culminating in the great narrative poem in Old French rhyming verse by Benoît de Sainte-Maure, the *Roman de Troie*, which includes much baroque invention but still trumpets its supposed fidelity to the witness of Dares (Constans 1904–12; Burgess and Kelly 2017; cf. Solomon 2007). From the time of its composition around 1170, Benoît's achievement overshadowed every other account of the Trojan War, and it was re-adapted and re-translated in turn into all the major languages of Europe.

In Gaelic Ireland, however, something different happened. The same Latin base-text of Dares Phrygius was taken in hand by Gaelic *literati* at least as early as the time of composition of the *Anonymi Historia* – perhaps several generations earlier – and on this basis was composed the elaborate narrative work known as *Togail Troí*, 'The Siege of Troy' or (to use Stokes' translation) 'The Destruction of

Troy'.[2] As Brent Miles shows (2011 and Ch. 7 in this volume), the earliest surviving version of this text, Recension 1 or *TTr-H*, composed probably in the mid-eleventh century, recasts Dares' work so that it resonates in theme and style with *Táin Bó Cúailnge* 'The Cattle-Raid of Cooley' and other sagas on the wars and warrior personalities of the remote past of Ireland itself. Even considered apart from this intertextual resonance, *Togail Troí* is one of the finest examples of the artistry of rhetorically heightened and variegated Gaelic prose (Mac Gearailt 2000/2001). Alongside Recension 1 we have a version in the late twelfth-century Book of Leinster (*TTr-LL*), considered to be a witness to Recension 2 that has been enhanced by 'runs' of inflated and repetitive language (Ch. 8 below). Recension 2 is thought to be based on a lost forerunner of Recension 1, so that the relationship between the two is not direct. The text was further extended in the later Middle Ages to yield Recension 3, which is preserved in its fullest form in two fifteenth-century manuscripts (Clarke 2014a: 25–9, and Ch. 9 in this volume). To complete the set, the Book of Ballymote version, in a manuscript of about 1390 (Dublin, Royal Irish Academy MS 23 P 12), is intermediate between Recensions 2 and 3. We thus have evidence for at least four distinct campaigns of rewriting and embellishment, perhaps stretching over several centuries.[3] Astonishingly, the evidence suggests that the earliest version of the work was created without the slightest awareness of the Continental literary movement that gave us the *Anonymi Historia* and its kin, despite the fact that in terms of genre and aesthetics there is a precise analogy between the two schools of translation and adaptation (cf. O'Connor, Ch. 2, p.19).

The poetic fragment beginning *Luid Iasón in a luing lóir* 'Jason went in his ample ship . . .' stems from an early stage in this long history of composition and adaptation.[4] The prose of *Togail Troí* has here been rendered into Middle Irish verse. The selection printed above is about one-third of what survives, but it is a reasonable guess that in its original form the poem may have been long enough to narrate the entire sequence of the Trojan War. The first part of the fragment, like *Togail Troí* and the original work of Dares, tells of the expedition of Jason to win the Golden Fleece (see further Ch. 8); our selection comes from the final part, recreating Dares' account of the great battles fought on the plain of Troy over the ten years of the war.

There is just one manuscript witness, a stray gathering of six vellum pages from a late medieval manuscript that seems to have been a compilation of poems on historical and learned subjects.[5] The manuscript must once have been an artefact of some beauty. In the surviving pages the initial words of poems are illuminated with great skill, decked out with intricate interlace in the typical style of the fifteenth and sixteenth centuries. As well as our poem, the surviving items include a lament on the death of the legendary king, Conn of the Hundred Battles; a poem on disasters in Irish legendary history that happened on Tuesdays; a compilation of *dindshenchas*, the lore of place-names (cf. in this volume Chs 27–28); and a poem listing various examples of extraordinary kinds of conception (*coimperta*) – human, salmon, bee and dove. The manuscript must have been compiled as an anthology of learned poetry, perhaps to be the prestige possession of a noble house or a family of poets.

The poems gathered in this manuscript were examples of the art of the eleventh and twelfth centuries, which was already regarded as the supreme age of learned poetic composition of this kind. *Luid Iasón* is headed with the name of Flann Mainistrech, the master-poet of Monasterboice who died in 1056 and is best known for his dynastic and chronological poems on Irish dynasties and the kings of the ancient nations of world history (see Ch. 5 in this volume). Although the ascription may well be false, it shows that the poem was seen as characteristic of Flann's style and time; and this is corroborated by the fact that the choice of details suggests it was adapted from a rather early version of the prose *Togail Troí*, a forerunner of the version that survives in our Book of Leinster – in other words, it dates roughly from the late eleventh century.

Our poet uses a loose version of the metre called *deibide* (on which see Ch. 5, pp.74–75, and Murphy 1961). In casting the narrative into verse, our author was practising an art that had been developed in the Irish language for perhaps two centuries before his time. The supreme achievement of this art is *Saltair na Rann* 'The Psalter of the Quatrains', in which the entire conspectus of biblical history from the Creation to the end of time is cast into over five thousand lines of syllabic verse.[6] There are no examples on secular subjects to match the scale of *Saltair na Rann*, but there can be no doubt that it was a common practice to versify narrative in this way, akin to but distinct from the versification of catalogue-style information like the regnal lists of kings, synchronisms and the lore of place-names, as exemplified in the poems of Gilla Cóemáin and others in this volume (see Chs 4, 5, 24, 27 and 28, with Smith 2002; cf. Clancy 2008, Mac Eoin 2012, Clarke 2023). The entire textual tradition of *Lebor Gabála Érenn* 'The Book of Invasions of Ireland' (on which see Ch. 26) is characterized by alternation between prose and verse renderings of the same sections of subject-matter, in a mode corresponding to that known in Anglo-Saxon studies as *opus geminatum* or 'twinned composition' (cf. Mathis 2011). Versification of this kind was one of the crucial practices of medieval Irish historiography. Its purpose was to fix and crystallize the information transmitted in the corresponding prose, and to subject it to the jewel-like aesthetic of the syllabic metres used. Perhaps, as is sometimes argued, the purpose of such composition was mnemonic, to enable this lore to be memorized more effectively by students; but the very regularity and order of the metrical form lends a strange and unique aesthetic, even a kind of beauty, to what has been created (cf. Smith 2016, Clarke 2023: 108–9).

Our selection gives a distilled and elegant summary of events from a short section of Dares Phrygius' work corresponding to chapters 23–24, 33 and 34 of 'The History of the Destruction of Troy'. Events include Hector's onslaught against the Greeks; Andromache's premonitions; Hector's death at the hands of Achilles; Troilus' answering surge and his own killing by Achilles; and the strategem used against Achilles by the Trojans, who lure him to an ambush in the temple of Apollo by making him believe that he will be married there to Polyxena, princess of Troy, this being his reward for betraying his Greek countrymen. These are standard elements of the post-Dares tradition in all the medieval vernacular histories of Troy. However, it is clear that our author is working not from the Latin but from an early copy of the Irish-language *Togail Troí*, and probably from this alone. The principal sequence shadows the corresponding sections of the prose saga, item by item (*TTr-H* 1103 ff.), but other sections of *Togail Troí* have provided additional models. For example, the sequence of images in quatrains 73–6 is built up from elements in the hyperbolic description of the Greek fleet arriving at Troy and the riddling exchange between Priam and the messenger who reports their arrival at the coast (*TTr-H* 825–7, 847–911). Quatrains 93-7 are based on the vivid account of Troilus' onslaught and his death at Achilles' hands (≈ *TTr-H* 1351–1570 with much selection and amplification), while the account of the ambush plot (quatrains 98–9) again matches the corresponding section of *Togail Troí* (*TTr-H* 1592–1627, based in turn on Dares' Ch. 34).

However, differences of detail suggest that the poet's exemplar was distinct from any of the existing versions of *Togail Troí*. Particularly puzzling is the account of the prophecy or foreboding of Hector's death, which leads a sorcerer or 'druid' (*druí*) to urge Priam to restrain him – in vain, because the hero bursts his bonds and goes to battle anyway (quatrains 80–83). In *Togail Troí*, as in the Latin and Old French Troy texts of the period, the foreboding is prompted by Andromache's news of a dream she has had (*TTr-H* 1126 ff.), and there is no mention of the sorcerer. Perhaps the poet has reshaped what he found in his source; but it is more likely that his copy of *Togail Troí* included material that has not survived directly. Stray details suggest that his source was closer in some respects to the Book of Leinster version than to Recension 1. The idea that

Hector was physically restrained from going to battle is not stated in Recension 1, where the passage implies simply that they show him his baby son in order to 'constrain' him from fighting, as if the pitiful sight of the child will discourage him from throwing away his life (*TTr-H* 1136–1145; the key word is the verbal form *astád*, 'constrain'). However, the corresponding account in the Book of Leinster version includes the words 'they restrained him by force' *ra fastád ar ecin é* (*TTr-LL* 32739), which seems on the face of it to refer to physical compulsion. The verb seen here, *fastád*, is essentially identical to the *astád* of Recension 1, but the meaning in this context is distinct. Presumably this or a similar phrase in the source inspired our poet's image of Hector held down by fetters. Again, his account of the killing of Hector by Achilles (quatrains 83–4) is consistent with the version treated as authentic in the Book of Leinster (*TTr-LL* 32740 ff.) but differs from that in Recension 1, which centres on the strange story that the Greeks piled their clothes into a mound and put Achilles on top to lure Hector into single combat against him (*TTr-H* 1167 ff.).[7]

Our author, then, was selecting and refining what he evidently took to be the essential narrative events of *Togail Troí*. Since the poem as we have it is quite likely to be incomplete, we cannot form a full picture of his selection method. However, it is typical of the manner of Middle Irish historical verse that he also included elements of counting, enumeration, catalogue. The figures for Greek and Trojan casualties, for example, are authentic and go back to Dares (Ch. 44). Similarly, the enumeration of the five greatest heroes of the world – Samson, Troilus, Hector, Hercules, Achilles – is typical of the working method of the Irish chronologists in this period (cf. Ch. 25 in this volume, with Clarke and Ní Mhaonaigh 2020, O'Sullivan 2021). This quatrain, indeed, was remembered in later generations, and it is found as a marginal item on a page of the Book of Leinster, apparently added by a reader considerably later than the time the manuscript proper was written.[8] In such ways the versified Matter of Troy became part of the stock-in-trade of the Gaelic scholars in the later Middle Ages.

This poem, or fragment of a poem, opens a window on a genre whose aesthetic is very hard to accommodate to modern canons of poetic beauty, namely the casting of historical or pseudo-historical narrative into the precise syllable-count and verbal music of syllabic verse. As mentioned above, the effect may have been practical, with the count of syllables encouraging accurate transmission; but perhaps that is merely reductive. Is it possible instead to see such an artefact in terms of aesthetic excellence? The imagery of the poets themselves encourages it, as for example in the fragment that survives from another, probably closely related, poetic account of the generations of the royal line of Troy, quoted in the text of *Togail Troí* Recension 3:

Airdrí in domuin Sadurnd seang	Slender Saturn was high king of the world,
coimsing ar chách co coitcend:	master over all communally:
suairc sencus in rígh reabaigh	pleasant is the lore of the nimble king
mása fhír dá fhiledaib.	if his poets speak the truth.

Clarke 2014a: 48–9

The assertion that this lore is 'pleasant' (*súairc*) should be our guide in trying to reconstruct the significance of works like *Luid Iasón* as literary artefacts, however alien they may be from modern literary aesthetics – or, for that matter, from the recoverable aesthetics of ancient epic poetry in Latin, to which their kinship is so tenuous as to be virtually irrelevant for listening to their verbal music.

Notes

1   This is an attempt to reproduce the chime of sound between the proper name and the first element of the compound epithet in *Priaim primh-ghairg.*

2   The principal published sources are the editions by Stokes 1881, 1884. For surveys of recensions and editions see Clarke 2014a: 32–5, Szerwiniack 2018. The word *togail* is ambiguous between 'siege, struggle' and 'sack, destruction'. The main argument against regarding it as an exact equivalent for Latin words like *exitium* and *expugnatio*, which it glosses in Old Irish (see *eDIL* s.v.), is the fact that it is used repeatedly within *Togail na Tebe* to refer to the subject-matter of that work, the assault by the Seven against Thebes, which ended inconclusively without the city being penetrated (see Ch. 11, and Briggs 2024). For this reason, 'Siege' is the term preferred throughout this book, except in instances where the context dictates otherwise (see Ch. 10, p. 129 with n. 2).

3   Clarke 2016 adds the possibility that *TTr-H,* the surviving copy of Rec. 1, includes fourteenth- or fifteenth-century additions based on Latin or French sources in the *Roman de Troie* tradition.

4   The poem is edited with commentary in Irish and English translation in Mac Eoin 1961, on which I draw in what follows. See also Miles 2011: 53–4, 74–5.

5   Edinburgh, National Library of Scotland, MS 72.i.19: see Mackinnon 1912: 136, 200, 204, with Ó Macháin 1986.

6   The best introduction to *Saltair na Rann* is Carey 2002a: 97–123, with the edition and commentary of the Adam and Eve section by Greene, Kelly and Murdoch 1976.

7   The Book of Leinster copy mentions but rejects the story of the stratagem with the clothes, ascribing it to *Fergil* (*TTr-LL* 32841–2). There is no explanation of why this strange story was ascribed to Vergil, nor is it fully certain that this name refers here to the poet of the *Aeneid*; Miles 2011: 65–6 discusses the problem.

8   Dublin, TCD MS 1339, The 'Book of Leinster', p. 118, upper margin, noted by Mac Eoin 1961: 48.

7

Togail Troí 'The Siege of Troy', Recension 1

Brent Miles

The text of this excerpt has been reproduced from Whitley Stokes's edition of the copy of Recension 1 (also referred to as TTr-H) in Dublin, Trinity College, MS 1319 (formerly H.2.17), at Stokes 1884: 46–8, lines 1473–1519); corrections from Stokes's own list of errata, p. 142, as well as those in Mac Eoin (1960: 77–9), have been silently incorporated. In addition to the substitution of u for vocalic v, length marks in some forms have been altered to today's practices, and some italics, when the question of the correctness of the expansion is not in question, have been removed.

Text: The onslaught of Troilus
(revised from Stokes 1884: 46–8, lines 1457–1519)

O thánic, thrá, aimser an catha, rochoraigset Troi*andai* a slógh. Roecratar da*no* Gr*éic* a cath don leith aile. Is annsin roghab Achíl for *g*resacht na Mirmedonda colléir, ⁊ ros-faide 'na snadmaimm chatha do chathug*ud* fri Troi*andu* ⁊ fri Troil, ⁊ atrubairt fr*í*u dano ara tuctaís cend Troil dósum léo. Ásaidh comrac úathmar anachnidh et*ir* dá n-indna na cath. Rodásed imna Mirmedónaib; is bec na romid an tal*am* fo cossaib la fichud na feirge baí 'na mbruinnib. Ba méte léo ná fagebtaís a ndoithin debtha ⁊ urgaile co forcenn mbetha. Ba méite léo cech beim do*b*ertaís nothascairtaís na firu co talmain. Ba méte dano léo nothaféntais na Troi*á*ndu corice a cath*raig*. Ba méite dano b*éus* leo nóráinfidís ⁊ nobrufitís m*ú*ru na Troí. Manbad nert na fer doralatar fr[i]ú araídhe ní faílsaitís mani chobhrad Troil.

Intan dino atchonnairc Troil in dechradh romór ⁊ in luthbás ⁊ in búrach rofersat na Mirm[id]ónda, ⁊ antan rotheilcset a ngaí fair feisin, ros-lín bruth ⁊ ferg, ⁊ atraracht an lon láich asa éton combó comḟota frisin sróin, ⁊ dodechatar a dí ṡúil asa chind combat sith[ith]ir artemh fria chenn anechtair. Ropo cumma a ḟolt ⁊ cróebred scíad. Rofóbair an cruthsin na slógu, amal léoman léir lán lui*nd* letarthaigh reithes do thruchu torcraide. Romharb, thrá, trí cóicthu láth ngaile do Grécaib ⁊ Mirme*dónd*aib lásin cétrúathar míled ron-úc aran-ammus. Ataig cummasc íarsin forna slúagu uile ⁊ romill na Grécu ⁊ romarbh na Mirm[ed]ónda corici beolu na scor. Ocus rolá ár na slógh, ⁊ is do díármidhib na Togla an-romarb Tróil in láasin *nammá* dona Grécaib. Ocus is cuit péne má roéla nech don tslúagh uile úad nád bád baccach *no* dall *no* bodhar *no* cérr íarna thescad ⁊ íarna timdibe d'ḟorgab a gaí, do ghin a chlaidhibh, do bil a scéith, do ind a duirn, do bacc a uille, do remor a glúini, conad immále noimbred forru báirne na cloch, creta na carpat, cunga na ndam, cécht na n-arathar. Nógebed dano na scíathu ⁊ na claidbe ⁊ na sunnu ⁊ na homnada, cona bitís 'na láim acht a ter*ú*arsena íarna mbrisiud oc slaide a námat. Is sí a mét, trá, dochótar for techedh conidh is infechtain tárrasair Áiaic mac Telamóin daran-éise. Rothintaí Troil cona Throi*andaib* com-mórbúaidh ⁊ com-morchoscur fó tr*áth* fescoir día cath*raig*. Baí brón mór in n-aidchi sin i ndúnadh na ṅGréc tría ágh láma Troil. Tarthut léo a óete in mic ⁊ a laghad nofulngaitís forgla trenḟer ⁊ ḟeinedh íarthair in betha imbúaladh fris. Asbert cách uadhib fria chéle, díambád lán a fiche bli*a*dan nomairbhfed in slógh ule ⁊ ní ris*ed* fer innisi scéoil diib úad co tír na Gréci forcúlu. Diamad ḟer imm

Newly translated by the author

When the time for the battle came the Trojans arrayed their host. The Greeks, meanwhile, set their battalion in order on the other side. Then Achilles took to inciting the Myrmidons, and he sent them in their battle array to fight against the Trojans and against Troilus, and he told them to bring him back Troilus' head. An awful, unheard-of conflict arose between the two battle-lines. The Myrmidons became furious; the earth nearly burst under their feet with the boiling of the wrath that was in their breasts. They deemed that they would not get their sufficiency of fighting and battle before the world's end. They deemed that every blow delivered would cast men down to the ground. They deemed that they would hunt the Trojans back to their city. They deemed further that they would break down and smash the walls of Troy. Were it not for the strength of the men who met them (?), they would not have endured had not Troilus helped them.

Now when Troilus beheld the great fury and the vehemence and the rage that the Myrmidons displayed, and when they cast their spears at him, fury and anger filled him, and the *lon láich* [hero's light] arose out of his forehead until it was as long as his nose, and his two eyes came out from his head until they were as long as the measure of a fist around his head. His hair was like the branches of a thorn bush. He attacked the hosts in that form, like a vigorous lion full of lacerating ferocity that races to visit doom on a herd of boars. He slew one hundred and fifty warriors of the Greeks and Myrmidons at the first soldier's onrush which he brought against them. He visited confusion then on all the hosts, and overthrew the Greeks, and slew the Myrmidons as far as the entries to the camp. And he brought the slaughter of the host, and what Troilus slew of the Greeks on that day alone constitutes one of the 'unreckonable things of the Siege [of Troy]'. And it is hard to say[1] whether anyone from the whole host escaped from him that was not lame or blind or deaf or maimed, after being cut and hacked by the thrust of his spear, by the bite of his sword, by the edge of his shield, by the tip of his fist, by the crook of his elbow, by the thick of his knee; (so that) he plied them together with the fragments of the stones, the frames of the chariots, the yokes of the oxen, the beams of the ploughs (?). Then he took the shields and the swords and the clubs and the spears, so that only their remnants lay in his hand after they had been broken in the smiting of his foes. So great was the number that fled that scarcely did Ajax son of Telamon stand his ground in their wake. Troilus returned with his Trojans in great victory and great triumph that evening to their city.

formna a aíse, nobíad ós churada ⁊ trénferaib in talman ó turcbáil ngréne coa funedh, ⁊ nolínfadh in domhun dia ailgib ⁊ día gaiscedhaib ⁊ dia mórglonnaib, ⁊ doróscaighfedh ced do Ercoil ar neurt ⁊ chalmatus. Día sirtha fair combad tríchtach a ríghe na Troiandae nofollomnaigfedh for firu talman, othá crícha Iuenes co hinnsi na mBretan fri domun aníarthúaid. Robad óenrí, thrá, fó chetheora árda an domhuin.

Isin matain arnabárach dolluid Agmemnón cona slogh. Dollotar dano uli thoísigh na Mirmedonda cobágach bruthmar cechndíriuch arcind Throil. Ó rochomraicset immorro na dá chath, rofiged gléo garb ann. Dorochratar sochaide do cechtar in dá lethe. Robátar sist in cruth sin oc cathugud cech laí. Nos-fúabred Troil cach día, ⁊ focéirdedh an ár corici na scuru. Ocus rogab eill dona Mírmedondaib sech cách, conas-cirred láma díb co teigtís 'na les co Achíl.

Intan íarum atchonnairc Agmemnón na hilmíle do thotim día muintir ⁊ in fordinge dorat Troil forru, doch[ú]as uad co Príaim do chuinchidh ossaid tríchat laa fri adhnacul a marb, fri híc á crechtnaigthe. Dorat Príaim in n-ossad sin fóbíth a cétna do dénum.

There was great grief that night in the Greeks' camp out of fear of Troilus' hand. They marveled (?) at the lad's youth and how little the pick of the champions and warriors of the Western world were able to hold out in battle against him. Each of them said to the other that if he were to live to the age of twenty, he would slay the whole host and no man from among them would get back to the land of Greece to bear tidings. If he were a man in the prime of his age, he would be superior to the heroes and champions of the earth, from the rising of the sun to its setting, and he would fill the world with his memorials and his feats of arms and great exploits, and would surpass even Hercules in strength and bravery. But if his life were lengthened till he was thirty years old, the Trojans' realm would rule over the men of the earth from the bounds of the *Iuenes*[2] to the isles of the Britons in the north-west of the world. There would be a single king, then, to the four corners of the world.

The following morning Agamemnon went out with his army. All the leaders of the Myrmidons went out, in contentious, heated fashion, and headed straight for Troilus. When the two battalions joined, there was fought a harsh battle. A multitude from each of the two sides fell. They were for a period fighting in that fashion every day. Troilus attacked them every day, and visited slaughter on them as far as the camp. And Troilus got the better of the Myrmidons more than anyone else, and he would cut off their hands so that they would go back to their enclosure, to Achilles.

Now when Agamemnon saw the many thousands of his men who had fallen, and the crushing defeat which Troilus had over them, he had word sent to Priam to ask him for a truce of thirty days, to bury their dead, to heal their wounded. Priam granted that truce, because he wished to do the same.

Essay: Troilus, Cú Chulainn and an Irish Troy

Togail Troí 'The Siege of Troy' is among the most ambitious and successful Irish literary enterprises of the Middle Ages. As already noted in the previous chapter (Ch. 6), it is an Irish rewriting of the *De Excidio Troiae Historia* 'History of the Destruction of Troy', a late-antique history of the Trojan War attributed to a supposed eye-witness to the war named Dares Phrygius, and survives in several versions, the earliest of which, so-called Recension 1, can be dated to the eleventh century. Certain linguistic features throughout Recension 1 suggest it was a revision of an earlier version which does not survive, but may have existed as early as the tenth century (Mac Eoin 1960: 201). The latest thorough revision, so-called Recension 3, dates probably to the late twelfth century, while the bulk of medieval manuscripts date from the 'manuscript revival' that started in the fourteenth century, with evidence for continued revision and editing even in these late copies (see Clarke 2016). *Togail Troí*, then, is a convenient title to describe a substantial library of versions of a Middle Irish classic, including one version in verse in addition to the three distinct prose recensions (see Chs 6, 8 and 9).

Dares' text was the most common source for the narrative of the Trojan War throughout the Middle Ages, but it is an odd work, written in a bare, nearly telegraphic style, with none of the adornment that typically accompanies historical writing in Latin. The first iteration of *Togail Troí* was probably a fairly literal translation into Middle Irish from this simple Latin text, and likely shared some of its features. The excerpt above corresponds to Dares' chapter 32. As an example of the supposed initial simple translation, the concluding lines translate the second half of Dares' chapter 32 in short, concise sentences, with minimal elaboration, and these lines probably preserve the initial translation of Dares fairly faithfully. The first part of the excerpt, however, is more typical of *Togail Troí* as a whole. This passage renders the first half of the chapter, in which Dares describes an unusually fierce sequence of fighting where the Trojans are led by Priam's youngest son Troilus, who is only a youth at the time. The whole of chapter 32 is only 120 words in the Latin, but the description of Troilus's battle with the Greeks on the first days fighting amounts to no more than three lines:

> fit pugna maior, acriter saevitur. Troilus in prima acie Argivos caedit, Myrmidones fugat, impressionem usque in castra facit, multos occidit, plurimos sauciat. Aiax Telemonius obstitit. Troiani victores in oppidum revertuntur.
>
> Meister 1873: 38.

There is a great battle, the fighting rages fiercely. Troilus cuts down the Argives in the first ranks, puts the Myrmidons to flight, attacks as far as the camps, slays many, wounds a great many. Telamonian Ajax opposes him. The Trojans, triumphantly, turn back to the city.

tr. Miles

Against this model, a reviser of the original *Togail Troí* has constructed a greatly elaborated picture of Troilus's martial feats. The Irish description includes no new details of the battle itself, but the intensity of the fighting is conveyed through a number of rhetorical techniques. Notably, the Irish employs a formulaic language seen in largely opaque sequences like *noimbred forru báirne na cloch, creta na carpat, cunga na ndam, cécht na n-arathar* '[Troilus] plied them together with the fragments of the stones, the frames of the chariots, the yokes of the oxen' and so forth. The formulaic language includes features that may reflect actual Irish battle terminology, for example *ros-faide 'na snadmaimm chatha*, lit. 'he sent them in their knots of battle', by which is presumably is meant a specific troop formation. Praise for Troilus is expressed in the most flamboyant terms, for example the contention that, had he lived to the age of thirty, he would have ruled an empire that would span the known world, a claim that has no counterpart in Dares. With these embellishments, Troilus's stature grows in measure with the translator's creativity and presumed desire to show mastery in the art of medieval rhetoric.

Most idiosyncratically, the description of Troilus has features shared with Irish heroic saga, especially the portrait of the boy-hero Cú Chulainn from the Ulster Cycle. This native model is inescapable when comparing the account of Troilus' battle-rage with the phenomenon of Cú Chulainn's *ríastrad*, his so-called 'warp-spasm', as portrayed in *Táin Bó Cúailgne* 'The Cattle-Raid of Cooley' and other Ulster Cycle narratives.[3] In the excerpt above it is described how a *lon láich* is seen above Troilus' head. Whether this is to be understood as a supernatural light, a supernatural bird representing the coming slaughter, or a phantom presence of some less well-defined kind, it undoubtedly corresponds to the *lúan láith*, the so-called 'hero's light', emitted from Cú Chulainn's forehead during his *ríastrad*. Furthermore, Troilus's face undergoes a physical transformation that employs language identical to that found in depictions of the *ríastrad*, including, for example, the protruding of his eyes from his face.[4] This example of Troilus in *Togail Troí* can be taken as a striking instance of the accommodation of learned, classically derived narrative to the expectations of a specifically Irish textual and storytelling culture. Yet throughout *Togail Troí*, as throughout Irish classical narratives as a whole, such striking examples as

Troilus's '*ríastrad*' are not the norm. Rhetorically accomplished descriptions of battle and elaborate passages of heroic praise in largely formulaic language, both met in the excerpt above, represent much better what the classical texts and the native heroic corpus share. However, the early date for the proposed original version puts *Togail Troí* near the beginning of literary trends characteristic of Middle Irish especially, and throughout critical discussions there has been a consistent recognition that *Togail Troí* was likely an influential text in the development of a Middle Irish style that finds a parallel expression throughout surviving saga and historical writing of the period (see e.g. Mac Gearailt 2000/1). That is to say, a rigid critical distinction between native and learned has been impossible to maintain, and while it remains common sense to invoke Irish oral storytelling as an influence in Middle Irish narrative, Irish had been a supple, learned written language in Ireland for centuries before *Togail Troí* was penned, and the Irish men of learning had most likely been close readers of Latin, and of classical epic, in particular, throughout that long period.

Apart from this accommodation to native literary culture, *Togail Troí* displays an equally impressive addition of scholastic, especially mythological, material relevant to the ancient story of Troy as known to readers of ancient Latin epic. For example, to the narrative of Hercules' destruction of Troy in the time of Priam's father Laomedon, the Irish text added a list of Hercules' labours, to accompany a greatly expanded narrative of Jason and the Argonauts (see Ch. 8). Pre-eminent among the ancient sources drawn on by the Irish authors and revisers of *Togail Troí* were Virgil's *Aeneid*, and a wealth of ancient commentary on Virgil's poetry, including the Latin commentary by the ancient grammarian Servius, and so-called Servius Danielis, an expanded version of Servius' commentary which has been closely associated with medieval Irish scholars of the earlier Golden Age of Irish learning.[5] With generations of Irish scholarship behind it, *Togail Troí* represents a high point in Irish learning and literary endeavour.

Notes

1   Lit. 'It was a share (quota) of pain'.

2   Presumably a reference to the distant east of the world.

3   'Warp-spasm' is Thomas Kinsella's memorable coinage, used throughout his translation *The Tain* (1970).

4   *TBC* 1, lines 2272–4 for the *lúan láith*, 2256–8 for the eyes.

5   See Miles 2011: 66–144 for *Togail Troí*'s sources, and 23–8 for a Hiberno-centric review of the Servian tradition.

8

Togail Troí 'The Siege of Troy', Recension 2 from the Book of Leinster

Michael Clarke

The text is based on the diplomatic edition in Best et al. 1954–83, vol. 4 pp.1064–6, with a new translation by the author. Line numbers are those of Best et al.

Text: The Golden Fleece and its origins

30862] Ra genair trá rí amra airegda urdairc din chenél rigda-sain. Ra gab-side ardríge Gréc. Pelias a ainm-side. Pilopensirda ainm na rigcathrach i rrabi-side ic Lacrimonnaib. In dara tuath déc hí-side do Grécaib. Ra baí dano bráthair ace, Essón a ainm-side. Genair mac amra úad-side, Iasón a ainm-side. Ba lán tuascertleth na Eórpa dá anmum .i. ar féle ⁊ saíri ⁊ suithcernas ⁊ cundla ⁊ cenél, gaís ⁊ gaisced, ánius ⁊ urdarcus, ar einech fri cech n-oen, eter aichnid ⁊ anaichnid. Ba fálid friu ule Iasón. Conid aire-sin ras-carsatar uli. Comba ina thegluch no bítis meic inna ríg ⁊ rígthuísech, amus ⁊ ócthigern na ṅGréc, ⁊ duthractar combad é bad rí ⁊ bad trén ⁊ bad tigerna dóib.

30873] Ó'tchondcatar áes gráda in ríg in muin ⁊ in míad ⁊ in mormassi-sin do bith for Íasón, ba dóig leo marbad no athrígad in ríg dó. Ro bátar acá aslach for Pelias Iason do marbad arnach tissad friss he. Iss ed ra raid in ri riu na diṅgned fingail for mac a brathar. Rop ferr leis a ḟaídiud i tírib ciana do chungid allaid ⁊ étala, do thobuch cisa ⁊ bésa, do ṡiriud na sét n-inngnad n-anachnid no betís isin doman, co torsitis ri Íasón ar áis no ar écin co mbetis i tírib Gréc. Ar ro bai do mét menman in ríg Pelias narbo massech leis sét suachnid sainemail do bith issin [domun] cen ḟagbáil tri gais no gaisced. Ar ni rabi d' acmib no cenélaib fer talman ra sessad cutrummus fri Grecu issin amsir-sin ar línmaire a slúaig ⁊ ar primdacht a popul, ar méit a n-orddain, ⁊ ar anfóilli a n-airechais, ar immad a n-ecnai ⁊ ar aidbli a n-eolais, ⁊ ar nirt a nniath, ⁊ ar leitmigi a laech, ⁊ ar ḟebas a ṅgascid, ar a n-ani a n-allaid ⁊ a n-orddain ⁊ a n-airechais, ri saigthige a ríge ⁊ a flathiusa for ferannaib in talman.

30890] Conid aire-sin ra for-coṅgrad forsin n-óclach n-uallach, for Iásón, tíchtain d'acallaim in ríg Pelias. O do-riacht iaram Iásón, ra ráid Pelias ris, 'Atá sét ingnad ic Etta, ic ríg na Colach .i. croccend órda in rethi ra edbair Frixis mac

Translation by the author

30862] There was born a wonderful, authoritative, renowned king from that kingly kindred. He took up the high-kingship of the Greeks. Pelias was his name. Pilopensirda was the name of the royal city in which he lived among the Lacedaemonians; that is one of the twelve tribal divisions of the Greeks. He had a brother, his name was Aeson. A wonderful son was born to him, whose name was Jason. The northern part of Europe was full of his name, for liberality and nobility and good-lordship and prudence and kindness, wisdom and valour, excellence and renown, for honourable conduct towards everyone, both those whom he knew and strangers. Jason was welcoming to them all, so that for that reason they all loved him; so that in his household would be the sons of the kings and royal chieftains, the followers and young lords of the Greeks, and they desired that he would be king, and that he would be the powerful one and the lord over them.

30873] When the men of rank around the king saw the esteem and honour and great beauty that Jason had, it seemed likely to them that he would kill or depose the king. They were urging Pelias to kill Jason so that he would not come against him. This is what the king said to them: that he would not commit kinslaying on his brother's son. He would prefer to send him into distant lands to seek glory and wealth, to gather tribute and levies, to seek the wonderful unknown treasures that were in the world: so that these things would come to Jason, freely or by force, so that they would be in the lands of the Greeks. For such was the greatness of spirit of king Pelias, that he did not think it fitting for a famous and conspicuous treasure to exist in the world without obtaining it by wit or by valour. For there were none among the peoples or kindreds of the men of the earth that could stand as equals to the Greeks at that time, for the size of their host and the pre-eminence of their peoples, for the extent of their dignity, and for the greatness of their superiority, for the abundance of their wisdom and the excellence of their knowledge, and for the strength of their champions, and for the boldness of their warriors, and for the excellence of their valour, for the brightness of their glory and their dignity and their superiority, for the pursuit of their kingship and princedom over the lands of the earth.

30890] So for that reason the proud youth, Jason, was summoned to come to converse with king Pelias. When Jason arrived, Pelias said to him, 'Aeetes, king of the Colchians, has a wonderful treasure, namely the golden fleece of the ram that

Adamaint dona deib .i. do Dean ⁊ do Apaill i tempoll Ioib fil i cathraig Etta i tír
na Colach. Iss *ed* ass áil damsa co ndechais-siu do thabairt in chroccind-sin ó
Etta damsa ar ais *no* ar écin.'

30895] In tan ra chuala in mílid mórmenmnach co méit menman .i. Iason in
faídiud ⁊ in forcoṅgra, is ed ro ráid, na ragad ⁊ ba tol dó a dul, acht co mbeth
coṅgab a théchta aici do daínib ⁊ do lestraib. Ar ro-fitir no biad clú ⁊ urdurcus
mór dó-som de ⁊ do Grecaib archena da torsed leis in croccend órda a tírib na
Colach.

30900] Iss é-seo imorro fis ⁊ senchass bunaid in rethi cosin croccend na olla
órda. Adamans mac Olei fer soim saidbir sochenelach ro baí issin Assia. Ra
thussim in bandea Nimpha dís clainne dó .i. Frixis ⁊ Ellis a n-anmand. Tuc
Adamans mnaí aile .i. Míca ingen Diomíd hi-side. Raba miscais lé-side a
leschland ⁊ ra aslaig for Adamans a n-edbairt dona deib, árna losced-si gurtu ⁊
fínemna a fir cacha bliadna, combad móti no edbrad a maccu. Tanic de-side
gorta mór do Adamans ⁊ ro erail-si for sacardaib na ndea a rád is sí fergg na ndea
fotera in gorta-sin, ⁊ ní biad scor furri mani edbrad a maccu. In tan imorro rop
áill do Adamans a n-edbairt dona deib, tanic a mmathair Nimpa dia sáerad, tuc
lé rethi co n-olaind órdai fair ⁊ tricha traiged 'na fot. Ra chuir-si a claind fair ⁊
ras-imchuir in rethi dar murib ⁊ tírib co torchair Ellis de issin Muir Ellispontide.
Conid uad ainmnigthir in Muir Ellispontide. Ra-siacht imorro Frixis fora rethe
co tír na Colach ⁊ da-rat a chroccend i n-edbairt i tempoll Ioib i cathraig Etta.

30916] Do ṡíl chairech ingen Hisper ócian íarthardescertach in rethe-sin, ar is
accu-side ro bátar na treóit ⁊ dath óir fora n-alaind, ⁊ is uadib-side do-rat
Nimpha in rethe-sin do chobair a clainne. <Cindus ón> ⁊ Nimpha i tuasciurt in
betha ⁊ na caírig 'na desciurt? Dethbir ón, ar bá siur di Ollorba mathair dá ingen
Hisper .i. Frithis ⁊ Ospera a n-anmand-side. Cid fotera dath óir for olland cairech
ingen Hisper sech olaind caírech cáich? Ni hannsa. Immarbaig do-rala eter da
ingen Hisper ⁊ Erinés ingen Oirc ⁊ Fama ingen Terra. At-rubradatar na da ingin-
sin, Erinés ⁊ Fama, bá mó a cumachta for dúlib andas cumachta ingen Hisper. Na
huli catha ⁊ uilc, is í Erines fotera a ndenam. Brecscéla in betha, is sí Fáma fotera
a ndolbud. Da ingin Isper dano da-chuatar i mmunigin a ndruidechta ⁊ ro laiset

Phrixus son of Athamas sacrificed to the gods, namely to Diana and Apollo, in the temple of Jove which is in the city of Aeetes in the land of the Colchians. What I wish is that you would go to bring that fleece from Aeetes to me, with his will or by force.'

30895] When the great-spirited soldier with abundance of spirit, Jason, heard this mission and summons, he said this: that he would go and that he desired to go, provided that he would have with him the proper amount of people and vessels; for he knew that great fame and renown would come from this for him and for all the Greeks, if he would succeed in bringing the golden fleece from the lands of the Colchi.

30900] This indeed is the knowledge and fundamental lore of the ram with the skin of the golden wool. Athamas, son of Aeolus, was a rich wealthy man who lived in Asia. The goddess Nimpha bore two children to him, and Phrixus and Helle were their names. Athamas took another woman: she was Mica daughter of Diomede. Hateful to her were her stepchildren, and she tried to induce Athamas to sacrifice them to the gods, for she used to burn her husband's fields and vineyards every year, so that this would make him sacrifice his children. From this a great famine came to Athamas, and she urged the priests of the gods to say that the anger of the gods was the reason for that famine, and that there would be no end to it unless he sacrificed his children. When indeed Athamas began to wish to sacrifice them to the gods, their mother Nimpha came to save them, and brought with her a ram with golden wool upon it, and its length was thirty feet. She put her children on it, and it bore them over seas and lands until Helle fell from it into the Hellespontian Sea. And that is why it is called the Hellespontian Sea. Phrixus, however, reached the land of the Colchi on his ram, and he set up its skin as a sacrifice in the temple of Jove in the city of Aeetes.

30916] That ram was one of the offspring of the flocks of the daughters of Isper from the southwestern ocean; for they had the flocks with golden colour on their wool, and from among them Nimpha gave that ram in order to help her children. <How can it be that> Nimpha was in north of the world, and the flocks were in the south?[1] That is fitting, for her sister was Ollorba the mother of the two daughters of Isper: Frithis and Ospera were their names. What is the reason that there was the colour of gold on the wool of the sheep of the daughters of Isper, unlike the wool of all other sheep? Not difficult. A dispute arose between the two daughters of Isper, and Erinys the daughter of Orcus, and Fama [Rumour] the daughter of Earth. Those two daughters, Erinys and Rumour, said that their bricht i mbélaib a caírech i n-úair a comperta dona caírib. Is é dath ro thogsat fora n-olaind dath óir ⁊ tucad dóib sin. Trícha bliadan do síl na caírech fon dath-sain, ⁊ marba na caírig do brith a n-úan. I cind trichat ṁbliadan imorro at-bathatar sil na caírech-sin ⁊ da ingin Isper i n-oenaidchi riu.

power over natural things was greater than the power of the daughters of Isper. It is Erinys who brings it about that all wars and evils happen. The lying tales of the world, Rumour is the cause of their shaping. The two daughters of Isper, indeed, went to make use of their sorcery, and they cast a spell upon the sheep[2] at the time they were conceived. The colour that they chose for their wool was the colour of gold, and that was given to them. The offspring of the sheep spent thirty years in that colour, and the sheep died while giving birth to their lambs. At the end of thirty years, indeed, the offspring of those sheep died, and the two daughters of Isper died on the same night as them.

Essay: Mythographic gleanings in *Togail Troí*

Troy was besieged twice, by Hercules and by Agamemnon. In the Dares Phrygius version, and therefore in texts like *Togail Troí* that follow its authority, there is a causal linkage between the two. Hercules seized Hesione, princess of Troy, in the fall of the city and brought her back to Greece, and this justified Paris of Troy's abduction of Helen that sparked off the second war. But why had Hercules attacked Troy in the first place? Earlier still, explains Dares, when Hercules accompanied Jason as one of the Argonauts in quest of the Golden Fleece, they were insulted by Laomedon king of Troy, who refused to welcome them when they arrived there in the course of their voyage. Hercules, being who he was, could not allow this to go unavenged (Dares, ch. 3). In this way the origins of the Trojan conflict are rooted in the story of Jason and the Argonauts. Dares, accordingly, begins his narrative with Jason, recounting what happened with his usual air of lean, pared-back simplicity:

> Pelias, king in the Peloponnese, had a brother, Aeson. Aeson's son was Jason, outstanding in valour, and as to those who were under his rule, he had them all as guest-friends and he was loved very strongly by them. When king Pelias saw that Jason was so popular with everyone, he feared that he would work harm against him and expel him from the kingship. He told Jason that among the Colchi there was a ram's skin covered with gold, that was worthy of his valour: and he promised that he would give him anything he needed so that he would bring back the skin from there. When Jason heard this, being a man of very strong spirit, and because he wished to get to know all places, and because he thought that he would be more famous if he brought the golden fleece back from the Colchi, he told king Pelias that he was willing to go there, if strength and companions would not be lacking to him.
>
> Dares Phrygius ch. 1, tr. Clarke.

It is typical of *Togail Troí*'s compositional technique that this passage has been taken and expanded into the vastly more complex and nuanced narrative that we see in our extract. This section does not survive in what is usually known as Recension 1 (*TTr-H*, see Ch. 7), so our earliest surviving version is that in the Book of Leinster (*TTr-LL*), a manuscript of about 1160 CE. Comparison between all the surviving versions suggests that the Book of Leinster copy incorporates unique additions of its own, characteristic of the style of many narrative texts in this manuscript. Typical of these additions are long strings of ornamental synonyms and epithets, which heighten the style without adding material of real substance. However, since in every other respect our passage takes virtually the same form both in the Book of Leinster and in the manuscripts of Recension 3, we can be confident that we are dealing essentially with the work of the original scholar-author whose version underlies all the surviving copies.

Our author extends and deepens Dares' narrative of the dealings between Pelias and Jason, adding vividness of motivation and, in general, transforming the bare bones of eyewitness historiography (as it was believed to be) into a form deserving of the name of saga, comparable in mode and level to Middle Irish narratives on heroic subjects from indigenous tradition. Additionally, however, the flow of this narrative is interrupted to address what seem to be strictly mythographic questions. What was the Golden Fleece, and why was it golden?

In all known sources in Latin and Greek the origin-story of the Golden Fleece begins, like so many of its kind, with a crisis caused by a wicked stepmother. She uses a deceitful ruse to persuade her husband Athamas to put the children of his first marriage to death as a human sacrifice; at the last minute their birth-mother saves them, putting them on the back of a ram with a golden fleece, which flies away with the children on its back. One of the children, the girl Helle, falls off the ram and drowns in the sea that will henceforth be called the Hellespont; her brother Phrixus lands safely in Colchis and leaves the ram's golden fleece as an offering in the temple. So far, this corresponds to standard mythographic knowledge in the West in the period, and (for example) it is matched by the information set out by the Second Vatican Mythographer (*MVII* ch.157, Kulcsár 1987: 218–19, Pepin 2008: 153–4), a source whose information often matches that found in *Togail Troí*.[3] However, two oddities stand out. The usual name of Athamas' first wife is Nephele or Nubes, 'Cloud', but here it is Nimpha, clearly a form of the Greek-derived word *nympha* 'wife, deity, nymph'. Again, the expected name of the second wife is Ino, yet here we have *Míca ingen Diomíd*, apparently 'Mica daughter of Diomedes'.

There is one (and, so far as I know, only one) surviving authority for the name *Nimpha*, the commentary on Virgil's *Georgics* known as the *Brevis Expositio*, at *Georgics* 1.221 (Thilo and Hagen 1881–1902: 3.240). This commentary ultimately goes back to the work of Iunius Philargyrius in the later fifth century (on whom see Ziolkowski and Putnam 2008: 641–2), via unknown intermediaries. The *Brevis Expositio* is also unique in offering an explanation for *Mica*. According to the printed edition, the *Brevis Expositio* states, conventionally enough, that for his second marriage Athamas *Ino Cadmi filiam coniugem duxit* 'took as wife Ino, daughter of Cadmus'. This, however, is an editorial emendation; the text is corrupt in all the surviving manuscripts.[4] In each manuscript the posited original reading *Ino Cadmi filiam* has been replaced by a garbled sequence of letters and contraction signs. The most telling example for us is in manuscript G (Leiden, University Library, MS BPL 135), fol. 100r (see Figure 4). It is easy to see how a reader of this or a closely-related copy might have tried to make sense of the characters picked out in the oblong box. He reads the uprights *in* as *m*; he reads *oc* as *cc*, equally easily; and he takes the horizontal stroke over the *a* to represent *n* or *m*, as is conventional. The key words then resolve into as *miccam diomi filiam* – ready to be interpreted in turn as 'Mi(c)ca, daughter of Diomi(t).'[5] *Diomit*, neatly, corresponds to the usual Middle Irish form of the name Diomedes.

This is not the only case in which the *Brevis Expositio* matches *Togail Troí*. On entirely separate grounds, Miles has argued that Philargyrian material seen in this commentary matches *Togail Troí*'s later account of the tasks that Aeetes sets Jason as preconditions for gaining the Fleece.[6] If the *Togail Troí* author was working in this way, assembling his knowledge from a combination of standard mythographies and gloss commentaries on poets like Virgil, his method was typical of philological practice across Europe in his time, treating the annotated text as a repository of world-knowledge – including mythology, cosmography and so on – rather than simply as a resource for understanding the Latin poet (O'Sullivan 2016, 2018).

But what of the second part of the digression, where the origins of the ram with the golden fleece are traced back to a contest between the 'daughters of Isper' and their rivals Erinys and Fama, the Fury and the personification of Rumour? So far as I can find, this story survives nowhere else in any ancient or medieval source.[7] Nonetheless, it is not mere invention, and the account of the characteristics of Erinys and Fama has the hallmarks of the use of a genuine mythographic source.[8] The description of Fama here is standard, including the detail that she is daughter of Earth (Virgil, *Aeneid* 4.178), but that of Erinys requires a closer look. The Furies of the Underworld do not normally concern themselves with the mortal world at all, except to ensure that solemn curses are fulfilled. However, the deity known in Greek as *Eris*, 'Strife', is indeed aptly described as 'responsible for all wars and evils', including the Trojan War itself (Clarke 2019: 166–70). Our author or his source has again slightly misread a source, mistaking the Greek name *Eris* for a contraction of the more common *Erinys*.[9]

Then a further clue comes into play. Figure 3 gives the family tree of the daughters of Isper according to the passage. Of all these names, only one seems recognizable: *Isper* is Latin *Hesperus*. The daughters of Hesperus, the *Hesperides*, were the girls – usually seven in number – in whose custody was the tree with

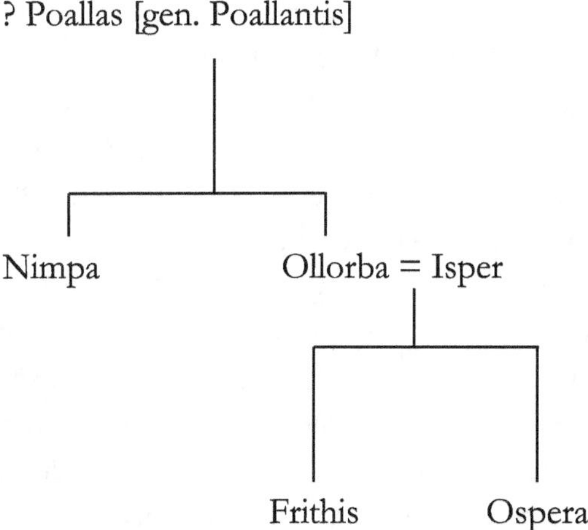

Figure 3 The family of Isper, according to *Togail Troí* in the Book of Leinster.

golden apples, celebrated in the story of the labours of Hercules. In rationalizing explanations of mythology, it was common to explain this story on the grounds that Greek *mēla* 'apples' is formally indistinguishable from *mēla* 'flocks'. Already in the first century BCE Diodorus Siculus claims that these sheep were called 'golden' as a way of signalling their excellence, although he says others hold that they were literally golden-coloured (*Library* 4.27, Oldfather 1933–67: 4.428–9; cf. Hawkes 2014: 127 ff.). Although the rest of his story does not match that in *Togail Troí*, we can be confident that our author is drawing on a source that began on the basis of the same explanatory strategy and merged the two stories into one.

Strikingly, the closest identifiable parallels to our passage are in Greek rather than Latin. Here, for example, is the opening of the story in Palaephatus, *On Unbelievable Tales*, a text that originated in the fourth century BCE and was commonly used by Byzantine scholars throughout the Middle Ages:

> There was a man of Miletus named Hesperus who dwelt in Caria and had two daughters called the Hesperides ['daughters of Hesperus']. Now Hesperus had beautiful, fleecy sheep – the kind which can still be found in Miletus. For this reason they were called 'golden', for gold is the finest metal, and these were the finest of sheep. The herds were also known as the 'apples of his eye'.[10]

Although the resemblance is not sustained as the story continues, the match between the two openings is enough to confirm that our author was working with an authentic source whose version of the story was cognate with this one.[11]

To what degree is this scholarly activity typical of medieval mythographic narrative, and to what extent is it uniquely Irish? While the Trojan war narratives of the European mainstream, beginning with the *Roman de Troie* of Benoît de Sainte-Maure, resemble *Togail Troí* in expanding and developing Dares' account of Pelias' reasons for sending Jason in search of the Fleece (Burgess and Kelly 2017: 55), none of them include anything like this digression on its origins. To that extent at least, we seem to be looking here at a species of text-production that belongs to Gaelic tradition alone. More strikingly still, the *Brevis Expositio* itself has demonstrable Irish affinities. In the four surviving manuscripts it sits alongside a commentary on the *Eclogues*, the *Explanatio in Bocolica*: the two probably are excerpted from a common source, as Brent Miles shows (2011: 28–32). Across the two texts in three of these manuscripts there survive numerous Old Irish words, evidently glosses in the exemplar which were misunderstood and written out *plene* by the scribes.[12] This can only mean that the transmission, and probably the origins, of the text were among speakers of Old Irish.

This leaves us with two distinct possibilities for our reconstruction of the sources used by the *Togail Troí* author in (probably) the early eleventh century. He may have encountered materials from the *Brevis Expositio* randomly as part of a collection of scholarly Latin manuscripts, coming from international sources like any other: in that case, the fact that it had Irish antecedents is merely coincidental. Alternatively, he may have been able to access a set of sources that had been held continuously in Ireland – presumably one of the more secure monasteries – for many generations beforehand, perhaps as far back at the period of heightened classical learning characteristic of those who were to emigrate and re-emerge as the learned Irish *peregrini* on the Continent.[13]

A decisive choice between those reconstructions seems unattainable. In this case, however, one crucial piece of evidence points in the direction of the former possibility. Between the four manuscripts of the *Brevis Expositio*, the Leiden manuscript G (illustrated below) is the one whose wording most obviously invites misinterpretation as *Micam Diomi filiam*, the source of *Togail Troí's* version. However, this manuscript differs from the others in the group precisely in the fact that here the Old Irish glosses have been dropped throughout. In other words, the most promising candidate for our author's source is also the one that is furthest away from the Irish stage in the transmission of the glosses. In its small way this adds to the suggestion that the flowering of classical text-production in Middle Irish, however distinctive in the wider European context, did not necessarily emerge directly from the earlier Gaelic classicism of

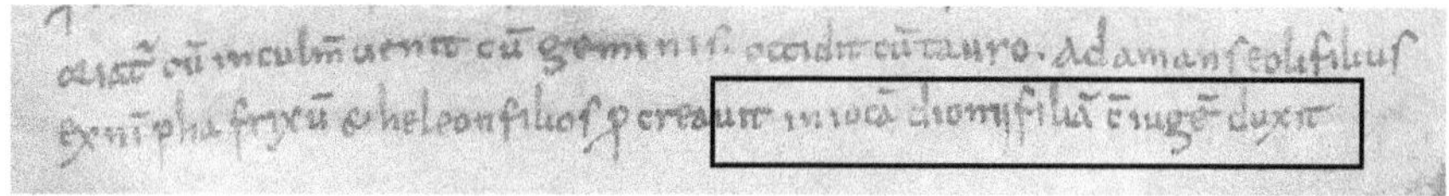

Figure 4 Leiden, University Library MS BPL 135, fol. 100r, detail: from the *Brevis Expositio* on the *Georgics* of Virgil. Reproduced under a Creative Commons licence by courtesy of University of Leiden Libraries.

the much earlier period when the learning of Irish scholars first came into prominence at the Carolingian courts and monasteries.

Notes

1 The words that I have supplied in angle brackets are missing in the Book of Leinster copy but are found in the later manuscripts of *Togail Troí* at this point (e.g. Dublin, Royal Irish Academy MS D.iv.2, fol. 25ra 37). The sense is incomplete without them, and they were evidently omitted in error by the scribe.

2 Or more literally 'in the mouths of the sheep'.

3 The terms 'First, Second and Third Vatican Mythographer' are purely conventional: they refer to three closely-related compilations of mythological information that were originally published by Angelo Mai in 1831 from manuscripts in the Vatican Library, Rome. The Latin edition of Kulcsár 1987 matches the translation in Pepin 2008.

4 The manuscripts are as follows, with the usual sigla used in the specialist articles. N = Paris Lat. 7960, ninth or tenth century, Auxerre; P = Paris, Bibliothèque Nationale, MS 11308, from Reims, second quarter of the ninth century; G = Leiden, University Library, MS BPL 135, second quarter of the ninth century; L = Firenze, Biblioteca Laurenziana, MS 45.14, from France, first half of the ninth century; V = Leiden, University Library, MS Voss F 79, ninth century.

5 In Dublin, RIA MS D.iv.2, representing the Third Recension of *Togail Troí*, the spelling is *Micca* throughout. This may well go back to the original.

6 Miles 2011: 72–3 shows that the list of tasks in the *Brevis Expositio* at *Georgics* 2.140 corresponds closely to that in *Togail Troí*. However, since the materials are also similar to those in the Vatican Mythographers (*VMI* ch. 25, *VMII* ch. 159, Kulcsár 1987: 13, 220–1; Pepin 2008: 24, 164–5), the identification of the source in this case is not decisive.

7 After looking in vain in every mythographic source known to me, I circulated a translation of the passage on the online Liverpool Classics List and asked subscribers to contact me with suggestions. While this led to many instructive suggestions,

which are acknowledged in footnotes below, no-one could find a source or close analogue for the story.

8 I thank Richard Martin for the observation that follows.

9 Erinys is familiar in Latin sources at (e.g.) Virgil, *Aeneid* 2.337, 573; 7.447, 570. Elton Barker suggests to me (pers. comm.) that the account of Erinys in our passage could be derived from Virgil's description of Allecto (*Aeneid* 7.325–6), but the match is inexact and it seems more economical to posit that the source was a glossary entry that originally described *Eris*.

10 Translation from Stern 1996: 49. I am grateful to Greta Hawkes and Elton Barker for bringing the passage to my attention.

11 In the Philargyrian *Explanatio in Bocolica*, which accompanies the *Brevis Expositio* in the manuscripts, we find (at Virgil, *Eclogues* 6.61) a reference to the Hesperides and their golden *mala* 'apples'. It is tempting to speculate that the original Philargyrian commentary from which this is excerpted might have had a discussion of the issue of apples and sheep.

12 Most of the Old Irish words are in the *Explanatio in Bocolica* commentary on the *Eclogues*; for the two in the *Brevis Expositio* (located at *Georgics* 1.171, 361) see Lambert 1986: 105, cf. Miles 2011: 29. MS P, probably the oldest, includes two Old Irish glosses not found in any of the others; the best explanation is that they were omitted by subsequent copyists. For a selection of the Old Irish items in the *Eclogues* scholia, see Ziolkowski and Putnam 2008: 698–700.

13 See Ch. 1 above, with the important discussion by Miles 2011: 10–11, drawing on Herbert's reconstruction of a revival of interest in earlier texts among Irish monastic scholars around the year 1000 (Herbert 2001).

9

Togail Troí 'The Siege of Troy', Recension 3

Michael Clarke

The text has been edited by the author from Dublin, RIA MS D.iv.2, fol. 32vb37 ff., with supplementary evidence from Dublin, King's Inns MS 12, fol. 17ra5 ff., following on the edition by Ó hAodha 1979.[1] As usual, the two manuscripts are referred to in the notes as D and K respectively.

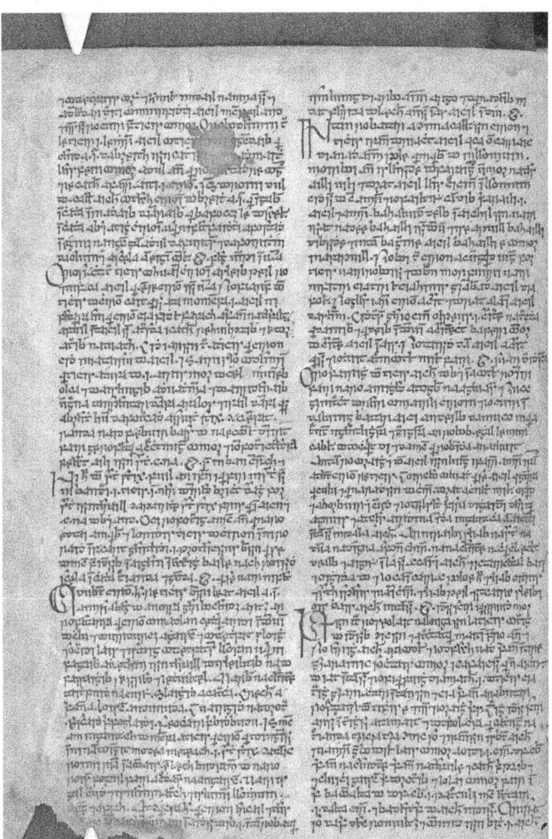

Figure 5 Dublin, Royal Irish Academy MS D.iv.2, fol. 32v: from *Togail Troí* Recension 3. Image from ISOS reproduced by kind permission of the Royal Irish Academy.

Text: The cross-dressing of Achilles

(1) Iar sin trat ro seolait na longa sin la Tichis co traigh indsi Scir iar siriudh mor do indsibh conic sin ⁊ atrrachtatar maitin forro ann. ⁊ ro eirigh Aichil asa codladh ⁊ ro d'fhech uadh ferann in tíre gusa rainic. Sochtais co mór icá faicsin ar nir aichnedh dó iat in tan-sin ⁊ ro fiarfuigh día mathair .i. do Tíchis cia traigh gusa riachtar in tan-sin ⁊ cia ferann a rabutar. Ro fregair dano Tichis é ⁊ iss ed ro raigh fris: 'Traigh indsi Scír', ar si, 'in traigh-si atámait ⁊ dot fholach-sa ar cathugad na Troianda tucusa tusa conic so.' ⁊ is annsin isbert Aichil ría máthair gurbo doilig lais co mór a oidi .i. Ciron d' facbail ⁊ ferann na cendture ⁊ ferann na Tesaile ⁊ cathugad fri pestib ⁊ cluichi gaisced fri torotraibh. ⁊ Ro lái co mór fair in fer ba comalta dó do facbail .i. Patroculus mac Echtair .i. dalta Ciron ⁊ ba deithfer do Aichil indí-sin. Ar is iat-so da fer dec rob fherr comultus ⁊ comund isin bith .i. Aichil [fol. 33ra1] ⁊ Patroculus, Téis ⁊ Periotus, Oiristeis ⁊ Paladies, Tétheus ⁊ Pollaniceis, Castor ⁊ Pullux, Nisus ⁊ Berialus. Ro gab dono Tichis ic agallam Aichil ⁊ iss ed ro raidh fris: 'Ata bandtracht suairc solus do nach feas firu na ferrdacht na tochmarc riam isin indsi-sea', ar si, '⁊ ata oigrighan a ndingbala a tigernus ⁊ a forlamus forro .i. Didhamia ingen Licomit .i. ingen rig indsi Scir ⁊ gé ro derrscaig Giunuind cruthach tar mnaib in domuin ar deilb ar ailli ar ai-sin tra is ailli co mór in ingen-sa inás. Ocus is ail dam-sa', ar si, 'tusa do gábáil étaigh mna umut ⁊ do beth a richt ingine atura sin ⁊ ní mebul duit-siu sin do denum ar ro gab prim-gaisgedach ⁊ cathmiled in domuin uimi étach mna .i. Ercail mac Aimpitnionis dia tard gradh do Ghoile .i. d' ingin righ indsi Lid ⁊ ro boi Ercail ic ciradh olla isin indsi-sin ⁊ e a ndeilb mna. Ro gab Liber pater imorro etach mna uimi ⁊ dono ro boi ac sním in abruis. Acus nar mebail le tigerna na ndee ⁊ lena rig .i. le hIoip mac Satuirrn delb mna do beth fair', ar si, 'co mboi ic uaim ⁊ ic cuma étaig. Ro gab Feneius in gaiscedach urrdairc do Grecaib eccusc bánda fair amlaid-sin ⁊ cid ima badh mebal lat-su, a mic', ar Tícis, 'in ní do-ronsat-sin do denum ⁊ nibud fata bes tu a ndeilb mna itir ar not-bertar for culu co Ciron cruiteri ⁊ ni findfa Ciron delb mna do gabail duitsiu fort itir'. Ro boi amlaid-sin ica radh fris ⁊ is-bert ann:

Translation by the author

(1) Then indeed those ships were sent by Thetis to the shore of the island of Scyros, after she had searched many islands before that; and morning arose upon them then. And Achilles rose up from his sleep, and he gazed upon the land of the country to which he had come. He was amazed when he saw it, for these things were unknown to him at that time, and he asked his mother Thetis what shore they had come to, and what land they were in. Thetis answered him, and this is what she said to him: 'The shore of the island of Scyros', she said, 'is the shore at which we are, and I have brought you here to hide you from the battle of the Trojans'. Then Achilles told his mother that he was sad to be leaving his foster-father, namely Cheiron, and the land of the centaurs and the land of Thessaly, and battling against beasts, and contests of valour against monsters; and that it weighed upon him greatly to leave behind the man who was his foster-brother, Patroclus son of Actor,[7] Cheiron's pupil; and that was appropriate for Achilles. For these are the twelve men that were best for foster-brothership and companionship in the world: Achilles and Patroclus, Theseus and Pirithous, Orestes and Pylades, Tydeus and Polynices, Castor and Pollux, Nisus and Euryalus.[8] Then Thetis began to converse with Achilles, and this is what she said to him: 'There is a lovely bright band of women in this island', she said, 'who have never known anything of men or masculinity or wooing', she said, 'and in lordship and command over them there is a young queen who is worthy of them, Deidamia daughter of Lycomedes, the daughter of the king of the island of Scyros; and although lovely Juno excels all the women of the world for shape and beauty, nonetheless this girl is much more beautiful than she is. And it is my wish', she said, 'that you should put woman's clothes upon yourself, and be among them in the form of a girl; and it is no cause of shame for you to do that, for the prime warrior and battle-soldier of the world put woman's clothes upon himself, namely Hercules son of Amphitryon, when he gave his love to Belly/Goile,[9] that is, the daughter of the king of Lydia, and Hercules was carding wool on that island, while he was in the form of a woman. Liber Pater [= Bacchus] put woman's clothing upon himself, and indeed he was spinning thread. And it was no cause of shame for the lord and king of the gods, Jove, son of Saturn, to have the form of a woman upon himself', she said, 'so that he was stitching and making clothing. Caeneus,[10] the famous warrior of the Greeks, likewise took a female appearance upon himself; and why would it be any cause of shame for you, my boy, to do the thing that they did? And indeed you will not be in woman's form for long, for you will be brought back again to Cheiron the harper,[11] and Cheiron will not find

(2) Dena orm, a Aicíl,
a romra co rathcheill,
fer[a][2] *for ga*ch flaithfeind,
at muir *ta*r *ga*ch múr.
Geb egcosc mna moiri;
dena[d] edbairt t' oíge,[3]
cath cu*m*aidh na gloire,
Deda*m*ia 'na dú*n*.

Ro gab Ercail am*ra*
étgúd a mh*ac*sa*m*la
ni bái cui*n*g bud calma –
et*ir* ba*n*tracht mi*n*
co *m*boí ic ciriudh olla
– giarsat garg a ghlon*n*a
it*ir* tír is ton*n*a –
tigh righ indsi Lit.[4]

Ro gab Lib*er* pater,
gerbo t*r*om a thaigidh,
nochon †ernachaiter†[5]
gersat laích re lá,
co *m*boi ic sni*m* in abruis
do tsluagh b*eth*adh barrglais;
dena i*n* ní na*ch* derrnais
i richt ga*ch*a mná.

Ro gab Ioip ba harn*aidh*
gidh e ba *t*reisi *ar* talmui*n* –
rob é i*n* t-*arm* os *ar*maibh
annsoraidh[6] gu se –
dia *m*boi ic cu*m*a i*n* étaigh
do tsluagh talmun tredaigh
i*m*an mnai do Grecdhaib
noco *n*dech*aid* de.
Dena.

out that you took on woman's form.' She was speaking to him in this way, and
then she said:

(2) Obey me, Achilles,
O you great ocean of prosperous sense,
may you pour (battle) against every princely warrior:
you are the sea against every rampart.
Take the form of a grown woman;
may she make an offering to your youthfulness,
the glorious battle of sorrow,
Deidamia in her fort.

Illustrious Hercules
put on the same kind of clothing
(there was no more valorous champion)
among the soft womanhood
so that he was carding wool
(though his deeds were fierce,
on both land and waves),
in the house of the king of the island of Lydia.

Liber pater wore (such clothes),
though his pursuit was difficult,
he was not refused…[*words obscure*]
though they were heroes in their day;
so that he was spinning yarn
for the host of green-topped world.
Do the thing that you have never done,
in the form of a woman.

Jove, the harsh one, wore (such clothes)
though he was the strongest one on earth –
he was the warrior above all warriors
unfortunate, up to the present time –
when he was fashioning clothing
for the host of the teeming earth,
in company with [or 'because of'] the woman of the Greeks,
until he departed from it.
Obey.

(3) Cid *tra acht* ba hainmin égcen*n*us ag*ar*b Aichi*l* fria m*athai*r an ta*n*-sin ⁊
ni*r*bo usa a cen*n*sug*ad* ina leomu*n* a tír na Tesalta *no* æ*n* do siled Sátuirn*n* ica
cétcuidbiug*ad* i*m* ca*r*pat. ⁊ rob iat-sidhe rob eccendsa isi*n* do*m*un. I*n* tan *tra* ro
boi Aicíl ⁊ a mh*athai*r i*con* imacalla*m*-sin, is an*n* do-rala Deda*m*ia .i. †d'† ingi*n*
Licoimit tiachtai*n* assin dún a*m*ach *con*a ban*n*trocht do denu*m* edp*ur*ta do*n*a
deib. O*cus* o'tc*on*airc Aichi*l* in i*n*gen-sin .i. Déda*m*ia ro lín a gr*ad*h ⁊ a hailgius é
o mull*ach* co tal*man* gerbo fata at*ur*ra ⁊ is i ro cláechlá delb ⁊ dat*h* do Aich*i*l
indsi*n*. Ro fairig Ticis *tra for* Aicil co raibi gr*ad*h na hi*n*gine ica treghd*ad* ⁊ ica
tr*a*scai*r*t ⁊ ica t*r*aethad co mor ⁊ is treisi dhi ro fhasl*aigh* fair étach mna do gab*ai*l
uimi i*n*d ni-sin.

(3) But indeed Achilles was harsh and ungovernable and rough towards his mother at that time, and it was no easier to subdue him than a lion from the land of Thessaly, or one of the seed of Saturn when first being fitted to a chariot; and those are the ones that were the most ungovernable in the world. But when Achilles and his mother were holding that conversation, then it happened that Deidamia, the daughter of Lycomedes, came out of the fort with her womenfolk, to make a sacrifice to the gods. And when Achilles saw that girl, Deidamia, love and desire for her filled him from top to bottom, though there was a great distance between them, and she changed Achilles' form and colour/appearance at that time. Thetis indeed observed in Achilles that love of the girl was greatly piercing and overthrowing and subduing him, and all the more for this reason she persuaded him to put on woman's clothing.

Essay: Statius and the expansion of the Trojan saga

Recension 3 of *Togail Troí* is a vastly expanded and elaborated version of the Trojan War narrative. It was probably composed in the twelfth or thirteenth century, on the basis of an earlier version that is now lost. The principal manuscripts, D and K (see above for details) are very closely related. They include an account of the boyhood of Achilles and his eventual journey to Troy to fight in the war, which must have been added to *Togail Troí* after the text seen in the earlier recensions was substantially complete. This episode has come to be known, misleadingly, as 'The Irish Achilleid', as if it were a translation of Statius' poem of that name. As we will see, however, what we have here is a mass of partially Statian material that has been seamlessly absorbed into the style and narrative sequence of *Togail Troí*, with no internal indication that it is separable from its context or that it comes from a specific Latin original.

Here, even more clearly than with *Togail Troí* Recension 1 (see above, Ch. 7), the author is exploiting a typological parallel with indigenous heroic tradition. The subject-matter of the earlier part of the episode (§§6–22) is named later on as Achilles' *macghnimurtha* 'boyhood deeds' (§43), echoing the flashback episode of *Táin Bó Cúailnge* on the *macgnímrada* 'boyhood deeds' of Cú Chulainn.[12] Seemingly, then, our text invites us to set it alongside this section of the *Táin*, which would already have been canonical at the time of composition.[13] As it continues, we learn how Achilles' mother, the sea-goddess Thetis, fearing that her son would die if he went to fight at Troy, disguised him as a girl and hid him among the followers of Deidamia, princess of the island of Scyros; but emissaries from the Greeks eventually exposed him by a ruse, talking in the girl-troop's presence of the outrage done to the Greeks and later displaying weapons for them to see, all in order to seize on the one whose reactions would reveal his warlike masculinity. The implicit allusion to Cú Chulainn continues in the description of his reaction to the weapons (§§39–40). They include a shield inscribed with the text or perhaps picture of a 'battle-tale' (*scél catha*), on reading which Achilles is physically transformed – hair grown wild, face reddened, shape distorted – in ways that recall the preternatural distortion (*ríastrad*) of Cú Chulainn in the *Táin*.[14]

In outline, the story of Achilles on Scyros could have been gleaned from a creative engagement with the Latin mythographic handbooks, as with many of the other episodes of the antiquity-sagas treated in this book. However, we have here a more complex form of intertextuality, because the episode is partially based on the epic poem *Achilleid* by Statius, composed in the late first century CE.[15] The relationship is covert, not explicit. The debt to Statius is not mentioned in the text, and direct verbal adaptations are relatively few, but the resemblance in outline is unmistakeable. Comparison between Latin model and Irish reworking offers sharp glimpses of the Irish author's engagement with this textual world. In our extract this is especially revealing with the speech in which Thetis uses a series of examples from earlier mythology to try to persuade Achilles to dress up as a girl. We will begin from the relevant Statian passage and see how it has been recreated in Irish, first as a prose speech and then in verse – an arrangement of the *opus geminatum* ('twinned work') type that is common, for example, in the presentation of detailed learning in the *Lebor Gabála* tradition (cf. Ch. 26 below) but rare in *Togail Troí* (for another example from the same recension, see Clarke 2014a).

Statius tells how Thetis has taken the sleeping boy Achilles to Scyros. He awakens, not knowing where he is, and she tries to persuade him to go along with her plan to disguise him as a girl, citing a series of examples from earlier mythology (on this passage see Heslin 2005: 121–5):

> cedamus, paulumque animos summitte viriles
> atque habitus dignare meos. si Lydia dura
> pensa manu mollesque tulit Tirynthius hastas,
> si decet aurata Bacchum vestigia palla
> verrere, virgineos si Iuppiter induit artus,
> nec magnum ambigui fregerunt Caenea sexus:
> hac sine, quaeso, minas nubemque exire malignam.

Statius, Achilleid 1.259–65

> Let us give way. Lower a little your manly spirit and deign to wear my raiment. If the Tirynthian carried Lydian wool in his hard hand and womanish spears, if Bacchus it beseems to sweep his footsteps with a gold-embroidered robe, if Jupiter donned a virgin's limbs, and doubtful sexes did not rob great Caeneus of his manhood, pray allow me this way to escape the threat and the baleful cloud.

tr. Shackleton Bailey 2003: 333.

The four mythological narratives mentioned here are of very different kinds. Hercules, 'the Tirynthian', when in love with the Lydian princess Omphale, exchanged clothing and gender roles with her and sat spinning wool, the quintessentially feminine activity of antiquity. Bacchus in the orgiastic ceremonies of his cult dressed in flowing robes like those of a woman. Jupiter, wishing to seduce or rape Callisto when she was a member of the girl-troop presided over by Artemis, took the form of Artemis herself and used that guise to insinuate himself into a close embrace with the girl, in due course leaving her pregnant. Caenis/Caeneus switched from female to male, and back again in the afterlife (see also Virgil, *Aeneid* 6.448–9; Ovid, *Metamorphoses* 12.171ff.). The essential elements of many of these stories could well have been present in the Irish author's manuscript in the form of glosses.[16] However, there is no *a priori* guarantee that a given medieval reader would have been in full control of the allusive references in this passage. What balance between knowledge, guesswork and creativity can be seen at work here in *Togail Troí*?

Our author gives Thetis' speech twice over: first in prose, then in syllabic verse in the metre *ochtfhoclach mór*, which is often used in Middle Irish narrative for a speech of persuasion put in the mouth of a character.[17] Since there is nothing of substance in the verses that is not also in the prose, it is a reasonable guess that the latter was composed first and that it will provide more immediate clues to the author's response to his Latin materials.

First, the author has full command of the story of the 'Tirynthian' and the Lydian princess. Hercules dressed as a woman and spun wool in his efforts to woo her. This could have been understood, for example, if the author were working from a manuscript with glosses similar to those in the corpus edited by Clogan (1968: 50, glosses on *Achilleid* 2.260–1), whose base manuscript dates from the thirteenth century. But there is a curiosity here: the expected name of the princess is Omphale, yet our text calls her *Goile*. What is going on? The clue comes not from the *Achilleid* commentaries but from the wider mythographic reference library of the period. In the text of Carolingian origins ascribed to the 'Second Vatican Mythographer', whose materials are often encountered elsewhere in the Irish antiquity-sagas, we read an etymological explanation of the name: Greek *omphalon* [i.e. *omphalos* in the accusative form] corresponds in meaning to Latin *umbilicus* 'navel', and since *libido enim in umbilico dominatur mulieribus* 'desire in the navel has control of women', so the whole story of Hercules and Omphale can be read allegorically, as lust overcoming previously unconquered virtue (*MVII*, ch. 178, Kulcsár 1987: 237, Pepin 2008: 173–4).[18] The range of meaning of Irish *goile* extends from 'hunger' to 'belly, womb, bowels' (*eDIL* s.v.). The Irish word has been chosen to replace Omphale's name, because its polysemy exactly matches that of the name in the classical source. Thus the author has not only understood the Statian allusion perfectly, but has also allowed another text on the same topic to draw him into an allegorizing translation.

So far, so ingenious. But the picture changes in what follows. As Thetis continues, she speaks of *Liber pater* putting on women's clothing, and Jupiter putting on 'a woman's form', both accurate enough within their limits as evocations respectively of Bacchus' effeminate robes and Jove's ruse in the seduction of Callisto. In both cases, however, this leads into an image of the god spinning and making clothes in womanish fashion – images that have no basis either in Statius or, as far as I know, in any source for the two myths in question. Our author is padding out these stories in a spirit of creative guesswork, modelling them on his fuller knowledge of the story of Hercules and Omphale. The last example, Caeneus taking on *eccusc banda* 'female form', corresponds well enough to the mythographic authorities, though it is so vague as to remain obscure in context – which may be why the verse omits it altogether.

In short, this passage shows us a scholar-author using a rich but uneven knowledge of Latin epic and mythographic material to embellish and extend the text of *Togail Troí* as he inherited it. *Togail Troí*, as we have shown elsewhere in this book, began its history as a work of elevated historiography, rooted in its origins in the supposed eyewitness account of Dares Phrygius. Here, at the latter end of its creative development, its generic horizons are extending into the realm of pure poetry, taking imagery and story from a dramatized dialogue in a work that the Gaelic scholar-author could only have seen as a creative, even fictionalized, embellishment of the mainstream traditions about the Trojan War. That he used Statius to variegate and extend his narrative, while clothing it so decisively in the narrative forms of Irish-language saga, is a testament to the vigour and autonomy of the genre up to the thirteenth century and perhaps beyond.

Notes

1   I am grateful to Máire Ní Mhaonaigh for help and discussion on this difficult passage, and to the postgraduate group in Ancient Classics at the University of Galway for their insights and encouragement in seminar.

2   The transmitted line is a syllable short. Taking the verb to be from *feraid* 'pours', the emendation proposed here gives a future or subjunctive: 'you will/may pour . . .'.

3   The transmitted text cannot stand: *dena edbairt t'oighe*, translated by Ó hAodha as 'sacrifice your virginity', does not make sense addressed to Achilles. I suggest that the manuscript reading *déna* is an error for *dénad*, imperative 3rd singular: 'Let her make . . .', referring to Deidamia. (The scribal error may have been encouraged by eyeskip to *Dena* higher up.) Given that *óige* can mean either 'youthfulness' or 'virginity', the further possibility arises that the words which come next could be

read as *edbairtt óige*, with the two t's a mere orthographic doubling. The meaning of the sentence would then be 'let Deidamia make a sacrifice of her virginity'. I suspect this was in the archetype; but the scribe of D has clearly written the two t's as if divided between two words *edbairt t' óige*, so I translate accordingly.

4   The manuscript reads *i tigh* . . ., which gives one syllable too many. I take the *i* as a scribal error, leaving *tigh* as simple locative dative.

5   This line is unexplained and may be corrupt.

6   I suggest tentatively that this is *soraidh* 'fortunate, happy', with the negative prefix *an-*.

7   The manuscripts have *mac Echtair*, which looks like 'son of Hector' but evidently began as 'son of Actor', that being the expected name of Patroclus' grandfather.

8   The manuscripts seem to read *Berialus*, but this is evidently a scribal error in the archetype.

9   The expected name is Omphale, as discussed in the accompanying essay below.

10 The manuscripts have *Feneius*, evidently an error in the archetype.

11 Or 'lyre-player'; in medieval Irish the two instruments share identical vocabulary.

12 See *TBC* 1 lines 388–824, O'Rahilly 1976a: 13–26, 136–48. *TBC-LL* is similar for this passage.

13 But compare Miles 2011: 59, minimizing the sense of an echo here.

14 For the similar distortion of Troilus elsewhere in the *Togail Troí* tradition, see Ch. 7 and Ch. 24: 316–17.

15 This seems first to have been recognised by Ó hAodha 1979, whose observations have been invaluable to me.

16 The *Achilleid* commentaries that I have consulted (Clogan 1968, Sweeney 1997, Jahnke 1898), while inevitably not complete, give a good sense of the apparatus of background mythographic knowledge of which elements might have been present in the copy of the Latin poem available to our author. See also Woods 2019: 49–103 for the reading strategies associated with such manuscripts.

17 The poem is found only in MS D; K omits it, as often with verse.

18 On the Vatican Mythographers see above, Ch. 8, p. 109 with n. 3.

10

Don Tres Troí 'On the Third Troy'

Brent Miles

The text survives complete only in the late fifteenth-century manuscript Dublin, King's Inns MS 12, though a substantial fragment survives in Dublin, Royal Irish Academy MS D.iv.2, among that manuscript's dossier of classical texts. The text, translation and notes have been adapted from Miles 2020: 90–9, with much of the italicization marking abbreviations removed. The line-numbers at the beginnings of paragraphs are taken from Miles 2020.

Text: The fall of Troy and its aftermath

40] Oc otharlighi Aichil immorro do bad*ur* Grecaig ac comroinn a creichi. M*ur* do bhad*ur* ann iarum co cualad*ur* an guth ard uathmar ingantach chuca a hichtar an adhnaicthi. 'A Grecca', ar sé, 'mebal daibh seoid ⁊ maine, mna ⁊ macaimh na Troigenach do roinn edraibh im fíadhn*uise* gan mo chuid do idhnacal damh dibh. Tabhridh dam tra Polixina ar son mo coda comhroinne ⁊ marbtar hí sunn fochetóir ar m'adhnacal ar daigh co rabh a hainim maille frim a ngrianbrogaibh ifirn. Air isin aeninadh ro budh duthracht linn beith an tan ro bam*ur* beo etir dhainibh ⁊ is uimpe fuar*us* ainfhir eccomhlainn do imbirt bais ⁊ oigheadha form. La sodhain n*us* geib Pirr Polixina ar[a] folt ina láim chlí ocus sáidhis an cloidhem a mbun a cíghi asa laim ndeis ar adhnacal a ath*ar* ⁊ ro cuiredh a corp isin comrair móir marmaire in ro cuiredh Aichil.

53] No gumadh é Pirr fen ro shanntaigh Polixína do mharbad air is uimpe do marbad Aichil ⁊ do bad*ur* ocá híaraid tar eis na Toghla daigh ros folaigh Enías uair do fhitir aininne Pirr do beth fria ⁊ dob eicen do Enias a haisec uadh gur ros marb Pirr.

57] Asa aithle sin atnaigh Andromacha aigi budhein ⁊ do-rat fir n-anacail don macoemh mbecc buí ina farrad .i. Astinactes m*ac* Eacht*uir* eisidhen. Is se an slicht gnáthach em sunn do réir Eirb ⁊ Uirghil Astinactes do mharbad do Uilixeis adhaigh na Toghla orrderca .i. a dibhruc*ud* do mhur na cathrach ⁊ a cheann roimhe um choirthibh ⁊ um chairrgibh an talman. Ocus andar lais ba deithbir dó an imirt sin do thabairt fair air do innis Calc*us* faidhshacart na nGrec dó co raibe a meanmain an m*eic* sin a aininne do inneachad for Grecaib; ⁊ d*no* at-clos on mhac budhein an cetna. Conad aire sin ro shirestair Uilixeis co féigh ⁊ co fuirechuir an mac a n-oidhchi na Toghla. No cumdis m*eic* oile do Eacht*uir* [...] tísadh do athchumdach na Troí .i. Elenus fáidh cona macaibh.

69] Acht ní ed at-beir Feirb ⁊ Or*us* ⁊ Béid uair is ed deimhnighit-side conadh é Astinactes do-chuaid ann ⁊ conid uime ro cumhdaiged an cathair; ⁊ o't-connairc a muintir do atherghi ⁊ an cathair do coimlinadh ro thaispen a aininne ⁊ ro fhuighill an ní sin do chach ⁊ do gell cona luighe co ndighelad for Greco gach n-olc ⁊ gach n-eccóir do-ronsat fria Troigenaib.

Translation by the author
adapted from Miles 2020

40] Now the Greeks were at Achilles' grave dividing their plunder. While they were there, they heard a loud, dreadful, strange voice coming from the bottom of the grave. 'O Greeks', it said, 'it is shameful of you that, in my presence, you have divided amongst you the wealth and the possessions, the women and the youths of the Trojans, without delivering up my share to me. Give me Polyxena for my allotted portion, and let her be killed at once here at my grave, in order that her soul may be with me on Hell's bright shores.[1] For it was our wish to be in the same place when we were alive among men, and it was on her account I encountered unfairness of unequal combat that brought my death and violent end'. Thereupon with his left hand Pyrrhus seized Polyxena by her hair, and with his right hand thrust the sword beneath her breast over the grave of his father, and her body was placed in the great, marble coffin in which was placed Achilles.

53] Or it was Pyrrhus himself who desired to kill Polyxena, as it was on her account that Achilles had been killed. And they searched for her after the Destruction,[2] for Aeneas had hidden her, because he knew that Pyrrhus' enmity was directed towards her; and Aeneas was forced to return her, with the result that Pyrrhus killed her.

57] After that, Pyrrhus took Andromache as his own wife and gave fair quarter to the small lad who was with her, Astyanax the son of Hector. Now the usual account according to Servius and Virgil is that Astyanax was killed by Ulysses the night of the famous Destruction, that is, that he was thrown from the walls of the city headlong onto the rocks and stones of the earth. And it seemed right to him to use him so, for Calchas, the prophet-priest of the Greeks, had told him that it was the boy's intention to visit his vengeful enmity on the Greeks; the same had, moreover, been heard from the boy himself. For this reason, Ulysses, keenly and alertly, sought out the boy the night of the Destruction. (And it was other sons of Hector [who recaptured the city, enlisting the help of another] to return to rebuild Troy, that is, the prophet Helenus with his sons.)[3]

69] But that is not[4] what Servius and Orosius and Bede say, for these latter assert that it was Astyanax who went there and that it was at his behest that the city was rebuilt; and that when he saw that his people were rising again and that the city was being repopulated, he made show of his enmity and he declared to everyone and pledged himself with his oath that he would take vengeance on the Greeks for every evil and every injustice they had perpetrated on the Trojans.

75] Ro-clos immorro co Greco an ní sin ⁊ do ling Ulixeis [...] slogh mor do longaibh ⁊ libhearnaib do shaigid na Troí ⁊ is ed ro raidhset: 'is aire do-[dech]am*ur*-ne ille do dhenamh comairle ⁊ caradraidh rut-sa a Astinactes; air gidh do Grecaib damsa is athimdha m'escarait im aireacht fein ⁊ beanait dib linaibh oc aithfe uilc cheacht*ur*dhe uainn for Greco'.

81] Ba maith tra la hAstinactes an ní sin ⁊ do-ronsat caradradh samlaid. Ro raidh d*no* Ulix*eis* re hAstinactes dul leis for múr na cathrach do fromhadh a radhairc. Ro bad*ur* d*no* an dias sin ann gurbhó dorcha an dubhaghaidh doibh ⁊ do-radadh leanna inmheasca dhoibh. Ac coimherghi doibh iarum [⁊] ag teacht don mur atnaidh Ulix*eis* araile primhloech da muintir sainnredh ⁊ tuc sraínedh n-angbhaidh n-aininneach for Astinactes co tarla-sidhe ⁊ cléithi a chinn a n-ícht*ur* roime co lárleacaibh talman gur fácaib gan inchinn gan anmain isin inat sin hé. Is annsin do-chúaidh Uilix*eis* cona muintir ina roen mhadma dochum a long an cein ro bás ag mothug*ud* an neich do-ronadh ann amail na budh é do-neth an gnim sin itir.

92] Ocus cumadh amhlaid iar Uirgil ⁊ íar Feirb oighidh Astinactes m*ei*c Eachtair. Madh iar n-araile immorro ní fír so amail derbhthar isin scel-sa sis.

95] An tan at-conairc Pirr focetoir an righan rochoemh roiscleathan .i. Anromacha ingen [...] d*us*-rat serc ndichra nduthrachtaigh di. Ocus do ainic aigi d*no* an primhflaith for*us*ta firaitech .i. Elenus faidh mac Priaim cona maithes ⁊ cona muintir ⁊ ruc leis amlaid sin dia thír bhudein. Ro gradhaigh immorro an flescmhnaí móir malachdhuibh (atces a forcomhal aigi) co mba hí ba coimhsherc céille ⁊ comairle dhó conidh edh ro fhás deiside guruo port toirismhe ⁊ cumhsanta ⁊ guruo hinneoin fhosaighi do Throigenaib uili Pirr o sin amach airet ro bhaí beó. Do-gnídh immorro Elenus faistinedha gan athcheodh gan éliug*ud* do Pirr.

105] Ro badar amlaid sin feadh fota. Araí sin trá ro léic Neptolmus a mhnaí .i. Andromacha ⁊ do-roine bhudhein a cura ⁊ a snadhmain re hElenus fáidh mac Priaim. Ocus do-rat hí co honorach dó ar ba hinmain co mor le maithib Grec an faidh sin fata re toghail Troi ar a mhéd do-righne do dheghfhaistine doib. Ocus is ed on ro comailled amail ro geall-sum. Ocus do-ratsat ferann et*ur*ra fein ⁊

75] Word of that made it to the Greeks, and Ulysses leaped [to action and led] a great host of ships and galleys towards Troy. And he spoke thus: 'This is the reason we have come hither, O Astyanax, to advise you and to enter into an alliance with you; for though I am a Greek, very numerous are my enemies among my own vassal chiefs, and they strike on either side, avenging the wrongdoing committed by both of us against the Greeks'.

81] That seemed good to Astyanax, and so it was that they made an alliance. Ulysses said to Astyanax that he should go with him onto the wall of the city to make a test of what they could see. The two of them remained there until they were surrounded by dark night and intoxicating drink was poured out for them. As they rose together and approached the wall, Ulysses brought a certain preeminent fighter from his own people, and he visited a ruthless and angry overthrow on Astyanax so that he was thrown down, headfirst onto the flag-surfaced earth. And they left him in that place, lifeless with his head smashed wide open. At that point, Ulysses, in the company of his people, fled towards his ships, while people looked with amazement at what had been done there, and he made as if it was not him at all who had done that deed.

92] And so that was the death of Astyanax son of Hector according to Virgil and Servius. According to others, however, this is not correct, as is attested in the account which follows.

95] When Pyrrhus saw that very beautiful, broad-eyed noble woman Andromache, daughter of . . .[5] for the first time, he fell zealously and fervently in love with her. And he took into his protection the settled and circumspect eminent prince, the prophet Helenus son of Priam, with his goods and household; and he brought him thus to his own country. However, Pyrrhus fell in love with that slender, tall woman with the dark brows (who only seemed in bondage to him[?])[6], with the result that she became a beloved source of good sense and counsel to him; and it was from her influence that it came about that Pyrrhus became a haven of refuge and repose and an anvil of support for all Trojans, from that time forward for as long as he lived. Helenus, moreover, used to prophesy with neither opposition nor rebuke from Pyrrhus.

105] They remained thus for a long time. Nevertheless, Neoptolemus [= Pyrrhus][7] released his wife Andromache, and himself prepared her marriage contract and bound her over to Helenus the Prophet, son of Priam. And he gave her to him with honour, for that prophet had been greatly liked by the Greek nobles long before the destruction of Troy, on account of the quantity of accurate prophecy he had made

Grecaib dó ria toghail Troí ⁊ do bhídh aitreabh mor aigi a ferann na hEibire. Achtchena ni lughaide no bidh-sum maille re Grecaib ⁊ re Troigenaib ina athardha dhilis cein coro lanmhilled ⁊ coro lomaircedh an Troi.

123] Ro thuisimh d*no* Andromacha chloinn ndighainn nderscnaidhigh do Elenus co mbatar m*e*ic imdha et*u*rra. Ro forbuirseat-side gurbat géraiti gaiscidh ⁊ gurba curaidh eccomlainn. Ro thinoil Elenus iar sin a fuair do Throigenaib isin Greic arna cedug*ad* do Pirr do ⁊ do maithib Grec airchena. R*us* dídin ⁊ *rus* deighleasaigh ⁊ *rus* toccaibh arna timsug*ud* ⁊ do-rigne ardaireacht righdha romhor dibh im Astinactes mac Eachtair; ar níro ghein a comaimsir fris do shluagaib na talman enairsidh amail Astinactes tar éis a athar.

123] Do-ronadh iar sin comairle mhaith mhóirmhenmnach ag Elenus ⁊ ag Andromácha ⁊ is ed ro raidhset: 'Is cóir sochar ar cl*ainn*i ⁊ ar cinil do denam bhudhesta .i. athnuaidhight*her* uainn Ilium, .i. an Troí, doridhisi; ⁊ cuirim coimthinol cl*ainn*i duaibhsighe danardha Dardáin im Astinactes ara hamas ⁊ im macaibh caidi m*e*ic Priaimh ⁊ fam macaib-si budhéin', ar Elenus. 'Ocus tabhrem lointi lansaidhbre doibh ⁊ liberna luchtm*u*ra. Tabrem d*no* innmh*us*a ilardha doibh etir ór ⁊ airceat, ⁊ tabhrem etaighi ⁊ erredha ailli ingantacha doibh. Cuirem cloidmi c*r*uaidhgera ⁊ laighne lethanglasa ⁊ luireacha treabraid tredhualacha ⁊ cathscéith shoillsi shechtfillte ⁊ boghadha blaithi bennchruaide ⁊ saighde semnecha sóereitecha doibh. Tabrem d*n*a eocha ⁊ asana, muca ⁊ coercha doibh ⁊ ba bennchoema ⁊ dumha daingne deghoib*r*i ⁊ gach ní ara mbía esbhaidh no airbhire acu; do neoch ricfait a leas teacait ara ceann. Ocus erghit in da uaithne catha ⁊ irgaili ⁊ in da colamain comlainn ⁊ an dá inneóin fhosaithi gacha deabhtha ⁊ gacha dibergi etir gaiscedachaib Grec .i. dá mhac poinnidhe primhárrachta Pirr m*e*ic Aichil re hAndromacha .i. Molaus ⁊ Alaxanndair a n-anmanna-sidhe ⁊ bíd maille re macaib a mathar ⁊ re hAistinactes an cein bhes ag cumdach na cathrach ⁊ ag daingniug*ud* an dingna'.

for them. And as he promised, that was fulfilled. And (even) before the destruction of Troy they had given him territory which lay situated between themselves and the Greeks, and he had an extensive possession in the territory of Epirus. However, in spite of that he remained with the Greeks and the Trojans in his own native land, until Troy was wholly overthrown and despoiled.

115] Andromache, moreover, bore Helenus numerous distinguished children, until there were many sons between them. They grew until they were champions in feats of arms and warriors of unequal combat. After that, Helenus assembled all he could discover of the Trojans in Greece, after receiving leave from Pyrrhus and from the rest of the Greek nobles. He sheltered them and reared them and, bringing them together, raised them up and made them into a very great, noble, royal assembly around Astyanax son of Hector. For there was not born in his own time from the hosts of the earth an outstanding champion the like of Astyanax, after the death of his father.

123] Thereupon, a goodly, high-spirited council was held by Helenus and Andromache, and this was what they said: 'It is proper to assert the rights of our children and our people from this time forward. Let Ilium, that is, Troy, be restored by us again; and to that end let us send for an assembly of the terrible, fierce children of Dardanus, together with Astyanax, and with the harsh sons of the son of Priam and with my very own sons', Helenus said. 'And let us give them very abundant provisions and well-manned galleys. Let us give them moreover all sorts of goods, both gold and silver, and let us give them garments and beautiful, wondrous vestments. Let us offer them harsh, keen swords and broad, grey spears and plaited, thrice-woven breastplates and bright, sevenfold battle-shields and polished, steel-tipped bows and riveted, nobly-winged arrows. Let us give them also steeds and mules, pigs and sheep, and lovely-horned cows and secure heaps of items of fine workmanship, and everything which they will need, or the lack of which will be a cause of reproach to them; of whatever items they will need, let them come for them. And let there rise up the two pillars of battle and combat, the two columns of contest, the two anvils of support in every strife and every pillaging among the armed warriors of Greece, that is, the two powerful, resolute sons of Pyrrhus son of Achilles by Andromache, namely Molossus and Alexander. And let them be with their mother's sons and with Astyanax for as long as the city is being built, and the stronghold strengthened'.

Essay: Legends of exile and return

Don Tres Troí 'On the Third Troy' is unique in medieval literature. As if the capstone to a 'Trojan Cycle' in Irish, *Don Tres Troí* recounts how the city destroyed in the time of Priam, as portrayed in *Togail Troí*, was rebuilt by Hector's son Astyanax. This Troy corresponds to the town Ilium of the classical period, whose presence in the historical record is scant, though its third and final destruction in the Roman era by the general Gaius Flavius Fimbria is recounted by Augustine in his *City of God* (3.7). The Irish text draws on Augustine for its closing sections, but the narrative of the city's refoundation itself has been pieced together in our text from clues primarily in Servius Danielis' commentary to Virgil (on which see further Ch. 7), in addition to Virgil's portrait of the fate of Trojan captives in Greece in the *Aeneid* itself. Unusually among the classical texts in Irish, *Don Tres Troí* recounts at several places its sources, including Virgil, Servius, Orosius, Bede, Augustine and (dubiously) Varro. Apart from the last name, all these can be verified (Miles 2020: 7–8). Uniquely among the Irish antiquity-sagas, *Don Tres Troí* also preserves the name of its author, 'Flannacán', in its concluding words.

The excerpt above, which represents roughly a third of the entire text, highlights both the learned character of *Don Tres Troí*, as well as its more fanciful literary embellishments. Strikingly, the passage recounts multiple competing versions of Astyanax's death, including the author's own novel interpretation of the sources that permitted him to claim that Astyanax survived Troy's capture to re-establish Troy in adulthood. Beginning with the sacrifice of Polyxena by Achilles' son Pyrrhus the night after Troy's fall, the excerpt shifts to the conundrum of there being multiple conflicting ancient accounts of Astyanax's fate. The text settles on the claim that the boy was taken captive to Greece in the household of Pyrrhus. Once grown to maturity, there he is able to connect with other Trojan captives in Greece and prepare for a return to Asia Minor. The latter episode draws heavily on the account of Helenus and Andromache from *Aeneid* 3. The council of Trojan refugees that concludes this passage was the Irish author's own invention. With the wealth of attention paid to the history of the Trojans prior to the refoundation of Troy, *Don Tres Troí* only briefly recounts the refounding itself, in a single sentence (not included in the excerpt above). The event, apart from being nowhere explicitly described in any ancient source, was clearly less important to the Irish author than the scholarly investigation that was needed to reconstruct the path taken to achieving it.

Notes

1   *Grianbroga ifirn* translates literally as 'the sun-lands of hell/the infernal regions', but there is a possible ambiguity or word-play between *grían* 'sun' and *grian* 'gravel, sand, sea or river bottom, land' (Miles 2020: 117–19). This is reflected in the translation adopted here.

2   Wherever the text refers to the *togail* without modification, this has been taken to be an intertextual reference to *Togail Troí* itself. In the present passage, *destruction* has been preferred to *siege* because the reference is so clearly to the siege's conclusion: cf. Ch. 6, n.2.

3   Text has been supplied from the model of an entry on the refounding of Troy in Bede's *Chronica Maiora*.

4   The wording before emendation is 'Et is *ed*' 'And that is what. . .' However, the authors quoted are not a source as such for this claim of Astyanax's return, though they are the principal sources for the claim of a Trojan refoundation of one kind or another.

5   There is a space left in the manuscript where the scribe, presumably, meant to go back and supply the name of Andromache's father.

6   The translation is speculative.

7   The names Pyrrhus and Neoptolemus alternate in Graeco-Latin tradition.

Part Four

Adaptation of Latin Epic

11

Togail na Tebe 'The Siege of Thebes'

Mariamne Briggs

Text revised by the author from Calder 1922: 2–5, ll. 1–82, on the basis of London, British Library MS Egerton 1781, fols 87r a1–87v b15[1]. Section-numbering in the text is the author's; in the esssay following, references to other parts of the text are listed according to the line-numbering system of Calder 1922.

Text: The foundation of Thebes and the fate of Cadmus

1. Aroile righ uasal oirmuindnech onorach rogabh forlamhus ⁊ ferandus ar an ardcathraigh n-aibind n-alaind .i. Teibh isin nGreic darua comainm Laius ⁊ is do-sidhe robo mac Eidhip ⁊ is on Eidhip sin ro cindset na da mac aildi oiregda .i. Polinices ⁊ Etioccles ⁊ is iat na braithri-sin romarb a chele isin cathugud mor na Tiabhanta ⁊ na nGrec ic cosnum righe na hardcathrach na Teibhe do cechtar leithi.

2. Acht cena is and-sin tainic ar menmain do Stait don airdfilid Frangcach sochinelach bunadh-indruim na Tiabanta, indus ro cinset o Caithim, mac Aghenoir ⁊ is e ant Aighenoir-sin rop airdrigh na Tirde ⁊ na Sidondoine ⁊ is aice ro ui in ingen sochinelach darua comainm Eoropa. Is di tuc Iob in gradh ndermair, corob hecin do tiachtain i richt tairbh da breith leis tar muinchind mara ⁊ morfaircce ⁊ o ro siacht darin muir-sin cu Cred, do-chuaidh 'na richt fen. Ro uai in ingen-sin aige co morgradhach ⁊ is don ingin-sin tuc Iop in tirfochriacc n-adhbul .i. tres primrand in betha do ainmniugud uaithi .i. Eoraip.

3. Agenoir immorro ro gabh fercc ⁊ londus adhbul ⁊ toirssi mor o fuair esbaid a ingine Eoropa morgradhaigi.

4. IS i immorro comairle do-rinne and-sin Aghenoir, a mac morgradhach do chur ar fud mara ⁊ tire do iaraidh a sheathar uan doman ⁊ is ed ad-bert ris, muna fadhbad a shiair, can tiachtain aris ⁊ gan a fhaicsin dosum.

5. IS and-sin immorro ro sirastar Caithim dingnada in domain ⁊ oilena ingantacha na haibheisi moraidhbhle thimchellas in bith. Fuair mor do dhuad ⁊ do dochar ⁊ do ghaibther mora ⁊ tire sechnon in domain iter muir ⁊ tir ⁊ ni fuair in ingin risin ré-sin, ger ces mor d'imnedh. Is ed ua-dera sin nar fédedh taidhecht i n-aigid Ioip mic Shatruinn, cend na dee, a ghradh goiti d'fis fair ⁊ o nach fuair-sium a shiair, is i comairle dos-rat ina menmain trena ghais, dul co tempall Apaild, dei na faistine, d'iarraidh fhessa ⁊ eolais uadha cuith a roiphi in ingen ⁊ is ed ad-bert Apaill ris, gan a sirthain, uair ni bfuidhbedh, acht eirghedh amach amarach isin magh minscothach maighreidh moradhbul amach ⁊ tæceradh bó bendach bithalaind duit isin magh minalaind sin ⁊ len-sa hi nocon luighe. In baile a luighfea, cumdaigther letsa cathair caomcumdachta co muraib moraibhle ⁊ co tigibh righ*dha* rofarsenga ⁊ co griananaib seimidhi solusglana, comad

Translation by the author
revised from Calder 1922: 3–6, ll. 1–82.[2]

1. A certain noble, revered and honourable king had assumed supremacy and proprietorship over the pleasant and splendid supreme city, that is, Thebes in Greece. His name was Laius and he had a son, Oedipus, and from Oedipus there came the two fair distinguished sons, that is, Polynices and Eteocles. They are the brothers who killed one another in the great war between the Thebans and the (other) Greeks, as they contended on each side for the kingship of Thebes, the supreme city.

2. Now at that time there came to the mind of Statius, the noble Frankish high poet, the original beginning of the Thebans: how they descended from Cadmus, son of Agenor, and he is the same Agenor who was high-king of Tyre and Sidon, and it is he who had a noble daughter who was named Europa. Jove felt deep love for her, so that it was necessary for him to go into the shape of a bull to carry (her) off with him over the wide sea and ocean; and when he had crossed that sea to Crete, he changed into his own form. He bestowed upon that girl great love, and to her Jove gave a large gift: namely, that the third principal division of the world should be named after her, that is, Europe.

3. Then anger, intense rage, and immense sorrow took hold of Agenor when he discovered the loss of his well-beloved daughter Europa.

4. Indeed, the plan Agenor then formed was to send his well-beloved son over sea and land to search for his sister throughout the world, and he told him, unless he found his sister, not to come back or be seen by him (again).

5. Then, in truth, Cadmus traversed the world's high places and the wondrous islands of the vast ocean that encompasses the earth. He experienced inordinate difficulty, misery and dangers of sea and land throughout the world both by sea and by land, and did not find the girl during all (that) time, although he endured much suffering. The reason was that he could not go against Jove, the son of Saturn,[3] head of the gods, to find out from him his (Jove's) stolen love.[4] And when he did not find his sister, the plan he formed in his mind as a result of his wisdom was this: to go to the temple of Apollo, the god of prophecy, to seek knowledge and guidance from him as to where the girl was. And Apollo told him this: not to search for her, for he would not find her, 'but' [as Apollo said] 'you must set forth the next day on the smooth, flowering, extensive, open plain, and a horned beautiful cow will meet you on that smooth-beautiful plain.[5] Follow

cathair ordain ⁊ oirechtais na nGrec in cathair-sin ⁊ comad e a hainm .i. Boetia no Tebae tre nertudh ⁊ tre forgill in dei Apaill.

6. Ro an-sum and-sin ⁊ ro gabh itaidh ⁊ ro cuirther techtaire tairisi uadha ar cend dighe, co sithil alaind umaidhe co n-imdenum oir ⁊ airgit umpi, co huamaidh adbul imdorcha uai a comfogus do, ar lar fualascaigh coirneacdai ⁊ tobar firalaind fondfuar ar a lar, o ro siacht an techtaire dochum na tibra ⁊ tuc a sithil uan usci. As and-sin tainic in naithir nemhnach a hiarthar na huama, co ceithri cendaibh moraidhbhle furri ⁊ co tri linaibh fiacul in cach cend fo leth ⁊ co ndeilbh torathair o hiarthar co hoirther.

7. O do-chonairc in techtaire os cind na tibraid, tuc beim da glomraib a n-aen*fh*echt cuige, go ro fagadh can anmain and-sin.

8. O ropo fada iarum le Caithim, mac Aghenoir, roui a fer muinntuire, ro faidhestar fer eli da muinntir dochum na huama ⁊ dochum in usque ⁊ tuc *in* naithir in aradhain cetna fair.

9. Cidh tra acht coica oclach torchair da muinntir amlaidh-sin.

10. IS and-sin ro eirigh Caithim, mac Aghenoir, ⁊ ro ghabh a ededh ⁊ ro trealaim a arma, co mbruth miled, co feirg leoman, co neimh nathrach co dorus na huama da digail ar an ti ro marbh a mhuinntir. O rainic, ad-connairc an nathraigh ndigfrecra ndimoir ⁊ do-rinne sduagh luib moir di o iarthar co hoirther, amal seolcrand lunga lanaidhbhle.

11. O 't-chonnairc in fer mor da hindsaigidh, ro cathaighset aræn and-sin co fuilech guinech crechtach crolinntech and-sin ⁊ torchuir a*n* naithir fadheoidh ⁊ do-chuaidh a neimh ar nemhfni.

12. Tainic-sium roime iar tain co tempoll Apaill, ⁊ ro raidhset na dei ris ar do denum isin moigh ar marbad an nathair; ⁊ a silad in air-sin o fhiaclaib na nathrach, ro eirgetar fir fon armghaisced arin tulaigh. Ro threabh in n-uir roime ⁊ do cathaighsit co feg, feochair, fercach; ⁊ ro marbh cach dibh a chéle acht æncoicer nammá; ⁊ is lesin coicer-sin ro chumdaighedh in Teibh, maræn re Caithim, mac Aghenoir. Ba he oenta oiregdha in cuiger-sin [ ] .i. Echion rouoi *ac* cumdach na Teibhe maræn re Caithim, mac Aghenoir.

her until she lies down. Where she lies down let a beautiful city be built by you, with huge walls, with spacious palaces and with sunny chambers bright with pure light', so that this city might be the city of pre-eminence and power of the Greeks, and that the name of it should be Boeotia or Thebes, through the will and through the authority of the god Apollo.

6. (Cadmus) remained there and he became thirsty. And a faithful attendant was sent by him to find a drink, with a beautiful bronze pail with gold and silver decoration around it, into a vast pitch-black cave that was near to him, in the middle of an overhanging grove, with a very pleasant earth-cool spring in the midst of it. When the attendant had reached the spring, and put his pail under the water, there came a venomous serpent from the back of the cave, with four enormous heads on it, and with three rows of teeth in each individual head, and with a monstrous shape from tail to head.

7. When it saw the attendant above the spring, at once it struck him with its muzzle, and he was left there lifeless.

8. When it seemed long to Cadmus, son of Agenor, that his attendant was (away), he sent another of his attendants to the cave and to the water, and the serpent dispensed the same treatment to him.

9. Indeed, fifty attendants from his household died like this.

10. Then Cadmus, son of Agenor, rose and took his armour and made ready his arms, with a soldier's heat, a lion's rage and a serpent's venom, (and went) to the entrance of the cave to avenge himself on the one that had killed his people. When he arrived, he saw the immense huge serpent and it made a great arched coil of itself from tail to head, like the mast of a vast abundant ship.

11. After it saw the great man (coming) to attack it, they fought together there a bloody, wound-dealing (fight) streaming with blood, and the serpent fell in the end, and its poison came to nothing.[6]

12. Afterwards he proceeded to the temple of Apollo, and the gods told him to plough the plain where the serpent had been killed, and from the sowing of that ploughland with the serpent's teeth men arose equipped with arms upon the hill. He tilled the land before him, and they fought keenly, fiercely, angrily. Each one of them killed the other except five men alone, and Thebes was built by these five along with Cadmus, son of Agenor. Those five were a pre-eminent fellowship [ ],[7] that is, Echion was building Thebes together with Cadmus, son of Agenor.

13. Cid tra acht ro chumdaighedh in Teibh amlaidh-sin re Caithim mac Aghenoir ⁊ ro uoi co soinmech setach innte re ré foda, co *fh*uair doinmed e uadheoidh, uair rosoad e fen ⁊ a shetigh a ndelbaibh nathrach co cend secht mbliadan, noco tainic craidhi na ndei forro uadeoidh ⁊ co roighsit *in*na corpaib fen iar sin, ⁊ is do shil ind fhir-sin ro chinseat na righa tromglana Thiabanta uili ⁊ is da sil Eidip mic Lai.

13. At all events Thebes was built by Cadmus, son of Agenor, and so that prosperously and richly he lived in (that city) for a long time, until misfortune found him in the end; for he himself and his wife were turned into serpent-shapes for the duration of seven years, until the gods were moved by them in the end, and so they turned into their own bodies; and from that man's descendants came all the powerful and pure Theban kings, and from his offspring was Oedipus, son of Laius.

Essay: The pseudohistorical prologue to the Middle Irish *Thebaid*[8]

The Middle Irish *Thebaid* is a prose retelling of the ancient Greek myth of the civil war between Oedipus' sons, Polynices and Eteocles, over the sovereignty of Thebes, as found in Statius' Latin epic *Thebaid* (*c*. 92 CE).[9] This war culminates in the fratricide of the brothers, which is described in the Middle Irish text as an act of *fingal* 'kin-murder' (cf. *TTeb* 4491), and this leads to a second conflict at Thebes in which Creon is overthrown by Theseus. The Irish narrative is frequently referred to in modern scholarship as *Togail na Tebe* ('The Siege of Thebes') after Calder's edition of the text. This title was Calder's own creation, and in the present contribution the narrative will be referred to as the Middle Irish *Thebaid* (see further Briggs 2018: 17–36 and 2019: 179–8). The text survives in two manuscripts, which date from the fourteenth to fifteenth centuries: Edinburgh, National Library of Scotland, MS 72.1.8 (hereafter, Adv. 72.1.8), fols 1r–27v and British Library, MS Egerton 1781 (hereafter, Egerton 1781), fols 87r–128r.[10] Modern scholars usually consider the text to date to the twelfth century, but little has been done up to now to determine a more concise date for the language (see O'Connor 2014b: 14; Calder 1922: xi; Bergin 1923: 321; Thurneysen 1928b: 28). Statius is identified in the Irish narrative as the *airdfili Frangcach* 'high poet of the Franks'. This is a misidentification which appears to have developed from a confusion with the first-century rhetorician, L. Statius Ursulus of Toulouse. The association was a common one and recurred throughout the medieval *accessus* tradition of the *Thebaid* and the *Achilleid*.[11]

The Middle Irish *Thebaid* retains the main outline of Statius' epic and essentially renders every part of the original text into Irish. Some sections are relatively close translations of Statius' original passages, but there are considerable additions, abbreviations and digressions from the Latin *Thebaid* in the Irish version. I will focus on an extensive section of supplementary material at the start of the work, part of which is quoted in the accompanying extract. *Thebaid*, 1.1–45, which forms Statius' proem, a type of preface which was an essential element of the Greek and Latin poetry tradition, was not rendered into the Irish narrative. Instead, the Middle Irish *Thebaid* begins with a brief genealogy of the Theban kings, Statius' decision to compose the work, the abduction of Europa, Cadmus' foundation of Thebes, and his subsequent reign.[12] The history of Oedipus and a summary of the quarrel between Polynices and Eteocles follows; and the Irish narrative then picks up from Statius' epic at

Thebaid, 1.46, Oedipus' prayer to Tisiphone (see Briggs 2018: 67–109; Harris 1998: 71; Meyer 1962: 691). This new material can be seen to constitute a pseudohistorical prologue, similar to that found at the start of *Imtheachta Aeniasa*, the later versions of *Togail Troí*, *In Cath Catharda*, and the early Irish legal compilation, *Senchas Már* (see respectively Poppe 1995: 6–7, with Ch. 13 in this volume; Myrick 1993: 162–3 and Clarke 2014a; Ch. 14 in this volume; Carey 1994a, with Ch. 1 in this volume, p.4). The addition of this type of prologue to the Middle Irish *Thebaid* appears to be indicative of the medieval readers' narrative expectations. By providing the background history of Thebes, the conflict between Polynices and Eteocles was set in the broader context of Theban history. This is a mode of scene-setting which is conspiciously absent from the Latin original (Briggs 2019: 185–7; cf. Kershner 2019: 102–5).

The opening lines of the Irish text appear to form a type of abbreviated *accessus*, a preface to the narrative, providing *locus* ('place'), *tempus* ('time'), *persona* ('person'), and *causa scribendi* ('cause of writing'; definition based on Irvine 1994: 121–2). The place is Thebes; the time was during Lauis' proprietorship, the person was Statius, and the cause of writing was that the origins of the Thebans came to the poet's mind. This type of *accessus* was known to medieval scholars from the Latin commentary tradition, including the works of Donatus and Servius.[13]

The identification of Statius as 'high poet of the Franks' in the Middle Irish *Thebaid* may indicate that elements of this pseudohistorical prologue were drawn from an *accessus* to the *Thebaid*, which was part of the manuscript culture in which Statius' *Thebaid* and *Achilleid* circulated during the Middle Ages.[14] Commentaries on the texts, such as that ascribed to Lactantius Placidus on the *Thebaid*, and mythological prefaces giving the background history of Thebes, were also a part of this manuscript tradition.[15] While no direct connection can be made with a specific *accessus* on the *Thebaid*, the Irish author's inclusion of an *accessus* seems to be a strong indicator of his knowledge of this tradition and his engagement with it as part of medieval rhetorical practice.

Further evidence that the author of the Middle Irish *Thebaid* may have had access to supplementary material in the Latin exemplar that he worked from can be found in the inclusion of the material about Europa and Cadmus narratives in the prologue. This material derives originally from Ovid's *Metamorphoses* (2.842–75, 3.1–130, 4.563–603), although it is likely that this was translated into Irish from an intermediate source.[16] Variations on these Ovidian narratives are known to have circulated in the mythological prefaces to the *Thebaid* and, so far, have been identified in four manuscripts of the *Thebaid*, three of which also include introductory material on Oedipus.[17] The Europa and Cadmus myths were also elucidated in the glosses and scholia that circulated with the *Thebaid*, including the commentary of Lactantius or Pseudo-Lactantius (Sweeney 1997: 1–4, at lines 16–28, 74–5). Abbreviated versions of these Ovidian narratives are also found in the Carolingian works of both the First and Second Vatican Mythographer.[18] The narrative related in the Middle Irish *Thebaid*, however, diverges from the variants known to date in the mythological prefaces and the Vatican Mythographers' accounts, which are themselves varied in their retellings.[19]

In each section of the extract quoted, the author can be seen to employ the kind of descriptive alliteration that is found so often throughout the Middle Irish antiquity-sagas. For instance, *tar muindchind mara ⁊ morfaircce* 'over the wide sea and ocean' (for *per aequora ponti* 'on the open sea', *Metamorphoses* 2.872) and *bó bendach bithalaind* 'a horned beauteous cow' (for *bos* 'heifer', *Metamorphoses* 3.10). Apollo's instruction to Cadmus *moenia fac condas*, 'build your city's walls' at *Metamorphoses* 3.13, is also elaborated upon and supplemented with alliterative phrases, providing a much more detailed image of what the city should look like: *cumdaigther letsa cathair caomcumdachta co muraib moraibhle co tigibh righdha rofarsenga co griananaib seimidhi solusglana,* 'let a beautiful city be built by you, with huge walls, with spacioius palaces, and with sunny chambers bright with pure light'.

Cadmus' venture into the woods and fight with the serpent from *Metamorphoses* 3.50–94 is heavily abbreviated and reworked in the Irish vernacular. In the *Metamorphoses*, Cadmus' companions are sent into a grove where there is a cave to obtain water for a sacrifice to Jove; the serpent there, which belongs to Mars, kills them (*Metamorphoses* 3.26–49). Ovid's detailed description is pared down in the Irish, where Cadmus develops a thirst and the serpent kills the fifty attendants sent to bring him water (see sections 6–9). When none of his men return, Cadmus sets out to look for them. Ovid placed emphasis on Cadmus' weapons as he set out to find his companions: *tegumen derepta leoni | pellis erat, telum splendenti lancea ferro | et iaculum teloque animus praestantior omni* 'For protection, he has a lion's skin; for weapon, a spear with glittering iron point and a javelin; and, better than all weapons, a courageous soul' (*Metamorphoses* 3.52–4). In the Middle Irish version a string of metaphors is used to develop the scene, describing Cadmus as he arms: *co mbruth miled, co feirg leoman, co neimh nathrach* 'with a soldier's heat, a lion's rage, and a serpent's venom'. Similar metaphors appear elsewhere in medieval Irish narratives. In the

Book of Leinster version of *Togail Troí* during an attack on the Greeks, the anonymous narrator of the tale bemoans the fate of any man who encountered the Trojan warriors Pelias, Telamon, and Hercules in battle, *Uair bá lathrach leomain ⁊ bá neim nathrach ⁊ bá comferg curad leo* 'For they had a lion's strength and a snake's venom and a hero's wrath' (*TTr-LL*, 314560–1). A similar description is used to portray Achilles as he goes into battle with Hector (*TTr-LL*, 32819–21). The *Imtheachta Aeniasa* 'The Wanderings of Aeneas' also adopts this type of imagery when describing Aeneas' reaction to Pallas' death (lines 2567–70, Calder 1907: 160–1). The inclusion of the string of metaphors in the description of Cadmus above may imply the author's familiarity with the conventions of arming-scenes in Middle Irish narrative on indigenous subjects (see also Chs 13 and 15).

Therefore, while the pseudohistorical prologue to the Middle Irish *Thebaid* can be seen as part of the wider medieval manuscript culture associated with Statius' epic, there are stylistic aspects of the translation, such as the use of alliteration and strings of metaphors, which demonstrate that the author was using literary techniques from the pre-existing corpus of Irish literature and classical adaptation texts. The author's use of these techniques in rendering the Middle Irish *Thebaid*, therefore, may denote an awareness of established conventions for translating classical literature within an existing corpus.

Notes

1 In the Egerton 1781 text, the Tironian symbol ⁊ (normally standing for *et, ocus*) often seems to function as a graphic marker for a sentence-break. This is reflected in the text and translation given here.

2 I would like to express my thanks to Michael Clarke and Erich Poppe for their helpful suggestions and comments on the text and translation, and to Marie-Luise Theuerkauf for her advice on the text and suggestions on the essay.

3 For 'Shatruinn' read 'Shatuirnd'.

4 The phrase appears to depend on Ovid, *Metamorphoses*, 3.6–7: *quis enim deprendere possit / furta Iovis?* 'for who could search out the secret loves of Jove?'.

5 Calder's edition has Apollo's direct speech to Cadmus start from '⁊ *tæceradh bó bendach . . .*', 'and a horned beauteous cow . . .'. I have taken it to start from '*acht eirghedh amach amarach . . .*', 'but to set forth the next day', echoing Ovid, *Metamorphoses*, 3.10–13. The alliterative description of the *mag* 'plain' (*maigh*, section 5) appears to reflect the word *arva* 'fields, plains' (*arvis, Metamorphoses* 3.10).

6 I am very grateful to Michael Clarke for his suggestions on translating the description of the fight in this section.

7   There is an erasure of text here at Egerton 1781, f.87v b.1. It seems likely that the lost text would have corresponded to the Ovidian narrative: *Iamque brevis vitae spatium sortita iuventus | sanguineam tepido plangebat pectore matrem,| quinque superstitibus, quorum fuit unus Echion* 'And now those youths, who had enjoyed so brief a span of life, were beating the breast of their mother earth warm with their blood – all save five. One of these five was Echion'; see Ovid, *Metamorphoses*, 3.124–6.

8   This essay has been developed with additional research from Briggs 2018: 67–109.

9   The edition used in this contribution is Shackleton Bailey 2003.

10 Calder used both manuscripts for his edition. Two fragments can also be found in Trinity College Dublin, 1298, pp. 457–8 and 459–60; the only edition to date is Meyer 1967: 121–32.

11 See Anderson 2009: 3.2, 31–2. Anderson proposes that the original error may have come from confusion over references to L. Statius Ursulus of Toulouse in Suetonius's *De Rhetoribus* and Jerome's translation of Eusebius's *Chronica*.

12 This section is known only from the Egerton 1781 manuscript, the text on the first page of the Edinburgh manuscript (National Library of Scotland, MS Adv. 72.1.8) is illegible.

13 See Irvine 1994: 121–2. For further evidence of the use of the *accessus* in medieval Irish literature see Sims-Williams and Poppe 2005: 309. Poppe 2016a: 119–20, on Lucan's *Civil War* in Ireland, demonstrating the range of learned traditions on which the Irish author(s) drew and highlights that they may have used *accessus* material and scholia from a manuscript of Lucan's epic. On the significance of scholia, see further Ch. 16 in this volume.

14 See Anderson 2009, vol. 3, which explores the *accessus* in the manuscript tradition of the *Thebaid* and *Achilleid*. For a broader overview of the reception of Statius's works in the Middle Ages, including the *accessus* tradition, see Battles 2004: 1–17.

15 Lactantius Placidus, *In Statii Thebaida Commentum* (Sweeney 1997). Material from the commentary was used extensively by the medieval Irish translator of the *Thebaid*, see Briggs 2018: 111–48; Edwards 2015: 497–511; Punzi 1990: 7–43.

16 For more on the use of Ovidian material in medieval Ireland, see Miles 2007; Miles 2011: 18–19, 58–9, 76–7, 91–3, 106, 109, 171 n.70, 220; Miles 2020: 7–10.

17 The manuscripts are Leiden, University Library, MS GRO 70, fol.1v; Leiden, University Library, MS BPL 136 K, fols 15r–v; Rome, Biblioteca Vallicelliana, MS C.97, fol 1v; and Wrocław, University Library, MS R.124 (formerly Breslau University Library, Rehdugeriana R. 124), now lost (hereafter BU, R.124). At present research on the first three of these prefaces is sadly lacking, although a brief overview of each can be found in Anderson 2009: 1.160–2, 169–70, 364–5. On the preface to the *Thebaid* in BU, R.124, see Schmidt 1866 and Punzi 1990.

18 See *MVI* chs 145, 146, *MVII* chs 96–8, Kulcsár 1987: 60–1, 169–71, with English translations at Pepin 2008: 68–9, 137–8. See Punzi 1990: 17, 24, 33, 38 for brief

observations on elements of the Europa and Cadmus myths known to the author of the Irish translation and also the Old French *Roman de Thèbes*, which are also found in the account by the Second Vatican Mythographer.

19 For further information on the associated source material and *Thebaid* manuscript culture, see Punzi 1990 and Briggs 2018: 67–92.

12

Riss in Mundtuirc 'The Tale of the Necklace'

Brent Miles

Riss in Mundtuirc *has been preserved whole in one manuscript, Dublin, Royal Irish Academy, MS D.iv.2, in that manuscript's dossier of classical materials. The copy is damaged due to loss of parchment at the bottom of several columns, and the conclusion in this copy is lost. Fortunately, however, the* Riss *happens to be quoted in* Togail na Tebe *(on which see Ch. 11), inserted at the point where Statius introduces the necklace. The conclusion printed below has been supplied from this version. The excerpts printed here have been adapted from Miles 2007: 86–8, 90–2, the only significant difference being the removal of much of the italicization marking manuscript contractions. The conclusion excerpted from* Togail na Tebe *is from Calder 1922: 52. Throughout, square brackets [ ] represent text lost due to the damage to the manuscript, while angle brackets < > enclose editorial additions supplied for omitted text.*

Text extracts

Amphiaraus and Eriphyle

. . . Ocus at-bert Adhruist re Poilinic dul dochum an tshacairt .i. Aimpiair a ainm,
⁊ a altug*ud* buidhi fris co ndernadh faistine do dhía fis cinnus do bhiadh
iardaighi in chatha ro chuir*fed* fria brait*hir*, no an budh sor*aid* a thurus.

Is é dono int Aimpiair sin do-nidh faistine ⁊ célmuine do Adruist do righ na
Greci Bigi; ⁊ do-rigni in sacart iar sin faistine do Polinic, ⁊ is ed ro raidh, dia
tuctais cath dona Tiabantaib nach tic*fed* duine dib i mbethaidh acht Adruist .i. rí
Grec ina aenur. A haithle na faistine sin do dhenum, do theich Aimpiair ar
imgabail in chatha ⁊ ro fhoiligh é ⁊ nirbo eolach duine gusan folach sin acht a
ben ⁊ sé fein.

Tainic iar sin Airgia ingen Adruist .i. ben Poilinic m*aic* righ na Tiabanda ar amus
Aimpiair celmuinigh da rada ris dul isin chath ⁊ niro hadmadh don ingin e; ⁊ is
ed robo dhoigh leo-san dia ndechadh in sacart isin chath conadh leo no b*eth*
buaidh in chatha ⁊ <. . . .> in chelmuine uadhibh.

Tainic iar sin Airgia co hairm i mboi ben Aimpiair [. . . .] di sain [. . . .] ina eccmuis
Airgia ic iar*aid* atmala a fir f*urr*i ⁊ boi oca guidhi co mór ar daigh co ndechsat
Aimpiair isin cath. Ro f*h*regair immorro ben Aimpiair ⁊ at-bert dia tucad Airgia
di in munntorc mirbulda do-righni Ulccan di, no biadh le imon *fath* sin. 'Do-
berthar', ar Airgia. Ro gres a ben in sacart iar sin im thaidhecht isin cath imailli
re Grecaibh i n-aig*id* na Tiabanda. At-bert Aimpiair nach rachad ar setaib na ar
mainib in domuin isin cathug*ud* út sech cach, uair ro <fh>etir nach biadh do
shaeg*ul* aigi acht co ndechad isin cath. At-bert in ben fris nach bia<d> a comrac
fris acht muna dhechsadh isin chath don chur sin.

'A ben,' ar se, 'ni coir i nd-i co n-aslaidhi form masa ferr let mo b*eith*-si beo na
marb, ⁊ gemadh mhor do mainib ⁊ d'innmus do-ghébtha ar mu dul-sa isin
chath, robam ferr-sa nait sin uile.' Ro chinn in ben cona luighi nach biad a comrac
muna dechad i n-aig*id* na Tiabanta. Ro cuiredh isin chath in sacart iar sin gerbo
lesc leis ⁊ tuc Airgia in munntorc n-oir iar sin do mnai Aimpiair ⁊ ro chuir sí a
fer ar éicin isin cath.

Translations from Miles 2007: 87–9, 91–3

Amphiaraus and Eriphyle

… And Adrastus told Polynices to go to the priest, whose name was Amphiaraus and to give him thanks so that he might make a divination for him to discover what would be the outcome of the battle which he was to fight against his brother, or whether his expedition would be successful.

It was Amphiaraus, moreover, who used to prophesy and augur for Adrastus, king of Little Greece;[1] and the priest prophesied to Polynices, and what he said was, if they waged battle against the Thebans, no one of them would come back alive except Adrastus, the king of the Greeks, alone. After making that prophecy, Amphiaraus ran off to avoid the battle and hid himself, and no one knew the way to his place of hiding except his wife and himself.

Thereupon Argia, Adrastus' daughter and wife of Polynices, the son of the Theban king, came after the augur Amphiaraus to tell him to enter the battle, and his whereabouts were not disclosed to the girl; and they believed that if the priest entered the battle that the victory in battle would be theirs, and […] of the augury from them (?).

Argia came after that to where Amphiaraus' wife was [……..] from that [……..] in his absence, Argia beseeched her to disclose the whereabouts of her husband, and she earnestly pleaded for Amphiaraus to enter the battle. Amphiaraus' wife answered and said that if Argia gave her the wondrous necklace which Vulcan had made for her, she would assist her on that account. 'It will be given', said Argia. Thereupon the priest's wife urged him to go to battle with the Greeks against the Thebans. Amphiaraus responded that he would not join that battle beyond all others for (all) the riches and wealth of the world, because he knew that he would lose his life as soon as he went to fight. The woman told him that she would not have sex with him unless he went to battle at that time.

'Woman', he said, 'what you urge upon me is not right if you prefer me alive to dead, and although you would get much wealth and treasure by my going to the battle, I (alive) would be better than all that'. The woman pledged with her oath that she would not have sex with him if he did not go against the Thebans. Thereupon the priest was sent to the battle, and Argia gave the golden necklace to Amphiaraus' wife, and she sent her husband to the battle under compulsion.

Alcmaeon and Eriphyle

Aimpiair dono in faidh .i. sacart Adhruist rí *Grec* immorro eisidhe, ro facaib-side
mac maith, Ailmeon dono a ainm-sidhe, ⁊ o ro chuala-sidhe a athair do marbad
⁊ a corp do bhathadh iarna marbad i cath na Teiphi, ro marb a mathair fein .i.
Eirifilia, ar is i fodera a athair do marbad .i. Aimpiair.

Ros-cab iar sin cuchach Almeon a haithle a *mathar* do marbad do. Ro chuinnigh
iar sin a ben for Almeon m*a*c Aimpiair in mundtorc n-ordha ro boi ica mathair-
sium ar ba doigh lé co fuibidh Almeon slainti dia scaradh in mundtorc fris.
Tuccadh dissi iar sin in munntorc ⁊ araí sin tra ni fuair Almeon slainte on
chuchach. Tainic athair a *mathar* cugi-sium iar sin .i. Peilic a ainm-side ⁊ ro
marb in Peilic sin Almeón a cinaigh a ingine do marbad .i. a mathair fein.

Ro thothlaig iar sin ben Almeoin .i. Caillioire ar Iop co ro choimétadh a dha m*a*c
di no co tisadh dibh digail a n-ath*ar* forin tí ros marb. Ren ⁊ Soicc anmann in da
m*a*c sin Almeon. Atrachtatar sin iar ngabail nirt ⁊ *ferainn* a n-ath*ur* ⁊ ro thinoilsit
sloigh mora diairmi dirfreccartha dochum Peilicc ⁊ ro fhuaccairset cath fair.

Ro tinoil dono Peilicc a muintir ⁊ a curadha ⁊ a clann ⁊ a lucht dingmala catha
dhe. Arai sin do cuinnigh Peilic cairdi bliadna gan chath do chur frisin re sin.
Atrubratar mic Almeoin co tibritis cairdi do dia tucadh-som a cenn doib risin
mbliadain sin iarna tescad dia mhéidi amail ro ben-som dia n-aith*ir*-sium .i. do
m*a*c a ingine fein. At-bert Peilic nach tibredh a cenn dia deoin doibh.

O nach fuair Peilicc cairdi ona macaib ro chuirsit fa cetoir <cath> co fichdha
fuilech feochair fergach leth ar leith ⁊ ro marbait sloigh dhírime dimhóra at*ur*ra;
araí sin tra ro mebaidh a[....] e[....] acht Peilicc etir. Ro-siachtata[r in da mac
sin Almeoin] gusin inad a raibi Pe[ilicc]

[....] adubratar [....]

Alcmaeon and Eriphyle

The prophet Amphiaraus, however, a priest of Adrastus king of the Greeks, left a good son, Alcmaeon by name. And when he heard that his father had been killed and his body engulfed after he had been killed in the battle for Thebes,[2] he[3] killed his own mother Eriphyle, for it was she who caused his father Amphiaraus to be killed.

Alcmaeon was seized by madness after he had killed his mother. Thereupon his wife asked Alcmaeon, son of Amphiaraus, for the golden necklace which had been his mother's,[4] for she thought that Alcmaeon would recover his sanity if the necklace were taken from him. Thereupon the necklace was given to her, but in spite of that Alcmaeon had no recovery from the madness. His mother's father, whose name was Peilicc,[5] came to him after that, and that Peilicc killed Alcmaeon in vengeance for having killed his daughter, that is, his own mother.

Callirhoe, Alcmaeon's wife, then besought[6] of Jove that he guard her two sons until they were able to avenge the death of their father on the one who had killed him. Ren and Soicc were the names of those two sons of Alcmaeon.[7] After seizing their father's authority and domains, they rose up and gathered innumerable, incomparable great hosts against Peilicc, and challenged him to battle.

Now Peilicc gathered to himself his household and his champions and his children and his bodyguards. In spite of that, Peilicc requested a year's truce, in which no battle would be waged against him. The sons of Alcmaeon said that they would grant him a truce if, within that year, he gave them his head cut off from his neck, as he had cut <the head> off from their father, that is, from his own daughter's son. Peilicc said he would not give them his head of his own accord.

When Peilicc did not receive a truce from the youths, immediately they joined battle furiously, bloodily, savagely, wrathfully on both sides, and countless, great hosts were killed between them; in spite of that [...] was defeated [...] at all except Peilicc, and [those two sons of Alcmaeon] reached the place where Peilicc was [...] they said [....][8]

Conclusion as quoted in *Togail na Tebe*

Aráoi romeabaid in cath for Pleigi, ⁊ rosiachtatar da mac Almeon chuige, ⁊ adubhratar ris: 'In tucais let,' ar siat, 'Almeon?' 'Ní tucus,' ar sé, '⁊ da mbeith agum doberoind'. Robensat iar sin maca Almeon a cend do Pleigi, ⁊ tucsat ár dermháir for a muinntir macaibh mnaibh. Tancatar iar sin da tigh ar mbreith buada ⁊ coscair. Finit do Scel an Mundtuirc.

Conclusion as quoted in *Togail na Tebe*

In spite of that Phegeus was defeated, and Alcmaeon's two sons came towards him and said to him: 'Have you brought Alcmaeon with you?' 'I have not', he said, 'and if I had him, I would bring him'. Thereupon the sons of Alcmaeon cut off Phegeus' head, and they visited a grievous slaughter on his household, sons and women. Afterwards they went to their homes, having had the victory and the spoils. Here ends the Story of the Necklace.

Essay: *Fingal* 'kin-slaying' and the Theban Cycle

At just under 1,500 words, *Riss in Mundtuirc* is the shortest of the texts in Irish adapted from the works of the Roman epic poet Statius. Derived primarily from Statius' *Thebaid*, the *Riss* purports to recount a series of misfortunes that befell the possessors of a cursed necklace crafted by Vulcan originally for the goddess Harmonia, divine progenitor of the Theban royal line. This *longa series malorum* 'long sequence of evils' is the subject of a substantial digression in Statius' *Thebaid* (2.265–305).

While Statius' interest was chiefly the Theban royal line, the *Riss* concerns mostly the effect of the curse on the family of Amphiaraus, an Argive soothsayer and one of the Seven against Thebes who fights for the claims of the exiled Theban prince Polynices, in the army led by Polynices' father-in-law Adrastus. The necklace is introduced when Eriphyle, Amphiaraus' wife, accepts the necklace as payment for her help engineering her husband's participation in the doomed expedition against Thebes, thus ensuring his death. This incident forms the subject of the first excerpt, which begins at the point where Polynices has just requested that Adrastus join his campaign against his brother at Thebes. The second excerpt concerns Amphiaraus' son Alcmaeon, who murders his mother in revenge for his father's death; it continues with the subsequent killing of Alcmaeon by Eriphyle's father, and then, finally, the killing of the latter by Alcmaeon's two sons. With this succession of killings within Amphiaraus' line, the true interest of the *Riss* is seen not to be the cursed necklace so much as the story's revelation of the scope of *fingal* 'kin-slaying' in ancient narrative. A concern for *fingal* runs through the 'native' corpus of Middle Irish narrative almost as an obsession, characteristic of a literature preoccupied with contests for power among sons of princes, even violence between children and parents, as exemplified by the haunting tale *Fingal Rónáin* 'The Kin-Slaying of Rónán'.[9] While the term *fingal* is not actually used in *Riss in Mundtuirc*, the text suggests that the term's scope included a wife having a hand in her husband's death, and the author has assigned this event a prominence in his epitome of the *Thebaid* that many moderns might miss altogether. However, Eriphyle's treachery towards Amphiaraus happens to be the feature of the story most commented upon in antiquity, so the Irish author was not idiosyncratic in the choice of this feature to be the narrative's emotional centrepiece. Accordingly, in this detail the Irish text reproduces a world view of the ancients, while it remains characteristic of the prominence of *fingal* in medieval Irish literary culture as a whole.

While much of *Riss in Mundtuirc* is an expert epitome of Statius' *Thebaid*, the author seems to have drawn on ancient scholia to the poem by Lactantius Placidus, and additionally on Servius Danielis' commentary to the *Aeneid*, at Virgil's mention of Eriphyle (*Aeneid* 6.445). The most surprising source is Ovid's terse recounting of this whole narrative in the *Metamorphoses* (9.403–15), from which the Irish author extracts the entirety of the section between Callirhoe, Alcmaeon's widow, their sons and Eriphyle's father. In the latter section, especially, the author had trouble conveying clearly the complexity of this family struggle, that is, who is killing whom, and the text shows signs of a reviser trying, with only partial success, to make sense of the complexity with glosses and notes.

Notes

1   The term 'Little Greece' probably refers here to Argos and the environs.

2   Amphiaraus was swallowed through a chasm in the earth down to Hades (Statius, *Thebaid* 7.818–19).

3   The manuscript adds *Almeon dono* 'Alcmaeon moreover'.

4   The manuscript (incoherently) adds *a Caillioire* 'Callirhoe's'.

5   This name stands for Phegeus, whom classical sources give as the father of Alcmaeon's first wife Arsinoe (the error originates with an unclear description in Ovid, the Irish author's source here).

6   The manuscript adds *Peilicc*.

7   These names, which seem to have no basis in the Latin sources, remain unexplained.

8   The conclusion has been lost due to damage to the vellum.

9   Edition by Greene 1955: 3–11; translation, Koch and Carey 2003: 274–82. Relevant studies include Mac Gearailt 2006/7. Cf. Ch. 19 in this volume, pp. 246–7.

13

Imtheachta Aeniasa 'The Wanderings of Aeneas'

Erich Poppe

The texts are reproduced from Calder 1907.[1] In the essay and notes, references to the Irish text are indicated by the letters IA followed by Calder's line-number.[2]

Text extracts

The opening of the narrative
(Calder 1907, lines 1–66)

O thairnic tra do Grecaib slad ⁊ inrad ⁊ dithlaithriugud rig cathrach na Frigia .i. in Træ, cend ordain ⁊ airechais na huili Aissia isside, tancadar rigraid na nGrec co dind Minerba isin Trae, ⁊ dorochtadar i n-æn baile uile ⁊ rofiarfaig Aigmenon, int airdrig dib, ca comairle dobertais do arin forind romairn in cathraig, no in comaillfitis friu. Doraidset foirend do Grecaib ni bud coir a comall friu, uair ni her ar ngrad-ni acht ar ar n-omun ⁊ ara n-anacul fen domairnset in cathraig, ⁊ doronsat, gen co rancadar, olc rind, ⁊ dogentais aris, dia cæmsad leo.

Roraid Nestor dono iarsin: 'LX bliadan,' ar se, 'gusin aimsir-sea, o thanac-sa ⁊ Pelias ⁊ Tailimon ⁊ Castur ⁊ Pullux ar æn re hErcail, lucht VII long im luing Argo, co roairgsim in cathair-seo, ⁊ co tuc*sam* fo gin gæ ⁊ claidim gach æn rob inmarbtha inti, co rucsam i mbroid ⁊ a ndairi gach æn na romarbad, ⁊ co rucsum a huili indmus esti, ⁊ co tarrdsim tenedh tairsi iarsin. Don-farraid Laimidon iarsin, *&* dorad cath dun, co torchair dono Laimidon lind cona tri maccaib isin cath sin .i. Pulus ⁊ Foclointis ⁊ Aimpiter. Dorochradar dono forgla rig ⁊ tasech ⁊ trenfer na Troianu imailli fris. Rofucum [sic] lind i mbroid mac ⁊ ingin Laimidoin .i. Esiona ⁊ Priaim ⁊ robai in Trai fas iarsin fri re ar omun na nGrec. Dorat dono Earcail iarsin tar cend set ⁊ maine deonugad do Priaim teacht dochum na Trai ⁊ a hathnuigedh dorisi, acht na dernad aris cogad fri Grecaib, ⁊ rochomaill Priam indi sin cen robo beo. O robo marb Ercail, ⁊ o'tconnairc Priaim daingni a cathrach ⁊ nertmhairi a sloig, ron-gab meit menmun ⁊ dimus ⁊ nir'bo maisi les cena gan a aincridi do iarraid for Grecaib, co rofaid a mac .i. Alaxandair ⁊ Ainias for creich go Grecaib, co roinirsiut inis Cheithiria, ⁊ co tucsat leo Elleand Legata. Tancamar-ne dono co lin ar sochraiti i ndiaidh ar creichi, ⁊ ni dernad acht nemthni dind, ⁊ ni thucad aissic dun tar cend ar sida, ⁊ rotinoilit moirneart na hAisia inar n-aigid, ⁊ atrachtadar co bagach brigach borrfadach righa ⁊ taisig, curaidh ⁊ caithmilid ⁊ laith gaili na n-uili Assia, ot*ha* in Scethia thuaiscertaig, ⁊ in n-Innia n-oirrtheraig, ⁊ i n-Eitheoip ndeiscertaigh, i cath inar n-aigid, co ndorchradar leo hilar *ar* rig-ni ⁊ ar tusech ⁊ ar cathmiled, co ndorchradar-sum uili lendi, ⁊ co ndorchair Priam fen cona coecait mac ⁊ ingen ⁊ clemnad, ⁊ cona

Translations

The opening of the narrative

Translation revised from Calder 1907: 3–7.

When the Greeks had finished the plunder, devastation, and destruction of the royal city of Phrygia, namely Troy, the foremost in dignity and importance of all Asia, the kings of the Greeks went to the citadel of Minerva in Troy, and they all assembled, and Agamemnon, their over-king, asked them what counsel they would give him concerning those who had betrayed the city and whether they should fulfil (their promise of security) to them.[4] Some of the Greeks said that it would not be proper to fulfil (that promise) for them, 'because it was not for love of us, but for fear of us and for their own protection that they betrayed the city, and they did us evil as long as they could, and they would do it again if it were possible for them'.

So Nestor then said: 'It is sixty years ago', he said, 'when I came, with Peleus and Telamon and Castor and Pollux together with Hercules, the crew of seven ships including the Argo, and we ravaged this city, and we put to the spear and sword everyone who was fit to be killed in it, and we brought into bondage and captivity everyone who was not killed, and we carried off all its treasure, and afterwards we set fire to it. Laomedon then overtook us and did battle against us, and then Laomedon was killed by us in this battle together with his three sons, Pulus [= Hypsipilus], Foclointis [= Volcontis], and Aimpiter [= Ampitus].[5] There also fell the best of the kings and leaders and heroes of the Trojans together with him. We brought with us in bondage Laomedon's son and daughter, namely Hesione and Priam, and Troy was deserted for a time afterwards for fear of the Greeks. After that, in return for treasure and valuables, Hercules gave Priam permission to come to Troy and to restore it again, provided that he did not make war against the Greeks again, and Priam fulfilled this as long as he [Hercules] was alive. When Hercules was dead and Priam saw the strength of his city and the fortitude of his host, self-confidence and arrogance seized him, and furthermore it did not seem fitting for him not to seek (redress for) his wrong from the Greeks. He sent his son, namely Alexander, and Aeneas on a raid to the Greeks, and they devastated the island of Cytherea and took Ledaean Helen with them.[6] We came then with a large number of our armies to recover our booty, and we were ignored, and no restitution was given us in return for peace with us. But the mighty strength of Asia was assembled against us, and the kings and leaders, the fen cona coecait mac ⁊ ingen ⁊ clemnad, ⁊ cona uilib curadaib ⁊ caithmiledaib, rigaib ⁊ taisechaib ⁊ særclandaib na Trae and, acht lucht in braith nama .i. Ænias ⁊ Antinor cona muintir. Ba he sin dered cardusa Priaimh fri Grecaib. Is demin daibsi, dono, ni ba ferr cairrdius Ænias ribsi dia facbaithi isin Trai, inas in cairdis sin Priaim fri Grecu. Is mairg Greca dobera tairisim fair; ar is nama Grec dogress Ainias. Sochaidi do curadaib ⁊ do caithmiledaib ⁊ d'anrudaib Grec torchair lais dia laim fen isna VII cathaib LX ar C dochuiredh rinde oc diden na Trae.'

O rochualatar tra Greca na haithesca sin roraid Neastor, is i comairli roraid*set*seom ⁊ roner*t*sat, in Trae do fasugud, ⁊ æs in braith do indarba esti gan a mbasugad, uair tucad enech Pirr friu fria *n*-anacul ar brath na Trae. Fororchongairt Aigmenon iarsin i comairli na nGrec for Ænias ⁊ for Aintinor, in Trai d'fagbhail fas, ⁊ Antinor do dul co hIleric, ferand fuil etir Grecu ⁊ Etail siar. Doluid immorro Ainias, gusin lucht rolen, co Sliab Ido – sliabh esside for ur mara Torrian co fidbaid cain and. Ba maith do cumdach long in fidbad, ⁊ cumdaigther lais XX long andsin, ⁊ o tairnic do cumdach a long, doluid la tosach soinindi i tus samraidh for muir Torrian, ⁊ a athair .i. Anaichis, ina senoir, ⁊ a mac .i. Ascan, ⁊ gach æn rolen d'a æs cumtha, immalle fris. Ba bronach dubach derfadach toirrseach imsnimach inn imirci sin. Ba leasc in turus docuas and. Ba truag tra in gair ghuil ⁊ basgairi ⁊ mairgnighi ac fegadh a tiri ⁊ a n-atharda duichi iarna n-indarba dia naimdib uathi. Roseolsat iarsin co Traicia . . .

A battle scene adapted from Virgil, *Aeneid* 9.691–777
(Calder 1907, lines 2280–321)

Rosoich iarsin co Tuirnd in daingin do fhoslugud ⁊ na Troianu do thiachtain as amach, ⁊ maidm rompo forna Rudultaib ⁊ beth doibh ac cor a n-air. O rochuala dono Tuirnd na briathra borbuathbasacha sin fagbais ant inadh a raibi ic toghail in dunaid ⁊ dos-fig a gal curud ⁊ a bruth miled ⁊ a nert niadh ⁊ doshoigh cona warriors and soldiers and heroes of all Asia, from Scythia in the north and India in the east and Ethiopia in the south, arose resolutely, forcefully, vigorously in battle against us, so that a multitude of our kings and our leaders and our soldiers fell at their hands, and they all fell at our hands, and Priam himself fell there with his fifty sons and daughters and sons-in-law, with all his warriors and soldiers, kings and leaders and nobles of Troy, except only the traitors, namely Aeneas and Antenor with their followers. This was the end of Priam's alliance with the Greeks. You can be certain then that Aeneas' alliance with you, if you leave him in Troy, will be no better than Priam's alliance with the Greeks. It will be bad for any Greeks who will put trust in him, because Aeneas is always an enemy of the Greeks. A multitude of warriors and soldiers and nobles of the Greeks fell by him by his own hand in the 167 battles that were fought against us in the defence of Troy.'

When the Greeks heard these words that Nestor had spoken, they spoke and confirmed the following counsel: to devastate Troy and to expel the traitors from it without killing them, because Pyrrhus' honour had been pledged to them to protect them in return for the betrayal of Troy. In the counsel of the Greeks Agamemnon then ordered Aeneas and Antenor that Troy must be left deserted and that Antenor must go to Illyricum, a country in the west between Greece and Italy. Aeneas, however, went together with those who followed him to Mount Ida – a hill on the shore of the Tyrrhenian Sea with a fine wood. The wood was good for constructing ships, and twenty ships were built there by him, and when the ships had been built, he set out on the Tyrrhenian Sea at the first fine weather at the beginning of summer, along with his father Anchises, an aged man, and his son Ascanius, and every one of his followers. Sorrowful, gloomy, tearful, grievous was this band of emigrants. Unpleasant was the journey on which they went. Sad was the cry of weeping and lamenting and wailing when they looked at their country and their hereditary fatherland from which they had been banished by their enemies. They then sailed to Thrace . . .

A battle scene adapted from Virgil

Translation revised from Calder 1907: 143–7

Then [word] reached Turnus that the stronghold had been opened and that the Trojans had come out and were overwhelming the Rutulians and slaughtering them. Then when Turnus heard these cruel and dreadful words, he left the place where he was attacking the camp, and his hero's valour, his soldier's fury, and his shochraite lais a n-aighidh in madhma. Ocus merbaid focetoir inti Patenus dorala do a ndiaidh na himghona. Marbaid dono Meropen milid, ocus Eirimantha ocus Petien milid, a comruc deisi. Maidm remhi iarsin forna Troianaib dochum in dunaidh, ⁊ nos-lenand Tuirnd cona Rudultaib ac cor a n-air co ndeochaid ina ndunadh, ⁊ luidh Tuirnd ina ndhiaidh isin dunadh ⁊ nir' len nech dia muintir he, uair ni fhedatar a techt uaidhib a cumasc a namad. Robo turus gan tindtudh dosan sin, muna beth Iunaind aga imchoimhet. In tan tra adconnairc Pindarus a brathair do marbad .i. Peidias, ⁊ maidm fora muintir, adnaigh a formna re comlaidh in dorois ⁊ dunaidh frisna Laitintiu ⁊ forfagaib forind dia muintir fen frisin dorus, ⁊ tic foirend ele dib isin dunad. Ocus adconnairc tra Pindarus Tuirnd isin dunadh ic tafand na Troiandach. Fa forbailigh leis a tharrachtain Tuirnd i n-ecomland, ar ba saint lais a brathair .i. Petias do dhighail fair, ⁊ roraid fris: 'Is tu is maith lend do beith amal atai. Ni hinund duit ⁊ beith i righdhai Amata ⁊ a cathraigh Duin .i. i n-Airdea. I scoraib do namhad atai, ⁊ ni bera 'h anmain lat.' Ocus daleg chuigi in gai romor robai ina laim. Cocerd dono Iunaind in gai sech Tuirnd cor'bean a ndorus in dunaidh .i. isin ursaind. Dobeir immorro Tuirnd bem do cloidem dosamh cor'dluig a cend fair ar do co ntorchair marb andsin. In tan adconncatar na Troiandaigh Pindarnus do toitim, nos-gebh eagla ⁊ omun, ⁊ techid sechnon in dunaidh ria Tuirnd. Dia maid edh dogned Tuirnd andsin, in dorus d'foslugud ria muintir, dotæthsaitis Troiandaigh uile de, ⁊ robad e sin la dedinach na cathrach. Acht ceana ni hedh sin doroine, uair tainic a bruth ⁊ a brigh ⁊ a morferg miled in churad co croda comrumach cosgurach cathbuadhach, ⁊ ros-geb for sraiglead ⁊ esorgain, leod ⁊ leadrad, brud ⁊ brisiudh ⁊ basagadh na Troianach gu mbenad bond fri medi aigi gach conair dotheigedh sechnon in dunaidh. Marbaid ar tus Pallemerus caithmilid, ⁊ Gigen ⁊ hAlimus ⁊ Frigia. Ocus marbaid dono iarsin in lucht-sa robatar ac cathugud dona muraib amach, ⁊ nach feadatar a beith sin isna muraib ac cor air na Troiannach. Ocus marbaid ochtur sær soicheneoil do Troianaib ⁊ rosoigh in sgel sin co taisecha Troianach .i. Tuirn do chur air Troianach.

champion's strength seizes him and he proceeds with his host to the place where they were being overwhelmed. And at once he kills Patenus [= Antiphates] who came upon him after the slaughter. He also killed the soldier Meropen [= Meropes] and the soldier Eirimantha [= Erymas] and the soldier Petien [= Bitias] in single combat.[7] The Trojans then scattered before him to the camp, and Turnus with his Rutulians pursued and slaughtered them until they went into their camp, and Turnus went after them into the camp, and none of his host followed him, because they did not know that he had gone from them into the midst of their enemies. This would have been a journey without return for him, had Juno not protected him. When Pindarus [= Pandarus] saw his brother Peidias [= Bitias] killed and his host routed, he thrusts his shoulder against the valve of the gate and closed it against the Latins and left a group of his own host at the gate. And another group of them came into the camp. And Pindarus then saw Turnus in the camp putting the Trojans to flight. He was very glad to find Turnus in distress, because he wished to take vengeance on him for his brother Petias, and he said to him: 'We are glad that you are as you are. It is not the same for you as being in Amata's royal dwelling and in Duin's [= Daunus'] stronghold, Airdea. You are in the camp of your enemies, and you will not escape alive.' And he thrust at him the huge spear that was in his hand. Juno then directed the spear past Turnus so that it struck in the gate of the camp, in the door-post. Turnus, however, deals him a stroke of his sword so that he split his head into two, and he fell down dead there. When the Trojans saw Pindarus fall, fear and terror seized them, and they fled before Turnus through the camp. If Turnus had then opened the door for his host, all the Trojans would have fallen because of this and this would have been the stronghold's last day. However, he did not do this, because his fury and his vigour and his great warrior's wrath came upon him fiercely, contentiously, triumphantly, battle-victoriously, and he took to attacking and smiting, hacking and felling, crushing and breaking and slaying the Trojans so that sole touched neck on every path that he took throughout the camp. First he kills the battle-soldier Pallemerus [= Phaleris] and Gigen [= Gyges] and Halimus [= Halys] and Frigia [= Phegeus]. And he then kills those who were fighting from the walls and did not know that he was inside slaughtering the Trojans. And he kills eight free and noble men of the Trojans, and this news reached the leaders of the Trojans, that Turnus was slaughtering the Trojans.

A battle scene with no Virgilian model
(Calder 1907, lines 2477–513)

O ruscaig doib tra a catha do corugud ⁊ a sloig do nertadh ⁊ do gressacht, ⁊ o rogabsat a n-idhna catha forro, ⁊ rocomfoicsigh cach dib dochum a chele co talcar tren tarpthech, ⁊ co brigmar borrfudach, ⁊ ba failidh badb derg dasachtach ac imchosait etir in da chath sin, ba trom sceo nemi ⁊ aingceoil ⁊ duabus for sluaghaib Rudultaib in la sin. [...]³ Ba hadhuathmhar edigh in buiridhach robuirsed damraidh daghchalma na Troianach ⁊ *na* n-Eodruisdegda ⁊ na n-Arcaidegda do chath fri Rudultaib. Roferad tra cuibleng croda crolinteach fuileth guinech gabalach crechtach crolintech etarru 'sin chath sin. Ba brisc fidbuidh a lamhaib læch lanchalma isin cath cetna. Rochlos and dresachtach na n-nar*m* ⁊ tulguma na sgiath ⁊ sgredgairi na ngai ⁊ fedgaire na cloidem ⁊ siangairi na soighed. Adceasa andsin sruthana fola fordhergi a hindaib laigin lanfhuiltech ⁊ colg nded nduaibseach n-aigthide imamnus ⁊ a hindaib cloidem corr coindealta corcordha. Dorochradar andsin tra don tslogh chechtardha gleri laech londghuinech for inchaib a tigernadh. Dorochradar and fos oirrigha ana ilardha don tshlogh cobsaid cechtarda sin. Ba haigthidhe aduathmhar, ⁊ ba cobsaidh curata in fhobairt tuc Ænias for slogh na Rudulta, ⁊ se ⁊ luirech trebraid tredhualach alaind umaidhe uime, ⁊ cathbarr fororda fora cind, ⁊ sgiath sechtfillti fora chliu, ⁊ claidem cruaidhgher colundledartha, is e daingen degfhæbrach særdenmach sechtleghtha co demin ina des laim aga slaidhi ⁊ iga slechtadh, ica leodh ⁊ ica letrad aga ndhichendadh ⁊ aga n-athcuma co mbenadh bond fri medi aigi gach conair rotheghedh tresin cath. In tan tra bai Ænias forsin luinde sin, dorala chuigi ina aighidh in cur croda comrumach .i. Telon cathmilid ....

A battle scene with no Virgilian model

Translation revised from Calder 1907: 155, 157.

When they [the Trojans and the Rutulians] had finished arranging their battalions and strengthening and exhorting their hosts, and when they had taken up their arms of war and approached each other ruthlessly, strongly, vigorously, and powerfully, boldly, and frenzied red Badb was joyous at stirring up strife between these two battalions, the abundance of evil and bad omen and ill-luck was heavy on the hosts of the Rutulians that day. [. . .] Dreadful, horrible was the shouting that the most valorous warrior-host of the Trojans and Etruscans and Arcadians shouted for battle against the Rutulians. A gory, wound-inflicting, violent, murderous, blood-stained [?], gory, bloody contest was fought between them in this battle. Brittle in this battle were the spears in the hands of very valorous warriors. There was heard there the clatter of arms and the clashing of shields and the screaming of spears and the hissing of swords and the whistling of arrows. Streams of red blood were seen there from the points of gory spears and of very fierce, awful, dreadful, ivory-hilted swords and from the points of purple, shining, pointed swords. The finest fiercely wounding warriors from the host of either side fell there for the honour of their leaders. Numerous splendid kings from the steady host of either side fell there also. Fearsome and terrible, steadfast and valiant was the assault that Aeneas made upon the host of the Rutulians, and he was wearing beautiful, triple-plaited woven mail armour of brass, with a gilded helm on his head, and a sevenfold shield on his left arm, and a body-wounding, hard and sharp sword, which was solid, sharp-edged, nobly fashioned, surely seven-times refined, in his right hand, striking them and cutting them down, hacking them and felling them, beheading them and maiming them, so that sole touched neck on every path that he took throughout the battle. When Aeneas then was engaged in this fierceness, the trophied, valiant warrior, the battle-soldier Telon [= Theron], happened to come upon him. . . .

Essay: A creative translator at work

Imtheachta Aeniasa 'The Wanderings of Aeneas' can be, and has been, described as an Irish 'translation' of Virgil's *Aeneid*. It follows the latter's basic events, so that the two texts can be placed side by side, as is shown by Calder's cross-references to lines in the *Aeneid* in his edition of the Irish text (Calder 1907). More detailed comparisons and gaps and irregularities in these cross-references bring out significant differences, even when a parallel for the Irish target text can be identified in the Latin source, as in our second extract, indicating that the target text deviates substantially in approach and style in the way the basic events are put together and told. Furthermore, some passages in the Irish text have no parallel in the *Aeneid*, as seen in the first and third excerpts. It is therefore perhaps prudent to call *Imtheachta Aeniasa* an Irish 'adaptation' (or a 'rewriting'/'retelling' or a 'paraphrase') of Virgil's *Aeneid*.[8] The appropriate term for the agent behind it is more difficult to determine in view of the creative translator's author-like responsibility for the orientation and form of the adaptation.[9] Exploiting the resulting fuzziness, both 'author' and 'translator' will be used in the following, depending on the perceived proximity of the status of the agent behind *Imtheachta Aeniasa* relative to that of an author responsible for a work or to that of a translator committed, even if only somewhat indirectly, to a source.

On the macro-level, Virgil's hexameters became Irish prose, the preferred medium for narrative in Irish textual culture. The Irish author furthermore added two framing passages, an introduction and an epilogue.[10] Whereas the *Aeneid* begins with Aeneas' travels in the Mediterranean Sea, the Irish narrative starts with Aeneas' expulsion from Troy and a survey of its history, which in relevant details deviate from Virgil's account in Book 2 (see below). Only after about fifty lines of printed text does it begin to follow Virgil's Book 3, with Aeneas' retrospective report at Dido's court about the first stages of his travels after leaving Troy, but in *Imtheachta Aeniasa* this is retold in the narrator's voice. The second framing passage, the brief epilogue, contains about ten lines of printed text. Whereas the *Aeneid* ends abruptly with the death of Aeneas' antagonist Turnus, the Irish passage outlines the future of Aeneas, his wife Lavinia, and his son Ascanius, and, looking ahead even further, describes them as the ancestors of 'Roman rulers and kings, and of governors of the world from then onwards until the Day of Judgement' (*IA* 3206–15).[11] The introduction and the epilogue together locate the events of *Imtheachta Aeniasa* in universal history, in which the destruction of Troy and other events from ancient and biblical history were important chronological points of orientation. Clarke and Ní Mhaonaigh (2020: 476) highlight the importance for medieval Irish scholars of 'syncretistic historiography, based on systematic correlations between events in Irish history (and mythological pseudohistory) and contemporaneous events in the histories of the great nations of the classical and biblical world'.[12] The Irish interest in the history narrated in the *Aeneid* was therefore one motivation for the production of its vernacular adaptation, while another motivation was the ongoing interpretative engagement of medieval Irish *literati* with it (compare Miles 2011). This does not conflict with the specific aesthetic and stylistic concerns of its Irish translator, which will be discussed in greater detail below.

For the date of *Imtheachta Aeniasa* Mac Gearailt thinks the thirteenth century to be most likely.[13] The text belongs to a second phase of the adaptation of classical tales in Ireland, postdating especially the first Irish adaptation of the *De Excidio Troiae Historia* 'History of the Destruction of Troy', supposedly by Dares Phrygius, as *Togail Troí*; it is thought by Miles (2011: 144) to represent 'the "school" of classical translations at an advanced stage'. It is extant in three manuscripts, namely in the final section of the late-fourteenth-century Book of Ballymote (Dublin, Royal Irish Academy, MS 23 P 12, fols 249r–267r), which also contains a version of *Togail Troí* (see Ch. 6 on the different recensions), *Merugud Uilixis* (see Ch. 18), and the Alexander compilation (see Ch. 21), and in two fifteenth-century manuscripts (Dublin, University College Dublin, MS A 11, fols 24r–49v, and Dublin, King's Inns, MS 13, fols 1r–25v, both defective at end) where it is transmitted together with other Irish versions of classical materials. (On the King's Inns MS see also p. 407 below, with n. 6).

For the purpose of this anthology, three excerpts from *Imtheachta Aeniasa* have been selected. The beginning of the Irish adaptation has been chosen as the first extract because it provides the historical setting for the narrative with an account of the role of Aeneas in the fall of Troy which significantly deviates from Virgil. The second excerpt retells a part of the siege of the Trojan camp by the Rutulians and is intended to show the basic fidelity of *Imtheachta Aeniasa* to the sequence of events in Virgil's *Aeneid* (9.691–777) on the one hand (even the eight nameless Trojans summarily killed can be identified in Virgil by name) and the stylistic differences between them on the other. It needs to be stressed that it cannot claim to be representative of the overall relation between the two texts. The third extract presents a section of another battle scene which has no parallel in the *Aeneid*. It is the Irish author's creative invention and gives an impression of the aesthetic and stylistic effects being sought in a specific narrative situation. It is part of a longer passage (*IA* 2436–503) sandwiched between Virgil's accounts of Tarchon's shipwreck and of the first meeting in battle of the Rutulians and the Trojans with their respective allies, expanding on Virgil's two-line reference to Turnus reassembling his army against the Trojans (*Aeneid* 10.308–9). It begins with Aeneas and Turnus mustering their respective armies and inciting them to battle with rousing speeches, then, in the section reproduced here, the general battle starts, until the narrative returns to Virgil's account at *Aeneid* 10.310–12 with the meeting of Aeneas and Theron (on this passage see also LeBlanc 2019: 216–20).

Imtheachta Aeniasa's introduction starts with the council convened by Agamemnon after the destruction of Troy in order to decide the future of those who had betrayed the city to the Greeks. The Irish author then expands the scene by inserting a long speech fittingly attributed to Nestor, who is characterized in *Togail Troí* in the Book of Ballymote as *trebar i comairle* 'prudent in counsel' (Breathnach 1952: 82). Nestor summarizes the main events of Troy's history in the sixty years between its first and second destruction and identifies Antenor and Aeneas as traitors.[14] This is blatantly different from Aeneas' own account in the *Aeneid*'s Book 2, according to which he fled from Troy after fierce fighting with the Greeks at the behest of his mother Venus, but parallels Dares' *De Excidio Troiae* chapter 42.[15] Nestor's argument in favour of banishing Aeneas, however, that he will always remain an enemy of the Greeks, deviates from that of *De Excidio Troiae* chapter 43, in which his expulsion is said to result from his having hidden Polyxena. At the point when Aeneas has ships built at Mount Ida and then sails towards Thrace, *Imtheachta Aeniasa* finally takes up Aeneas' own account of his travels in *Aeneid* Book 3, but in the narrator's voice. The narrative then continues with a paraphrase of *Aeneid* Book 1, at the end of which Aeneas has arrived at Dido's court. His own account of the destruction of Troy, as in *Aeneid* Book 2, and his fifteen-line summary of his travels, told in *Aeneid* Book 3, follow. The new Irish introduction provides the narrative with historical contextualization and chronological sequentiality at the expense of consistency, because it does not replace Aeneas' own, and conflicting, report about his role in the fall of Troy at Dido's court in Book 2, which is retold at its original place in *Imtheachta Aeniasa* (*IA* 408–654). The Irish translator's acquaintance with the representation of Aeneas as traitor in Dares' *De Excidio Troiae* (and in *Togail Troí*) may have influenced and complicated his perception of Virgil's *pius* Aeneas. Dido's accusations that he is a liar receive greater emphasis in *Imtheachta Aeniasa* (see *IA* 835, 895–6, 910). On the other hand, medieval Irish authors and audiences would seem to have been less concerned than modern critics with the tensions arising from contradictory versions.[16]

Since our first and third excerpts have no parallel in Virgil's text, the discussion of the stylistic intentions of the Irish translator will proceed from our second extract.[17] A comparison with Virgil's corresponding passage (*Aeneid* 9.691–777) reveals instructive and far-reaching differences in presentation. Virgil's style has been said to aim for 'producing an emotional response, often one of pathos or sympathy' (O'Hara 1997: 253). Otis (1963: 88) has described it as 'empathetic-sympathetic': 'Virgil not only reads the minds of his characters; he constantly communicates to us his own reactions to them and to their behaviour'. He labels this a 'subjective' style, contrasting it with Homer's 'objective' one. *Imtheachta Aeniasa*'s style could also be characterized as objective, in which the author (to quote Otis on Homer's approach) 'is letting his characters speak and act for themselves' (Otis 1963: 62). The differences in rhetorical strategies between the Latin and the Irish passages are nicely encapsulated in their presentations of the death of Pandarus. Virgil gives a dramatic and emotive account in altogether seven lines of verse (*Aeneid* 9.749–55), whereas the Irish translator provides a swift, detached, and unemotional description: 'Turnus however deals him a stroke of his sword so that he split his head into two and he fell dead there' (*IA* 2306–7).[18] Other noteworthy features include the omission of Virgil's elaborate description of Bitias' death with its extended simile (*Aeneid* 9.710–16),[19] and the clarification of the sequence of events after Turnus' intervention. The Irish translator explains that the Rutulians did not follow Turnus into the Trojan camp 'because they did not know that he had gone from them into the midst of their enemies' (*IA* 2212–13), whereas Virgil, from a different, subjective perspective, blamed Pandarus for having overlooked Turnus' incursion (*Aeneid* 9.728–9). The Irish translator adds a pithy proverbial phrase to characterize the risk for Turnus' life, that, had not Juno intervened, it had been *turus gan tindtudh* 'a journey without return' for him (on this phrasing see Poppe 1995: 25).

The narrative in both our first and second excerpts proceeds swiftly, but it is not without conspicuous retarding ornamentation, which links it to the specific strand of medieval Irish literary style often called 'bombastic' or 'florid' (Ní Mhaonaigh 2006a: 41–2). The density of such ornamentation is significantly greater in the elaborate descriptions given in our third extract. Typical forms of ornamentation are figures of repetition of sound, sense, and structure. These may be phrases which are (near-)synonymous or belong to semantically related fields, and they often alliterate. Syntactic structures are also repeated in adjacent sentences. Turnus' intervention in battle, for example, is marked with three semantically similar noun phrases with parallel internal structures: *dos-fig a gal curud & a bruth miled & a nert niadh* (*IA* 2284–5) 'his hero's valour, his soldier's fury and his champion's strength seizes him' (expanding on Virgil's *immani concitus ira* 'impelled by a giant's fury', *Aeneid* 9.694). The concept of a warrior's fury is a heroic *topos*, a conventionalized and formulaic phrase in medieval Irish literature; the phrase is repeated, with the addition of another noun phrase, at *IA* 2145–6, and the concept reappears later in the excerpt with somewhat different wording: *tainic a bruth & a brigh & a morferg miled in churad* (*IA* 2312–13) 'his fury and his vigour and his great warrior's wrath came to the hero'. The collocation *bruth ocus brígh* 'fury and vigour', often in combination with further nouns, is frequently employed in *Imtheachta Aeniasa* (cf. e.g. *IA* 284, 1110, 1693–4, 1998, 2138–9, 2853). Its formulaic character is brought out by its expanded repetition in a longer heroic set piece (*IA* 2565–74) which describes Aeneas' fierce advance in battle in quest of Turnus (it has no immediate parallel in Virgil, beyond *ardens* 'fierce', *Aeneid* 10.514): *doerigh a bruth & a brig and, & a fherg & a gal curudh* (*IA* 2566) 'his fury and his vigour and his wrath and his hero's valour rose'.[20] Other formulaic phrases employed in the excerpts are the descriptive medieval Irish *topoi* of the triple-plaited woven mail armour with its helmet and of the sevenfold shield and the heroic *topos* of 'sole touching neck', discussed together with their possible Virgilian background below.

Small stretches of rhetorically elaborate and heightened language are used in *Imtheachta Aeniasa* in order to highlight significant narrative situations. In our second extract, such language is appropriately reserved first for Turnus' intervention in battle (*IA* 2284–5, quoted above), then for the moment when his sudden and irrational impulse not to open the gate of the Trojans' camp and allow his followers to come in, but to continue fighting on his own, prevents an eventual Rutulian victory.[21] In a single sentence (*IA* 2312–16), the Irish translator finds room for three pleonastic phrases – the *topos* of the warrior's fury quoted above, four alliterating adverbs, and a sequence of seven nouns realized as two doublets and a triplet[22] – as well as for the image of 'sole touching neck', a heroic *topos* to describe turmoil and slaughter in battle, which also occurs in a similar context in the third extract.[23] Miles (2011: 239–41) argues that this formulation originally arose in Irish from imitation of a Virgilian phrase in *Aeneid* 10.361 (*haeret pede pes densusque viro vir* 'foot cleaves to foot and man is pressed densely against man') and then acquired a literary life of its own. In *Imtheachta Aeniasa*, the phrase does not render its Virgilian original (a pleonastic doublet *co dur ⁊ co dichra* 'hard and fervently', *IA* 2527–8, is used instead); in the three instances in which it occurs in *Imtheachta Aeniasa*, it has no immediate Latin equivalent, and this supports Miles' contention that it had become part of the Irish stock of formulae for the description of battle scenes.

In our first excerpt, the stylistically elaborate passages are the descriptions, first, of the battle between Trojans and Greeks which comprises the emotional highlight of Nestor's speech, and second, of the sorrowful departure of Aeneas and his followers from Mount Ida, which expands the reference to Aeneas' weeping in *Aeneid* 3.10. Heightened language is functionally motivated.

Our third excerpt has no parallel in Virgil's *Aeneid* and is part of an extended rhetorical showpiece created by the Irish author, which relates the mustering by Aeneas and Turnus of their respective armies and the beginning of the battle between them. Its high density of figures of repetition determines its overall aesthetic effect. Other such elaborate showpieces in *Imtheachta Aeniasa*, significantly also without analogues in Virgil, are the mustering of Evander's hosts (*IA* 1904–18), the ekphrases of Pallas and of Nisus and Euryalus (*IA* 1921–37, 2060–4), a description of battle between the Trojans and the Rutulians (*IA* 2197–212), and the council of the Etruscans, with Tarchon's speech, and the departure of their host (*IA* 2373–408).

Besides the topos of 'sole touching neck', which characterizes the results of Aeneas' onslaught, another descriptive formula with Virgilian associations in the third extract is the 'triple-plaited woven mail coat' (*luirech trebraid tredhualach*, *IA* 2497). This is ultimately related to the *Aeneid*'s *auro trilix lorica* 'cuirass triple-meshed in gold' (5.259–60), translated as *luirigh tredhualaigh* (*IA* 1030, acc.sg.), but, as convincingly argued by Miles (2011: 202), its entry into the Irish narrative repertoire predates *Imtheachta Aeniasa*. Its use independently of the *Aeneid* in *Imtheachta Aeniasa*, as in the third extract (and in six other instances), shows that it too has become a topos.[24] The collocation *badb derg dasachtach* (*IA* 2480) finally may conjure up further classical associations. *Badb* is an Irish word for a crow and also for a female figure of war, and in combination with the adjectives *derg* 'red' and *dasachtach* 'mad, violent' it may here denote a Fury, or more generally a demonic phantom associated with war.[25]

The stylistic differences between the second and third extracts – both battle scenes, the first sparingly, the second densely ornamented – can be ascribed to different narrative strategies. The third excerpt is part of an elaborate showpiece reporting the initial stages of an important battle. The second extract, on the other hand, is a passage taken from a longer description of a battle which itself does not require continual narrative highlighting; more elaborate stylistic ornamentation is, as is functionally appropriate, reserved for the beginning and for the sentence which describes a decisive moment in the battle.

The creative translator of *Imtheachta Aeniasa* retains Virgil's plot, but changes the mode of presentation overall, from Virgil's 'empathetic-sympathetic', subjective style to a predominantly detached report, which, however, does not eschew aesthetic effects. He employs various figures of repetition for small-scale narrative highlighting and inserts some extended and stylistically highly elaborate showpieces of his own creation. This makes *Imtheachta Aeniasa* less Virgilian than the *Aeneid* and less classicizing than the classicizing prose of *Togail Troí* and those parts of *Táin Bó Cúailnge* in which Miles has identified reflexes of a medieval programme of Irish classicism (see Miles 2011: 99, 143–4). Even though the specific contexts for the translators' attitudes and strategies remain opaque to modern readers, *Imtheachta Aeniasa* and the corpus of the antiquity-sagas nevertheless provide an instructive, and fascinating, window on the creativity of medieval Irish *literati*.[26]

Notes

1 I wish to thank the Council of the Irish Texts Society for permission to use excerpts from Calder's edition.

2 For their helpful advice on this essay and the translation of the excerpts from *Imtheachta Aeniasa* I wish to thank Michael Clarke, Uáitéar Mac Gerailt, Maio Nagashima and Ralph O'Connor.

3 One sentence omitted whose meaning is not clear.

4 This refers to the pact arranged in Dares Phrygius, *De Excidio Troiae Historia* 'History of the Destruction of Troy', Ch. 40.

5 These are Laomedon's three sons in Dares Phrygius, Ch. 3.

6 Compare *Aeneid* 7.364, *Ledaeam… Helenam*, and *IA* 1649, *Eleand Legata ingen Tinair*, and see also Ch. 19 in this volume, pp. 244, 245.

7 Note the retention of the Latin case forms here from the accusatives *Meropem, Erymanta, Bitian* (*Aeneid* 9.702–3).

8 For the 'paraphrastic' approach of the Irish translator, compare Slotkin 1978–9: 444–7.

9 For a characterization of modern 'creative translators', see Bantinaki 2020: 315: they 'can be seen to freely appropriate existing literary works to create new literary works, ignoring, as it were, the commitment to produce a constrained representation of the original'. For the concept of 'constrained representation' in translation, see Bantinaki 2020: 312. I wish to thank Ralph O'Connor for pointing me to Bantinaki's discussion.

10 In a few instances, small-scale complementary information is derived from commentaries on the *Aeneid*, see Kobus 1995: 79–80.

11 The concept of *translatio imperii* echoed here is also present in the extended genealogy of Aeneas' son Ascanius, inserted by the Irish author at *IA* 2365–6, where

it is noted that 'he was the origin of the sovereignty and the overlordship of the world, because from him sprang the emperors of the word'.

12 On the historical focus specifically of the Book of Ballymote as the framework of its reception of *Imtheachta Aeniasa*, see Ní Mhaonaigh 2018, 2022. For the wider context, see O'Connor's introduction to this volume.

13 I wish to thank Uáitéar Mac Gerailt for his thoughts on the date of the text; previously (Mac Gearailt 2018: 137) he had opted for an earlier date in the mid- to late-twelfth century.

14 For the wider context of the tradition that considers Antenor and Aeneas to have been traitors, see Clark 2020: 65–76.

15 Compare, for example, *Togail Troí* in the Book of Ballymote: *O tainic, tra, in raind sin ro fiarfaid Agmemnon duna Grecaib, in comaillfidis a mbreithir risin aes mbraith. Ba h-í a comairli, firindi du comallad friu* (Breathnach 1952: 170–1) 'When the division of the plunder was finished, Agamemnon asked the Greeks whether they would fulfil their promise to the traitors. It was their counsel to observe righteousness to them'.

16 Harris (1998: 105) argues that the accusation of treason can be satisfactorily explained with reference to Aeneas' own account given at Dido's court and that his treason consists in having led his own family and followers to safety and thus having deserted Troy and its king. This suggestion underestimates the clear affiliations of the introduction to Dares (for instance, the number of Aeneas' ships is derived from *De Excidio Troiae*, which gives it as twenty-two), as well as the prominence of *Togail Troí* in medieval Irish textual culture.

17 See further Poppe 2004a, 2014b.

18 See also LeBlanc (2019: 207) on the presentation of Nisus avenging Euryalus: 'The Irish text shifts focus to Nisus's martial ability, away from Virgil's subjectivity'.

19 In his adaptation of Book 3, the Irish translator substituted stylistically refined descriptions for Virgil's three extended similes, see Poppe 2004a: 79–87, also Poppe 2014b: 34. The approach of the Irish translator of *In Cath Catharda* 'The Civil War', who often reproduces Lucan's similes, is therefore strikingly different, on which see Miles 2011: 58 and Nagashima in Ch. 15 in this volume, with further references. The foxglove simile discussed by Nagashima occurs in *Imtheachta Aeniasa* (1924–34) as part of an extended description of Pallas, which has no analogue in Virgil, but interestingly it does not occur in the Irish version of the relevant simile used at *Aeneid* 12.67–8, compare *IA* 2925–7.

20 Compare, in the same passage, *Ba ferg nathrach ferg Ænias in tan sin. Ba bruth miled ⁊ ba luth leomain, ba gal curudh . . . lais* (*IA* 2567–9, 'The wrath of a serpent was the wrath of Aeneas at that time. His was a soldier's fury and a lion's power, a hero's valour . . .') with *co mbruth miled, co feirg leoman, co neimh nathrach* ('with a soldier's heat, a lion's rage and a serpent's venom') in the excerpt from the Middle Irish *Thebaid* (Ch. 11 in this volume).

21 Compare Virgil's *Aeneid* 9.757–61 and the Irish narrator's comments at *IA* 2309–12.

22 The doublet *leod & leadrad* is found again as *ica leodh & ica letrad* in our third
    extract, as well as in two other places in *Imtheachta Aeniasa* (*IA* 546, 2229).

23 For some examples from other texts, see Poppe 1995: 26 and LeBlanc 2019: 212–13.

24 *Lúirech thredúalach*, with or without *trebraid*, also occurs in other Irish texts as a part
    of a hero's equipment, including *Togail Troí*. For examples and discussion, see Poppe
    2004b, 2023. It is also found in the excerpt from *Don Tres Troí* in this volume
    (Ch. 10, p.132) in the form *luireacha treabraid tredhualacha*, together with sevenfold
    shields, possibly another descriptive topos.

25 Compare Borsje 1999: 244–8, Clarke 2014b: 114–17 and, for the *badb* in the Middle
    Irish *Thebaid*, Briggs 2018: 168.

26 It is worth recalling here Windisch's dictum in his note to Stokes' posthumously
    published edition of *In Cath Catharda* 'The Civil War', 'dass sich die Eigenart des
    irischen Geistes nirgends deutlicher hervorhebt, als in der irischen Bearbeitung
    eines fremden Stoffes' (Stokes 1909: IX, 'that the character of the Irish mind is
    nowhere more evident than in the Irish treatment of foreign matter'). Windisch's
    intuition productively links to recent insights on characteristics of medieval
    strategies of translating, as reflected, for example, in Bampi's (2022: 31–2) comments:
    'the notion of translation in the Middle Ages allowed various forms of reshaping and
    rewriting of the source text according to the norms that were dominant in the target
    culture. If translation can be defined, on a general note, as a negotiation involving
    two cultures rather than merely two languages, it may quite often be described as a
    manipulation, whereby both the wording and the meaning of the source text may
    undergo such major changes that the final result could be defined as an outright
    rewrite. What drives the manipulative process of the amendments of the source text
    is generally to be found in the target system.'

14

In Cath Catharda 'The Civil War': The Prologue

Brigid Ehrmantraut

The text is reproduced from Stokes 1909: 1–11, lines 1–102. The translation is revised by the author from Stokes' facing translation.[1]

Text: The pseudohistorical prologue to *In Cath Catharda*

Do Chogadh Síuialta na Romhanach, dia ngoireid Gaoidheil in Cath Cathardha.

1. Sé h-istudha flatha ro gabh*us*tar flaith*ius* ⁊ forlamh*us* ar crichaibh ⁊ ar cennadh[ch]aibh na c*r*uinne domhanta a llos neirt ⁊ niachais isin aimsir anall .i. flaith*ius* alaind na n-Assardha, am*ail* atb*er*t in fili:

Righ na n-Assardha ria cach,
do ghabh in flaith*ius* fírgnath.
fer co cas cluimh, co ceill n-gle,
Assur m*ac* Seimh m*aic* Noé.

2. O*cus* flaith*ius* mor-uasal na Med. *Ocus* flaith*ius* primhda na P*er*s. Ocus fla*ithius* cruthglan na Callacda. Ocus fla*ithius* gargmor na n-Grécc. O*cus* in senadh ríghdha Rómhánach in sesedh fl*aithius*.

3. Tos*ach* ⁊ tinnscedal na h-airdrighi n-Assardha cebé ní is as gabhar, ó Nín m*ac* Béil m*aic* Ploisc do c*l*annaibh Sem m*aic* Noé m*aic* Lámhiach. IS leis sen ro c*um*daighedh in primhcathair airde*r*c .i. Babilóin. Adhbhul méd na ca*th*rach sin, cethar-ochair a cuma, c*ét* n-dor*us* n-umaidhi f*u*irre. LX m*íle* cémenn ina timthacmang. L cubat a tighe a múir. CC cubhat ina h-airdi. Da line lanmora do tighibh ar mullach a múir: imriadhaitis XX cetherriadh it*er* na da sreth sin re tighe in múir fós. IStudh flatha ⁊ indeoin f*or*ais ⁊ ár*us* righ Nin m*aic* Béil ⁊ righ na n-Asardha uili in cathair sin.

4. Nín m*ac* Beil c*étrí* na n-Assardha ⁊ Tonus a rig dédhenach. Sé XX ⁊ c*ét* ⁊ m*íle* fad a flaithiusa.

5. IX mbli*adn*a cóicat f*or* dibh cétaibh fad flaithisa na Med. Ocht*ur* ro gabh ríghi dibh. Arbait a c*étrí* ⁊ Astighages a rí dédhenach.

6. Cir mac Dair, c*étrí* Pers didu, mac sen in*gine* do Astighages. is é ro athrígh athair a m*áthar*. is leis ro toghladh in Babiloin, ⁊ ro h-orta a rí Ballastair, ⁊ ro tuaslaic do mac[aib] Isr*ael* asin daire LXX i m-Babiloin, corus-léicc uadh do Ier*us*alem *co* n-adhmib tempail Solman léo .i. V m*ili* lest*ur* d'ór ⁊ ceit*hri* c*ét* lestur n-airgit.

Translation

Concerning the Civil War of the Romans, which the Gaels call *In Cath Catharda* ['The Civil War']:

1. Six abodes of rule took possession of sovereignty and supremacy over the territories and the lands of the earthly globe in consequence of strength and valour in former times, as follows: The beautiful empire of the Assyrians, as the poet said:

> The king of the Assyrians before everyone,
> took the true, well-known sovereignty;
> a man with curly hair, with clear sense,
> Assur son of Shem, son of Noah. –

2. – and the very noble empire of the Medes; and the pre-eminent empire of the Persians; and the brightly-formed empire of the Chaldeans; and the formidable empire of the Greeks; and the sixth empire was the royal senate of the Romans.

3. The start and beginning of the high-kingship of the Assyrians, however, was initiated by Ninus, son of Belus, son of Plosc, of the descendants of Shem, son of Noah, son of Lamech. The famous, foremost city, Babylon, was built by him. That city's size was great, its shape had four edges, and a hundred bronze doors were in it. It was sixty thousand paces in circumference. Its walls were fifty cubits thick and two hundred cubits high. There were two full lines of houses upon the top of the wall; they also used to drive twenty four-horsed chariots between those two rows because of the thickness of the wall. That city was a seat of rule and an anvil of knowledge and the residence of King Ninus, son of Belus, and the king of all the Assyrians.

4. Ninus son of Belus was the first king of the Assyrians, and Tonus was their last king.[2] The duration of their empire was 1220 years.

5. The duration of the empire of the Medes was 259 years. Eight men of them took kingship. Arbaces was their first king and Astyages was their last king.

6. Moreover, Cyrus son of Darius, the first king of the Persians, was the son of Astyages' daughter. It was he who deposed his mother's father. Babylon was destroyed by him, and its king, Belshazzar, was killed, and he freed the Children of Israel from the captivity of seventy years in Babylon, and he allowed them to go to Jerusalem with the implements of Solomon's Temple, that is, 5,000 vessels of gold and 400 vessels of silver.

7. Darius in rí dedhenach o Persaibh, dá rí décc a righi díbh. CC. XXX bli*adn*a fot a flatha.

8. *Cé*trí gasraidhe Grécc *immorro* Ala*x*ander m*a*c Pilip, ardrí in domhain uili o Espain an*í*ar co hInnia sair, ⁊ o Etheoip andes co sleibhtibh Rifi fotuaidh. Is leisin Ala*x*ander sin ro fáidhedh in cobhlach f*or* in muir tentidhi do ḟis in mesraighthi deis*c*ertaigh, uair nír' folartnaigh leis fis in mesraighthi tuais*c*ertaigh namá. hI cind a dá bli*adan* decc ro triall Ala*x*ander insaighidh. Da bli*a*dain XXX a oes intan ros-marbh neim isin Babiloin. Pilip *immorro* rí dédhenach na n-Grecc.

9. Tinnscedal in ríghfl*aithiu*sa Romhanta *immorro* ba saine modh leis ⁊ lasna h-ardfl*aithiu*saibh romhaind, uair ni o[c] ardrighaibh tarrasair f*or*lamh*us* na Romha it*er*. Ro ordaighset airigh in t-senaidh ⁊ lu*cht* cemenn ⁊ gradh n-onorach acco do tobhach a císsa doibh a cinedhach*aib* coimighthibh ⁊ do indsaighi f*or* finibh fodhaltaibh in domain do ḟollamhnug*ud* ⁊ do stíuradh in righrechta gebe tan budh adhlaic.

10. Decán iar*um* slonnudh ḟir in ceime ba h-isle dona cemendaibh sin. Taísech *dech*nebhair eisséin; f*er* sein nó díghladh gach gaid ⁊ gach slad ⁊ gach sarug*ud* dognithi isin cathair ar medhón.

11. Cenntuir uasin décán, taísech *céit* an fer sin.

12. Trebhunn uasin cenntúir, taisech dá chét *no* tri chét eisséin.

13. Vicair uasin trebhunn, fer sin no *con*gbadh feidhm in comit intan téighedh in comit do agallaim in rígh.

14. Comit uasin uicair, taísech aencat*h*rach eisséin.

15. Taíssech uasin comit, da cathraig déc fáe sen.

16. Patric uasin taissech, f*er* le*th*lamha rígh nó impir eisséin,⁊ bá h-é a modh, bretha ⁊ uirghill do dhenam tar éis in airdrigh intan ba h-emhilt in rí féin.

17. Rí uasin patric, tri ciniudha a ferann.

18. Imp*er* uasin ríg, *acht* cena ní bíth in céim sin ic Rómánachaibh *nocor'* gabh Iúil Césair a los a lámha mar indeósus in scél inar ṅ-diaidh. In t-imper *immorro*, ardrí in domain eisséin uas chách ⁊ ní bid nech úasa.

7. Darius was the last king of the Persians. Twelve kings of them were in kingship. The duration of their empire was 230 years.

8. The first king of the warriors of Greece, moreover, was Alexander son of Philip, high-king of the whole world from Spain in the west to India in the east, and from Ethiopia in the south to the Riphean mountains in the north. It was by that Alexander that the fleet was sent upon the torrid sea to discover the southern temperate zone; for he did not think it sufficient to know only the northern temperate zone. At the end of his twelfth year Alexander began his endeavours at conquest. He was thirty-two years old when poison killed him in Babylon. Philip, moreover, was the last king of the Greeks.

9. The beginning of the royal Roman empire, however, had a different manner from those of the aforementioned high empires; for the supremacy of Rome did not reside with high-kings at all. The leaders of the senate along with the people of rank and honourable degrees gave orders to levy their tribute for them from foreign peoples, and to invade the divided nations of the world, to govern and direct the royal rule whenever it was needful.

10. At that time *Decanus* was the title of the lowest of those ranks. A *Decanus* was a commander of ten men. He was the man who used to punish every theft and robbery and outrage that was committed in the city.

11. *Centurio* was above the *Decanus*, that man was the leader of a hundred.

12. *Tribunus* was above the *Centurio*, he was the leader of 200 or 300.

13. *Vicarius* was above the *Tribunus*. That man used to assume the function of the *Comes* when the *Comes* would go to speak with the king.

14. *Comes* was above the *Vicarius*, he was the leader of a single city.

15. *Tóisech* ('leader') was above the *Comes*; there were twelve cities under him.

16. *Patricius* was above the *Tóisech*; he was the right-hand man of a king or emperor. His work was to make judgments and decrees in place of the high-king when the king himself was weary.

17. *King* was above the *Patricius*; his territory comprised three peoples.

18. *Emperor* was above the *King*, but the Romans did not have that rank until Julius Caesar took it by means of his hand, as the tale will tell subsequently. The *Emperor*, moreover, was high-king of the world above everyone, and there was no one superior to him.

19. Bá dá gradh *immorro*, ceim *Con*sail ⁊ ceim Dictatóir. IN *consul immorro* aenbli*a*dain dó ina céim ⁊ a atharr*ach* i f*or*cind na bli*adn*a arna gabhadh dium*us* na méd menman é ar tenne a neirt ⁊ ar airdi a graidh. Da tecmadh comadh soirbh dó in bli*a*dain sin ina *con*sul*ach*t no ordnighthe doridhisi isin ceim *cét*na dor*éir* in t-senaidh ⁊ airicc in popoil. Unónius Brutus is é *cét*na ro gabh in ceim sin la Romhanchu.

20. IN Dictatóir *immorro*, cíamadh maith saich dogníedh, ní h-athraighthe asa céim co cenn V m-bliadan, ⁊ dá madh buidhech cách de intan sin ni h-at*h*raigthe it*er*. G*ur*ub eisséin céim is cadchasaighi bói leó-son cin co tarr*us*tair n*er*t imp*ir* f*or*ro.

21. Ro scail tr*a* ⁊ ro lethnaigh in ríghe Rom*án*ta fó ceit*h*ri h-airdibh in domain amhl*aid* sin, cor' f*á*s dium*us* ⁊ innócbáil inntibh siun féin de sin, cor' ergedar debtha d*er*mara ⁊ cocadh cathordha it*er* ar*a*ill d'áes na cemenn sin isna cenna[d]ch*aib* a m-bidis a sechnoin in domain imuich ⁊ araill isin Roim fein ar medhón ar méd a n-diumais ⁊ a llos in neirt romoir ro-adhbhail ro gabhsat f*or* ciniudhaibh ⁊ f*or* cinélaibh na cruinne.

22. Tarr*us*tar ríghfl*aith*is na Romhán fri ré trí m-bl*ia*dan *cóec*at f*or* díbh *cét*aibh fon inn*us* sin gen imp*er* gen aenrígh f*or*ro, *acht* lu*ch*t na cemenn n-exam*ail* sin ic stiur*ad* a fl*aith*isa occo. *co n*-dernadh leo-san fecht n-aen ann tri cindiudh in t-senaidh ⁊ tria comairle in popoil, uair issí in dictatoire*cht* éncéim ba h-uaisle ⁊ ba h-onóraige búi occo.

23. Tríar comard do h-ordnedh léo intan sin, ⁊ in doman uile do roind et*ur*ru da tabairt ar áis *nó* ar éccin fó cís ⁊ fó cain na Romh*á*nach. *Ocus* is aire ro ordaighset triar isin céim sin, ar dáigh cé bé dibh no ardadh a n-aig*id* in t-ṡenaidh co m-beith in tres fer ic sídh et*ar*ru ⁊ ardaigh na com-aentaighidís a tríur im ardadh in agidh na h-athardha, uair ní gnáth comann comáentadhach la triur it*er*.

19. There were two more grades: the rank of *Consul* and the rank of *Dictator*. The *Consul* held his position for a year, and at the end of the year he was replaced lest he should become proud or arrogant from the strength of his power and the elevation of his rank. If it happened that he was successful that year as Consul, he was reappointed to the same rank by the will of the senate and the decision of the people. Junius Brutus was the first among the Romans to have that rank.

20. The *Dictator*, however, whether he did well or ill, was not removed from his rank until the end of five years. If everyone was thankful for him then, he was not replaced at all. Thus that rank was the most esteemed that they had until the power of an emperor overtook them.

21. Thus the Roman realm extended and spread out then to the four quarters of the world, so that pride and arrogance grew among them on account of it, and vast quarrels and civil war arose among some of those nobles in the provinces in which they dwelt throughout the world outside [of Rome], and among others inside Rome itself, because of the greatness of their pride, and because of the exceedingly great power which they had acquired over the nations and peoples of the globe.

22. For the space of 253 years the royal rule of the Romans remained that way, without an emperor, without a single king over them, but people of various ranks directed their government. Until at one time [a Dictator] was made by them by the decision of the senate and by the advice of the people, for the dictatorship is the one rank they had that is highest and most honourable.

23. Three people of equal rank were then appointed by them, and the whole world was divided among them to be put under the tax and tribute of the Romans, willingly or by force. And this is why they appointed three to that rank, so that if two rose up against the senate, the third man would keep peace between them, so that the three of them would not agree in rising up against the state, for any agreement between three people is rare.

Essay: Lucan transformed in a Christian world

In Cath Catharda adapts Lucan's epic poem *De Bello Civili* 'On the Civil War' (commonly also called *Pharsalia*), which narrates the events of the Roman Civil War between Caesar and Pompey in 49–48 BCE. It is one of the three longest works of medieval Irish prose, together with *Táin Bó Cúailgne* 'The Cattle-Raid of Cooley' and *Acallam na Senórach* 'The Colloquy of the Ancients'. At over 6,000 lines, it is commensurate in length with Lucan's poem, although the Irish text only adapts the first seven books of Lucan, and ends with an account of the climactic Battle of Pharsalus that seems to have been freely composed for the purpose.

In Cath Catharda survives in nine manuscripts, only one of which is complete, as well as a series of glossed extracts in Dublin, TCD MS 1337 (formerly H.3.18). Whitley Stokes edited and translated the text towards the end of his life, basing his edition on four manuscript witnesses (Stokes 1909). It was published posthumously in a condition that was likely not yet ready for publication, and a new edition is needed. Linguistically, the text itself probably dates from the late twelfth or early thirteenth century. The death of the poet Flann Mainistrech in 1056 provides the earliest potential *terminus post quem* (as he is quoted in the prologue), although Erich Poppe has identified the late twelfth-century Arnulf of Orléans as a source for some of the scholia on Lucan incorporated into *In Cath Catharda*, requiring a later *terminus post quem*, at least for the inclusion of this material.[3] The popularity of *In Cath Catharda* continued into subsequent centuries, and it was drawn on in the fourteenth century by the author of *Caithréim Thoirdhealbhaigh* 'The Triumphs of Turlough', which recounts a series of recent wars between the O'Brien dynasty and the Anglo-Norman family of de Clare (O'Grady 1929). Compared to many other medieval Irish adaptations of classical texts, the author or authors of *In Cath Catharda* took a relatively conservative approach to rendering the source material into Irish, and retained much of Lucan's imagery and phrasing. Those changes they did make are often stylistic, including Middle Irish literary features or explanatory digressions, which incorporate background material from scholia and commentaries, as discussed in Chs 15 and 16.

A major departure made from Lucan's text by the Irish author(s) is the addition of a pseudohistorical prologue, which replaces Lucan's opening praise of Nero. The first section of this prologue here is quoted here. The prologue situates the Roman senate as the sixth *flaithius* (ruling entity) of the world; it includes an explanation of various Roman political and military offices, a description of the death of Crassus, probably drawn from Florus, *Epitome of Roman History*, I.46 (Forster 1984: 208–14), and a summary of Caesar's invasion of Britain, probably drawn from Bede's *Ecclesiastical History* I.2 (Colgrave and Mynors 1969: 20–3), or its Irish translation (Stokes 1909: vi; O'Hogan 2014: 26–7). The prologue also quotes from Flann Mainistrech's *Poems on World-Kingship* in the stanza included in the passage given here (for more detail on these poems, with a focus on the Romans, see Ch. 5).

However, *In Cath Catharda*'s specific system of six world empires, encompassing the Assyrians, Medes, Persians, Chaldeans, Greeks, and the Roman senate, is unique to the present text. The prologue synthesizes elements of Augustine's series of six ages of the world represented elsewhere in medieval Irish literature (e.g. *Sex Aetates Mundi* 'The Six Ages of the World', Ó Cróinín 1983), with Eusebius-Jerome's synchronistic view of history from the *Chronicle*, and Orosius' succession of world empires from his *Histories against the Pagans*.[4]

Orosius himself models his four-empire scheme on that ultimately rooted in the Book of Daniel, with its twin prophecies, first of the statue made of contrasting substances – gold, silver, bronze, iron, and iron mixed with clay – and then of four great beasts emerging from the sea (Daniel 2:31–40, 7:17; Glorie 1964: 787, 838–48). Daniel's prophecies were traditionally read by Christian commentators as referring to a sequence of four world empires, culminating in the empire of the Romans. Jerome's interpretation was the most influential of all, interpreting Daniel 2.40 as follows:

Regnum autem quartum, quod perspicue pertinet ad Romanos, ferrum est quod comminuit et domat omnia. Sed pedes eius et digiti ex parte ferrei, et ex parte sunt fictiles, quod hoc tempore manifestissime comprobatur. Sicut enim in principio nihil Romano imperio fortius et durius fuit, ita in fine rerum nihil imbecillius: quando et in bellis civilibus, et adversum diversas nationes, aliarum gentium barbararum indigemus auxilio.

Glorie 1964: 794–5.

'Indeed the fourth empire, which clearly pertains to the Romans, is iron, which crumbles and overcomes all. But its feet and toes are part iron and part clay, which is most manifestly demonstrated at this time. For just as there was in the beginning nothing stronger or harder than the Roman empire, accordingly in these last days there is nothing weaker, since we need the help of various barbarian tribes both in our civil wars and against foreign nations'.

tr. Ehrmantraut.

For a medieval reader or adaptor of Lucan well-versed in Jerome, the Roman poet's *Bellum Civile* 'Civil War' is very likely to have been read in the light of the Church Father's comments about *bella civilia* 'civil wars'.

The conflict of *In Cath Catharda* is thus situated within a chronology of salvation history stretching from Creation to the Eschaton. In contrast to Orosius and Jerome, however, in our text the Roman *senate*, rather than empire, constitutes the last *flaithius*.[5] This gives it a new eschatological spin: as the final *flaithius* of the world, the Roman senate occupies the age immediately preceding Judgment Day. The erosion of the independent power of the Roman senate under the emperors who come to power in the aftermath of the Battle of Pharsalus may thus be read as the decline of the sixth age of the world in the period leading up to the Eschaton. At the same time, the rise of Roman rule corresponds to the rise of Christianity, especially within the medieval historiographical structure of *translatio imperii*, or the translation of power from the ancient world to successive polities.

This eschatological perspective and concern for the place of the Roman Civil War in world history are echoed elsewhere in *In Cath Catharda*. The text has a tendency to increase the role and agency of infernal beings such as the necromancer Erichtho. It also frequently compares the events of the Battle of Pharsalus to biblical catastrophes such as the Flood and Judgment Day (see further Ehrmantraut forthcoming, Chs 4 and 5). The significance of the Battle itself is magnified by virtue of the fact that it forms the climax of the work, since *In Cath Catharda* does not adapt the final three books of Lucan's text. *In Cath Catharda* relies on the perspective of its Christian audience, living in the era after the events Lucan portrays, as well as after the coming of Christ and the Fall of Rome, to frame the central conflict as a key turning point in salvation history as the pagan world of old is washed away in the blood of Pharsalus to make way for the Christian age to come. While *In Cath Catharda* is usually comparatively faithful to Lucan's original narrative, structure, and often (if not always) phrasing, the addition of the pseudohistorical prologue reframes Lucan's epic entirely. The Battle of Pharsalus is caught in the space between the final world *flaithius* embodied by the destruction of the Roman senate and the future *flaithius* represented by the Kingdom of Heaven.[6] The interest demonstrated by the authors of the prologue in chronology and synchronism is shared with many other texts examined in this volume (see especially Chs 3, 4, 5, 17), reminding us that figures and events from Mediterranean antiquity were as much a part of the larger, salvation-oriented narrative of world history as those in biblical or indeed in Irish history.

Notes

1   I am grateful to the Harding Distinguished Scholars Programme for supporting this research, and to Máire Ní Mhaonaigh, Michael Clarke, Erich Poppe, Isabelle Torrance, Maio Nagashima, and John Carey for their suggestions and editorial observations; any errors or infelicities remain my own.

2   Tonus here is for *Thonos Concoleros*, given by Eusebius-Jerome as an equivalent for the name Sardanapalus.

3   O'Hogan 2014: 24; cf. Stokes 1909: 3–8; Poppe 2015: 431–40. See also Sommerfelt 1915–23.

4   See Clarke and Ní Mhaonaigh 2020 for contextualization of the six ages of the world in medieval Ireland.

5   There is some discrepancy as to how many world empires there are in different manuscripts of *In Cath Catharda* itself. Dublin, TCD MS 1298 and Dublin, RIA MS D.iv.2 list six (although D.iv.2 specifies the Roman senate as *in ceathramadh* 'the fourth' despite it being listed sixth), and Dublin, UCD Franciscan MS A17 lists four. Nonetheless, the Roman senate is the final *flaithius* in all manuscripts.

6   Indeed, the term *flaithius* is often applied to the Kingdom of Heaven. For attestations, see *eDIL* s.v. *flaithius*.

15

In Cath Catharda 'The Civil War': Literary Techniques

Maio Nagashima

The texts are based on Stokes 1909 with revisions as noted at the head of each. Translations from the Irish text are by the author.[1]

Text extracts

Learned imitation of a simile

The text is revised from Stokes 1909: 44, lines 567–70, in light of the author's transcription from Dublin, Royal Irish Academy, MS D.iv.2, fol. 5vb22–31

Ro gab grém trā in gressacht-laīdiudh sin dobert Curiō fri Cesair; air amail arduighter aicneadh ⁊ mēduigter menma ind eich Ēlīussecda ina coimling tre nūall ⁊ tre gāirib in lochta bīs uimi do gach leith, ce beith ic brisiudh a uchtcrand remi a saint in retha, is amlaid sin ro mēdaiged saint ⁊ āilgus in catha i cridhi Cesair tre nertad intī Curió fair, gurbo mían ⁊ gurbo laind leis fēin rēim in catha do tabairt.

The Latin source: Lucan, *Civil War* 1.291–5

> sic postquam fatus, et ipsi
> in bellum prono tantum tamen addidit irae
> accentique ducem, quantum clamore iuvatur
> Eleus sonipes, quamvis iam carcere clauso
> inmineat foribus pronusque repagula laxet.

The saga and its subdivisions

The text is from Stokes 1909: 322, lines 4304–12, with minor changes.

Conidh remscél do remscélaib Catha Móir na Tesāili conicci sin. Echtra Poimp Sext, ⁊ Taircetla Ericto Tesālta, ⁊ Fāistine inn Arrachta Ifernaidhe ainm in scéoil sin. IS é sin dano reimscél dēidinach Catha na Tesáili. Conidh comāirem .x.u. remscél conicci sin. Scéla immorro ⁊ turtechta ⁊ eitirdeilighthi in catha móir fēin, ⁊ tinnriumu na laechraide i(n) n-ellach inn imairicc mōir i m-muigh na Tesāili fēin, is īat atfīadur sīsana fodhesta. Cath Mōr Muighe na Tesāili innso.

From the arming scene of Pompey

The text is from Stokes 1909: 350, 352, lines 4703–12, 4733–9, with minor changes.

§1 Ro gabh a inncomarta imperechta[2] .i. a minn ríg, ūasa sin uili imma cenn. Minn ōir buide eisside, ⁊ bil-cimsu ōir deirg fris co sreith cristail ⁊ gem cōem

Translations

Learned imitation of a simile

That urgent incitement which Curio had imposed upon Caesar took effect; for just as the spirit and mind of the Elean horse in its race are raised and heightened through the clamour and shouts of those who are around him on every side, although he is already breaking the breast-high starting-barrier[3] in his eagerness to run, so the eagerness and desire for war was heightened in Caesar's heart through the encouragement which that man Curio had given to him so that he himself became eager and desirous to undertake battle.

The Latin source: Lucan, *Civil War* 1.291–5 (Duff 1928: 24–5)

Eager for war as Caesar was already, these words of Curio increased his rage and fired his ardour none the less; so the race-horse at Olympia is encouraged by the shouting, although he is already pressing against the gates of the closed barrier and seeking to loosen the bolts with his forehead.

The saga and its subdivisions

Thus far, one of the preliminary tales of 'the Great Battle of Thessaly'. 'The Adventure of Sextus Pompeius' and 'the Prophecies of Thessalian Erichtho' and 'the Augury of the Infernal Spectre' is the name of that story. That, then, is the last preliminary tale of 'the Battle of Thessaly' so that fifteen is the number of the preliminary tales thus far. The stories and descriptions and divisions of the great battle itself, and the accounts of the warriors engaging in the great conflict on the plain of Thessaly itself, these are what are related from here onwards below. 'The Great Battle of the Plain of Thessaly' follows.

From the arming scene of Pompey

§1 He [sc. Pompey] raised his imperial insignia, that is, his royal diadem, above all those things around his head [sc. hood, helmet and nosepiece]. It was a

carrmoccail ina mórtimcill ann. Coimhrinnadh comcoitcenn do dhelb*aib* ēn ⁊
ethaiti ⁊ anmann n-anaichentae n-ingantach fair ōsin amach, *co* n-dib
benncob*r*aib blāthsnaidthibh do leccaib tog*aid*ib tīre na hInnia airt*her*aige ūasu
*co n*deilb uvuill Affracda, *con*a cairchi cīuil ann for inn cacha benncobair dib,
co mba binnith*er* tēta m*en*dcrot binnḟoghroghudh na n-ubullcairchi-sin ic a
foglūas*acht* la cach cēim no cinged int airdrī fēin ⁊ la hardlūth a eich.

§2 Tucc*adh* cuicci īarsin each midhach m*er*dāna mōraicc*intech*, lonn lūath
lūthm*ur* lēimn*ech* leab*ar*mongach, tenn, tailc taīblebar torannclesach, airdcond
allata et*er*būasach u*cht*letan, gobcāel cosremhar, bolccsrōin baisletain bolccsūil*ech*,
*con*a cetair crūa īarnaide foī, *con*a srīanglom*ur* airg*did*e f*r*iss, *con*a suidedīllait
ōrdha f*or*a muin. Ro cing Poimp i ndor*us* a pupaill f*or* in each-sin d'ord*ug*hadh a
slōgh *ocus* do córug*ud* a cath.

Pompey's army advances into battle

The text is from Stokes 1909: 368, 370, lines 4972–5004, with minor changes.

A mbat*ar* ann ic f*or*csi in maigi cētna co facat*ar da* saig*id* in lebarbrōin lānmōir
lethanfota d'óc*caib* fon armgaisg*edh ocus* a n-ucht uili friu i fairsingi ach*aid*, *ocus*
a ndlūs fidb*aidh*e, *ocus* a mēt cat*h*rach no caistēoil .i. an sen*adh* rīghdha
Rōmānach arna n-ordug*ud* ⁊ arna cōrug*ud* .i. na ho*cht* catha *ocus* na ceit*h*ri
*fich*it cath do curad*aib*h cengailte *ocus* na dā .xx. mīle traigtech 'na trī lorg*aib*h,
d*r*uim ar d*r*uim, co mberadh g*ach* lorg fri araile dib ina mbūaili bodba *ocus* ina
crō catha ⁊ ina n-innellaigh, *con*a tuighi do clethcoillt*ibh* āigh, *ocus* d'fidb*ad*aib
neime, ⁊ do sleg*aib* crainnleab*r*aib snasta slinnsolsi ūastib, *con*a sonncaistēl cotat
comdaingen do cūarscīethaib cetraimteachaib *ocus* do chlārscīat*h*aibh aladaib
ūacht*ar*fairsing*aib*h mōraib ina timchioll, comba lōr d'*ur*gairdiug*udh* a n-aisgin
indara fe*cht* re himat dath n-ēxamail a n-arm ⁊ a n-ecradh ⁊ a n-ētgadh, re
gristaitnem ⁊ re gleōrdealr*adh* na grēini ina c*er*tag*aid* friu, re somaisi na m*er*gedh
⁊ na minn rīg*da* roietroct, ⁊ na cathbharr crūan-cumhtaighthi, ⁊ re geild*er*gi
gruadh na mīl*ed* am*al* cnāim ōeingel elifainti īarna tumma i corc*ur*, ⁊ re
sol*us*ruid*edh* na sāerchlann soicinēoil ōs bilib na scīath ar n-*ē*rgi na rūaidgrīsi
romōiri sin in aigt*ibh* na n-anr*adh* n-ast*ar*ach re hannaime a n-imte*cht*a ⁊ re
c*um*ga na crōbuail*edh* cathae i mbat*ar* ic mallascnam in maigi fonnglais for*ū*aine
darar' cingset. In fe*cht* n-aill im*morro* ba lōr d'ūathbās ⁊ c*r*idenbas a forccsi re

diadem of yellow gold with a rim of burnished gold, and a row of crystal and of beautiful gems of carbuncle all around it. Above that, there was regular engraving of forms of birds, flying creatures, and strange unknown animals, with two beautifully-fashioned pinnacles of precious stones from the land of eastern India above them, and the figure of an African apple with a musical chime on the end of each pinnacle; so that the resonance of those apple-chimes was as sweet as the strings of a harp, when it was set in motion by every step that the overlord himself would take, and by the vigorous motion of his horse.

§2 Then was brought to him a horse – strong, bold and brave, high-spirited, fierce, swift, vigorous, bounding, long-haired, stout, stiff, long-sided, thunder-feat-performing, high-headed, famous, leaping aloft, broad-breasted, slender-snouted, thick-legged, bag-nosed, broad-hoofed, bulge-eyed, with its four iron shoes under it, with its silver bridle-bit, with its golden saddle-cloth on its back. Before his tent Pompey mounted that horse to order his hosts and to arrange his battalions.

Pompey's army advances into battle

When they [sc. Caesar's followers] were there observing the same plain, they saw coming to them the lengthy, very great, broad and long band of armed warriors [sc. Pompey's followers], with their breasts all set towards the expanse of the field, with the density of a forest, and with the extent of a city or castle, namely, the royal Roman senate, ordered and arrayed, that is, the eighty-eight cohorts of serried heroes, the forty thousand foot-soldiers in their three arrays, back to back, so that each array was bearing down upon another in their warlike enclosure and in their fold of battle and in their arrangement, with their covering of the wattle-woods of battle, and of deadly forests, and of long-shafted, polished, bright-bladed spears above them, with their hard, very firm, strong citadel of quadrangular curved shields, and of great, speckled, wide-topped flat shields around them, so that at one time it was a sufficient pleasure to see them, because of the abundance of variegated colours of their weapons, their ornaments and their garments; because of the fiery glare and the bright radiance of the sun shining directly upon them; because of the beauty of the banners, of the brilliant royal diadems and of the helmets adorned with red enamel; because of the bright red of the cheeks of the soldiers like an elephant's white bone [i.e. ivory] dipped in purple; and because of the shining ruddiness of the well-born noble families hadūath na n-arm ⁊ re hūathgrāin na sochaidhe *ocus* re fost*acht* a cēime *ocus* re tr*eise*c*ht* a tocimme *ocus* re hadmaire a n-innill; re n-aidble *ocus* re n-imatlinm*uirecht* fodēin *ocus* re mēt ro gapsat fōtha don muigh rēidh rofairsing f*o*rsa rabat*ar, ocus* da*no* risna hammaitip āerdaip *ocus* risna heltadaib adhūathm*u*raib do duibēnoip dorchaidhib bat*ar* ina n-urlenm*ain* ic urn*aid*he a fola *ocus* a n-apaige n-escoman d'fagbāil gan uiresb*aid* i n-ell*ach* in mōrcatha *ocus* i(n) n-ot*har*lig*ib* na n-ānr*ad*h isin ārm*aig*'ar trioll.

over the rims of the shields, after the rising of that great ruddy glow in the faces of the journeying warriors because of the strangeness of their march and the density of the battle array in which they were slowly passing the bright green soil over which they stepped. At another time, however, it was sufficiently horrible and terrible to observe them, because of the awfulness of the weapons, and because of the dread horror of the multitude, and because of the steadiness of their step, and because of the strength of their advance, and because of the valour of their array; because of their own vastness and great number, and because of the expanse that they covered, of the smooth, spacious plain upon which they were, and also because of the phantoms of the air and the horrible flocks of black dark birds which were following them, expecting to get their blood and their foul entrails copiously, in the engagement of the Great Battle that followed, and in the graves of the warriors on the battlefield.

Essay: Learned art and rhetorical strategies:
From *De Bello Civili* to *In Cath Catharda*

A detailed reading reveals *In Cath Catharda* to be the product of an innovative and learned author, who mined Lucan's *Civil War* epic for materials, emulating the Roman poet's hexameters and deploying a variety of artful rhetorical strategies to compose the Irish version of the battle narrative. Aspects of the technique include the reorganization of the narrative structure, the reproduction of elaborate epic similes, the amplification of battle scenes with extended *ekphrases*, and the use of formulaic phrases that sometimes derive from indigenous tradition and sometimes from direct emulation of the Latin.

In order to understand the overarching concept for the narrative, we must first examine our second excerpt. This comes just after the scene corresponding to the end of Lucan's Book 6. It describes the preceding passage as a *remscél* ('preliminary tale', traditionally rendered 'foretale'), applying a technical term that was used by medieval Irish scholars to characterize a sequence of prose that is associated with and complementary to another narrative that follows it. Formulaic statements similar to what we have in our second passage ('One of the foretales . . . thus far. Such and such is the name of that story . . .') recur throughout *In Cath Catharda*.[4] Together, these demonstrate a desire to recast the original poem of Lucan by dividing it into two parts: first a series of *remscéla* ('foretales'), and then the *cath* ('battle-tale') proper entitled *Cath mór muighe na Tesaili* ('The Great Battle of the Plain of Thessaly'). This twofold division is important for understanding not only the narrative structure that has been produced, but also the two distinct rhetorical strategies that have been applied to the earlier and later parts of the Irish work (Poppe 2016a: 101–4, Poppe 2016b).

Our first excerpt presents a typical example of learned imitation of Lucan's Latin in the *remscéla* part of the narrative. The greater part of this passage was not printed by Stokes, who seems to have judged it spurious, but it is here reproduced in full based on my own transcription from Dublin, Royal Irish Academy, MS D.iv.2, fol. 5vb22–31.[5] Reading it alongside *Civil War* 1.291–5, where the epic poet likens Caesar to a race-horse straining to burst out of the gate, the Irish version reproduces the simile in language that is striking in terms of both syntax and phraseology. Lucan's correlative construction *tantum . . . quantum . . .* ('so much . . . as . . .') is replicated faithfully with *amail . . . is amlaid sin . . .* ('just as . . . so . . .'), and even his concessive *quamuis . . .* ('although') within the subordinate clause finds its counterpart in *ce . . .* ('although'). The Irish *saint ⁊ ailgus in catha*

('[Caesar's] eagerness and desire for war') picks up *saint in retha* ('[the horse's] eagerness to run'), just as the Latin *in bellum prono* ('[Caesar being] eager for war') does *pronus* ('[the horse being] eager'). The Irish author's desire for accuracy extends to the coining of a compound noun *uchtchrand*, a *hapax legomenon*. I have argued elsewhere that this must have been a neologism based on Lucan's *repagula* and triggered by a gloss by Arnulf of Orléans in his annotations to the passage, so that its meaning should be 'breast-high (starting) barrier' (Nagashima 2019: 75–7).[6] The author, however, is not merely paraphrasing Lucan's verses, but effects a creative emulation, ornamenting his prose with figures typical of medieval Irish florid literary style. These include both alliteration and semantic and syntactic parallelism (Ní Mhaonaigh 2006b: 12–16): *arduighter aicneadh ⁊ meduigter menma* ('spirit is raised and mind is heightened'), *tre nuall ⁊ tre gairib* ('through clamour and through shouts'), *saint ⁊ ailgus* ('eagerness and desire'), *gurbo mían ⁊ gurbo laind* ('so that he became eager and so that he became desirous'). By way of contrast, it should be noted that the Latin poet's simile is simply omitted in *Li Fet des Romains* and *Rómverja Saga*, the near-contemporary Old French and Old Norse works containing adaptations of Lucan.[7]

According to Brent Miles (2011: 58), '[a] striking feature of *In Cath Catharda* is how often the author reproduces Lucan's involved epic similes, a challenging task encountered much less frequently in the other classical tales'. The data reveals how peculiar the text is. *Imtheachta Aeniasa* reproduces only one Virgilian simile (Glennon 1996–97: 216–17, cf. Poppe 2014b: 34–7); the Middle Irish *Thebaid* has 28% of Statius' similes (Briggs 2018: 184); *In Cath Catharda* imitates 56–80% of Lucan's similes, according to my calculation.[8] What makes the text even more exceptional, however, and hence more important in medieval Irish literary history, is the great number of similes introduced by the author with no models in Lucan: twenty-five in total. While eight take their cue from phrases in the base texts (seven from Lucan and one from Bede[9]), seventeen are independent, the author's own creations. All of these occur after the structural and stylistic juncture (see above) between the *remscéla* part and the *cath* proper. Although linguistic features encourage the hypothesis that the entire work is the creation of a single author (Mac Gearailt 2022: 75–77), it is evident that a distinct compositional strategy has been introduced into the latter part of the narrative. There the verbal linkages between the Latin and Irish text become minimal, and Lucan's 630 verses (*Civil War* 7.1–630) are expanded to three times their original length, making 1855 printed prose lines. In narrating the climactic Battle of Pharsalus, what has been perceived as 'absence of visualised action' in Lucan's work is transformed in the Irish version with a series of extended flamboyant *ekphrases* 'in the mode of hyper-realistic visualisation' (Clarke 2022c: 26). Our third and fourth extracts give a flavour of this stylistic movement.

In the third excerpt we see two separate sections of the *ekphrasis* of the arming of Pompey (*CCath* 4660–739). This scene takes its cue from Lucan's passing mention of Pompey's troops attending to their weapons (*Civil War* 7.139–43). The adaptor creatively composed this passage and its longer counterpart, the *ekphrasis* of the arming of Caesar (*CCath* 5203–335), by building on the traditional arming scenes (known as 'arming-runs') that are a familiar feature of earlier Irish saga composition.[10] Thus the lavish portrait of Pompey's dress and arms opens with a formulaic string of repetitions of *ro gab* ('he put on') just as the arming of Láeg and Cú Chulainn does in an episode of *Táin Bó Cúailnge* ('The Cattle-Raid of Cooley'),[11] achieving its effect 'from an ekphrastic tour-de-force of relentlessly listing exotic items of armour, often enhanced by alliterating adjectives' (Poppe 2016b: 13).

Pompey first puts on five different pairs of greaves (*Cath* 4662–70), then three different mantles (4670–5), a pair of gauntlets (4675–6), two different hauberks of mail (4676–82), a baldric (4682–6), a sword (4686–93), and a crested helmet (4694–702).[12] The first section of the third excerpt comes last in this sequence of *ro gab*, and features one of the most exotic items, a diadem which the author considered worthy of an almost hundred-word description. It is not an ordinary jewelled golden crown with engravings. It is adorned with twin pinnacles of Indian gems and musical chimes upon pinnacles extending from what is depicted as an African apple. Significantly, India and Africa are the two most distant places in the known world of the period when *In Cath Catharda* was composed. These geographical references also follow the literary tradition of arming-scenes, which at moments of heightened description invoke exotic locales, sometimes factual and sometimes otherworldly.[13] Furthermore, this familiarizing topos is strengthened by the incorporation of a simile independent of Lucan: *co mba binnither teta mendcrot binnfoghroghudh na n-ubullcairchi-sin* (4710–11 'so that the resonance of those apple-chimes was as sweet as the strings of a harp'). The author here has recourse to a formulaic phrase featuring a Gaelic musical instrument and a number of linguistic archaisms.[14]

The second section of our third excerpt similarly derives from traditional Irish *ekphrases* concerning horses. Triggered by Lucan's brief reference to a nameless soldier tacking up his horse, *auget eques stimulos frenorumque artat habenas* (*Civil War* 7.143 'the horseman enlarged his spurs and tightened the straps of his bridle'), the adaptor describes Pompey's imaginary horse with densely alliterating adjectives (*m. . . m. . . m. . . l. . . l. . . l. . . l. . . l. . . t. . . t. . . t. . . t. . . a. . . a. . . e. . . u. . . g. . . c. . . b. . . b. . . b. . .*), many of which are stock phrases recurring in the portraits of heroes' horses in earlier Irish sagas.[15] This string is followed by a syntactically parallel prepositional triplet, each consisting of *cona* ('with its') + a piece of horse tack + its metallic material + another prepositional phrase referring to a body part of the horse. By employing the topoi and rhetorical technique common in high-register Middle Irish prose, the adaptor has transformed his Latin model into a passage that resonates closely with the traditions of Irish heroic literature on indigenous themes.

Our final extract forms part of another extended familiarizing *ekphrasis* which combines with 'a classicizing aesthetic' (Miles 2011: 103). Here a verse of Lucan's is amplified expansively: *conspicit in planos hostem descendere campos* ('[Caesar] saw his enemy come down to the level plains', *Civil War* 7.237) becomes an 85-line description of how Pompey's troops look to the eyes of Caesar's men. It accumulates seven parallel passages all beginning with the phrase *a mbatar ann ic forcsi. . . confacatur. . .* ('when they were there observing ... they saw ...'), gradually extending in length. A remarkable literary heritage lies behind the simile, *re geildergi gruadh na miled amal cnaim oeingel elifainti iarna tumma i corcur* ('because of the bright red of the cheeks of the soldiers like an elephant's white bone [i.e. ivory[16]] dipped in purple'). In ekphrastic passages in earlier Irish literature, it is common to compare a character's blushing cheeks to a foxglove. The translator of the Irish *Thebaid* uses such a formula to render Statius' description, without a simile, of the blush of Adrastus' daughters: *ua deirgither losa liac gnuisi 7 aichthi na n-ingen sin* 'as red as foxgloves were the faces and countenances of those maidens' (*TTeb* 479–80).[17] By contrast, ivory is rare in medieval Irish imagery. This ivory-dipped-in-purple simile, I argue, ultimately originates from Homer's *Iliad*:

Ὡς δ᾽ ὅτε τίς τ᾽ ἐλέφαντα γυνὴ φοίνικι μιήνῃ
Μηονὶς ἠὲ Κάειρα, παρήιον ἔμμεναι ἵππων . . .
τοῖοί τοι, Μενέλαε, μιάνθην αἵματι μηροὶ
εὐφυέες κνῆμαί τε ἰδὲ σφυρὰ κάλ᾽ ὑπένερθε.

Iliad 4.141–7

'Like when a woman stains ivory with purple dye, some woman of Maeonia or Caria, to make a cheekpiece for horses, . . .: just so, Menelaus, your thighs were stained with blood, your well-formed thighs and your legs and your beautiful ankles below.' [Translation revised from Murray 1919–1925]

However, the Irish author is unlikely to have derived it directly from the Greek text; instead he is likely to have acquired it through classical learning continued in the vernacular period, the movement which Brent Miles has defined as medieval Irish 'classicism'.[18] This Homeric simile has a long history of reception and emulation in Latin poetry: Ennius, Catullus, Virgil, Ovid and Statius (Sfyroeras 2014). Most frequently cited by later grammarians was the first part of Virgil's famous double simile describing Lavinia's blushing cheeks in *Aeneid* 12.67–8: *Indum sanguineo veluti violaverit ostro / si quis ebur* ('as when someone stains Indian ivory with crimson dye'). Intriguingly, Diomedes Grammaticus and Marius Plotius Sacerdos (Keil 1855–80: 1.463, 6.464) list it as a representative simile *per colorem* ('through colour'), and the adaptor includes the Irish version of the simile opportunely in an ekphrastic passage focusing on 'the abundance of variegated colours' (*CCath* 4985 *imat dath n-examail*).[19]

The same excerpt also demonstrates the author's consistent attentiveness to historical sources. The information that Pompey's troops arranged eighty-eight cohorts, or forty thousand men, in three arrays (*CCath* 4976–8) corresponds with Orosius, *Histories against the Pagans* 6.15.23, which was incorporated into a gloss in *Commenta Bernensia* ('Bern Scholia'), one of the published collections of medieval glosses to Lucan.[20] The author here supplements Lucan with an additional historical detail while displaying his own creative imagination, shortly after describing the army as 'countless, numberless and immeasurable' (*CCath* 4970 *can rimh can airem can airdmes*).

After a passage corresponding to Lucan, *Civil War* 7.628–30, *In Cath Catharda* ends with a brief epilogue (*CCath* 6159–67), which is not found in the original.[21] The Latin verses following the Battle of Pharsalus are omitted, and the narrative is reconfigured to conclude with a major battle in line with Irish vernacular tradition. In this way, Lucan's epic on a war (*bellum*) is transformed into an antiquity-saga culminating in a decisive battle (*cath*). Under this programme our author, adopting a traditional structuring technique, has displayed one set of rhetorical strategies in the *remscéla* sequence and another in the sequence of the *cath* proper. In the foretales he has imitated the artistic qualities of ancient epic, and in the core of the battle tale he has amplified the narrative through ekphrastic set pieces and formulaic heroic similes, both Gaelic and classical in their affinities. Their programmes being different throughout, Lucan's subjective apostrophes have been objectified, his declamatory speeches have been simplified, and his poetic language has been replaced with the elevated language in alliterating style that was traditionally deployed in high-register Middle Irish prose.[22] *In Cath Catharda* is not so much a translation into the vernacular as an adaptation into a new cultural milieu: a creative rewriting by the hand of an engaging, philological artist, bearing witness to the broader intellectual environment of his age.

Notes

1　I am grateful to the Gates Cambridge Scholarship for supporting this research, and to Máire Ní Mhaonaigh, Erich Poppe, Isabelle Torrance, Michael Clarke, Brigid Ehrmantraut and Jesse Harrington for their helpful comments on earlier drafts of this essay.

2　I have deleted the second *a* of Stokes' *a inncomarta a imperechta* ('the insignia of his empire'), which in fact is to be found in none of the surviving manuscripts of *In Cath Catharda*, and I have construed *imperechta* as an attributive genitive.

3　For the meaning of *uchtcrand,* a *hapax legomenon,* here given the explanatory gloss 'breast-high starting-barrier', see the essay, p.201.

4　Eight further instances are directly parallel: *CCath* 2261–2, 2593–4, 2858–9, 3208–9, 3247–8, 3386–7, 3768–9, 3874–5. Our excerpt references fifteen instances, and further passages for comparison include the narrative units headed with a title at *CCath* 382, 522, 818, 1085, 1192, 1528. Other titles at *CCath* 148, 205, 346 can be considered divisions within what is virtually an Irish version of *summa historiae* placed before 'the story itself' (*CCath* 380).

5　For the textual problem in this passage, see Nagashima 2019: 71–5.

6　The adaptor's use of glosses to Lucan is discussed in Ch. 16 of this volume by Cillian O'Hogan.

7　See respectively Flutre and Sneyders de Vogel 1938: 1.352; Þorbjörg Helgadóttir 2010: 2.238.

8　The range of the proportion in the case of *In Cath Catharda* is due to the nineteen similes excised along with the passage in which they occur. The reasons for these omissions do not necessarily involve the similes at all.

9　The relevant passage is *is remhithir ré sliasait ferócclaich cech bun díbh* (*CCath* 191–2 'each of the stakes is as thick as a warrior's thigh'), which takes its cue from wording found in Bede, *Ecclesiastical History* 1.2 (Colgrave and Mynors 1969: 22–3).

10　The arming scenes of Pompey and Caesar have been studied by Poppe (2016b: 12–14) and Clarke (2022c), respectively. For the literary tradition of the formulaic languages used in the arming scenes in *Táin Bó Cúailnge* and *Togáil Troí*, see Miles 2011: 199–207.

11　*TBC 1* 2189–203, 2213–44; *TBC-LL* 2205–19, 2230–61. So also the arming of Fer Diad in another episode of *Táin Bó Cúailnge* (*TBC-LL* 3246–63), that of Conchobhar at *Cath Ruis na Ríg* 'The Battle of Rosnaree' §27 (Hogan 1892: 80), and that of Conn

Cétchathach at *Cath Maighe Léna* 'The Battle of Mag Léna' §81, 1468–85 (Jackson 1938: 57–8) .

12 For *lúirech* and *assán*, here translated 'hauberk of mail' and 'greaves' respectively, see Clarke 2022c: 30–6 and Poppe 2023.

13 Examples include *CCath* 4671–2, *TBC 1* 2244–5, *TBC-LL* 2259–61, *Cath Maighe Léna* 'The Battle of Mag Léna' §81, 1470–2, 1479–82 (Jackson 1938: 57) and *Cathcharpat Serda* 'The Scythed Battle-Chariot' 29–32 (O'Rahilly 1976b: 197). The description of Pompey's diadem, however, might not be a purely imaginative, literary product of the intertexual dynamic, but might resonate with contemporary reality, just as the description of Caesar's armour could, as argued by Clarke (2022c). The reference to India and winged creatures associates the diadem with the toupha, the Byzantine-style crown of peacock feathers sent by Pope Urban III to Henry II of England in 1186 as part of an abortive project to crown John as King of Ireland. One of the papal legates who accompanied this crown, Gerard, may have been cardinal priest of S. Stefano al Monte Celio, a Roman basilica which had strong associations with Irish sovereignty. I owe this idea to Jesse Harrington, who discusses the mission of the crown and its later memory in Ireland in Harrington (2024, forthcoming). I am also grateful to Michael Clarke for reminding me that the seemingly eccentric description of two pinnacles projecting from Pompey's diadem might reflect the contemporary visual culture of international knighthood. See, for example, the Topfhelm mit Zimier (Vienna, Kunsthistorisches Museum, Hofjagd- und Rüstkammer, B 74) and the illustrations of helmets in the so-called Codex Manesse (Heidelberg University Library, Cod. Pal. German 848).

14 According to *eDIL* s.v. *mennchrott*, the word is used '[o]nly in g[enitive] p[lural] in heroic and poetic literature in stereotyped similes'. The uses of Old Irish equative suffix *-ithir* and accusative of comparison in such a fossilized phrase are thus not surprising. For the use of archaisms or pseudo-archaisms in *In Cath Catharda*, see Mac Gearailt 2022.

15 Comparable examples include *TBC 1* 2286–91, *TBC-LL* 2914–25 and *Tochmarc Emire* 'The Wooing of Emir' §12–13 (Van Hamel 1933: 24).

16 Medieval Latin scholars used to explain ivory as elephant's bone: e.g. Bede, *In Canticum Canticorum* 'Commentary on the Song of Songs' 5.23, PL 91: col. 1167) *Ebur autem os est elephantis* ('Ivory, then, is an elephant's bone'). This tradition seems to have been followed by the Irish as here and at *O'Mulconry's Glossary* 700 (Moran 2019: 222) *Ibar .i. ab ebore .i. ó cnáim elefante* ('*Ibar* ['ivory' in Irish], from *ebur* ['ivory' in Latin], i.e. from an elephant's bone').

17 Other comparable examples include *Mesca Ulad* 'The Intoxication of the Ulstermen' 588–90 (Watson 1941: 26), *Togail Bruidne Da Derga* 'The Destruction of Da Derga's Hostel' §2.21 (Knott 1936: 1), and *Imtheachta Aeniasa* 'The Wanderings of Aeneas' 1925–7. For the literary tradition of this foxglove simile, see Briggs 2018: 209–15.

18 See Miles 2011, esp. 131–9, for the imitation of similes from classical epic in medieval Irish adaptations. For the continued importance of classical rhetoric in late antique and early medieval Ireland, see Stone 2022.

19 It must be noted that *Imtheachta Aeniasa* replaces the original double simile with descriptive sentences in the corresponding passage (2926–7): 'she blushed, and beautiful was the flush of countenance that stole over her, and it was the blush of noble breeding in her' (cf. Ch. 13 in this volume). Briggs (2018: 213–14) hypothesizes that the adaptor of *Togail na Tebe* modelled his double simile of blushing maidens on the Virgilian one (*TTeb* 479–82, whose first part is the aforementioned foxglove simile).

20 Usener 1869: 240, at Lucan, *Civil War* 7.460. The same happens at *CCath* 5391–4, where the author details Caesar's army; see Nagashima 2021: 11. Cf. also Ch. 16 in this volume.

21 This epilogue is likely to derive from the medieval tradition of *accessus ad Lucanum*, for which see in general Sanford 1934, which remains valuable, and Munk Olsen 2009: 84–7.

22 In his study of the language of *In Cath Catharda*, Mac Gearailt (2022: 77) recognizes 'a style ... belonging to early schools of *senchas* in the late 12th or the 13th century.'

16

In Cath Catharda 'The Civil War': The Influence of Scholia

Cillian O'Hogan

The text is reproduced from Stokes 1909: 64–8, lines 818–91.

Text: Portents on the eve of war

Dearbairdi in Catha Catharda

Isin ecmung na rea sin ⁊ na haimsire sin ro faillsighit dona Rom*án*chaib faistineada ⁊ remtirchanta na n-olc ro badar arcind doib, air ro línadh in neam uasu ⁊ in talamh futhu ⁊ in muir do gach aird umpu do taidbhsibh ingnaitighibh, ingantaibh ⁊ do de*r*bairdibh ic tairngire ⁊ ic taircedul in Catha Catharda do gnim acco.

It e inso na h-airdi aitchesa doib .i.

Ro artraigset isna h-aidhchibh sin accó renna anaichinti na ro artraigset in nim remi sin riam, ⁊ nar' artraigh barsamail re met ⁊ re n-imat ⁊ re n-urg*r*ain.

Atc*on*ncadar da*n*o clar gorm glainidi na fi*r*maminti neamda do bith 'na h-aencorthair lassar ⁊ tened os a cind.

Atc*on*ncadar araili rind ann co ruithnibh roed*r*ochtaibh ⁊ co t*r*illsib tendtidib *for* esrediudh ass, in retlu mongach insin, ⁊ ni ro artraigh sen riam *acht* la cumscugudh flaiti*u*sa, na clodh catha, *nó* la bás airdrigh. Ro tirchanait in t*r*iar sin don cur-sa isin Roimh, air ro cumscaighead Poimp re Cesair asa flaithi*u*s, ⁊ ro srainead cath mor maigi na Tesaila *for* Poimp beos. Is t*r*iana acais in catha sin fuair Poimp bas ⁊ fuair cidh Cesair ara cind.

Atc*on*dcadar athainni tenntidi ⁊ locharna lasamnacha ⁊ ilbrectad dealb n-ecsamhail na saignen taitnemach sechnón in aeoir as gach aird. Doraitni ann aensaighnen dib ro de*r*csaigh de uilibh tenntib nimhi aircheana ar met ⁊ sol*u*stacht ⁊ dene. Ro gab sen asin tuaiscirt atuaidh docum na Roma. Ro tecluim ⁊ ro tinoil ina h-uili teinti aerda leis g*ur*o bloscastar im ceand na Capitoli rigda ⁊ tempuill Ioib isind Roim. Is*ed* ro tircanadh t*r*itsin: Cesair do tide*cht* a tuaisciurt in domhain do gabail na Roma.

Ro artraighset ann na retlanda aidhchidhi im-midi medonlae. Atceas ircra eisci acco i lansoilsi na .xu.

Atc*on*ncadar fordorcad *for* ruithnib sol*u*staib na g*r*eni i c*er*tmedon lae, ⁊ ba met na dorcadad i sein gonar' sailseat la gona lanshoillsi do taithneamh tre bithu doib.

Translation

lightly revised by the author from Stokes 1909: 65–9

The sure signs of the Civil War

At that time and period, auguries and prophecies of the evils that were ahead of them were shown to the Romans; for the heaven above them and the earth below them and the sea in every direction around them were filled with strange and wondrous signs, and with vast sure signs, foretelling and predicting the Civil War that would be fought by them.

These are the signs that were seen by them:

In those nights there appeared unknown stars that had never appeared in the sky before then, nor had any like them in size and number and horror appeared before.

Then they saw the blue, clear surface of the heavenly firmament as a fringe of flame and fire above their heads.

They saw a certain star there, with brightest gleams and fiery tresses spreading from it: that is the hairy star [i.e. a comet]; and it has never appeared except at the changing of a reign, or defeat in battle, or death of a high king. Those three things were then foretold in Rome, for Pompey was removed from his reign by Caesar, and Pompey also lost the great battle on the plain of Thessaly; and because of that battle Pompey died, and even Caesar afterwards.

They saw fiery torches and blazing lamps and a variety of different types of bright lightning-bolts throughout the sky from every direction. One of the lightning-bolts that shone there surpassed all other fires of heaven in size and splendour and speed. It came south to Rome from the north. It gathered and collected all the other fires of the air, so that they crashed around the head of the royal Capitol and the temple of Jove in Rome. Through this it was prophesied that Caesar was coming from the north of the world to capture Rome.

The night-time stars appeared in the middle of midday. They saw an eclipse of the moon in the full light of the fifteenth (day).[1]

In the very middle of the day they saw a darkness on the bright rays of the sun, and the darkness was so great that they did not expect the full brightness of day ever to shine upon them again.

Rosceastar sliabh n-Ethna sruaim tened trichemruaid isin tslis ba comnesa do tír na h-Edaili, *gu ro* lae ar daini ⁊ cet*h*ra ann. Ro artraigh ann da*no* for*d*ath fuilidhi *for* saebcori mara T*u*rrein *f*ri headh lae go n- aidhchi.

Ro scailead ⁊ ro fodladh i ndib blogaibh lassar in tenead bithbi no bith i teampull Uesta na bande. Is *ed* ro tircanad tritsin, in flaithi*us* Rom*á*nach do roind i ndó *eti*r Poimp ⁊ Cesair.

Ro erig crith mor ⁊ fogluas*acht* fircalma i fothaibh ⁊ i slutraigib in talman, *gu*ro fas talamcumscugudh trenadbul de, ⁊ ba he met in tal*am*cumscug*tha* sin, *gu*r croithestair slíabh n-Elpa uadh ina mbui da moilib sena sneachtaidi im- madmandaib a sliabh ⁊ i nglaccaibh a tulach, *gu*ro tuitseat i n-aenfecht de *fo*r fíadmaighibh ⁊ *for* fanglenntaibh na tiri ba comneasu dó.

Ro erig commbogad ainbtini d*e*rmairi dona *f*rith samail *nó* cosmuilli*us* riam i c*r*isluch mara T*u*rrein, guro línsatair ruadbhuindi robarta ⁊ barruactar a tonn tulgorm taebed*r*ucht clethi na da n-ardsliabh filet impi do gach leith .i. sliabh Cailp isinn Edail ⁊ sliabh nAthlaind i crichaibh Aiffraici.

Atc*í*tis dealba ⁊ imaigni na ndéi adhartha ic cai ⁊ ic d*e*rfadhaigh and. Atc*í*tis tolada mora alluis ac siliud a slesaibh ⁊ a *f*raightibh gacha tighi isin Roimh, ic fiug*r*ad in morsaethair no foidémtais 'artain.

Tainic airmc*h*rith mor i n-uilibh templaibh na ndéa isin Roim, *con*na roibi slegh *nó* claid*eb* no caithsciath *for* alcuing intib nach drocair *f*ri lar talman.

Atcitis na hethaidi aidhchidi acco ic foluam*ain* i soilsi in lae seachnon na cat*h*rach .i. in écthach ⁊ inn iatlu ⁊ in bubo. Ticdis ois ⁊ allta ecendsa na ndit*h*reb comfog*us* co ndentais leptha ⁊ cubacla doib *for* larmedon na Roma gach n-aidhchi. No feartais coin ⁊ cuanarta ⁊ meic tire na hEtaili ualla mora sechnon na cat*h*rach gach n-oidhchi. No labraidis na ceit*h*ri tre glor ndaenda acco, uair inniste*r* isna sdairib intan bui araili Rom*á*nach ic gresacht a ogdaim ⁊ a eri arba fair, ro labair in t-ogdam *f*ris *co* ndebairt: Cid tai dom t*r*engresacht, a oglaich? ol se, uair is taescu atbelat na Rom*á*naig innas domelat ina fil d'arbannaibh acco.

Mount Etna spat out a river of rushing red fire on the side nearest to the land of Italy, so that it brought destruction on men and cattle. Then for a day and a night the eddies of the Mediterranean[2] sea took on the colour of blood.

The flame of the eternal fire which was in the temple of the goddess Vesta was scattered and divided into two pieces. Through this it was prophesied that the Roman dominion would be divided in two between Pompey and Caesar.

A great shaking and strong commotion arose in the foundations and in the depths of the earth, resulting in a vast earthquake, and the extent of that earthquake was so great that the Alps shook off the ancient snowy masses in the crevasses of their mountains and in the forks of their hills, so that they fell together on the plains and the glens of the land that was closest.

An enormous shaking storm rose, the like or semblance of which had never been found within the confines of the Mediterranean sea, so that the strong burst of the flood tide and the summit of its blue-browed, bright-sided waves filled the tops of the high mountains about it on each side, namely Mount Calpe in Italy and Mount Atlas in the ends of Africa.

The statues and images of the gods they worshipped were seen wailing and shedding tears. Great floods of sweat were seen flowing out of the sides and walls of every house in Rome, indicating the great trouble which they would afterwards endure.

A great shaking of arms occurred in all the temples of the gods in Rome, so that there was no spear nor sword nor shield on any rack inside them that did not fall to the floor.

Nocturnal birds were seen flying throughout the City in the light of day, namely the night-owl and the bat and the owl. Every night, deer and the savage wild beasts of the neighbouring wildernesses came to make lairs and sleeping-places in the middle of Rome. Every night, the dogs and hounds and wolves of Italy uttered great howls throughout the City. Cattle spoke with human voice, for it is told in the histories that when a certain Roman was goading his ox with its load of corn upon it, the ox spoke to him and said: 'Why are you goading me, young man? For the Romans will perish before they consume all the corn they have.'

Essay: The use of scholia in *In Cath Catharda*[3]

In the Middle Ages, canonical texts circulated accompanied by a variety of materials intended to facilitate their study and interpretation. These ancillary materials could take the form of a prologue (*accessus*), which usually included a brief life (*vita*) of the author, and/or marginal notes, usually referred to in modern classical scholarship as scholia, but among medievalists as glosses, and known in medieval Latin scholarship as *commentarii, commenta, glossae,* or *glossemata* (cf. Teeuwen 2003: 235–6, 277–8). These explanatory annotations (philological, historical, literary) were keyed to specific lines of a canonical text, and could travel independently, compiled into separate manuscripts[4] or alongside the text, usually in the margins, as in Bern, Burgerbibliothek MS 45, a ninth-century manuscript containing the text of Lucan with marginal commentary.

As one of the major classical Latin epic poems that was studied in the Middle Ages, as well as virtually the only detailed source for information about the civil war between Pompey and Caesar available north of the Alps, Lucan's *Civil War* was extensively studied and annotated.[5] Two apparently independent sets of substantial commentaries were published as the *Commenta Bernensia* (Usener 1869) and the *Adnotationes super Lucanum* (Endt 1909, Cavajoni 1979–90), though these titles misleadingly imply that these commentaries are stand-alone compositions from late antiquity, whereas in fact they frequently overlap, and likely were compiled in the Carolingian age.[6]

In addition to these collections, another major body of work on Lucan is the *Glosule super Lucanum* of the twelfth-century scholar Arnulf of Orléans (for text and commentary see Marti 1958). A full study of Lucan's reception in the Middle Ages, or even a survey of medieval commentaries on Lucan, remains a major *desideratum*. Recent research on *In Cath Catharda* has indicated the dependence of the Gaelic composer on the so-called *Commenta Bernensia* and *Adnotationes* (O'Hogan 2014, Poppe 2015, 2016a, 2016b), as well as on Arnulf (Poppe 2016a, 2016b, Nagashima 2019). Attempting to pin down the exact set of scholia available to the author may well be a fool's errand. At the very least, it requires considerably more foundational work to be done on the transmission of Lucan and the Lucan scholia in the high Middle Ages.

With the exception of a very small number of canonical commentaries (e.g. that of Servius on Virgil), scholia are fluid texts. They do not have named authors, and change considerably over the course of their transmission, as comments are added or removed as necessary by successive copyists (Tosi 2014). Scholia can be grouped into families, but there is frequently cross-pollination between different traditions, most often because scholar-scribes were willing and able to copy simultaneously from multiple source manuscripts. As a result, in the case of the Lucan scholia, it seems virtually impossible to construct a reliable stemma for their transmission (Werner 1994). The scholia on Lucan run the gamut from straightforward explanatory glosses (e.g. where Lucan uses an obscure or unusual word) through to historical comments or clarification on matters where Lucan is vaguely elliptical. In a number of cases, the scholia appear to have incorporated material from standard encyclopaedic texts (Isidore's *Etymologies*, for example), or even from other commentaries (see e.g. La Bua 2018).

Recent studies have emphasized the centrality of school-texts, and of learning materials, to the production of medieval literature, be that in Latin (Woods 2019, Haynes 2021) or in High Medieval vernaculars such as Middle English (Baswell 1995). Scholars of medieval Irish are finding rich materials for similar questions in *In Cath Catharda*. This text is a productive testing-ground for identifying the influence of scholia and other commentaries since, unlike the other Irish redactions of Latin epic such as *Imtheachta Aeniasa* and *Togail na Tebe*, when the author of *In Cath Catharda* is translating rather than engaging in free composition, he often remains remarkably faithful to the Latin original. Similes are frequently translated, for instance, something that occurs more rarely in other texts (see Ch. 15). At moments when there is deviation from or (in particular) expansion on the Latin original to include additional information, it very often appears to be the case that there is direct engagement with a scholion.

The text in the passage shown above presents a retelling of Lucan's narrative of the portents accompanying the imminent arrival of Caesar in Rome. The sudden bolt from the blue is described by Lucan as follows:

> emicuit caelo tacitum sine nubibus ullis
> fulmen et Arctois rapiens de partibus ignem
> percussit Latiare caput . . .

> *Civil War* 1.533–5

> A silent lightning-bolt shone from the sky, without any clouds, and gathering fire
> from the Northern regions it struck the Latian peak . . .

Lucan's original is elliptical (see further Roche 2009, note on the passage). The lightning appears without accompanying thunder (*tacitum*) or clouds (*sine nubibus ullis*); it 'gathers fire' from the North, clearly signifying Caesar's approach from the north; and then strikes the Mons Albanus (*Latiare caput*, literally the 'Latian head'). *Latiare caput* is particularly challenging, and in the author's translation we can see how the scholia are drawn on to expand and explain this problem for a medieval audience. The author states

> *bloscastar im ceand na Capitoli rigda ꝛ tempuill Ioib isind Roim*

'they struck round the head of the royal Capitol and the temple of Jove in Rome.'

The scholia read as follows:

> 'LATIALE CAPUT Romam' (aA); 'PERCUSSIT LATIALE C. Albanum montem dixit ubi est Iouis Latialis' (Commenta Bernensia)

> 'LATIAN PEAK Rome' (aA); 'IT STRUCK THE LATIAN PEAK he speaks of the Alban mountain where Jove Latialis is' (*Commenta Bernensia* on *Civil War* 1.535, Usener 1869: 35).

The reading *Latialis* for *Latiaris* is common in manuscripts of Lucan, and this change is not hugely significant.[7] The author translates Lucan's text reasonably literally. 'Royal' is slightly ambiguous, but it may point to a lost note on the nature of the term *Latiaris*, which, as Roche (on 198) notes, 'underscores a personal connection shared by the god and Caesar through Iulus, the founder of both the Julian line and Alba Longa'. This is expanded into 'and the temple of Jove in Rome'. In other words, the Mons Alba is mistranslated as the Capitoline (confusion with *caput*) and then this is explained by reference to a temple: the temple of Jupiter Latiaris on the Mons Albanus would not have been well known, but the Capitoline would have been familiar. Moments where the author appears to go astray, then, can often point to the author in fact consulting a scholion instead. Throughout this passage, there are further signs of certain or possible influence from the scholia: the list of items portended by a comet (lines 831-38); the misidentification of Calpe as being in Italy, rather than in Spain (lines 871–2, cf. *Civil War* 1.554–5); the expansion of nocturnal birds at lines 881–2 (cf. *Civil War* 1.558).[8]

A final example can be seen at the end of the passage quoted, when the author recounts the tale of the talking ox. This well-known story finds its fullest account in Jerome's *Chronicle,* but is preserved in varying versions by the scholia. As Nagashima (2021) has demonstrated, the likeliest direct source for the redactor is Arnulf of Orléans' comment on line 1.561:

> NUNC PECUDUM Aliud prodigium contra naturam quod lingue soluebantur in uoces hominum. Legitur enim in Romanis historiis de quodam cui nimium urgenti iuuenca locuta est: 'quid me urges? Prius deficient homines quam frumenta.'

NOW AS FOR CATTLE Another marvel against nature, that [their] tongues were loosened for human speech. For it is read in the Roman histories about a certain man who was too harshly urging on his heifer, who said to him 'Why are you hassling me? Men will die out before the crops do.'

The Irish scholar's prefacing of the tale with the remark 'for it is said in the histories' (*uair innister isna sdairib*) very closely echoes Arnulf's *legitur enim in Romanis historiis*, as Nagashima points out, and follows other syntactical aspects of the gloss. It is unusual for the author to mark a conscious break from the text of Lucan in this way. One of the more remarkable aspects of *In Cath Catharda* is the way in which it relatively seamlessly incorporates additional information from the scholia, something that contributes to the unmistakably learned and scholarly character of the text and its intended audience.

Notes

1 The specificity of the fifteenth day has no basis in the text of Lucan or any commentaries; might it be a memory of the Ides of March?

2 Here and below the author uses the word *Torrian*, ostensibly 'the Tyrrhenian sea', but used here and elsewhere to refer to the Mediterranean as a whole.

3 Translations of Lucan and the Lucan scholia are my own, previously published in O'Hogan 2014 (with occasional modifications or corrections).

4 Examples are the commentaries on Lucan in Bern, Burgerbibliothek MS 370, and Cologny, Fondation Martin Bodmer, Codex Bodmer 182 (cited in Endt 1909 as Wallerstein I 2).

5 Orosius was usually available, though the treatment of the civil war is brief (6.15); Caesar was little read before the fourteenth century, and where he was known it tended to be for the *Gallic Wars*, rather than the *Civil Wars*; see further Brown 1976: 88–91.

6 Additionally, however, they doubtless preserve some individual annotations that date back to antiquity, cf. further Gotoff 1971 and Werner 1994.

7 *Latiaris* is usually connected with Jupiter, whereas *Latialis* is more properly related to Latium, but it is unclear how keenly the distinction was observed in practice: see Bruggisser 2002. *r* and *l* are occasionally confused in Latin (see e.g. *fragrantia/ flagrantia/fraglantia* at Vergil, *Aeneid* 1.436). The original word may have been *Latialis* (on the analogy of *Quirinalis* and *Mucialis*) which changed to *Latiaris* through liquid dissimilation, cf. de Melo 2019: 284–5, 693, on Varro, *De Lingua Latina* 5.52, quoting *Sacra Argeorum* fr. 3).

8 For expansion on these see O'Hogan 2014.

Part Five

Mythography and Pseudohistory

17

How Samson Slew the Gesteda

Brigid Ehrmantraut

The text is reproduced from Marstrander 1911: 150–4, lines 88–142.[1]

Text: Samson's messengers encounter the Gesteda

Rocuiredh iarsin luing romoir a crichaib na nEbraidhe ar merugud ⁊ arna combat[h]adh co caladhport na nGeistedhda .i. lucht luingi do ócaib treibi Dán mic Iacoip .i. indara treb deg do macaib Israel. Robatar dano dá ardtaisech .x. do aes gradha Samsoin mongaid mic Manua iarsin isin luing sin. Tangatar iarsin lucht na luingi a tir otchualatar in morchomdhail roboi isin tir i tangatar. Doriachtsat do acallaim in rig. Rogabad fachetoir iat uili icon ri[g] ⁊ ro[iarf]*aig* in ri scela doib iarsin ⁊ roinnsitar gorbo [. . .]

. . . Israel [. . .] '. . . do acallaim Priaim mic Laimidhoin ⁊ Echtair mic Priaim ⁊ Æniasa mic Anachis mic Thinair ⁊ na maithedh archena fuiledh icon Trai. Daig ata Elina faidh mac Priaim fri re bliadna anosa a farrad Samsoin ica thoghairm do fortacht na Troian i naigid na nGrec ⁊ is da fis tiagmaitni in creitit na Troianadh do dia adhrus Samson ⁊ adhrait mic Israel ⁊ dia creitit radhitsium dia saeradh ar n*ir*t na nGrec ⁊ muna adradh don aendia uilichumachtach ní chathfidisium tara cend.'

Atbert in rí iarsin: 'Isi bar conair coir tancabair ⁊ bermid a buidhi rer ndéib coimriachtain frib'.

'Cidh on' ar siat 'cret fa tathar duinn no cia holc doronsam?'

'Laighid bar mbrighi linn ar ansatu bar nathardha frisna gentib dia támni ⁊ da bar nidhpairt dona deib gach laei co cend da mis ⁊ rotmuirfidersi amlaid sin dona deibh .i. da fer .x. gach laei noco tairsit uilid ⁊ rotibrait uili dona deib fa dheoigh'.

Atbertsat lucht na luingi iarsin: 'Is olc' ar siat 'in comairli doníthi .i. ar marbadni ar notmuirbfider sib fein inn gusna huilib Geistedhaibh feraib macaib mnaib sceo ingenaib'.

Adubairt in rí: 'Cia dodenadh no cía dofétfadh in morgnim sin do dhenum?'

'Ar tigernani bodhein .i. Samson mongach mac Manuagh .i. fer dúrdha dodaing doiligh ise morghalach meargnimach ise badhach brut[h]mar co spirait na

Translation

based on Marstrander 1911: 151–5,
with style and wording modernized

Then a huge ship from the lands of the Hebrews, after going astray and being shipwrecked, was driven to the harbour of the Gesteda. The ship's crew were of the warriors of the tribe of Dan the son of Jacob, one of the twelve tribes of the Children of Israel. In that ship were also twelve noble leaders from among the counsellors of long-haired Samson, son of Manoah. The crew of the ship then came ashore, having heard of the great assembly in the land to which they had come. They came to speak with the king. They were all taken at once before the king and then he asked news from them, and they related that [...] '[We have come from] Israel ... [...] to speak with Priam son of Laomedon, and Hector son of Priam, and Aeneas son of Anchises son of Tinar, and the other nobles who are at Troy. For the seer Helenus, son of Priam, has been for a year now with Samson, entreating him to aid the Trojans against the Greeks, and we ourselves have come to find out whether the Trojans believe in the God whom Samson worships, and whom the Children of Israel worship, for if they believe they will go to free them from the strength of the Greeks, but if they do not worship the one omnipotent God, they would not fight on their behalf'.

Then the king said: 'It is the correct way that you have come, and we give thanks to our gods for encountering you'.

'What is this?' said they, 'why does calamity befall us, or what evil have we done?'

'Your value weakens in our opinion, because of the troubles your ancestors [inflicted] upon the Gentiles from whom we are [descended] and [we will] sacrifice you to the gods every day until the end of two months, and thus you will be sacrificed to the gods: that is, twelve men each day until you all have been seized and you all have been offered up to the gods at last'.

The crew of the ship said then: 'It is an evil counsel' they said 'that you have taken, that is, to kill us, for you yourselves will be killed because of it, together with all of the Gesteda, men, sons, wives, and daughters'.

The king said: 'Who would do, or who would be able to do that great deed?'

'Our own lord, that is, longhaired Samson, son of Manoah, a stern, hard, austere man, great in valour, and quick in action, warlike, violent with the spirit of divine sonairti diadha ann ⁊ isé mét na sonairti na fétfaitis fir in betha uili a fulang ina [a] frestal im sroighledh no im dhebaidh no im esorgain no im irghail ar ni tarla fris riam tren na taetsat leis. Acht c[h]ena' ar siat 'doberamni comairli maith duitsiu .i. legar aen don da thóisech .x. fuil acainn do breith fiadnaisi ⁊ fesa scel do Samson ⁊ dia ndilsigisen sine marbh*thar* sinn iarsin. Madh dia tí immorro Samson benaid cach re ceile acaib ⁊ denaid imurbágha ⁊ madh calma duitsiu ina dósom marbthar sinne uili ⁊ idhbrait dona [deib] iarsin. Dia tecma immorro comadh calma do Samson inas duitsiu ar isedh bias ann co deimin notsaerfaidhthea thu fein ⁊ do muintir dia mairmisni imṡlán agat. Madhé ar marbad immorro doghneis notmuirfider fein feraib macaib mnaibh.'

Atbert iar sin in ri:

'Leicfidht*er* aen uaibhsi do acallaim bar tigerna acht chena muirfidht*er* da fer .x. gach lai im ardtaisech agaib ⁊ tidnaicfidht*er* dona deib cein fogébt[h]ar in coimlín sin ann no co toir bar tigerna cugaib ⁊ dia toir sidhe muirfider fachetoir in lin doragha'.

Roleigedh iarsin aentaisech dib as ⁊ curach ⁊ lón leis ⁊ tainic reime co treib Dain .i. gusin cathraig daridhthi diarbo ainm B*er*sa [. . .].

strength in him. So great is that strength that the men of the whole world could not withstand him or oppose him in striking, or in strife, or in slaughtering, or in conflict, for no champion ever came against him who was not killed by him. However', said they, 'we will give you good counsel: Let one of our twelve leaders go to bear witness and bring news to Samson, and if he rejects us, then let us be killed. But if Samson comes, let each of you strike the other and do battle and if you prove stronger than he, then let us all be slain and sacrificed to the gods. But if Samson should prove to be stronger than you – which is certainly what will happen – both you and your people may be saved, if we remain unhurt among you. If, however, you kill us, you yourselves will be killed, men, women, and children'.

Then the king said: 'One of you will be released to speak with your lord, but twelve men of you including a leader will be killed every day and offered up to the gods, as long as that number is found there, or until your lord comes to you, and if he comes he shall be killed at once, and all who come with him'.

One of their leaders was then released with a boat and provisions, and he came to the tribes of Dan, to a certain city called Bersa [. . .].

Essay: Creative mythography in action

Like several other classically-inspired texts discussed in this volume the short narrative *How Samson Slew the Gesteda* is found in Dublin, RIA MS D.iv.2. No other copy is known. It follows *Fingal Chlainne Tantail* 'The Kin-Slaying of the Family of Tantalus', *Merugud Uilixis* 'The Wandering of Ulysses', and *Sgél in Mínaduir* 'The Story of the Minotaur' in the manuscript, and is itself directly followed by *Riss in Mundtuirc* 'The Tale of the Necklace' (see, respectively, Chs 19, 18, 20 and 12). The manuscript gives the narrative no title and I shall refer to the text as *How Samson Slew the Gesteda*, the name under which it was edited by Carl Marstrander in 1911. (The translation above is based on Marstrander's work, with minor updating and modernization.) The text dates linguistically to the late twelfth century or early thirteenth century.[2]

A plot summary will be necessary before we proceed any further. At the outset of the tale, the land of the Gesteda (which probably represents the land of Goshen in Egypt) faces a terrible drought because the angry gods have concealed its waters.[3] A priest named Proiss arrives, having been banished from India by his wife after raping his stepdaughter. Despite learning the cause of Proiss' exile, the Gesteda seek his advice concerning their drought. Proiss tells them to begin sacrificing their learned men to the gods, and to move on to other victims when they have exhausted these. At the point where the excerpt given here begins, a ship from the land of the Israelites washes up in the land of the Gesteda. Prior to this, Priam's son Helenus had come to request Samson's aid against the Greeks in the Trojan War. Samson sends messengers to Troy to ascertain whether the Trojans worship the same god as the Israelites. En route, his messengers are shipwrecked in the land of the Gesteda and the king begins sacrificing them. Upon learning the fates of his messengers, Samson rushes off to fight the Gesteda. He wields his camel jawbone, two beams of light shoot from his eyes, and he jumps on the floor of the palace so that it shakes, prompting everyone inside to fall upon their own weapons in fear. Samson forces the king, queen and Proiss to watch the waters return before killing them too. Samson thanks God and the text ends with a note that the priest Nehemias recorded the events.

How Samson Slew the Gesteda recounts the story of a legendarily strong hero killing a king who has been sacrificing visitors to the gods in order to avert a drought. As I have argued elsewhere, the Irish narrative is ultimately a version of the classical myth of Hercules and Busiris, recast to star the biblical Samson (Ehrmantraut 2022). In the classical myth Busiris, the king of Egypt, struggles with a terrible drought and, at the advice of a foreign seer Thrasius, begins sacrificing his guests to the gods. Hercules later arrives in Egypt between his Labours and kills Busiris, ending the drought. I have suggested that the details of the Busiris storyline were sourced from Ovid, a scholiast on Ovid, or Hyginus, as only these authors contain all the correct plot elements and names mentioned in *How Samson Slew the Gesteda*. I have also argued that *How Samson Slew the Gesteda* draws from the story of Philomela for Proiss' backstory, probably due to the fact that Orosius discusses Philomela directly after Busiris in his *Histories against the Pagans* as examples of bloodshed and moral depravity in earlier pagan eras.[4] At the same time, *How Samson Slew the Gesteda* also makes use of Irish historiographical material. Ultimately drawing on the historical synchronisms such as those in Eusebius/Jerome's *Chronicle*, which place Samson, Hercules, and Troy in the same time-period, a passage in the Book of Leinster version of Recension 2 of *Togail Troí* postulates that Samson might have been able to defeat Achilles had he fought at Troy (Best et al. 1954–83: 4.32823–5).

Like the other short adaptations of classical mythology beside it in RIA MS D.iv.2, mentioned above, *How Samson Slew the Gesteda* fashions an original narrative out of references in longer works and historical speculation. All five texts represent creative approaches towards historiography and mythography, supplementing classical narratives where details are unknown or where Irish and biblical material can reveal new levels of meaning. While *How Samson Slew the Gesteda* incorporates biblical material into its retelling of a classical storyline far more explicitly than do any of the other adaptations that accompany it in RIA MS D.iv.2, its inclusion amongst them clearly indicates that the compilers of the manuscript intended for it to be read alongside these other tales set in Mediterranean antiquity.

However, the historiographical methods at work in *How Samson Slew the Gesteda* involve a bolder sense of cross-cultural fusion than those in any of the other short classical adaptations found alongside it. Samson does not merely live at the same time as Hercules or as the Trojan War, he takes on the role of Hercules himself. We might even say that Samson functions as a type for Hercules (or Hercules as a type for Samson). This reflection of an ancient Greek hero as typologically resonant with a biblical character has its parallel in *Togail Troí* in the Book of Leinster (Recension 2), when baby Jupiter floats down the river Nile in a boat made of hide, much like Moses does in Exodus 2.3–10 (Best et al. 1954–83, 4.30827–34). Jupiter is given a literal biblical pedigree in the prologue to *Togail Troí* by virtue of his descent from Noah and Cham, but also a figurative pedigree via his adoption into the narrative based on Exodus. In the late eleventh-century Irish *Sex Aetates Mundi* ('The Six Ages of the World'), Romulus and

Remus are similarly set afloat in a cradle upon the Tiber (Ó Cróinín 1983: 87). While the Roman narrative probably ultimately stems from the authoritative tradition represented by Ovid's *Fasti*, 2.407, it was also likely understood by Christian authors and audiences in light of its typological similarities to the Biblical story of Moses. Typology thus emerges alongside synchronism as a major strand in the adaptation and interpretation of classical material: Jupiter is a type for Moses (and by extension Christ) in the *Togail Troí* passage mentioned above, just as Romulus and Remus are in the Irish *Sex Aetates Mundi*, and Samson is for Hercules in *How Samson Slew the Gesteda*.

Despite the claim that Nehemias recorded the events of *How Samson Slew the Gesteda* 'i nanaltaib na nEbraidhi co mairenn fos isna lebraib amail atclos' (Marstrander 1911, lines 228–9), 'in the annals of the Hebrews, so that it still remains in the books as it has been heard', it is unlikely that any reader of *How Samson Slew the Gesteda* thought that they were dealing with straightforward *historia*. However neither is it entirely a work of *fabula*. Instead, *How Samson Slew the Gesteda* provides a way for audiences to think about world history and the production of historiography. As in the case of the Moses-like episodes in *Togail Troí* and *Sex Aetates Mundi*, *How Samson Slew the Gesteda* employs the kind of typological methodology primarily used to explicate and interpret the Bible and applies it to classical figures, incorporating the classical world into the larger course of salvation history and exemplifying medieval Irish scholarly creativity.

Notes

1   I am grateful to the Harding Distinguished Scholars Programme for supporting this research, and to Máire Ní Mhaonaigh, Michael Clarke, Erich Poppe, Isabelle Torrance and John Carey for their helpful editorial suggestions; any errors or infelicities remain my own.

2   Marstrander 1911: 146; Ehrmantraut 2022: 40.

3   See Marstrander 1911: 145 and Ehrmantraut 2022: 41 for the identification and location of the land of the Gesteda.

4   Orosius, *Histories against the Pagans* 1.11.1–3.

18

Merugud Uilixis meic Leirtis 'The Wandering of Ulysses Son of Laertes'

Barbara Hillers

Three excerpts from the text presented here are edited by the author from Dublin, Royal Irish Academy, MS 23 P 12 (The Book of Ballymote), fols 247ra–248rb (hereafter B; for other manuscript abbreviations see n.5 below). Contractions (including whole word contractions) have been silently expanded; potentially ambiguous expansions are indicated by italics. Missing letters have been supplied in square brackets. Lenitions marked in the manuscript are rendered as Roman 'h' (except in the case of ḟ and ṡ, where the punctum delens *has been retained); lenition marks omitted in the manuscript have been suggested by italic 'h'. Length marks, absent from the manuscript, have been added throughout.*

Text extracts

Ulysses sets out from Troy

Iar n-indrad ⁊ díscaíl*ed* Tro*í*ana, turt*h*echta na nGréc tánic cách díb doc*h*um a chríchi [⁊] a f*h*eraind dílis féin. Tánic trá Uilixes mac Leirtis dá c*h*rích ⁊ dá f*h*erann co n-acca uad slébti a f*h*erainn féin.

'Is doilig lind imorro in ní fogébam and siút .i. in rígan álaind áilgen ro ḟácsamar and a beith ag fir eili inar fiadnaisi ⁊ ríg eli ar ar crích ⁊ ar ferand do bheith aigi, ocus ar séna fén im ar ndelb gid ar fírindi beam'.

'Ná cuirid fort-su sin', ar a muinntir fri hUilixes, 'uair fogébum uili int olc sin'.

Is and sin im*orro* ro t*h*aescair in gáeth forro-som ⁊ ro cuirid i falc mara móir amach dorigisi. Co ro bádar bliadain ar in mescmerugud sin nó co ráncadar in oilén mór ⁊ fuaradar cáerchu ollacha móradhbli ⁊ ro marbsatar trí cáerc*h*u díb ⁊ ro cuirid a pupaill tairrsib ⁊ ro tarlait a teinnti ⁊ ro hurrlamaigid a caírig. Trí lá ⁊ trí haidc*h*i dóib ann. Iar sin imorro adbert Uilixes:

'Is mit*h*ig dún imt*h*echt', ar sé.

'Ní cóir i n-aprai', ar siat, a muinnter, re hUilixes, 'uair atá ar ndaíthin co brát*h* ina fil do c*h*aírib sund'.

'Nocho dingnem foraib', ar sé, 'gan dula d'iarr*aid* ar n-athart*h*íri bunaid féin'.

The Judge of Truth

Táinic iarum Uilixes a tír co tarladar meic ingairi dó oga n-almaib. Ba fear fiamach fírglic trá in fear sa ⁊ ba coitc*h*endbérla, uair ro foglaimthea leis bérla cac*h*a tíri a teigid ⁊ ro f*h*iarfaid scéla tresin bérla ro f*h*ogain dóib ⁊ is ed fuair acco gurb é Brethem na Fírindi robo airiuch isin c*h*rích sin.

'Cá fírindi fognus dó?' ar Uilixes.

Translations by the author

Ulysses sets out from Troy

After the spoiling and dispersion of the Trojans, as to the Greeks, each of them went to his country and his own dear land. Ulysses son of Laertes for his part set out for his country and his land until he saw before him the mountains of his own land.

'What we will find there seems hard to us, namely that another man should in our presence possess the beautiful gentle queen we left behind there, or that another king should rule our country and possess our land, and that we should be denied because of our appearance, even though it is really us'.

'Do not let that weigh on you', Ulysses' companions said to him, 'for we will all suffer the same ill treatment'.

At that moment however the wind gushed on them and they were thrown back out to the open sea. And in that way they spent a year lost and adrift, until they came to a big island; and they found enormous big woolly sheep and killed three of them. And their tents were put up over them, and their fires were lit and their sheep cooked. They spent three days and three nights there. Then however Ulysses spoke.

'It is time for us to leave', he said.

'What you say is not right', his companions said to Ulysses, 'for there are enough sheep here to last us forever'.

'We will not refrain from going to seek our own native fatherland for all you say', he said.

The Judge of Truth

Then Ulysses went ashore, and he met some herdsmen with their flocks. Now that Ulysses was astute and very clever and he was a polyglot, for he used to learn the language of every land he would come to, and he asked their tidings in the language they used, and he found out from them that the Judge of Truth was ruler in that country.

'What kind of truth does he practice?' Ulysses asked.

'Ga*ch* duini doní a *fh*oglaim aigi ro *s*hoich a dúth*aig* fo *ch*étóir', ar iatsum.

'Cidh dam-sa', ar Uilixes, 'na*ch* dingnind foglaim aigi?'

'An bail a acfainn agad?' ar in freisnésid, 'uair ní fadbaidt*er*[1] aicept in áenláe gan deich n-uingi fichet do deargór dó. ⁊ tusa', for iat-som, 'cársa cúich thú?'

'Do éloicht*h*ib na Troíana dam-sa', ar sé, ⁊ taínic uaidib ar amus a luingi ⁊ ro *fh*iarfaigedar a muinnter scéla de ⁊ ro indis dóib feib adcuala ⁊ ro baí'ga ráda riu foglaim do dénum, ⁊ is ed ro ráidsiut ar sin na*ch* roibi a *t*hoisc accu a dénum, 'uair ro *t*huitsidar ar fuilt ⁊ ro theimligedar ar ruisc ⁊ ro dor*ch*aidsedar ar ngnúisi ⁊ ro glasadar ar ndédbaigi; ní bud oir*ch*es dún ar n-ór ná ar n-innmus do *t*habairt ar *fh*oglaim na*ch* tuillfid dún do dénum'.

'Cá ferr daíb', ar Uilixes, 'a *f*ágbáil ar bernadaib báegail nó ar doirrsib aideda, nás a *t*habairt ar *fh*oglaim *t*huillfeas daíb bidéin'?

The homecoming: Penelope tests Ulysses

'A daíne maithi', ar in rígan, 'cársa cia [d]íb-si etir?'

'Uilixes mac Leirtis misi', ar sé.

'Ní tú int Ulixes rob aichnid dúin-ne', ar sí.

'Indésad mo *ch*omartha', ar sé.

⁊ Do*ch*uaidh ina rúinib ⁊ ina comráitib ⁊ ina derridib.

'Caidi do delb ⁊ do muinnter', ar sí, 'masa tú Uilixes?'

'Do*ch*uadar amugu', ar sé.

'Cráed fo derid dud' *ch*omart*h*aib ro *fh*ágais agum-sa?'

'Delg óir', ar sé, '⁊ cend airgid fair ⁊ rucus-[s]a do delg-su leam ag dula dam isin luing ⁊ is and sin ro impóis-siu uainn'.

'Is fír trá sin', ar sí, '⁊ dam*a*d tú Uilixes, do *f*iarfóchtha do *ch*ú'.

'Nír *s*haílius a marthain etir', ar sé.

'Everyone who is taught by him reaches his country at once', they said.

'Why should I not be taught by him?' Ulysses said.

'Do you have the means for it?' his respondent answered. 'For you will not receive a single day's instruction from him without thirty ounces of red gold.[3] And you', they asked, 'where are you from?'

'I am one of the Trojan fugitives', he said, and he went away to his ship, and his people asked him tidings, and he told them what he had heard. And he was urging them to receive instruction, and they said that they did not want to do that, 'for our hair has fallen out, our eyes have grown dim, our faces are weathered, and our teeth have become discoloured. We ought not give away our gold and our wealth for the sake of instruction that would do us no good'.

'What do you prefer', Ulysses asked, 'to leave it in the gap of danger and on the doorstep of death, or to give it in exchange for instruction which would benefit you?'

The homecoming: Penelope tests Ulysses

'Good people', the queen said, 'who are you then?'

'I am Ulysses son of Laertes', he said.

'You are not the Ulysses we know', she replied.

'I will prove it', he said.

He went into their secrets and their talks and their confidences.

'What has become of your looks and your people, if you are Ulysses?'

'They have gone astray', he replied.

'What was the last of the tokens you left with me?'

'A golden brooch with a silver pin on it', he answered, 'and I took your own brooch with me as I was boarding the ship, when you turned away from us'.

'That is quite true', she said, 'and if you were Ulysses you would ask after your dog'.

'I did not expect her to be alive at all', he said.

'Dorónadh brochán aísi dí agum-sa', ar sí, 'uair do ráthaigius a grád co mór ag Uilixes. Ocus cia halt con hí etir in cú sin?' ar sí.

'Dá tháeb glégela aice', ar Uilixes, '⁊ druim gléchorcra ⁊ tairr círrdub ⁊ earball uainegda'.

'Iss í tuaruscbáil in chon', ar sí, '⁊ didiu ní lamund duine isin baili a cuid do thabairt dí acht misi ⁊ tuso ⁊ in rechtaire'.

'Tabar in cú asdeach', ar sé.

⁊ Ro éirgetar² ceathrar ara cend ⁊ tucsat leo asteach hí ⁊ amail ám adcuala sí fogur gotha Uilixis tug builli ara slabrad co tuc in cethrar ina laigi ar fad in taigi ina degaid gur ling in ucht Uilixis ⁊ guro ligh a gnúis ⁊ a aigid. Ó'dconncadar muinnter Uilixis sin ro lingsiud chuigi; in duine díb nach roiched a chneas re phógad, do phógad a édach. ⁊ nír gluais a ben ris-sin.

'Is tú Uilixes', ar sí.

'Is mé', ol sé.

'Is imda lucht na cumachta', ol sí, '⁊ taiscfet-sa m'áentuma co tí do dealb duit-siu'.

Sechtmain dó and in tan tuc-si aichni for a delb ⁊ ro áentaigedar iar sin.

'Cilfing beag agam', ar Uilixes, 'tuc m'oidi dam ⁊ adubairt rium a tabairt id' láim-siu gan fioslugud furri nó co tuccaind duit-siu hí'. Ro fioslaig furri fo chétóir. Deich n-uingi ⁊ cethra fichet tucustair-sium ar in foglaim is ed ro baí innti ⁊ tinni óir ar a uachtar do choiméd a fírinde fair.

Conid é Merugud Uilixis ó thús co derid co sin.

'I made a gruel of long life for her', she said, 'because I knew how much Ulysses loved her. And what kind of dog is that dog at all?' she asked.

'She has two pure white sides', Ulysses replied, 'and a bright crimson back, and a jet-black belly, and a greenish tail'.

'That is the description of the dog', she said, 'and moreover no one in the house dares to feed her but you and me and the steward'.

'Let the dog be brought in', he said.

And four men went to get her and took her inside, and when she heard the sound of Ulysses' voice, she gave a tug on her chain so that she pulled the four men on their backs all through the house behind her and jumped up at Ulysses and licked his cheeks and his face. When Ulysses' people saw that, they crowded round him, and anyone who was not able to kiss his skin, kissed his clothes instead. But his wife did not come to him.

'You are Ulysses', she said.

'I am', he replied.

'Many are the Mighty Ones', she said, 'and I will keep to myself until you look more like yourself'.

When he had been there for a week she recognized his looks, and then they slept together.

'I have a little bag which my teacher gave to me', Ulysses said, 'and he told me to put it into your hands, and not to open it until I gave it to you'. She opened it right away. Inside it were the ninety ounces he had paid for the instruction, with a gold cover on top to keep them intact.

And that is the Wandering of Ulysses so far, from beginning to end.

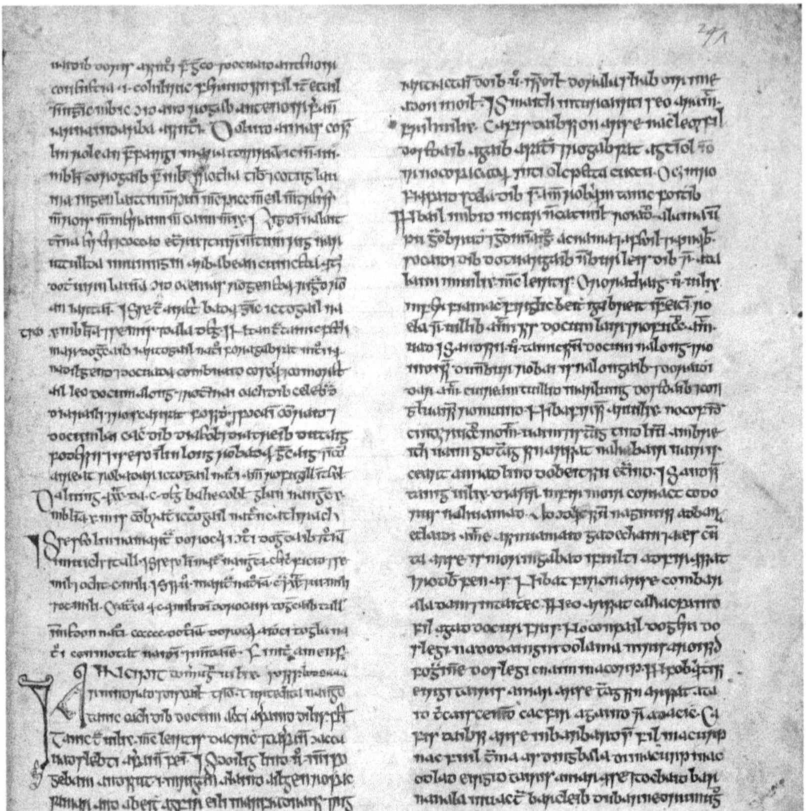

Figure 6 Dublin, Royal Irish Academy MS 23 P 12, the Book of Ballymote, fol. 247r, the opening of *Merugud Uilixis*. Image from ISOS reproduced by kind permission of the Royal Irish Academy.

Essay: Ulysses between book-culture and oral tradition

Merugud Uilixis meic Leirtis ('The Wandering of Ulysses son of Laertes') is a short Middle Irish prose saga of less than 300 lines, composed by an anonymous author working in an ecclesiastic milieu around the end of the twelfth century.[4] The text is extant in three late-medieval manuscripts, the oldest of which is the Book of Ballymote.[5] The language of the text is late Middle Irish.

The saga is one of the earliest vernacular retellings of the *Odyssey* in medieval Europe, and critical interest in the saga has always focused on its relationship to Homer's epic. The Latin West had no first-hand access to the Homeric epics until texts of the *Iliad* and the *Odyssey* were brought to Italy in the wake of the fall of Constantinople. Knowledge about Ulysses was mediated through Latin, and medieval readers knew of him primarily as a participant in the Trojan War; some of his Odyssean adventures were known as tropes from patristic writings and mythographic digests (Stanford 1976a; Clarke 2014b: 111). *Merugud Uilixis* throws light on the mediation and reception of classical sources in Ireland (cf. Ahl 1989). The saga draws on Virgil's *Aeneid* as well as a Virgilian prose digest, the *Excidium Troie* 'Destruction of Troy' (Clarke 2020). Far from vilifying Ulysses, as Virgil does, however, the Irish author casts him as a proto-Christian everyman and wisdom seeker. This sympathetic treatment suggests the author was familiar with allegorical interpretations of the hero espoused by late-antique and medieval churchmen (Hillers 1999a). Even more surprisingly, the saga incorporates an international folktale well-known in Irish oral tradition, The Master's Good Counsels (ATU 910B).

The first excerpt quoted above (Ulysses sets out from Troy) illustrates the saga's historiographical orientation. All three manuscript copies of *Merugud Uilixis* occur in a cluster of tales about Troy,[6] and the saga clearly functioned, among other things, to flesh out the 'historical' events of the Trojan War. Michael Clarke (2020) has shown that the author of *Merugud Uilixis* drew on the anonymous post-classical *Excidium Troie*.[7] The *Merugud*'s first sentence ('After the sack and the destruction of the chief city of the Trojans ...') closely follows the Latin text,[8] and the description of the homeward-bound Ulysses being tossed by winds out to the open sea is also drawn from the *Excidium*. It is at this point that the Irish hero's *merugud* ('going astray', 'wandering') commences, and his much-curtailed journey (Uilixes only visits three places on his homeward journey) captures something of the spirit, if not the letter, of the *Odyssey*. It should be stressed that, except for the Cyclops episode, which is mediated via Virgil and the *Excidium*, no sustained and detailed parallels can be established between the saga locales and the fifteen-odd stops on Odysseus' homeward journey.[9] The first excerpt concludes with Ulysses' visit to the Island of the Sheep, an episode whose Odyssean ambience has led critics to draw parallels between this island and various Homeric episodes, in particular the Oxen of Helios and the Lotus-Eaters (*Odyssey* 12 and 9, respectively). Robert Crampton has pointed to the use of the word *atharthír* 'fatherland' in this episode, comparing it to Odysseus urging his companions to be mindful of their *nostos* 'homecoming' (Crampton 2014: 64–8).[10]

Our second excerpt (The Judge of Truth) marks the point where the saga narrative pivots to the folktale of The Master's Good Counsels (ATU 910B, Uther 2004). The tale was told throughout Europe and further afield (Pichette 1991), and was particularly popular in Ireland, where almost three hundred versions were collected from oral tradition in the twentieth century (Hillers 1999a, 2014). The folktale hero is a poor man who gives up his wages in lieu of three pieces of advice from his good master. By following each counsel, the hero reaches home safely and is further rewarded by having his money restored to him. *Merugud Uilixis* skillfully grafts the plot of the folktale onto the story of Ulysses. The role of the good master is played by the Judge of Truth, who sells Ulysses three pieces of advice and sends him on his way home with a parting gift for his wife. The advice Ulysses receives from the Judge of Truth preserves him from falling into the hands of marauders, and, later on, from killing his own son. Thanks to the Judge's good counsel, Ulysses, like the hero of the folktale, is able to control his impulse to kill the young man whom, in a fit of jealous fury, he takes to be Penelope's lover.

In the final excerpt quoted here (the homecoming) the saga author draws on several Homeric motifs (Penelope's reluctance to believe the stranger is her husband, *Odyssey* 22, and Ulysses' description of the brooch he wore as he left for Troy, *Odyssey* 19), skilfully weaving them into the plot of the folktale. As in Homer's epic, the hero's homecoming is defined by mutual testing between husband and wife. In the saga, Penelope assumes a dominant role, questioning and testing her husband. Even Ulysses' encounter with his old dog (*Odyssey* 17) is repurposed as a final test. Penelope asks the stranger to describe the dog, and once Ulysses has correctly and in detail identified its unusual coloring, the dog is brought inside to test whether it will recognize the stranger. Odysseus' recognition by his old and decrepit dog Argos is in the Irish saga Transformed into a dramatic scene of public recognition. The dog leaps up and licks Ulysses' face, and his people crowd around to welcome their master home.

For its happy conclusion, finally, the story returns to the folktale denouement. Like the good master of the oral tale, the Judge of Truth restores the hero's money; the purse he gave Ulysses as a gift for his wife turns out to contain the precise sum of money the hero paid for the three good counsels.

The transformation of the good master of the folktale into the mysterious and lightly allegorized figure of the Judge of Truth reflects the author's ecclesiastical milieu and worldview (Hillers 1999a). The author has endowed the Judge with Christ-like attributes; his teachings include the precept to always adhere to the right path and to forego vengeance, and his parting gift to Ulysses is referred to as *timna* which can mean 'testament' as well as 'keepsake'. The saga is imbued with words for wisdom, knowledge, teaching, and particularly truth (*fírinne*), which occurs multiple times in the short text.

W. B. Stanford suggested half a century ago that the saga's undeniable charm was due to the manner in which 'classical and folklore motifs are skillfully combined' (1968: 286). The use of an oral folktale in the learned and literate context of the classical adaptations is certainly intriguing, and Michael Clarke calls the saga 'an unsolved puzzle' (2020: 95). *Merugud Uilixis* suggests that the world of the ecclesiastically educated author was not hermetically closed off from the world of the oral storyteller: he drew on written and oral lore, and imbued his pagan tale with meaning derived from his own Christian belief system.

Notes

1 *fadbaidter* is supplied from D, the verb being omitted in B.

2 Reading from D. B has *epgidar*.

3 The compound word *dergór* ('red gold') occurs frequently in early Irish literature. *Derg* ('red') may refer to objects of an orange or tawny hue, and 'purified gold' is the equivalent suggested in *eDIL* s.v.

4 Editions: Kuno Meyer (1886); Robert T. Meyer (1958); Hillers (forthcoming). The saga was previously known as *Merugud Uilix*, following the editions of Kuno Meyer and R. T. Meyer. Ulysses was known in Ireland by the Latin form of his name (*Ulixes*, in Irish texts often spelt *Uilixes / Uilixeis*). In two of the three manuscripts of the saga, the hero's name is abbreviated (*Uilix.*), and the editors took this abbreviated form to be the hero's name. However, it is clear that the scribes of all three manuscripts of *Merugud Uilixis* understood the hero's name to be trisyllabic, since the bisyllabic *Uilix* is consistently marked as an abbreviation (Hillers 2014: 86).

5 Dublin, RIA MS 23 P 12, fol. 247r (B); the other MSS are Dublin, RIA MS D.iv.2, fol. 67 (D) and Dublin, King's Inns MS 12, fol. 41 (K). The three excerpts chosen here are

cited from my edition (Hillers, forthcoming), based on B, with occasional variant readings from D.

6   In B, *Merugud Uilixis* occurs between *Togail Troí* and *Imtheachta Aeniasa*; in D it follows *Togail Troí, Don Tres Troí* and *Fingal Chlainne Tanntail*, and in K it comes between *Togail Troí* and *Fingal Chlainne Tanntail*.

7   The *Excidium Troie* (Bate 1986) is a prose paraphrase of the *Aeneid* (with supplementary episodes from Apollodorus), and Clarke suggests it may have supported classroom study of Virgil (Clarke 2020: 110; see also Miles 2011: 85–6 and 2020: 10 for use of the *Excidium* in Ireland).

8   *Et dum Troia expugnata vel incensa fuisset, exinde omnes unusquisque ad provinciam suam reversi sunt . . .* (Bate 1986: 71; Clarke 2020: 104–5).

9   There is no echo, however faint, in the Irish saga of some of the most popular Odyssean adventures, such as the hero's escape from the Sirens and from Scylla and Charybdis, or his sojourn with the sorceress Circe and the nymph Calypso.

10 Rather than an echo of Homer's *nostos*, the rare compound *atharthír* is likely to be a calque on Latin *patria* and thus suggestive of a Latin context for the mediation of the tale (Hillers 2014: 88).

19

Fingal Chlainne Tanntail 'The Kin-Slaying of the Family of Tantalus'

Robert Crampton

The text is preserved in two fifteenth-century manuscripts, D and K. D = Dublin, RIA MS D.iv.2, fols 66vb–67va, edited and translated by Byrne 1927:16–33; K = Dublin, King's Inns MS 12, fols 43va–45va, edited and translated by Crampton 2010:16–45. The text extracts and translations below are based on Crampton's edition of K.

Text extracts

The sacrifice of Pelops (based on Crampton 2010: 16–19)

Peloip mac Tantail, is dó tuc a lesmáthair an grád ndermháir, .i. Moesia ingen Aiax mac Mirmedoin, deirbhsiúr athar í sidhe d'Achil échtach mac Peil. Ocus ro ob-sum an inghin co rus-dímicnigh co mór iarsin, cond-ebert Peloip: 'dia mbeidís mná an talmun a cóemthach mh'athar uili, ní edraidfinn én mhnaí díbh, ⁊ ní dhingninn míréir mh'athar.'

Ro fergaighedh an bhen ghusmar ghnáthúaibhrech accarbh aininnech annsin ima hopadh don gilla. ⁊ ro scaíl-si a folt ⁊ do rép a haghed, do tuaircc a hucht ⁊ a cighi, ⁊ tánaic dochum Tanntail ⁊ adfét a sárugad do Pheloip. 'Apair-siu, a ríghan', ar Tanntal, 'créd do-géntar fris'. 'Aderim', ar sí, 'a coscairt ⁊ a áidhedha do dhenamh dhe, ⁊ a brúith ⁊ a thabart dona déibh gan fhis dóib da chaithemh, co fesam indat dei iat iar fír.' Ar nir léicset cloinn doibh ⁊ is aire do ráidh sí sin. Ro gairmed iarsin na dei docum Tanntail gurro idhbradh a mac dóib.

How Aegisthus became Clytemnestra's husband (based on Crampton 2010: 24–7)

Fácbhais Aighmemnon a mhnaí agá thigh isin Gréc, .i. Clemestra. Is sí aireg menman for-fúair sí, .i. tuc grádh ndermháir do Eighist mac Teist ⁊ ro chuir fis air dia shaiged ⁊ is ed ro ráidh an techtaire fri hEigheist, 'Tuc ben Aighmemnoin grádh duit-si, ⁊ adbert rit dul dá saighidh ⁊ co faífedh let ⁊ cosain féin ríghi na Gréce friad naimdibh imalle fria-si. ⁊ dono dligi-si mhnaí is a ben suut, uair ruc a derbráthair súd do mnaí-siu ar éigin lais, ⁊ rot-innarpsat a ríghe na Gréce. 'Is fír sin', ar sé, '⁊ ragat-sa ar cenn mná Aighmemnoin, ⁊ coisénat rígi na Gréce fri macaib Aídir'. Tuc Eighist iarsin mhnaí Aigmemnoin leis ⁊ ro marb athair Aigmemnoin, .i. Aídir.

Translations

The sacrifice of Pelops

It was Pelops son of Tantalus whom his stepmother loved greatly, that is, Moesia daughter of Aeacus son of Myrmidon, she was the sister of the father of murderous Achilles son of Peleus. He refused the girl [i.e. Moesia] however, and then he rebuked her greatly, and Pelops said: 'Even if all the women of the world were my father's lovers I would not have sexual intercourse with a solitary woman of them, and I would not act against the will of my father.'

Then the fierce, angry, very violent, proud woman became enraged at her rejection by the youth. And she unbound her hair, and tore at her face, and beat her bosom and her breasts, and she came to Tantalus and declared that she had been raped by Pelops.[2] 'Say, o queen', said Tantalus, 'what shall be done to him'. 'I say', said she, 'that he should be slaughtered and dismembered, and crushed into pieces, and be given to the gods to be eaten without their knowledge, so that we may find out whether they are truly gods'. For they did not allow them to have offspring, and that is why she said that.[3] After that the gods were summoned to Tantalus so that his son might be sacrificed to them.

How Aegisthus became Clytemnestra's husband

Agamemnon had left his wife Clytemnestra in his house in Greece. This is the scheme she fixed upon: she developed a great passion for Aegisthus son of Thyestes and she sent for him to come, and this is what the messenger said to Aegisthus: 'Agamemnon's wife has given her love to you and she said to you to come to her and that she would go to bed with you, and that you yourself alongside her must contest the kingship of Greece with your enemies. And you are entitled to the woman who is his wife, for that man's brother took your own wife away with him by force, and they have expelled you from the kingship of Greece.' 'That is true', he said, 'I shall go and meet Agamemnon's wife and I shall contest the kingship of Greece against the sons of Atreus'. Then Aegisthus took Agamemnon's wife for himself and killed Agamemnon's father, Atreus.

Hermione, Pyrrhus and Orestes (based on Crampton 2010: 40–3)

Ermiona dono, ingen Menelaus mic Aídir ⁊ do Eillenn Leghdha, ben is caíme baí isin domun acht a máthair, ro naiscedh í re hOirist mac Aigmemnoin riasiu do marbad a athair, ⁊ iar marbad a athar ro innarb a mháthair ⁊ bráthair a athar é, amal ro rem-ráidhsemar. Tuc Pirr mac Aichil iar sin Ermionha dar sárugad Oirist, ó'tconnairc co hanbhfhann é iar marbad a athar ⁊ iarna innarbadh budhein. Ó ro gabh Oirist ríghi Grec baí oc iarrad a mhná for Pirr, ⁊ ní tuc Pirr freccru fair acht atbert co marbfed é féin dia n-imráidedh í[1] co bráth.

Do-cuaidh Oirist iarsin do accallaim sacairt tempaill Apaill co hinis Deil, ⁊ tuc seoda ⁊ maíne imdha dó ar Pirr do brath, ⁊ ro mairn an sacart Pirr do Oirist ⁊ dogabh Oirist teampall Apaill for Pirr, ⁊ ro marbhadh Pirr ann ⁊ ro gonadh Ermiona. ⁊ ro haincedh í iarna guin ara grádh ⁊ ar dáigh a tarberta. Ocus ro leadur sisi féin a crécht guruo marbh dhé fo cétoir, uair dob ferr le a hoighidh inas a faicsin do mhnaí oca namhaid.

Hermione, Pyrrhus and Orestes

As for Hermione, daughter of Menelaus son of Atreus and of Ledan Helen, the fairest woman there was in the world, except her mother, she had been betrothed to Orestes son of Agamemnon before his father had been killed but, after his father's killing, his mother and his father's brother [= Aegisthus] banished him, as we have said. Pyrrhus son of Achilles then carried Hermione off to the dishonour of Orestes, having perceived that he was very weak after his father's killing and his own banishment. When Orestes seized the kingship of Greece he constantly demanded his wife of Pyrrhus, but Pyrrhus gave him no answer but said he himself would kill him if he ever mentioned her.

Then Orestes went to the isle of Delos to speak with a priest of the temple of Apollo, and he gave him valuables and treasures aplenty in exchange for betraying Pyrrhus, and the priest betrayed Pyrrhus to Orestes, and Orestes took the temple of Apollo from Pyrrhus, and Pyrrhus was killed there and Hermione wounded. And she was saved after being wounded, because of the love he had for her, and moreover in order to carry her off, but she hacked at her own wound so that she died at once, since she preferred to die than to see herself become the wife of her enemy.

Essay: A tragic narrative reimagined

Fingal Chlainne Tanntail, 'The Kin-Slaying of the Family of Tantalus', is a twelfth- or thirteenth-century Irish account of the (mis)deeds and ultimate downfall of the classical dynasty whose members include Tantalus, Pelops, Atreus, Thyestes, Agamemnon, Clytemnestra, Menelaus, Helen, Orestes and Hermione. It is remarkable for its author's knowledge of what was arcane material for his own time and place, for his skilful reworking of the underlying narrative, and for a number of radical mythological interventions. He seems to have been engaged in filling perceived 'gaps' where the tradition available to him might have been considered incomplete; for example, our text provides details of the deaths of Pelops and Orestes that are unparalleled in any other known source. Even without knowing for certain the form in which the author received his information, we can see the shape he put upon it. He made thematic connections to link together the generations of the Tantalid clan, he provided clear motivations for the actions of the various characters, and in some cases he completed their biographies with otherwise unattested events.

The major effect of these interventions is to provide a new intergenerational moral template behind the action, remodelling tragedy in the terms of the author's own culture.[4] This process is bookended by the introduction of a specifically female 'original sin' at the tale's outset, namely the false accusation of rape, and by the similarly unique final replacement of the male Tantalids by the descendants of Achilles as rulers of Greece. Taken together, such novel elements ensure that our text offers a new version of the fate of Tantalus and his descendants. The Tantalid house lost the sovereignty because its members were immoral. That immorality originates in female agency, first through Moesia, then through Clytemnestra, leading in turn to internecine male violence. This succinct prose version of the narratives that tend nowadays to be most familiar in the form they take in Aeschylus' *Oresteia* (which was not itself available in medieval Western Europe) has been reimagined for a medieval Irish audience.[5] The three extracts presented here illustrate this process.

The murder of Pelops at the behest of his father Tantalus, in our first extract, is the dynasty's first kin-slaying, here as elsewhere in the mythological tradition. However, our text goes against the mainstream tradition in presenting this as the result of unrequited sexual desire on the part of Pelops' otherwise unattested stepmother, 'Moesia, daughter of Aeacus, son of Myrmidon'.[6] In the few extant sources to contain any motive, it is related simply that Tantalus wished to serve a special meal for the gods. If his sources did offer any justification for the murder of Pelops, the author of our text preferred the idea of a lustful stepmother's uncontrolled rage at her own rejection. The 'lustful stepmother' figure here echoes classical, biblical, and medieval Irish examples of this familiar trope or story-pattern, including the legends of Phaedra and Hippolytus, Joseph and Potiphar's wife, and the plot of *Fingal Rónáin* 'The Kin-Slaying of Rónán'.[7] *Fingal Rónáin* and *Fingal Chlainne Tanntail* are particularly close to the Phaedra-Hippolytus model as, in each case, a stepmother brings about the death of her husband's son by feigning rape after having been rejected by him. It seems probable, then, that our text borrows the motif either from *Fingal Rónáin* (which comfortably predates it, as is clear on linguistic grounds) or from some version of the classical story of Phaedra and Hippolytus.[8] It is impossible to specify which of these was the most probable inspiration, yet it is Seneca's *Phaedra* which offers the closest verbal similarity to the account presented in our text.[9]

The action of the remainder of the text exhibits several unique elements, showing female characters as the prime movers behind his tale's litany of kin-slayings; and the actions of Aerope and Clytemnestra follow classical models in broad terms but differ from them in certain key details, as we shall see below.

As we see repeatedly in the texts studied in this volume, the medieval Irish authors were often ready to intervene and elaborate in order to 'complete' an inherited narrative.[10] In the present text, we are told that Pelops ultimately dies at the hands of Aegisthus, an account for which there is no parallel. The text also seems to innovate as far as the Latin mythographic tradition goes by linking the two sets of incidents in which Aegisthus appears elsewhere. He is avenger on behalf of his father Thyestes, whose other sons (as many as fifty here, a deliberate exaggeration, I suggest, from the maximum of three elsewhere) were killed by his brother Atreus. Meanwhile, he is also the lover of Clytemnestra, wife of his cousin Agamemnon, the supreme king of the Greeks.[11] However, whereas the liaison between Aegisthus and Clytemnestra is presented as a *fait accompli* elsewhere, our author takes great care to describe it as the result of a deliberate *aireg menman* 'scheme', conceived by Agamemnon's faithless wife in order to gain political power for herself. It seems beyond doubt that the author's use of the term *aireg menman* is a clever wordplay on the Gaelicized *Aigmemnon*, which emphasizes the scheming element in his portrayal of Clytemnestra.[12] It is intriguing that Greek authors made similar plays using Clytemnestra's name in relation to the same literary incidents.[13]

Such examples of wordplay, combined with the introduction of novel details and inventions in places where extant sources are incomplete, highlight the impetus to create a newly integrated and coherent narrative.[14] In this episode, for example, we read that Helen, wife of Menelaus, had originally been Aegisthus' spouse before Agamemnon's brother had taken her from his cousin.[15] Aegisthus, we are further informed, had been 'King of Greece' before the sons of Atreus stole both wife and sovereignty. In this version, Clytemnestra is given significant agency in instigating the relationship with Aegisthus and has a political motivation that is paralleled in Aeschylus' *Agamemnon*. As with the agency of Moesia, however, the destruction connected to it casts the women in a negative light for a medieval Irish audience. Whereas, for example, it is possible to sympathize with the classical Clytemnestra's conduct towards Agamemnon – he has killed their daughter, Iphigenia, in a human sacrifice and brought his Trojan concubine Cassandra home from the war – there seems to be no room for such moral ambiguity towards Clytemnestra in the account presented in *Fingal Chlainne Tanntail* (Crampton 2010: 118–19).

Our final extract occurs towards the end of the narrative, at the point where Orestes, as in the familiar accounts of the story, has retaken the kingship by killing both his mother and her lover, his kinsman Aegisthus. What is remarkable here is the conduct of Hermione, daughter of Menelaus and Helen. The author begins by drawing the reader's attention to the physical similarity between Hermione and her mother, a theme that receives little attention elsewhere in Latin mythographic sources. This is surely intended to emphasize their similarly adulterous actions, for the author rapidly mentions thereafter that Hermione was initially *ro nasicedh* 'betrothed' to Orestes, before preferring Achilles' son Pyrrhus (also known as Neoptolemus).

As with the previous examples of faithless female characters in our text, violent enmity between male characters is directly caused by Hermione's infidelity. Again, there is little room for sympathy for any of the major characters of either gender, yet the episode's main female character is once more the instigator behind the calamity. The final collapse of the Tantalid dynasty after Aegisthus' son 'Aimpitir' kills Orestes at the climax of *Fingal Chlainne Tanntail* is primarily the responsibility of Hermione, who is presented as an adulteress.[16] Male characters are unable to control their violent impulses, a theme which clearly echoes the classical sources and continues their themes, yet the men's actions are secondary to the causal sin of Hermione and other females. The manner of the otherwise unattested suicide of Hermione recounted in our text is perplexing, however, in that it seems both honourable and physically brave, not attributes which are suggested by any of the surrounding descriptions either of Hermione or of any other female character in the tale. Nevertheless, as with the only other instance of a female suicide-for-love present in extant medieval Irish literature, that of Deirdriu in *Loinges Macc nUislenn* 'The Exile of the Sons of Uisliu' (Hull 1949; Gantz 1981: 256–67), such an act might not have been viewed sympathetically by a medieval Irish audience. Here, control over Deirdriu's marriage lies in the hands of her foster-father Conchobar, King of the Ulstermen, and it is he who orders first the killing of her chosen lover, Noisiu, then that she marry Noisiu's killer, Éogan mac Durthacht, for a year. In the Tantalid narrative, we are told that Hermione had been betrothed to (her cousin) Orestes, rendering her preference for Pyrrhus, later killed by Orestes, an act of rebellion against her family. In each of these literary incidents, the lawful course of action for the female character would have been to marry the man who had killed her own chosen lover. In each case, the female character prefers to commit suicide. No overt comment is passed by the authors on the conduct of either prominent female figure, yet each text highlights the tragic consequences for women who choose to act contrary to lawful authority in the context of marriage.

It is interesting to note that the two literary suicides discussed above are highly similar by circumstance, but dissimilar by method. Hermione tears open her wounds, as we have seen, whereas Deirdriu dashes her head against a stone.[17] Curiously, rather than resembling the suicide of Deirdriu, a story which, as a man of letters, the author of our text is very likely to have known, Hermione's rather grisly final act in the Irish text is highly resonant of perhaps the most famous act of suicide in Roman history, that of Cato the Younger in 46 BCE. Around a hundred years after the event, Seneca described it thus (*Epistula* 24.8):

> Inpressit deinde mortiferum corpori vulnus. Quo obligato a medicis cum minus sanguinis haberet, minus virum, animi idem, iam non tantum Caesari sed sibi iratus nudas in vulnus manus egit ...

> He inflicted a mortal wound upon his body. After the physicians had bound it up, Cato had less blood and less strength, but no less courage; angered now not only at Caesar but also at himself, he rallied his unarmed hands against his wound ...

> Gummere 1917–25: 1.170–1

Thus, the famous Stoic is alleged to have rent open his own wounds rather than 'live among the unfree', paraphrasing the words of Seneca, while the Hermione of our text is said to have performed a remarkably similar final act rather than be bound to her lawful fiancé, Orestes. Their motivations differ in that Cato's determined act was purely political whereas Hermione's motivation is said to have been romantic as well as political, in that Orestes is described as her *namhaid* 'enemy'. As with the tale's initial incident involving the lustful stepmother-figure, Moesia, there appear to be partial analogues for the novelty of Hermione's suicide from both a classical and a medieval Irish source. Although it is impossible to prove direct borrowing from either, the suspicion remains that the author may have garnered material from both types of possible source.[18] Whatever his models were, the author of *Fingal Chlainne Tanntail* took on a significant literary challenge in reworking the underlying Greek tragic narrative. The resulting work showcases both wide literary knowledge and a highly creative mind.

Notes

1 The independent object pronoun *í* is not in MS K and has been supplied here from the copy of the text in MS D. See Byrne 1927: 30, n.24.

2 To render her own appearance dishevelled is a relatively common – but not the only – literary device in narratives in which a woman makes a false claim that she has been raped. The closest analogue to this episode may be that found in Seneca's *Phaedra*; see Crampton 2010: 143–4.

3 There are several unique details present in *Fingal Chlainne Tanntail* which serve to offer a cause for a character's actions, where typically none exists in the Latin mythographic tradition. These offer a means to analyse the medieval Irish author's methods and purposes; see further Crampton 2010: 71–138.

4 Crampton 2014: 60–73.

5 A useful comparison is with the account of the Tantalids' travails as presented in Euripides' *Orestes*, see Kovacs 1994–2008: 5.412–17 and 600–1, at lines 5–45 and 1653–63 respectively. No complete account of the Tantalid cycle is present in Latin mythographic sources such as Hyginus or the Vatican Mythographers.

6 'Moesia' seems to have been introduced into the narrative to suit the medieval Irish author's purposes, since there is no other mention of any such figure in the extant record. The personal name Moesia may have been inspired by the connection between Achilles (Moesia's nephew, according to our text's story) and the Romanized place-name Moesia, see Crampton 2010: 51–2.

7 Edition by Greene 1955, translation at Koch and Carey 2004: 274–82.

8 For discussions of a possible connection between Seneca's *Phaedra* and *Fingal Rónáin*, see Mac Gearailt 2006/7; De Bernardo Stempel 2006 and 2016; Crampton 2010: 142–4; Clarke 2014c.

9 'She is preparing wicked charges against the innocent youth … she seeks credence with her torn hair, she mars the beauty of her head' (*Phaedra* 825–7, Fitch 2002–4: 1.514–5).

10 Some of these unique 'explanatory' details are highly unusual, including the statement that Helen had originally been married to Aegisthus before the sons of Atreus stole both her and the kingdom from him, mentioned in our second extract.

11 For a discussion of the 'fifty sons' of Thyestes found uniquely in this source, see Crampton 2010: 93–4.

12 This example of an unmarked play on a personal name is unusual in the context of medieval Irish scholarship, where explanation via explicit etymologizing is the norm. See for example *Cóir Anmann* 'Treatise on Personal Names' (Arbuthnot 2005–7).

13 Aeschylus, for example, see Sommerstein 2008: 2.131, n.237.

14 The author also makes a covert reference to the Trojan patriarch Laomedon in referring to the *lár medhón* 'epicentre' of a battle. Crampton 2010: 33–4.

15 Perhaps the most unorthodox detail present in the text is the statement that Teucer, the famous archer on the Greek side in the Trojan war, was barred from fighting for the Greeks by Hesione, who was daughter of Priam and thus a Trojan by birth. See Crampton 2010: 34–5.

16 Aegisthus' son, named as Aletes in other sources, is typically killed by Orestes. It is doubtful whether 'Aimipitir' is intended to be this figure.

17 *Do-lléici a cenn immon cloich co nderna brúrig dia cinn co-mbo marb* 'She dashed her head against the stone until she had made fragments of her head so that she died.' (Hull 1949: 51, 69, at lines 316–17).

18 Although we have no direct evidence for the works of Seneca in medieval Ireland, his philosophical works seem to have been available in the British Isles. Interestingly in the context of this incident in our text, Seneca's *Epistolae* 'Letters' are included in a medieval catalogue from the Cistercian house at Margam, Glamorgan (Mynors et al. 1991: 291).

20

Sgél in Mínaduir 'The Story of the Minotaur'[1]

Barbara Hillers

The text has been edited by the author from Dublin, Royal Irish Academy, MS D. iv.2, fol. 69 (hereafter referred to as D). Contractions have been silently expanded, italics being reserved for potentially ambiguous expansions (and whole word contractions even where these are unambiguous). Lenition marks – usually the punctum delens *– have been rendered as roman 'h', except in the cases of ḟ and ṡ, where the* punctum *has been retained. Lenition is marked only sparingly in the manuscript, and missing lenition marks have not been editorially supplied here. Editorial length marks have been suggested (ē, ā, etc), and missing letters have been supplied in square brackets in a few cases. For previously-published editions see Meyer 1903 and Hillers 1999b, with German translation and commentary; see also Miles 2011: 60.*

Text: The story of the Minotaur

Sgēl in Mhínaduir annso

[B]aī rí amra oiredha i n-Inis Crēit .i. Minósa a ainm-sidhēin. Buī rīghan caem crutach leis-[s]idhēin .i. Paisibé a h-ainm-sidhe, ⁊ tucustair grádh ndermair do Ioip mac Sátuirn. Boī *immorro* tarb ndermair suaichnidh soineamail accon rí sin, ac Minósa. Tuc *immorro* Paisibé grádh dó-sidhe, ar bá dōigh léi-sidhe gurb é Iop ro boī i richt in tairb, amail tāinic Iop fecht ele a richt tairb do saidhi Eorpta ingine Eghnoiris.

Boī *immorro* ollam cerda accon rí .i. ac Minósa. Ro gairmtea lé-si in cerd ⁊ atbert a comrád fris, in fuidhbi airicc dí, tresa rois*ed* in tarb do comaentug*ud* fris. Atbert in cerd co fuidhbedh. Is í airig foruair in cerd .i. bó cranda do dhénum dhí ⁊ Paisibé do cur isin deilb cranda sin, co nárbhudh lēir acht a h-iarthar aisti. Tucthá iarum in tarb a ndochum na bó coro aentaigi fria ⁊ ro toirrcid Paisibé de sin ⁊ ro boī *noí* mísa torrach, amail is dír.

Ro tuismedh araili ainmidhi adhuathmar cumuscdha ó dhuine ⁊ ó tharb .i. cend tairb fair ⁊ corp duinecda aigi .i. Mínaduir a ainm. ⁊ ó ro sill in rí fair, ro mhiscnidh é fa *chēt*ōir co narbodh āil leis a ḟaicsin ⁊ ro gairmedh ón rí in saer .i. Dedhail ainm in t-ṡaeir ⁊ isbert araili co ndernadh teadhais ndodaingin dō, ar nac fétfadh toidecht. Ar dá fáth*aib* ro hordaidedh in tegais-si accon rí don Mínaduir, .i. ar mét ⁊ ar truma a foghla for daīnib ⁊ cethrib na crīchi, ⁊ an fáth *ele* do*no*, ba nár leis duine beó dia ḟaicsin, ar bá dōigh leis cor hé fēin athair in Mínaduir. Ro airigh in saer iar sin in [n]-uaim n-aineōlaidh seacrānda ⁊ ro cuiraed in Mínaduir innti iar dain. Gach duine *immorro* dogníth cinta *nó* pudar frisin rí ro tidhnaicedh don Mínaduir co n-ithedh fa *chét*ōir ⁊ dobertha mōirseisiur cacha bl*iadn*a do macaib saercl*ann* na Grēci don rí, .i. do Mhinósa, a cum*ne* a athar, ⁊ doberdis iat-sidhe don Mínaduir conus ith*ed* iat, uair is iat Grēcaigh ro marb aith*ir* Minósa.

Is aml*aid* doníthea sin .i. cranncur doníthea eturra ⁊ gibé dā roiseadh, a tabairt ar tūs don Mínaduir; dobertha dó é. ⁊ Rosiacht a los cranncair do Théis m*a*c Ēig *m*eic Neptuin *m*eic Iop *m*eic Sátuirn in fer fa dheoig. Ar ba hé in *secht*mad fer ro boī isin ngiallaidecht ⁊ tuc ingen boī accon rí grádh dó-sidhe .i. do Théis ⁊ is ed isbert in ingen fris: 'Is duit-siu rosiacht do*no* do thidhnacul don Mínaduir', ⁊ ro

Translation

Here follows the story of the Minotaur

There was a great and famous king on the island of Crete; Minos was his name. He had a noble, beautiful queen; her name was Pasiphae. Pasiphae conceived a great love for Jupiter, son of Saturn. Now this King Minos owned a great, renowned and special bull. Then Pasiphae became filled with love for the bull, believing that it was really Jupiter in the shape of a bull, since Jupiter had on another occasion taken the shape of a bull in order to pursue Europa, the daughter of Agenor.

King Minos, furthermore, had a master craftsman. The craftsman was summoned by the queen, and she asked him in confidence whether he could contrive a device for her by which she might come to the bull to copulate with him. The craftsman said he could. The contrivance he devised was to construct a cow from wood for her, and in that wooden figure she could be accommodated so that only her back side was exposed. Then the bull was taken to the cow to mate with her, and Pasiphae conceived from that and was pregnant for the regular span of nine months.

She gave birth to a fearsome creature, half human and half bull: it had a bull's head and a human body, and it was called Minotaur.[3] And from the moment the king saw it, he was filled with instant loathing for the creature and could not bear to look at it. And the king summoned the craftsman – his name was Daedalus – who said he could build him an inscrutable[4] dwelling from which he could not escape. The king had two reasons to commission this dwelling for the Minotaur: first, on account of the extent and heaviness of its depredation against men and beasts of the country; and his second reason, moreover, was that he was ashamed of anyone seeing the creature, because he believed that he was himself the father of the Minotaur. So the craftsman built an impenetrable, mazelike souterrain,[5] and then the Minotaur was placed in it. Moreover, anyone who committed an offence or crime against the king was thrown to the Minotaur, who would devour him instantly. And each year seven young men of the Greek nobility were surrendered to King Minos, in memory of his father, and they would be thrown to the Minotaur to be eaten; for it was the Greeks who had killed Minos' father.[6]

This is how it used to be done: they would cast lots between them, whoever it fell on to be given to the Minotaur first; he was sacrificed to him. The last person the lot fell on was Theseus, son of Aegeus son of Neptune son of Jupiter son of Saturn,[7] for he was one of the seven hostages. And one of the king's daughters fell in love with Theseus, and the girl said to him, 'It is your turn now to be surrendered rāidh: 'Cia luagh nobērtha don t-í not saerfad?' Atbert Téis dia mbeth' na comung maith isin tal*main* dobēradh uadh ar a ṡaeradh. 'Atā *immorro*', ar in ingen. 'Abair é', ar Téis. 'Mo thabairt-si', ar sí, '⁊ mo beth d'aenmnaí agat'. Atbert Téis: 'Céin bemaid araen beó, doghēbud-su sin, dia tísadh mo saerad-su de'. 'Doticfa', ar in ingen.

Dobeir in ingen ceirtli dlūta dō ⁊ cloidhem a h-athar ⁊ itbert in ingen: 'Cengail cend in [t]-snaithi do dorus na h-uadma ⁊ tuinnmi lat in ceirtli it' lāim noco roisir in Mínaduir ⁊ dícend é iar sin'. Rosiacht-san trā dochum in Mhínaduir ⁊ do chath*aig* fris corus dícend é ⁊ tāinic iar tain a lenmuin in t-ṡnaithi *chét*na ⁊ ní h-innister nec do thíachtain *est*i dia ndech*aid* innti acht eisin ina aenur.

Iar sin trā ro fergaidhedh in rí .i. Minósa frisin cerd, uair is é ro ḟairig in mboin cranda ro boí ic Paisibé ⁊ ro gabad in cerd ⁊ a mac ⁊ ro ḟobair a marbad. Rob í trā comairli a muintiri dó, a ḟuirech, ⁊ grēsa ⁊ cumdaighi in rígh do dénum dóib ⁊ ro cuiredh i tech foriata iat ⁊ senistri anuas fair ⁊ ro bhátar isin tigh sin ic dénum grēssa ⁊ cumdaigh in rígh. ⁊ Araili fecht bátar macrad in rígh amuich ic imain ⁊ ro buail araili mac dīb in liathroit an airdi co tarla anuas gach ndīrech tar seinistir tighi in cerda ⁊ ro ghab in cerd in liathroit tall isin tigh ⁊ tāinic in fer ros buail ina diaigh. Ro gab in cerd uimpi. Tancatar in macrad uili iar sin do iar*aid* na liatroiti ⁊ rāidhis in cerd nach tibrad uaidh in liatroit *noc*o tuctais in macrad a breath féin dó. Ocus is í breath ro iar forro .i. lán glaici gacha ḟir dīb do eitib én do thabairt dó cech lāi co cend *noí* mís ⁊ doratadh dó-san sin tar cend na liatroiti ⁊ dorighni-sium dá éncheanaigh do na h-eitibh sin .i. dó féin ⁊ dia mac .i. do Iacair mac Dedail ⁊ ro ēloidhétar iar tain isna h-énchendach*aib* sin tar Muir Torrian a leith ⁊ atbert in cerd fria mhac co nach dighsedh suas co ro-ard uas gāith, nā sīs co ro-ísil 'acht len in firmamint medónach'. Ní dernaidh-sium sin acht dochuaidh suas co ro-ard, coro legh in cēir ro bī a[c] congbail na n-eitedh re teas na grēine, co torcair iar sin isin muir ⁊ is é ainm na mhara² sin ō ṡoin a *leth* Muir Iacair .i. Iacair mac Dedhail dotuit innti.

Rosiacht do*no* in t-aithair imslán tar in muir co riacht Magh Campain ⁊ dorighni temp*ul* do Apuill ann ⁊ is é sin senchus in Mínaduir ⁊ a oighidh. FINIT.

to the Minotaur'. And she asked, 'What reward would you give to the one who would free you?' Theseus answered he would give anything in the world to procure his freedom if it was in his power to give. The girl said, 'It is in your power'. 'Name your reward', said Theseus. 'To take me', she said, 'and to make me your only wife'. Theseus responded, 'You will be granted that, as long as we shall both live, if my freedom is won by it'. 'It will be', said the girl.

The girl gives him a ball of thread and her father's sword,[8] and she said, 'Tie one end of the thread to the door of the labyrinth, and unwind the thread in your hand until you get to the Minotaur: then cut off its head'. Then Theseus came to where the Minotaur was. He fought with it until he cut off its head, and afterwards he returned by following the same thread. And it is said that he alone of anyone who had entered the labyrinth ever came out again.

King Minos, however, became angry at the craftsman after that, because it was he who had designed Pasiphae's wooden cow, and the craftsman and his son were taken prisoner and they were about to be killed. But the king's attendants advised him to keep the craftsman captive, to fashion the king's ornamental artwork and adornments for them. They were put into a locked house whose windows were high up, and they remained in that house making the king's ornamental artwork and adornments. Another time the king's boy troop were out playing hurling, and one of the boys hit the ball up high and it fell down right through the window of the craftsman's house, and the craftsman caught the ball there inside the house. The boy who had hit the ball came looking for it. The craftsman refused to relinquish it. Then all the boys came to ask for the ball, and the craftsman said that he would not give up the ball until they would grant him the price he demanded. And the price he demanded from them was for each one of them to bring him a fistful of bird feathers each day for nine months. And that was granted to him in exchange for the ball. And from the feathers the craftsman fashioned two feather suits,[9] for himself and for his son, Icarus son of Daedalus, and in those feather suits they fled away across the Mediterranean.[10] The craftsman had told his son not to fly either too high up above the wind, nor down too low – 'but hold to the middle heaven'.[11] The boy did not do so: he went up too high, so that the wax holding the feathers together melted in the heat of the sun, and he plummeted into the sea then. And the name of that sea has been the Icarian Sea ever since, after Icarus son of Daedalus who perished there.

The father, however, crossed the sea safely and reached the Campanian plain, and he built a temple to Apollo there. And that is the lore of the Minotaur and his death. *FINIT.*

Essay: Book-lore and literary creation in the Minotaur legend

The 'Story of the Minotaur' (*Sgél in Mínaduir*) is found in a single manuscript, Dublin, Royal Irish Academy MS D.iv.2, which appears so often in this book as one of the most important compilations of Irish classical adaptations. The text has been reproduced in its entirety here. The language of the text is late Middle Irish; a number of features suggest a date in the second half of the twelfth century.

Sgél in Mínaduir is a short, well-told and action-packed narrative. It contains a heroic combat against a monster, a romantic encounter, and dysfunctional family relationships. The first part of the narrative deals with the Minotaur, the second part tells of the tragic death of Icarus; the two parts are held together by the figure of Daedalus, whose famous inventions are interwoven with the Minotaur's fate. The text follows the broad strokes of the story as told in the ancient sources. It opens with Pasiphae's unfortunate love for the famous bull, and how a bull-headed monster, the Minotaur, is born from their union; how Theseus kills the Minotaur and makes his escape from the labyrinth thanks to the help of the Cretan princess; how Daedalus is imprisoned by the king but makes wings for himself and his son to escape from Crete, and, how, finally, Icarus tragically falls to his death when he flies too close to the sun.

Both parts of the story have undoubtedly ancient roots in Greek mythological tradition (Hillers 1999b: 138–9). More relevant for our search for the Irish author's source, however, is the story's continued popularity in the Roman and post-Roman world and especially its circulation in the Latin literature embedded in the medieval curriculum. Our text does not appear to be indebted to Orosius' brief summary of the Minotaur story in his *Histories against the Pagans* (1.13), nor to Hyginus, whose *Fabulae* refer to various aspects of the legend (chapters 40–3). The clue to the Irish author's primary source can be found at the very end of the text, which concludes with Daedalus reaching the Campanian plain where he builds a temple to Apollo. In most classical accounts, including Hyginus and Ovid, Daedalus seeks refuge in Sicily. The Irish text's reference to Campania (the region around Naples) and the temple of Apollo leads us to Virgil's *Aeneid*. In Book 6, on his way to consult the oracle at Cumae, Aeneas visits the temple of Apollo, built, Virgil tells us, by Daedalus (*Aeneid* 6.14). On the doors of the temple, Daedalus had depicted the scenes of his adventures, including Pasiphae's love for the bull and the result of their union, the 'mongrel breed of the Minotaur'; the Athenians' 'yearly tribute' of 'seven living sons'; and the 'maze inextricable' of the labyrinth (*Aeneid* 6.20–30). Each of the scenes alluded to by Virgil is represented in the Irish text, which follows Virgil in many details, such as the *annual* rendering of tribute (every nine years in other sources), the fact that only male youths are mentioned (most sources refer to girls *and* boys), and the allusion to the drawing of lots to determine the victims.

The Irish author did not rely solely on Virgil, however, whose depiction of the episode is characteristically allusive. The Irish author was able to reconstruct the sequence of events with the help of Virgilian scholia, specifically the fourth-century commentary of Servius. In his notes to Book 6, Servius spells out the narrative in a passage which appears to be echoed by the Irish text:

> Igitur Pasiphae ... Minois regis Cretae uxor, tauri amore flagravit et arte Daedali inclusa intra vaccam ligneam, ... cum tauro concubuit, unde natus est Minotaurus. qui intra Labyrinthum inclusus humanis carnibus vescebatur ...
>
> Servius on *Aeneid* 6.4–8, Thilo and Hagen 1881–1902: 2.6

> Then Pasiphae ... the wife of Minos, king of Crete, fell in love with the bull: and by the art of Daedalus, enclosed within a wooden cow, ... she slept with the bull. From that [union] was born the Minotaur, who, enclosed within the Labyrinth, fed on human flesh ...
>
> tr. Hillers

The Irish author appears to have used Servius selectively. There is a good deal of additional relevant information in Servius' commentaries on the passage which is not reflected in our text. This selective use of Servian material may suggest that the Irish writer drew on a glossed text of the *Aeneid* with marginal or interlinear Servian glosses rather than having a complete text of the commentary before him.

The Irish tale's final episode – the famous flight and tragic death of Icarus – is omitted entirely from the *Aeneid,* and is supplied instead from Ovid's *Metamorphoses* (8.203–6). Miles has adduced substantial evidence for the use of Ovid in twelfth-century Ireland (Miles 2007: 74–6; Miles 2011: 76–7, 93; Miles 2020: 40; and see Briggs 2018: 60–2, 78, 80). Daedalus' warning to his son, not to fly too close to the water or too close to the sun, is so faithfully rendered into Irish that it seems certain the author had these particular lines – or at least a close paraphrase – in front of him. That does not, however, mean he necessarily had access to a complete text of the *Metamorphoses.* Miles discusses the circulation of Ovidian commentaries and paraphrases, such as the *Narrationes Fabularum Ovidianarum,* and points out that 'the availability of commentary obscures whether the classical poem itself has been read' (Miles 2011: 91). A comparison of the Irish tale with Ovid's account does not suggest that the author of *Sgél in Mínaduir* had a text of the *Metamorphoses* in front of him. There is little overlap between the details or the sequencing of the two narratives. The Irish author's access to Ovid appears to have been selective, and once again we may hypothesize that he was drawing on Ovidian marginal or interlinear glosses. In the absence of extant Ovidian commentaries such suggestions must remain speculative, but hypothesizing on the Irish author's access to a partial excerpt of Ovid, maybe in the form of a gloss, might help to explain why otherwise *Sgél in Mínaduir* is so strikingly independent of the Ovidian narrative.

The kind of source-critical analysis we have engaged in here provides us with an insight into the mediation of classical subject matter in medieval Ireland. *Sgél in Mínaduir* and other free adaptations were constructed by culling 'narratives from allusions and inset narratives in the epics' (Miles 2011: 60). It seems clear that the composition of *Sgél in Mínaduir* was prompted by Virgil's allusion to the story in the *Aeneid,* which the Irish author supplemented from glosses and explanatory commentary drawn from scholiastic literature. Miles has suggested that the work may in fact have played a role within the *Hilfsliteratur* that supported and facilitated the study of Virgil, arguing that it functioned 'as an aid to accompany the reading of Virgil' (2011: 60; see also 2020: 3).

Source-criticism also helps us gauge what portion of the text was the Irish author's own contribution and thus throws light on the creative process by which the author turned the classical material at his disposal into a well-told narrative that conformed to the conventions of Early Irish saga. In the brief space allowed here, I highlight just two instances of this process.

For all its brevity, our tale exhibits some of the characteristic features of early Irish saga style: its terse and understated tone; the alternation of action and dialogue; the use of the historical present. The Irish author puts flesh on the bare bones of the classical material by adding dialogue and realistic detail. The creative expansion is particularly striking in his treatment of the encounter between Theseus and the Cretan princess. Even though the princess remains nameless in the Irish text, it gives her far greater agency than Ariadne is given in the ancient accounts. Unlike Ariadne, who is rarely ever allowed to speak, the princess in our text is assigned five speeches (Theseus, by contrast, only speaks twice). It is she who provides the hero with the objects he needs to succeed and tells him what to do; it is she who initiates the conversation and propositions the hero, evoking the plucky heroines of Irish saga like Deirdre and Gráinne.[12] The saga author's use of dialogue in this passage lends motivation to the characters' actions and makes them come alive.

As a final illustration of the author's embrace of traditional saga style, let us look at the story's opening sentence: *Baī rí amra oiredha i n-Inis Crēit .i. Minósa a ainm* ('There was a great and famous king on the island of Crete; Minos was his name'). The underlying formula (*baí rí amra . . ., X a ainm*) was identified as a traditional opening formula by Karl Horst Schmidt (1960–61). It is used widely in Irish literature, including well-known sagas, such as *Togail Bruidne Da Derga* ('The Destruction of Da Derga's Hostel', Knott 1936) and *Scéla Mucce meic Dathó* ('The Story of Mac Dathó's Pig', Thurneysen 1935; Koch and Carey 2003: 68–75). It is worth noting that our tale is one of six narratives in MS D.iv.2 that employ the formula, including four native sagas as well as two classical adaptations: *Sgél in Mínaduir* and the extraordinary tale of *Samson and the Gesteda*, which fuses biblical and classical elements (Marstrander 1911; Ch. 17, this volume). We may read the formula generally as a statement of the narrator's performative gambit. It signals that what we are about to hear is considered history. The choice of the formula in the two classical tales asserts their 'truth value' as traditionary history. Both stories, like so many of the texts gathered in the present volume, stake out their authors' claim that the history of the ancient world, of Greece, Rome and Jerusalem, is part of their world. By the simple expedient of using the native formula, they declare to their audience that 'this, too, is our history'.

Notes

1　I am grateful to participants at the 2022 workshop on Classical Antiquity and Medieval Ireland at Aarhus University for comments on an oral presentation of this paper, in particular to Maio Nagashima and Ralph O'Connor, and to Daniel Watson for his helpful suggestions on the translation. I also wish to acknowledge the valuable feedback I received from William Gillies and Roibeard Ó Maolalaigh when I prepared the German edition of the text (Hillers 1999b), which proved useful once again in preparing this English edition.

2　*Ainm na mhara*: A *punctum* appears over the 'm' in the manuscript, although lenition would not be expected here.

3　Elsewhere in the text, the definite article is used with Minotaur. The spelling *Mínaduir* suggests that the name was interpreted as meaning 'unnatural', 'monstrous' (from *mí-* 'un-, ill' + nádúir 'nature') at some point of the transmission, though not necessarily by the author.

4　The MS has *dodaingin* which I take to be *dodaing(e)* 'difficult, intractable' here; a later scribe may have read it as *daingin* 'firm, solid, strong'; either word fits the context, see Hillers 1999b: 135.

5   *Uaim* usually refers to a natural cave, but in this text we are clearly dealing with a
    man-made structure; I have translated 'souterrain' in the first instance to convey
    the subterranean association suggested by *uaim*; further on I translate 'labyrinth'.

6   Classical sources agree that Androgeus, the *son* of Minos, was killed by the
    Athenians. Servius and Ovid both unambiguously identify the person who was
    killed as Minos' son. The Irish text might suggest that its author did not have access
    to the complete commentary of Servius or the full text of the *Metamorphoses* but
    relied on an ambiguous gloss which he re-interpreted.

7   This genealogy is problematic on two accounts. In some classical accounts Theseus,
    like other Greek heroes, is given a dual paternity, Aegeus being his human and
    Neptune/Poseidon his divine father. The Irish genealogy shifts the divine ancestry
    back to Theseus' father Aegeus. The appellation 'Theseus son of Aegeus son of
    Neptune' (*Téis mac Éig meic Neptuin*) appears elsewhere in the Irish classical corpus,
    e.g. in the Irish *Thebaid,* and might reflect a genuine scholiastic or mythographic
    variant tradition. The latter part of the genealogy, which makes Neptune the son
    (rather than the brother) of Jupiter may well be a later addition by an eager scribe
    insufficiently acquainted with the Greek pantheon.

8   'The girl gives': I leave the verb in the present tense here to draw attention to this
    instance of the historical present.

9   Michael Clarke defines *énchennach* as 'something that endows one with the overall
    shape and appearance of a bird, including the ability to fly' (2022b: 43). In the
    classical tales the term is used for Mercury's feathered *talaria*, conventionally
    translated 'winged sandals'.

10 *Muir Torrian*: The Irish term is derived from *Mare Tyrrhenum* (the Tyrrhenian Sea,
    to the west of Italy) but is used in medieval Irish texts for any part of the
    Mediterranean (no part of the story takes place in the Tyrrhenian Sea); cf. Ch.16 n.2.

11 I am indebted to Daniel Watson for suggesting this translation.

12 The language employed by Theseus in his promise of marriage may seem somewhat
    duplicitous. We cannot assume, however, that the saga author was aware of Theseus'
    abandonment of Ariadne on the island of Naxos (which is not alluded to in Servius'
    scholia on *Aeneid* 6).

21

Scéla Alaxandair 'The Saga of Alexander'

Cameron Wachowich

The text is a semi-diplomatic transcription from the Book of Ballymote (Dublin, Royal Irish Academy MS 23 P 12), fol. 274rb17 ff. (hereafter BB), cf. Peters 1967: 153–4. Translations are by the author.

Text: The division of Alexander's empire

[fol. 274rb17] Foceard cor *tra* do m*en*main ⁊ intle*acht*aig alaile ndainib, ced f*o*ruair do Alax*andair* am*al* ro bai a amaindsi ⁊ a glicca tuide*acht* ara cend o bais do Baibil*oin*. Ba cora do a n-i*m*gabail, *acht* comaidi*acht* don aitc*í*us ⁊ credem do f*o*ruai*r*. No doneo am*al* doi*m*muir †am† i mBaibil*oin* da radad nem do-som, *acht* is a mbailiu ailiu ⁊ is ind na-ti*m*nai a galar*um*. Tuccad sin iar*um* isin catr*a*ig ndaingin, i mBaibil*oin*. *C*eist tra di*diu*, ol attat na teora faid*h*isin faisdini deoda ⁊ faistini diabulacda. In faisti*n*e diada fir asb*e*ir-side dogres. In faisdini daenda *didiu* ⁊ faisdini demonda asb*e*ir-side fir ⁊ gai. Ge adb*e*rar faisdi*n*e do diabal? Dia *con*darolegea do faisdi*n*e, iss e doruasat a n-aicned. *C*ontuaisi di*diu* ac co*m*arlegud de siste and f*r*i coigedul faisdi*n*e ai*n*gel. *C*eist cia tarba ro bai 'san faisdi*n*e demnaccda do Alax*andair*. Ni*con* ro bi *didiu* tarba do inti, ol noco d*e*rna aith*r*ige, *acht* is eslaini m*en*man dorad in ḟaisdi*n*e demnacda so do fuillicht a pecca, ut D*avi*d d*ixi*t: Per angelos malos viam fecit semita iræ suæ. Dorat tarba do f*e*raib in beaṫa. Arrosir o crodattu IN tan ro ḟid*ir* fod a sægail, ar ro læd airfided cosin anall tesdi*n* fola dui*n*e.

[fol. 274rb38] Dori*m*t*er* di*diu* fogail a feraind do-su*m* and o taisechu in tan ro i lobra a gal*air*. Cet*r*i toisig t*r*ecad do taisecaib maitib. Rosuigided cetam*us* Ptholomeus i n-Alaxaindria i *n*-Egipt ⁊ *for* [ar] Araibia*m* ⁊ for arailiu tuat*ha* Af*r*aicci c*et*na accrundu. Ladon *didiu* for Siria*m*, Telenus *for* Cipciam, Filotos *for* Ilirios, Accrobatos *for* in Metha*m* is mo, Sromes forsin Metha*m* is lugu, Sunnus *for* Saman, Antegund*us* forsin Frigiam as mo, Merat*us* *for* Licciam ⁊ Parifiliam, Casander *for* Coiriam, Mimander *for* Lidiam, Leomaindti*us* forsin Frigiam as lugu, Lisamach*us* forsin T*r*aigiam ⁊ Pon*n*tum, Iumen*us* *for* Capadociam ⁊ Flagomam, suma c*us*trorom Seliucco; sdipatores ⁊ sateli Casandra; in der[1] in rig diatarda *for* Inecdaib ⁊ *for* Baict*r*ian*n*daib uch[2] for Bachtriandu, Talixes *for*si Serdu airt*er*achu, ⁊ Batona *fo*rana Indecda eli, Oixiaires for P*ai*rminos, Sippirites *for* Arcosos ⁊ Cedrosos, San*n*tanor *for* Dranceos, Amitas *for* Andrian*us*, Siccios for Sotian*us*, Etaccanor *for* Parthu, Pilip*us* *for* Arcandui, Scratafernis *for*

Translation by the author

Latin phrases in the original are given in *italics*; expanded wording added
for clarity to the translation is given in (round brackets).

[fol. 274rb17] The spirit and understanding of many people is now moved by
what caused Alexander – clever and wise as he had been – to go to Babylon to
meet his death. It might have been better for him to avoid it; but he was induced
(to go) by respect for the oracle, and by faith. Or, (it was because) he thought that
the poison would not be given to him in Babylon, but in some other place. But
that is where his illness brought him. He was taken, therefore, to the strong city,
Babylon. A question now arises because there are the three (kinds of) prophecy:
a divine prophecy,[3] a human, and a diabolical prophecy. Divine prophecy always
tells the truth. Human prophecy, on the other hand, and demonic prophecy, tell
both truth and lies. Why is prophecy said to be made by the devil? It is God who
permits him to prophesy; it is He who created his nature. He sometimes listens
there, by permission, to the chorus of the prophecies of the angels. A question
now arises: what benefit was in the demonic prophecy for Alexander? But there
was no benefit to him in it at all, for he did not repent, rather it is insanity that
brought this demonic prophecy, for the magnitude of his sins, *as David said: By
evil angels he made a way for a path to his anger* [Psalm 77:49–50]. (But) it
brought benefits to the men of the world. His cruelty continued, when he knew
what the length of his life would be, for up to that point he took pleasure in
shedding human blood.[4]

[fol. 274rb38] It is also related how his country was divided by the generals when
he was in the weakness of his illness. There were thirty-four from among the
good generals. First set up was Ptolemy in Alexandria in Egypt and over Arabia
and over other peoples of Africa, by the first lot. Then Laomedon (was set up)
upon Syria, Mitylinaeus upon Cilicia, Philotas upon the Illyrians, Atropatus
upon Greater Media, Sromes upon Lesser Media, Scynus upon the Susians,
Antigonus upon Greater Phrygia, Nearchus upon Lycia and Pamphylia,
Cassander upon Caria, Menander upon Lydia, Leonnatus upon Phrygia Minor,
Lysimachus upon Thracia and Pontus, Eumenes upon Cappadocia and
Paphlagonia, *command of the army* was given to Seleucus; *the retinue* and
bodyguard to Cassander. The kings who had presided over the Indians and
Bactrians beyond did not leave: Taxiles (was set up) upon the eastern Seres,
Python upon the other Indians, Oxyarches upon the Parapamenes, Sibyrtes

Arminios, Tleponmos *for* Persa, Pergestis for Baibil*oin*, Ballas*us for* Arcos, Anċelous *for* Mesopotaimia; is amlaid sin do roin*n*ed.

[fol. 2744va9] Is f*riss* (sa*m*lai*m*), ar Orus, Alax*andar con*a muint*ir fri* leoman mor laiges *for* preid*h* no for *m*art, *co n*-airrtet hilcoin i*m*on *p*reid sin no i*m*on m*a*rt ꝛ co coi*m*chirat ꝛ co co*m*le*t*trait he. Is e in leomun mor: Alax*andar*, ꝛ is e i*n* m*a*rt *no* i*n* preid: i*n* domu[n]. Finit.

upon the Arachosians and Gedrosians, Statanor upon the Dancheans, Amyntas upon the Bactrians, Scythaeus upon the Sogdians, Stacanor upon the Parthians, Philip upon the Hyrcanians, Fratafernes upon the Armenians, Tleptolemus upon Persia, Peucestes upon Babylon, Pelassus upon Archous, Archelaus upon Mesopotamia; it is in that way it was divided.[5]

[fol. 274va9] It is with this, says Orosius, that I compare Alexander along with his people: with a great lion lying on prey or on an ox, and many dogs fall upon this prey or upon this ox and tear and rip it to pieces together. The great lion is Alexander, and the ox or prey is the world. *It has ended.*

Essay: Sources and analogues of the Irish Alexander

Texts concerning Alexander are to be found in every corner of the continent in virtually every attested language of the medieval period in Europe. Richard Stoneman goes so far as to claim that the legendary biography of Alexander, in its various incarnations, was the most frequently adapted and translated text of the period after the four canonical Gospels (Stoneman 2008: 4). The Irish were no exception to this pattern. However, the surviving Irish material has been wholly omitted from all the most recent surveys of the medieval Alexander corpus (Stoneman 2008, Zuwiyya 2011 and Gaullier-Bougassas 2015). Only two modern surveys of the wider Alexander tradition mention the Irish material at all: George Cary's *The Medieval Alexander* of 1956, and D. J. A. Ross' *Alexander Historiatus*, first published in 1963 and largely based on Cary's work, and in both it is disposed of in a single short paragraph (Cary 1956: 69–70; Ross 1988: 75–6). Not only for those seeking to understand the Irish antiquity-sagas as a genre, but also for scholars working in other areas of Alexander literature, it is important to shed light on these texts.

The principal medieval Irish account of Alexander survives in three manuscripts. The earliest of these is Dublin, Royal Irish Academy, MS 23 P 12, the Book of Ballymote (hereafter BB). There the Alexander text is found at the very end of the manuscript as it currently survives, and it is immediately preceded by the series of other Irish classical adaptations including *Togail Troí*, *Imtheachta Aeniasa* and *Merugud Uilixis* (see Chs 6, 7, 8, 9, 13 and 18 in this volume). The Alexander text extends for some seven folios and an additional slip at the end. This is by far the longest witness of the text to survive, and it will be the main point of reference for the study below.[6]

Proceeding in order of age, the second manuscript witness is Dublin, Royal Irish Academy, MS 23 P 16, the Leabhar Breac (LB). The Alexander text occurs at a particularly fragmentary part of the manuscript and is preceded by a lacuna. The beginning of the text is missing and it opens in the middle of a description of Philip's army. A colophon at the end of the text indicates that it was copied from the Book of St Berchán of Cluain Sosta, a manuscript that is now lost. The last trace of it is in a catalogue of the library of the Earl of Kildare from the mid-sixteenth century (Byrne 2013: 151). The third and final witness to the text is Oxford, Bodleian Library, MS Rawlinson B512. Only a fragment of the Alexander text is present, namely the correspondence of Alexander and Dindimus; however, as it is integrated with the material around it, no loss of text is apparent in this instance.

Although none of the witnesses preserve contemporary titles, the title used here, *Scéla Alaxandair*, appears in a number of manuscripts and is the most common mode of reference to this text.[7] *Scéla Alaxandair* has been edited twice in the modern period. Kuno Meyer produced an edition and translation of a portion of the Leabhar Breac text for his PhD dissertation at the University of Leipzig (Meyer 1884). Three years later, he published the whole of the Leabhar Breac text with variants from the Book of Ballymote in the second volume of *Irische Texte* (Meyer 1887). The Ballymote text would have to wait until the 1960s when Erik Peters transcribed and translated it for his own dissertation at Galway. Peters' edition was published in the *Zeitschrift für Celtische Philologie* in 1967. He provided a semi-diplomatic transcription of the Ballymote text. Furthermore, he appears to have worked from the lithographic facsimile of the manuscript, rather than the original. Comparison of his text with the high-resolution digital images of the Book of Ballymote currently available on ISOS reveals that several sections that he considered to be illegible are now decipherable, including much of the marginalia. A fresh look at this material is merited (see further Tristram 1989, 1990; Miles 2011: 55; Roelofs and Groos 2007).

With the exception of two quatrains quoted near the beginning of the Ballymote text, the work is exclusively in prose. The language is mostly typical of the Middle Irish period which has given rise to a general consensus placing the composition of the text in the tenth or eleventh century. Most recently, Uáitéar mac Gearailt (2016: 104) has argued that elements of the verbal system suggest towards a tenth-century date. Even if the text were to be placed in the latter part of this date range, *Scéla Alaxandair* stands alongside Recension 1 of *Togail Troí* as one of the earliest Irish classical adaptations.

Compared to the other Irish antiquity-sagas, there are relatively few difficulties in the identification of the principal sources (see Robert T. Meyer 1949). The narrative proper is preceded by a historical prologue (BB fol. 268ra1–268vb11) broadly reminiscent of those found in *Togail Troí* and *In Cath Catharda* (see Ch. 14). The emphasis of this prologue is on Greek history, and it regards the Greeks' destruction of Troy with conspicuous approval. Then follows an account of Philip II of Macedon, and the biography of Alexander as far as the death of the Persian king Darius III (BB fol. 268vb11–271ra25); both are very clearly drawn from the latter part of book 3 of Orosius' *Histories against the Pagans* (3.12–14, 3.16–19). This is followed by Irish translations of the well-known *Epistola Alexandri ad Aristotelem* ('Letter of Alexander to Aristotle'; Boer 1973, BB fol. 271ra26–273rb30), and the *Collatio Alexandri cum Dindimo rege Bragmanorum* ('Correspondence of Alexander with Dindimus, king of the Brahmans'; Steinmann

2012, BB fol. 273rb31–274rb16). MS Rawlinson B512 contains only the Dindimus correspondence in a version closely corresponding to the text in the Leabhar Breac. In the other two witnesses, the text concludes with a return to the narrative as recounted by Orosius covering Alexander's death and the division of his empire (*Histories*, 3.23, BB fol. 274rb17–275ra11). A portion of this concluding section has been presented above.

The combination of Orosius with the *Letter* and *Correspondence* exemplify the heterogeneous nature of the Alexander texts available to the Irish translator. Orosius' moralizing narrative draws its content principally from Justinus' epitome of Pompeius Trogus' *Historia Philippicarum* ('Philippic History'), and thus is part of a tradition of historical accounts of Alexander that extends back to Arrian's *Alexandrou Anabasis* ('Anabasis of Alexander'). The *Letter* and the *Correspondence*, on the other hand, draw on the fantastical tradition ultimately traceable to the *Alexander Romance* of Pseudo-Callisthenes. The *Letter* is especially notable in this regard. The letter recounts Alexander's exploits in India; he and his army pursue the Indian king Porus and discover his palace to be surrounded by four hundred golden pillars; the army then nearly dies of thirst in the desert, but goes on to defeat in turn: giant snakes, giant crabs, a monster larger than an elephant with the head of a horse, a beast, possibly a hippopotamus, which may have two heads, and finally they encounter a pair of talking trees who foretell Alexander's death.

This tension, between the comparatively sober historical accounts and the fantastical, is also to be seen in certain areas of the medieval Latin tradition. A short biography of Alexander is found together with the *Letter* and the *Correspondence* in London, British Library, MS Royal 13 A I, an English manuscript from the last quarter of the eleventh century. Charles Russel Stone has argued that this grouping of texts is justified by a clear thematic unity that is itself indicative of the reception of Alexander in England at that time (Stone 2013: 17–24). The legendary conqueror is caught somewhere between the historical and mythical accounts of his career. Alexander is simultaneously an intrepid discoverer of many of the world's wonders and the prideful tyrant condemned by Orosius. Another analogue of interest here is the J^2 recension of the *Historia de Preliis* ('History of Battles'; Hilka 1976–77). In this, the rewriting of the Alexander romance attributed to Leo of Naples is heavily interspersed with passages taken nearly verbatim from Orosius. This recension is now generally believed to date from no later than the beginning of the twelfth century (Cizek 2015: 35–42). It will be noted that if *Scéla Alaxandair* is placed anywhere but on the lattermost extreme of its probable date range, this Irish composition predates these English and Continental analogues.

Although the possibility that the text is a faithful rendering of a Latin exemplar cannot be wholly excluded, it is at least clear that *Scéla Alaxandair* has a closer relationship to its sources than is usual in the genre of the antiquity-sagas. The text of the sources is abridged, but otherwise the translation is often comparatively faithful. In the Orosian sections, the text often takes on a heterogeneous character; in many sections one or two sentences are translated nearly literally from the *Histories* and then followed by material gleaned from other sources, suggesting that the translator may have worked from a commentary. In the section above, the first paragraph is not drawn from Orosius or any known adjacent source, whereas the other two are comparably faithful renderings (see *Histories* 3.23.7–13, 3.23.6 respectively). With access to such a literal rendering of the original Latin, the opportunity may therefore be afforded to attain some sense of the place of the sources in their respective manuscript traditions. Can the translator's exemplars be put into established reconstructions of the transmission? If so, this could elucidate historical information that would have a significant bearing on literary analysis. Virtually none of the classical sources for the adaptations discussed in this volume were written in Ireland, so where might they have come from? And when? How might this material aspect of transmission impact readings of the text?

Discussion of the relationship of *Scéla Alaxandair* to its exemplars both in Orosius and in the *Letter* can benefit from being informed by a considerable amount of work that has been done on very similar questions. A translation of the *Letter* and an adaptation of the whole of Orosius' text survive in Old English – a West Germanic language once spoken in parts of southern Britain. The efforts that have been undertaken to situate these translators' exemplars provide a useful framework for the questions at hand.

It should first be noted that there is no definitive proof that the Irish translator was working with a complete copy of Orosius' *Histories*. Although no exact Latin analogue to *Scéla Alaxandair* has yet been identified, it still remains well within the realm of possibility that the translator was working from an epitome, or a commentary, as suggested above, or a Latin manuscript that in its content already closely resembled the Irish text. However, in spite of its significant impact on the wider medieval Alexander tradition, Orosius' account of Alexander does not have a large, independent circulation that would suggest towards such a text. Very few copies of it are found independently of the rest of the *Histories*, in marked contrast to Orosius' geographic excursus and his account of Babylon (see Mortensen 1999–2000: 114).

Both the *Histories* and the *Letter* were widely copied during the European Middle Ages. According to the most recent catalogue, the *Histories* survives in some 249 complete or substantial fragmentary witnesses and at least fifty-two small fragments (Mortensen 1999–2000: 119–65). Some sixty-seven manuscripts of the *Letter* are noted in the most recent edition (Boer 1973: iii-xxi). These rich traditions invite the possibility that manuscripts related in some way to the translator's exemplar are still extant. Whereas medieval translations are often so liberal that variations in wording are difficult to trace and indeed any omission or expansion could reflect a deliberate choice by the translator, it stands to reason that names, and especially uncommon ones, are likely to be copied from an exemplar with greater fidelity.[8] The present work is informed in this regard by a similar study, produced by Janet Bately in 1961 and republished with minor revisions in 1980, in which Bately sought to ascertain the position of the exemplar used by the translator of the Old English *Orosius* (Bately 1961: 79, 86; Bately 1980: lvi-lviii).

Bately identified witnesses related to the translator's exemplar in the first instance by collating Orosius' *Histories* 3.23.7–13, in which the division of Alexander's empire after his death is outlined. Here the text lists Alexander's Diadochi – his successors – and the territories which they were allotted. While virtually all the geographical names are also found in book 14 of Isidore's *Etymologies* and other sources, the names of the Diadochi make for a soup of obscure Greek terms that would have been nearly indecipherable and otherwise unknown to most scribes working in Western Europe when *Scéla Alaxandair* was likely composed. Bately was able to use this passage for her purposes because it is translated largely verbatim in the Old English *Orosius*. Indeed, it is also found in *Scéla Alaxandair*, as shown in the excerpt above, and there it is so literal a rendering that many of the geographical names retain Latin accusative case endings.[9]

When one looks at the readings of *Histories* 3.23 reflected in *Scéla Alaxandair* one finds that they are broadly in keeping with those of Bately's witnesses. This does not necessarily suggest that *Scéla Alaxandair* and the Old English *Orosius* share source material; the two translators did not work from the same manuscript, but rather they both likely worked with manuscripts from a common but widely-dispersed tradition. The readings in *Scéla Alaxandair* are closest to those in the manuscripts Bately classified as her group C.[10] This group comprises thirty-seven witnesses of English and French provenance that are broadly indicative of the Channel-centric textual culture attested from the tenth through the twelfth centuries and associated with the advent of Caroline minuscule script in England (see Bischoff 1990: 124). This conclusion holds for the *Letter* as well. On the basis of the edition available to him, Peters noted several readings shared between the Irish text and the text of Leiden, University Library MS BPL 20, a manuscript produced in Normandy circa 1139 (Peters 1967: 86, Boer 1973: xi). Checking the text against the edition by Boer largely confirms this result. Boer places this manuscript in his group I, which again consists of witnesses of probable English or northern French provenance. It is clear enough that texts were being transmitted from France to England during this period, and thus it appears that Irish centres were recipients as well.

Finally, the conclusions offered here should not be regarded as firm, but rather as tentative observations. On the basis of the apparent affiliations of the manuscripts, the translator's copies of the *Histories* and the *Letter* appear to have come from a common source. The overall appearance is that the translator drew on a witness that seems to be affiliated with the cross-Channel exchange of manuscripts following the Carolingian period. This may be taken to suggest that the Latin exemplars, or exemplar, for *Scéla Alaxandair* came to an Irish centre not long before *Scéla Alaxandair* itself was composed. A skilled and learned scholar may have taken the latest works received from abroad and immediately set about rendering them into the indigenous language of Gaelic learning.

Manuscripts cited in this chapter

Cambridge, Corpus Christi College MS 23. Online:
https://parker.stanford.edu/parker/catalog/nz663nv2057
Dublin, Royal Irish Academy MS 23 P 12, the Book of Ballymote. Online:
https://www.isos.dias.ie/ga/RIA/RIA_MS_23_P_12.html
Dublin, Royal Irish Academy, MS 23 P 16, the Leabhar Breac. Online:
https://www.isos.dias.ie/ga/RIA/RIA_MS_23_P_16.html
Leiden, University Library MS BPL 20. Online:
http://hdl.handle.net/1887.1/item:1611194
Oxford, Bodleian Library MS Rawlinson B512. Online:
https://digital.bodleian.ox.ac.uk/objects/3ffc0cfc-ce63-4a6c-95c0-
547f36b4333d/

Notes

1   The sense of *in der* is not immediately clear. Peters 1967: 255 n. 806 suggests that there has been a corruption in transmission and that the original reading here was *ni derget*, cf. *eDIL* s.v. *do-érig*.

2   Peters regards this as a demonstrative adjective, cf. *eDIL ucut*.

3   This phrase, not found in BB, is supplied from LB.

4   The source of this passage is unclear.

5   This paragraph and the following are near literal renderings of Orosius, *Histories*, 3.23.7–13 and 3.23.6 respectively.

6   This witness is noteworthy as well for its extensive marginalia. Virtually every column features substantial notations in a contemporaneous or perhaps only slightly later hand.

7   In the Book of Ballymote, a later hand has added a title in the upper margin: *Iomtusa Alexandair Moir do reir an udair Laidne Iustinus bodein*, 'Concerning Alexander the Great according to the Latin authority, Justin himself'. The formulation *Stair Alaxandair* 'History of Alexander' is found in marginal notes in both the Book of Ballymote and the Leabhar Breac. *Scel Alaxandair* 'Tale of Alexander' is found several times in Ballymote, and *Scela Alaxandair* 'Report of Alexander' is found within the text in the Leabhar Breac (Peters 1967: 73, 103 n. 32). The final text listed in the first section in list B of the tenth- or eleventh-century Irish tale lists is entitled *Scéla Alaxandair maic Pilip* (Mac Cana 1980: 52).

8   Although it is not universally accepted, a very similar methodology has already been used in another study on medieval Irish translation literature; see Palandri 2018: 163–74 and Palandri 2019.

9   Whereas the version of this passage in BB is extremely close to the text found in certain Orosian manuscripts, the version in LB has clearly enjoyed many adventures along the way to its attested form. In LB, the personal and geographic names are split into columns and both show considerable variation: for example, Greater and Lesser Media, *Metham is mo* and *Metham is lugu* respectively in BB, are in LB instead *Iudeam is mo* and *Iudeam is lugu*; Peithon becomes Xerxes; the Bactrians become Cretae.

10 Cambridge, Corpus Christi College, MS 23 II (hereafter Co), written in the late twelfth century in southern England, will serve as a representative example of Bately's group C witnesses. Amyntas (Ἀμύντας), Philip's father, whom Orosius renders in the genitive as *Amyntae*, is written as *Aminicae* in Co and *Aminiċe* in *Scéla Alaxandair*. The city of Methone (Μεθώνη), which Orosius calls *Mothona*, is written in Co in the accusative singular form *Mathonam*, and in *Scéla Alaxandair* as *Mathonia*. Laomedon of Mytilene (Λαομέδων ὁ Μυτιληναῖος), Orosius' *Laomedon Mytilenaeus*, suffered the misfortune of having his home town reanalyzed as a

personal name: this is written as *Thelenus* in the great majority of witnesses in Bately's classification system, and as *Telenus* in Co and *Scéla Alaxandair*. The father-in-law of Perdiccas who was allotted lesser Media, and who in Orosius is merely *socer Perdiccae*, is named as *Stromen* in a handful of Bately's witnesses, as *Sinomen* in Co, and, finally, as *Sromes* in *Scéla Alaxandair*. Peithon (Πείθων), who was left in charge of the Indian colonies and whom Orosius called *Python*, is found in Co written as *Pitona*, while Bately (1961: 90 n.170) reports the same reading in Cambridge, Clare College MS 18: this is the closest to *Scéla Alaxandair*'s *Batona*. Finally, Tlepolemus (Τληπόλεμος), the general who was left in charge of Persia, is rendered *Thleponmos* (or, in Co, *Thleponinos*) throughout group C, nearly matching *Scéla Alaxandair*'s *Tleponmos*.

22

Stair Ercuil ocus a Bás 'The History of Hercules and his Death'

Gregory R. Darwin

The text is transcribed from Dublin, TCD MS 1298. Italics are used to indicate where potentially ambiguous abbreviations in the manuscript have been expanded; <angle brackets> indicate a gap or a dubious reading in the manuscript; (round brackets) indicate an omission from the manuscript; [square brackets] enclose an addition by the editor. All punctuation and capitalization has been added by the editor. Unambiguous abbreviations have been silently expanded.

Text: Two passages about the giant Antaeus

Passage 1

Dublin, TCD MS 1298, pp. 272a28–272b1, 273b26–274b36; cf. Quin 1939: pp. 50–52 lines 941–966, pp.56–60 lines 1038–1108.

Do-ronad iarum morsl*uaigh*edh mor la hErc*uil* [⁊] do-cuadh isin Libia dia hinnr*adh* ⁊ dia hargain. Iarna clos sin d'Anntenon, .i. ri na Libia, do thionoil a sl*uaigh* as gach aird a rabadar ⁊ tanicc a n-arrthaisc Erc*uil* ⁊ na nGregach ⁊ tugadar *cath* oghla ainnsergach ainiarmartach daroile. ⁊ tarrla *imorro* Erc*uil* ⁊ Anntenon, rí na Libia, da chéile isin *chath* ⁊ do-ronsad comhrac feram*ail* fuirtill fírarrachta ⁊ ro buail Erc*uil* builli brighmar borbnertmar don liurg inremar iarn*aidh*i a cenn Anntenon ⁊ ro thrasgair a cend ar a gualaind clé ⁊ tuc cnedh guasachtach fair.

Do-cuadar sl*uaigh* na Libia eturra do cab*air* Anntenon, ⁊ tangadar na Gregaigh do cabair Erc*uil*, ⁊ do rucadh o chéile aml*aidh* sin iat. Ro bui Erc*uil* iarum ag ledairt ⁊ ag lanmarb*adh* sl*uagh* na Libi ⁊ ro bui Anntenon ac marb*adh* na nGregach. Do bui *imorro* Erc*uil* ag scoltadh na scíath ⁊ ac marb*adh* na miled ⁊ ac leonad na læchr*aidh*i sechnoin in catha ag iarr*aidh* Anntenon. An uair *imorro* do cunnaicc Erc*uil* ina doch*um*, ro theith roime asteg in cathr*aigh* ⁊ ro lensat a muindter é iar mbrisedh orra le laim arrachta Erc*uil*. ⁊ ro badar Greg*aigh* aga marb*adh* co mithroccar no gur dúnsat in cathair orra. .xc. ⁊ da .xx.c. to[r]chuir le hErc*uil* do sl*uagh*aib na Libia an lá sin. ⁊ ro bai in rí Anntenon anbann eneirt o bemenaib arrachta Erc*uil* ⁊ a d*ubh*radar a lega nach beidh Anntenon slán co cenn mís. ⁊ ro *gh*abh Anntenon comosadh re hErc*uil* re fedh na mís sin. Conidh e sin an *chéd* cath do chuir Erc*uil* ar Anntenon.

[.........]

Ar caithem na mís sin doibh ba hogh[sh]lan rí na Libia ona othrus, ⁊ do *ch*uir a dirmada degslóigh ar æensl*igh*i ⁊ do gluais a coindi Erc*uil* ⁊ na nGregach ⁊ do-rindi tri coirighti comlunncruaidhi catha díbh. ⁊ do *ch*uir da mile d*eg uathu* sa *céd*corug*adh* ⁊ .xx. mili sa dara corug*adh* ⁊ .x. m. xx. sa treas corug*adh* ⁊ ro buí ri m*en*mach móraicenntach 'na cenn ar cach corug*adh* dibh, .i. rí na na Sisaile roimh an *céd*corug*adh* ⁊ rí Cotuli ar an dara corug*adh* ⁊ rí na Getuli ar an treas corug*adh*. Do-gní *imorro* Erc*uil* da chorug*adh* da muindter budéin ⁊ do *ch*uir se Afer .i. rí na Maigionda roim an *céd*corug*adh* ⁊ é fein roim an dara corug*adh*. ⁊

Translations by the author

Passage 1

Then a great host was gathered by Hercules, and he went into Libya in order to plunder and to pillage it. When Anntenon (that is, the king of Libya) had heard that, he gathered his armies out of every place in which they were, and he came against Hercules and the Greeks, and they gave one another fierce, hateful, deadly battle. Then Hercules and Anntenon, king of Libya, met one another in the battle, and made manly, mighty, and monstrous combat, and Hercules struck a powerful, harsh, strong blow against Anntenon with his broad iron-studded club, and knocked his head against his right shoulder, and gave him a perilous wound.

The armies of Libya went between them to aid Anntenon, and the Greeks came to aid Hercules, and so they brought them away from each other. Hercules then was maiming and slaughtering the armies of Libya and Anntenon was killing the Greeks. Hercules, for his part, was splitting the shields and slaughtering the soldiers and wounding the warriors all throughout the battlefield searching for Anntenon. Then, when he saw Hercules [coming] towards him, he fled before him into the city, and his supporters followed him, after they had been defeated by the mighty hand of Hercules. And the Greeks were killing them mercilessly until the city was closed against them. Five thousand fell by Hercules from among the armies of Libya on that day. And king Anntenon was weak and feeble from the powerful blows of Hercules, and his physicians said that Anntenon would not recover for a month. And Anntenon made a truce with Hercules for that month. And that was the first battle which Hercules waged against Anntenon.

[. . . . .]

After that month had passed, the king of Libya was fully healed from his injuries, and he brought together the soldiers of his fine army, and he moved against Hercules and the Greeks, and he made three hard-fighting battle companies. He put twelve thousand of them in the first company, twenty thousand in the second company, and thirty thousand in the third company, and there was a bold, high-spirited king at the head of each of the companies, that is, the king of Sisaile before the first company, the king of Cotuli before the second, and the king of Getuli before the third. Hercules, for his part, made two companies of his own

Do ruc ben Er*cuil* mac in tan sin ⁊ do *ch*uiredh coroin fona cin[d] iarna breit ar righacht na Libia ⁊ fuair a *math*air bas sul nar fagaibh Er*cuil* in tír sin. Do-cuadar na catha cechtarrdha fo ceile in tan sin .i. sluaigh línmara lancalma na Libia cona cairdib, ⁊ sl*uaigh* greannmara gaesmara na *Greig*e ⁊ tucatar cath niata naimdighi *nemh*carthanach daroile.

⁊ tarrla Anntenon ⁊ Er*cuil* da cheile isin cath ⁊ do-rónsat comruc dían disgir dána dasachtach ⁊ ro buail Anntenon builli orr*edh*a arrachta ar Er*cuil*, ⁊ ro *gh*err a sciath ar dó. Tuc iarum Er*cuil* buille ele ar Anntinon, ⁊ ro *th*rasgair he ⁊ do rugadar sl*uaigh* línmara lan*ch*ruaidhi na Libia Anntenon on læchmil*idh* gan malairt. Is ann sin do *ch*ruinnighedar gasraidhi greannmara grodgnim*ach*a ⁊ drechta dana dedhsluaigh saichi seghmar sárcalma a n-urtimcell Er*cuil* dia malairt ⁊ dia mormbarb*adh*. ⁊ tanicc Afer .i. ri mermenmach milita mordhalach na Maigionda do com(ur)fhurtacht Er*cuil* on hégin sin. ⁊ Tanic rí na Cotuli do cumnad la rí na Libia ⁊ tugadar in da rí 'sin cath diaroile ⁊ is naimdigi *nemh*chartanach do feradh in mórgleo sin ⁊ torchuir rí Cotuli co n-ilimud dia muindtir mar aon ris la hirgail arachta urunta Afer.

Tanicc *imorro* rí na Getuli .x. catha .xx. chucu fon am sin ⁊ tuc cath do rí na Maigionda ⁊ ní mór ro torchuir do muindter righ na Getuli sa cath sin in tan tainicc Er*cuil* do cumnadh d'Afer. Do thogaibh Er*cuil* os a gualainn in læchlorg inreamair iarn*aidh*i ⁊ in sust segmhar sarbuilleach ⁊ ro *gh*ab do beimennaib bedhgnima*ch*a bais *for* sluagaibh na Getuli no gur *bh*ris rian madhma ⁊ mormarbhta forra.

Do rug an aidhchi orra in tan sin, ⁊ do *gh*absat comosadh co mucha na maidni iarna marac ⁊ do-ronsat comnaidhi ar comhuir a ceile co maidin. ⁊ ro ba doigh la hEr*cuil* co fuighedh *cath* iarna márach o Anntenon. Is ann sin adub*h*airt Anntenon rena muindtir: 'Ní fuil sen maith catha oruind,' ar se, '⁊ ni tabhraid ar ndee lam linn, ⁊ torcair forgla ar muindtiri la hEr*cuil* ⁊ ní fuilmid lín catha do amarach, fagam in magh so, ⁊ ergem co cathr*aigh* na Morian anocht.' Do-ronsat saml*aidh*.

Dala Anntenon iarum, do tinol se na fir gorma mar æn ris ⁊ tainnic a fritheing 'na conaire c*édn*a. ⁊ tuc se rí na Tingi ⁊ ilimud do sl*uaigh*ib les ⁊ tucadar cath daroile. Tarrla Er*cuil* ⁊ Anntenon da cheile isin chath ⁊ do *ch*omraicsit co fortill firarra*ch*ta ⁊ ro bui Anntenon aca clæí isin comruc. Is ann sin do togair Anntenon imthecht re luas a retha o Er*cuil* ⁊ do rith Er*cuil* ina diaigh ⁊ do rug air ⁊ do followers, and he placed Afer, king of the Magionda, in front of the first company and himself in front of the second. Hercules' wife bore him a son at that time, and he was crowned king of Libya after he was borne. His mother died before Hercules left that land. Then each of the armies approached the other, that is the numerous and brave troops of Libya and their allies, and the fierce and clever armies of Greece, and they gave each other heroic, hostile, unfriendly battle.

And Anntenon and Hercules met each other in the battle, and made fierce, vigorous, bold, furious conflict and Anntenon dealt Hercules a mighty and monstrous blow and split his shield in two. Hercules then gave another blow to Anntenon, and knocked him down, and the numerous and mighty soldiers of Libya bore him away from the warrior unharmed. Then the fierce, quick-acting companies and impulsive bands of that mighty, violent, victorious host gathered around Hercules in order to slaughter and to slay him. And Afer, that is the impetuous, soldierly, proud king of the Magionda came to rescue Hercules from that danger. And the king of Cotuli came to aid the king of Libya, and those two kings gave each other battle, and great combat was waged hostilely and without friendship, and the king of Cotuli fell along with a great number of his people, on account of the valorous and victorious fighting of Afer.

Then the king of Getuli came with thirty companies and gave battle to the king of the Magionda, and not many of the king of Getuli's people had fallen in that battle when Hercules came to aid Afer. Hercules raised his broad, iron-studded hero's club above his shoulder, the victorious staff of mighty blows, and began to strike harmful and fatal blows against the troops of Getuli until they were routed and great slaughter broke against them.

Then night fell, and they made a truce until early the next morning, and they made camps opposite each other until morning. Hercules thought that he would receive battle from Anntenon on the morrow. Anntenon, then, said to his followers: 'We have no good omen of battle,' he said, 'and our gods will not help us, and the best part of our people have fallen to Hercules, and there are not enough of us to wage battle tomorrow, so let us leave this plain and flee to the city of Morian tonight.' So they did.

As for Anntenon, then he gathered together the Black men[1] with him, and came back by the same route. He brought the king of Tingi and a great number of warriors with him, and they gave each other battle. Hercules and Anntenon met in the battle, and they fought strongly and mightily, and Anntenon was being overcome in the battle. Then Anntenon made an attempt to flee from Hercules *c*huir ara gualaind é ꝛ do buail fo lig lanmoir e co nar fagaibh edh n-ord*l*a*i*g ina *c*horp gan combrugh*adh*, co fuair bas co hobunn. ꝛ torcuir rí na Tingi iarsin la hErc*uil* ꝛ ilimud do rigaibh ele mar æn riu, co nar eidir in magh do imthecht la himud na *c*orp crechtach cnaimgerrtha, ꝛ la falcaib fairsinge fírdoimni fola for fiarlaid in muighe.

Do hannluicedh Anntinon iar sin ꝛ ro ordaigh Erc*uil* delb alainn do denum do cnaim eilifinnti do Anntenon ꝛ a *c*hur osa cinn mar comartha cuimnighthi in coscair sin. Tuc *imorro* Erc*uil* righi na Libia d'Afer ꝛ is e recht ro buí isin Libia in n-inbiud sin .i. gan fer d'airigthi do beth ag mnai ann ꝛ gach ben do thoigeoradh fer isin tír sin do beth aigi ꝛ ní bidh a fis ag mnaim na crichi sin cía da meirdis a clann la himud fer ag luidi leo. ꝛ do-rinde Erc*uil* recht núa doibh .i. gnathug*adh* na nGregach .i. b*en* fosta ag gach æn dibh. Conidh am*l*a*idh* sin do choisc Erc*uil* díumus ꝛ *égoir* Anntenoin.

Passage 2

Dublin, TCD MS 1298, pp.296a28–296b; cf. Quin 1939: 122, lines 2378–2409.

Is and sin ro hinnsedh d<......>idh calma ꝛ trenfher ingnathach do beth ag fasug*adh* na c<ri>ch ꝛ na ferunn ꝛ se ag malairt ban ꝛ fer, óg ꝛ arr*s*aidh. 'Ca hainm in *c*huraid sin?' ar Erc*uil*. 'Ainntius mac Terra .i. mac do geinedh asin tal*main* gan ath*air* gan m*athair* coll*aidh*i aigi acht in tal*am*.' Iarna clos sin d'Erc*uil* do ullmaig é ꝛ do-cuaidh roime ina luing, ꝛ do g*h*ab cuan isin crich ina cual*aidh* Ainntius do beth ꝛ do bí ag siub*al* na crichi sin. ꝛ nir cían do co fac*aidh* in tulach ibhinn ꝛ ind locc alainn oirechtais os ur in cuain ꝛ do-cuaidh ar inn na tulcha ꝛ do bí ag féchain do gach tæbh de. ꝛ do chunnuic in fodmoir fortill fírarrachta, ꝛ delbh dubh duaibhsech diabl*aidh*i fair ꝛ do féch sé co hadh*uath*mar for Erc*uil*, ꝛ do smer sé a *c*horp le husc esgunn ꝛ le holuibh sleabhnaigtechta ele ꝛ tanic se co prap primurrlum a comdhail Erc*uil*, ꝛ ro iar spairn fair.

Erc*uil* iarum nír diultad*h* sin les ꝛ ro sínedar na fir *f*herrda sin na lamha læchdha lancalma tar taebhuib tenna tailce tarrletna aroile ꝛ tugadur cuir borba ꝛ snadhmanna arrachta. ꝛ do-ronsad gleic croda coimthenn curata re hadh ꝛ re hathaigh ꝛ ro thoguib Erc*uil* os inn a gualann in fodhmoir ꝛ do *t*hrascair co as fast as he could, and Hercules pursued him, and caught him, and threw him onto his shoulder, and struck him against a mighty flagstone so that not an inch of his body was left unbruised, and so that he died immediately. Then the king of Tingi fell by Hercules, and a great number of other kings with him, so that the field could not be crossed on account of the great number of wounded, broken-boned bodies, and the broad and deep rivers of blood flowing across the field.

Anntenon was buried then, and Hercules ordered a beautiful statue be made of elephant bone [ivory], and be placed above him as a memorial of that battle. Hercules then gave the kingship of Libya to Afer. And this was the law that was in Libya at that time: women would not have a specific husband, and the men in that country would have whichever woman they desired, and the women of that country did not know whose children they bore, on account of the number of men lying with them. And Hercules made a new law for them, the custom of the Greeks, that is, each man would have one wife. And thus, Hercules put an end to the tyranny and injustice of Anntenon.

Passage 2

Then it was related to (Hercules?) that a brave ... and unusual champion was laying waste to the nations and the territories, and slaying men and women, young and old. 'What is the name of that warrior?' said Hercules. 'Ainntius son of Terra, that is, a son borne from the earth without carnal father or mother, except for the earth itself.' After Hercules had heard that he prepared himself and went forth in his ship, and landed in the country where he had heard that Ainntius was, and he was walking throughout that country. It was not long until he saw a pleasant hill and a fair assembly site above the edge of the bay, and he went to the summit of the hill and looked out in all directions. He saw a mighty and monstrous giant, with a black, gloomy, diabolical appearance, and [the giant] looked fearsomely at Hercules, and covered his body in filthy grease and other slippery oils, and came to meet Hercules quickly and swiftly, and demanded that he wrestle.

As for Hercules, he did not refuse that. Those two virile men stretched their courageous champion's arms around each other's thick, rough, broad sides and gave each other powerful grips and vigorous attacks. They grappled each other bravely, powerfully, and mightily for a long while, until Hercules lifted the giant hainmín co talm*ain* he. Iar tastill na talm*an* do tanicc nert *céd* ann os cinn a neirt fein. Teora fecht ro t*h*rascair Erc*uil* mar sin hé co talm*ain* ⁊ tanic nert *céd* ann le gach uair dib. Iarna aithne d'Erc*uil* co tabrad in tal*am* fuill*edh* neirt ⁊ calmad*uis* d'Anntius, ro togaib Herc*uil* o talm*ain* itir a <di> lámaib é ⁊ tug fasgudh fortill <fedhmlaidir> firarachta fair et*er* a ucht ⁊ a <…>ma innus gur c*h*roith a dennmur ass <…> fagaibh edh n-ordl*ach* da c*h*orp gan bris*edh* <co fuair> bas mar sin. ⁊ do len Tulach na <Gle>cca in tulach o sin amach. Conid <a>ml*aidh* sin do thoit Anntius mac Terra la Herc*uil*.

above the point of his shoulder and threw him roughly to the ground. After he had touched the ground, the strength of a hundred men came to him, in addition to his own strength. Three times did Hercules throw him to the ground in this way, and the strength of a hundred came to him each time. When Hercules noticed that the earth was giving Ainntius more strength and courage, Hercules lifted him up from the ground between his two arms, and squeezed him strongly, forcefully, and powerfully between his chest and his (arms?), so that he shook the excrement out of him (and there wasn't?) an inch of his body that was left unbroken, and so he died. The hill was known as Hill of the (Struggle?) from then on, and that was how Ainntius son of Terra fell to Hercules.

Essay: From Raoul Le Fèvre to Uilliam Mac an Leagha

Stair Ercuil ocus a Bás 'The History of Hercules and his Death' is preserved in a single manuscript, Trinity College Dublin MS 1298 (formerly H.2.7), written by the scribe and scholar Uilliam Mac an Leagha, who most likely also authored the text, in the last quarter of the fifteenth century.[2] It differs from the other texts in this volume in two key ways: first, it was composed significantly later than the other texts discussed here (although it is roughly contemporary with many of the manuscripts in which these texts are preserved), and secondly, it is a version not of a Latin original but of a text written in another contemporary European language, and thus reflects an interest in, and familiarity with, other contemporary engagements with classical mythography.

The ultimate source for the text is *Recoeil des histoires de Troyes* 'Compendium of the Histories of Troy', written by Raoul Le Fèvre about the year 1463 (edited by Aeschbach 1987). Relatively little is known about Raoul Le Fèvre. He was also the author of *Histoire de Jason* 'The History of Jason' (*c.* 1460), and was chaplain to Philip the Good, third Duke of Burgundy (reigned 1419–67), for whom both works were written.[3] The *Recoeil* recounts, as its title suggests, the history and destructions of Troy, and draws upon a wide range of classical and medieval authorities, chief among which are Giovanni Boccacio's *Genealogia Deorum Gentilium* 'Genealogy of the Pagan Gods' and Guido delle Colonne's *Historia Destructionis Troiae* 'History of the Destruction of Troy' (Aeschbach 1987: 94–106). William Caxton published an English translation, *The Recuyell of the Historyes of Troye*, in Bruges *c.* 1474, which has the distinction of being the first printed book in the English language.[4] While Caxton's text is a fairly close, if not always accurate, translation of Le Fèvre's work (Quin 1939: xvii), the Irish author took considerable liberties with his source text – whether that source was Le Fèvre or Caxton.[5] He abridged his source considerably, freely altered the sequence of events at points, and removed material which did not directly pertain to the life and deeds of Hercules (Quin 1939: xxv-xxi). These interventions result in a greater focus on the exploits and heroic biography of Hercules, a difference which is foregrounded by the Irish title (see further Ross 1989 and 1995–7; Mac Eoin 2006; Poppe 2006).

The two passages presented here both deal with the giant Antaeus who, according to classical tradition, lived in Libya and forced travellers to wrestle with him, killing them when they were exhausted. This practice continued until Hercules overcame and killed Antaeus.[6] Some accounts add the further details that Antaeus was the son of the Titan Gaia, that he gained strength from touching the earth, and that Hercules was able to defeat him by holding him above the ground and crushing him to death.[7] Antaeus appears once in the *Recoeil*, but as two separate characters in *Stair Ercuil*. Both of these characters are giants dwelling in remote places where Hercules journeys in order to challenge and ultimately defeat them. By comparing both of these passages, we can arrive at some insights regarding Uilliam Mac an Leagha's understanding of, and attitudes towards, his source materials.

The first passage corresponds directly with one in Le Fèvre's (and Caxton's) text and, although it has been abridged considerably and rewritten in the elaborate and alliterative style typical of Irish heroic literature, it presents largely the same narrative as in the source text (Aeschbach 1987: 345–7, 352–6; Sommer 1894: 351–5, 361–6). Shortly after the death of Laomedon at the hands of Hercules and the second destruction of Troy, a king named Afer comes to request Hercules' aid in fighting the tyrant and giant Anntenon (Antheon in Le Fèvre and Caxton), who had been attacking his kingdom. In Le Fèvre and Caxton, Afer initially asks Hercules for aid in order to avenge his kingdom or the destruction caused by the tyrant Busire. Hercules agrees, and they set out to attack Libya where they are met by, and defeat, Antheon. This Busire is undoubtedly Busiris, an Egyptian king who, in classical tradition, sacrificed his guests to the gods until he was slain by Hercules and on whom Samson is modelled in the Middle Irish text *How Samson Slew the Gesteda* (see Ch. 17).[8] The Irish narrative is simpler: Afer asks Hercules for aid against the depredations of Anntenon. The Irish text also describes Afer as *rí na Maigionda Moire* 'king of Great Macedonia', while in both Le Fèvre and Caxton he is an Egyptian. In our text, Hercules and Afer bring a large military force into Libya, where a pitched battle ensues. After being wounded severely by Hercules, Anntenon requests a month-long truce in which to recover from his injuries. Hercules goes off to have other adventures and, at the end of the month, returns to Libya to give battle again. Hercules slays Anntenon, erects a memorial, gives the kingship of the country to Afer, and establishes the institution of marriage among the Libyans.

This passage demonstrates two prominent features of the *Recoeil*: firstly, the removal of nearly all supernatural or fantastic elements of the source material, and secondly, the unorthodox forms in which Latin names are presented (Sommer 1894: cxxvi). Latin *Antaeus* has become *Antheon* in Le Fèvre and Caxton, and in the Irish text it has become further transformed, perhaps under the influence of the name *Antenor*, into *Anntenon* (Quin 1939: xxxi–xxxii). While he is described as a *geant* 'giant' in Le Fèvre's (and Caxton's) text, there is no mention of his unusual ancestry, his particular connection with the earth, or even of his skill in wrestling. Because of these two characteristics of Le Fèvre's work, the connection between Antheon/Anntenon and the classical Antaeus is barely recognizable.

The second passage corresponds with nothing in Le Fèvre or Caxton. Hercules was informed that a giant known as *Ainntius mac Terra* 'Ainntius son of the Earth' has been causing devastation in some distant territory. Hercules set forth and, when he arrived in that territory the giant challenged him to a wrestling match. As in certain classical accounts, Ainntius' strength was restored upon touching the earth, and Hercules was only able to prevail over him by raising him above the ground and crushing him to death. The closest parallel to this account in classical tradition is found within Lucan's epic *Civil War* (4.588–655), when the Roman general Curio asks a Libyan guide to explain the meaning of the toponym *Antaei regna* 'Antaeus' kingdom'. In Lucan's account, however, Antaeus pours hot sand over himself prior to his fight, a further indication of his connection with the earth. In *Stair Ercuil* the giant smears himself in various oils. This, along with various textual affinities, suggests that Mac an Leagha's source for this episode was *In Cath Catharda*, the Middle Irish adaptation of Lucan (Quin 1939: xxxvi-xxxvii; on *In Cath Catharda*, see further Chs 14, 15 and 16 in this volume).[9] Mac an Leagha includes a further detail not found in *In Cath Catharda*, that Hercules squeezed all of the excrement out of his opponent; this was likely borrowed from (or at least inspired by) the combat between Cú Chulainn and Láiríne mac Nóis in the *Táin Bó Cúailnge* (*TBC 1* lines 1810–45; *TBC-LL* lines 1951–85).

This second episode appears towards the end of the text, shortly before events are set in motion which result in Hercules' death at the hands of the unwitting Deianira. One possible explanation for the insertion of this episode here was that the author was aware of Hercules' combat with Antaeus from some previous source and conscious of its absence in his source text. Unaware, however, of where it fits in the chronology of Hercules' life, he inserted it towards the end of his text. That the wrestling match and other details were not added to the episode involving Antheon/Anntenon indicates that Mac an Leagha did not recognize the classical antecedent behind that episode, as elsewhere the translator has not hesitated to supply additional context from classical tradition which is lacking in his source (Quin 1939: xxxviii-xxxix).

As noted above, the Irish author took considerable liberties with his source. Some of these interventions can be characterized as corrections to Le Fèvre's account: explicitly identifying the Olympian gods and others as divinities, and adding the important battle between Hercules and Antaeus. The new title may provide some insight into his attitude towards his main source and its truth-value: the *stair* 'history' of Hercules. These interventions are consistent with the medieval practice of historiography: sources are read critically and supplemented with readings from other authorities (cf. Toner 2000). Rather than appealing to a Latin authority, or even another French or English source, our adaptor made use of *In Cath Catharda*. Not only might a Middle Irish text have been more readily available to our adaptor, but we can also infer that it was regarded as equally authoritative.

In addition to *Stair Ercuil*, there are three other texts unique to this manuscript which were also likely composed by Mac an Leagha: *Stair Nuadat Find Femin* 'The Story of Nuada Find Femin' (Müller-Lisowski 1921), *Beathadh Sir Gui o Bharbhuic* 'The Life of Sir Guy of Warwick' and *Bethadh Bibuis o Hamtuir* 'The Life of Bevis of Hampton' (Robinson 1908).[10] The latter two texts are also translations of Anglo-Norman literary works, by way of their English versions. The contents of the manuscript point to a patron who was interested in the mainstream of late medieval Anglo-French literature, as well as a scribe who was well-acquainted with that same literature. Rather than faithfully translating more prestigious texts from the centre to the margins, however, the author's engagement with his sources is active and critical, casting their crusading heroes in a characteristically Gaelic mode, and reading their depictions of the ancient world in light of by then long-established tradition of Irish engagement with classical antiquity. While the most well-known products of this tradition took on their canonical forms in the eleventh and twelfth centuries, texts such as *Stair Ercuil* show that it continued to be a vital one in the later Middle Ages, invigorated rather than diminished by the presence of the Anglo-Normans and their literary culture.

Notes

1   *Na fir gorma*, corresponding with *moores* in Caxton and *Mores* in Le Fèvre. While the basic meaning of *gorm* is '(deep) blue, (deep) green,' it can also convey the sense of 'dark, swarthy, black' (*eDIL* s.v. *gorm* c). In Modern Irish the word is used like 'Black' in English, to refer to people with dark skin, especially those from Africa or of African descent. This passage is, to the best of my knowledge, the earliest unambiguous example of *gorm* used in this way.

2   A partial diplomatic transcription of this text was first published as Nettlau 1889. The first and, to date, only edition and translation is Quin 1939. On the identity of the translator, see Quin 1939: xxxviii–xl.

3   Edited by Pinkernell 1971. Le Fèvre's biography is discussed there (32–5); see also
    Aeschbach 1987: 17–23.

4   Edited and discussed by Sommer 1894. Sommer also discusses the authorship,
    sources, and manuscript content of the work, although much of this discussion is
    superseded by Aeschbach 1987.

5   Quin (1939: xvii–xxiv) argues, on the basis of the treatment of proper names, that
    Stair Ercuil is derived from Caxton's translation rather than Le Fèvre, although
    neither of the English printings which were available when it was written can explain
    all of the features of the Irish text. For the sake of the current discussion, it is not
    particularly important whether it is directly derived from Caxton or Le Fèvre as,
    while Caxton does present variant spellings of proper names, the content of his text
    is practically identical to that of Le Fèvre.

6   See, for example, Plato, *Laws* 7.796a; Plato, *Theaetetus* 169b; Plutarch, *Sertorius* 9.3;
    Pausanias 9.11.6; Diodorus Siculus 4.17.4; Hyginus, *Fabulae* 31.

7   See Statius, *Thebaid* 6.893–6; Ovid, *Metamorphoses* 9.181–4; Lucan, *Civil War*
    4.588–655; Apollodorus, *Library of Greek Mythology* 2.5.11.

8   Classical sources for the story of Hercules and Busiris, often in sections that also
    mention the Antaeus story, include Ovid, *Metamorphoses* 9.181–4; Diodorus Siculus
    4.18.1; Hyginus, *Fabulae* 31; Apollodorus, *Library of Greek Mythology* 2.5.11.

9   Another possible verbal parallel not mentioned by Quin is the place-name *Tulach na
    Glecca* 'the hill of struggle' (*CCath* lines 2889, 2988), corresponding with *Tulach na
    <. . .>cca* in *Stair Ercuil*. Unfortunately, a tear in the manuscript means that it is
    impossible to determine how close this parallel actually is.

10 On the interrelationship between these texts, see further Poppe 1992; Poppe 1997;
    Poppe 2005. An intriguing possibility raised by Robert Crampton is that the
    inclusion of the Antaeus episode in our text, above other narratives about Hercules
    known in Irish sources, may have also been motivated by thematic similarities with
    the other romances in this manuscript. We may briefly note that the Irish lives of
    both Bevis and Guy feature episodes in which the hero hears a report of a monstrous
    being which has been despoiling the land, the hero sets out, engages the monster in
    single combat and, after a difficult fight, returns victorious (*Bethadh Bibuis* §5;
    Beathadh Sir Gui §32).

Part Six

World Knowledge and Indigenous Tradition

23

Auraicept na nÉces 'The Scholars' Primer'[1]

Nicolai Egjar Engesland

The text is transcribed from Dublin, Royal Irish Academy MS D.ii.1, the Book of Uí Mhaine (referred to below as M). This late fourteenth-century manuscript contains the second-oldest surviving copy of Auraicept na nÉces. *It is significant for the analysis of the textual tradition, as it represents an independent branch of the stemma (Ahlqvist 1983: 24–6; Engesland 2021: 52–65). The text from this manuscript is published here for the first time, reproduced with changes from Engesland 2020: 263–305. A full revision of that edition is forthcoming. This passage may be compared to the text in Calder's edition (1917) at B 1034–1134 and Y 3989–4228.*

The transmission of Auraicept na nÉces *is relatively complex. A crucial characteristic is that older sections have been expanded through the inclusion of glosses and commentary items that presumably accompanied the main text in the margins of earlier, lost manuscript copies. This poses considerable challenges to the establishment of a critical text. However, the extract presented here is an exception, because it is preserved as continuous text in all manuscripts that contain it (11 out of 12) and the variation between the manuscripts is relatively minor.[2]*

Letters have been supplied or removed only in cases where this is necessary for clarity in reading. Supplied letters are enclosed in angle brackets ⟨. . .⟩, and letters that should be removed are enclosed in curling brackets {. . .}. Other symbols are used in accordance with the general guidelines in the prefatory Guide to Editorial Practices in this volume. A few unambiguous and frequent contractions have been silently expanded. Length marks have not been supplied.

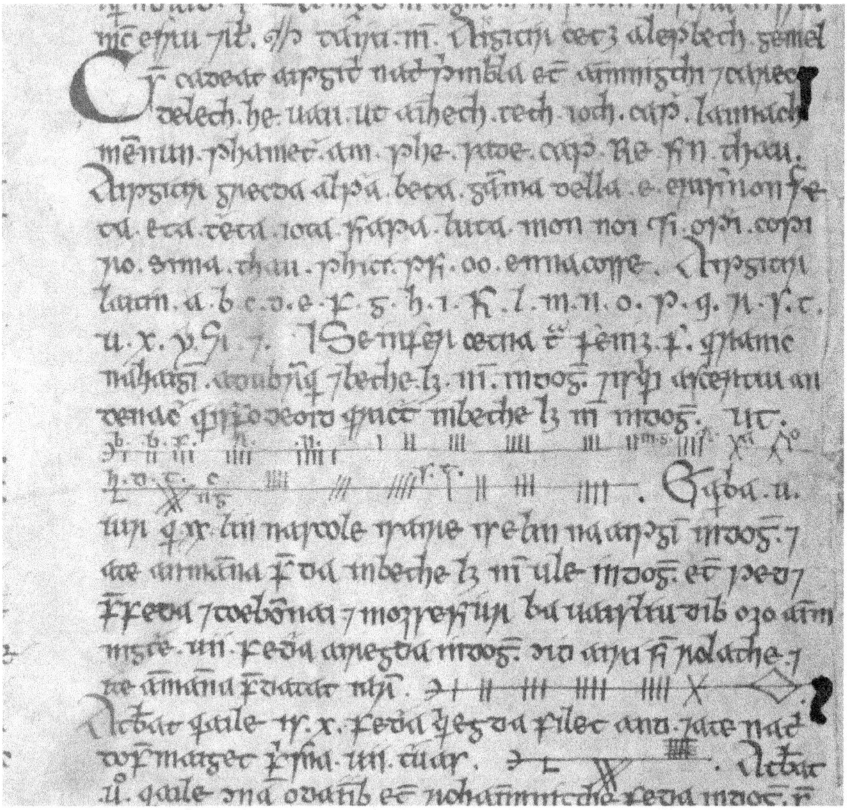

Figure 7 Dublin, Royal Irish Academy MS D.ii.1, the Book of Uí Mhaine, fol. 141v, detail, *Auraicept na nÉces*. Image from ISOS reproduced by kind permission of the Royal Irish Academy.

Text: On the origins of the Irish language

M 563–612 (fol. 141va-b); see Figure 7 on the previous page.[3]

Ceist: Cia ar-raníc a mberla Fene ⁊ cía aírm im-arnacht ⁊ cia aimser ar-richt? Ni ansae. Ar-raníc Feníus Farsaid oc Tur Nemruaid cind *deich* mbliadain iar scaíliud on Tur ⁊ is ca*ch* comberlaid do-cuaidh i suidhíu docu*m* a criche ⁊ ni ca*ch* comcenel, am*al* ro gab Cae Cainbretha*ch*, dalta Feniusa Far*said*, i*n* dara desci*bul* *sechtmogat* na scole. Ba do Ebrib a bunadas ⁊ bad g{h}o Edeptacdu ro foidhed fobíth is a*nd* batar a tu*st*idi ⁊ ba h-and ro alt. Is and ro an Feíníus fei*n* oco*n* Tur no co thoracht a scol chuchi as ca*ch* aird cind *deich* mbliadain ⁊ *con*-atgetar cosi*n* sui{*n*}d (.i. go Feínius) berla na beth oc neoch aile do thepe doib asna ilberlaibh acht co*m*bad leo a n-aenur no beth *no* ac neoch fo-gle*n*dad leo. Is a*nn*si*n* iar*um* do-reped doib in berla-sin isna ilberlaib.

Ro taiselbadh do oen dib co*n*id a ai*n*m side forda-ta in berla-sa, co*n*id Goedelg de side o{c} Goedíul m*ac* Ainginn, m*eic* Gluin(ḟ)ind, m*eic* Lam(ḟ)ind, m*eic* Etheoír, m*eic* Agnom*ain* do Grecaib. Ínu*n*d t*ra* Goediul m*ac* Aingin ⁊ Goedíul m*ac* Etheoír *acht* da ai*n*m badar *for* a athair .i. Aingin ⁊ Etheoir.

Is a*nn*si*n* iar*um* ro riaglad in berla-sa. A *m*ba ferr iar*um* in ca*ch* berla ⁊ a mba caimiu, is *ed* ro teped isin nGoedelg. Ca*ch* so*n* dona airnecht carechtaír isna aipgitrib ailib ar-ricta carechtairi doib isi*n* Bethe-Luís-Ni*n* ind Og*aim*, ut *est*: ᚛ᚋᚔᚂᚌᚎᚖ᚜.

'A mba ferr iar*um*' ⁊rl.

.i. ferr leo-som i*nt* etargna a mbíth muti uli *quam* a mbith muti ⁊ leathgutha*i* am*al* atat oco*n* Laitneoir.

'A n-aṡ coemiu' ⁊rl.

.i. coemiu les a *coic* fo fhut ⁊ a *coic* fo lanfogur ⁊ a *coic* fo cruaidi. Feda airegda insin. Coeimiu da*no* les a *coic* fo gair ⁊ a *coic* fo buca ⁊ a *coic* fo de<fh>ogur (*for*feada a*nn*sin) andas a n-oen cuiciur fri*u* ule.

Translation by the author

Question: Who invented the language of the Féni [i.e. Irish/Gaelic], and in what place was it invented and at what time was it invented? That is not difficult: Fénius Farsaid invented it at Nimrod's Tower at the end of ten years after the dispersal from the Tower; and those who went from there to their territory were all speakers of the same language, rather than all being members of a single kindred: as for instance Cai Caínbrethach, a pupil of Fénius Farsaid, one of the 72 students of the school. He was of Hebrew extraction, and he was sent to the Egyptians because his parents were there, and there he had been raised. It is there that Fénius himself stayed, at the Tower, until the pupils came to him from each direction at the end of ten years and asked of the sage (i.e. of Fénius) to form for them a language out of the many languages, one that would be held by no one else, such that only they would have it, or someone who would learn it from them. It is there, then, that this language was formed out of the many languages for them.

It was assigned to one of them, so that his name is the name of this language, so that *Goídelc* [Irish/Gaelic] comes hence from Goídel, son of Angin, son of Glunḟind, son of Lamḟind, son of Etheoir, son of Agnoman of the Greeks. Now Goídel son of Angin is the same as Goídel son of Etheoir, but his father had two names: Angin and Etheoir.

It is there, then, that this language was given its rules. What was best, then, of every language and what was finest was cut out into Irish. For every sound for which a letter could not be found in the other alphabets, letters were invented for them in the Beithe-Luis-Nin of the Ogam,[4] *thus:* ᚛ᚅᚌᚍᚓ᚜.

'*What was best, then . . .*'[5]

i.e. they preferred the interpretation that they [the letters of the Ogam] should all be mutes, rather than that they should be both mutes and semivowels, as they [i.e. the Roman letters] are for the Latinist:[6]

'*What is finest . . .*'[7]

i.e. he thought it more fitting that five should be long and five should be fully sounding and five should be voiced. Those are the vowels. He thought it more fitting that five should be short and five should be soft and five should be

'A mba lethíu'

.ị. 'galmarium' ⁊ 'glinula' ⁊ 'glamulum' *no* 'galinulum' lasin Laitineoir, 'gruth' ⁊ 'fascri' ⁊ 'grutrach' lasin nGoedelg. 'Grus' *uero* lasin nGoedel, ní fil a ⟨ḟ⟩recra lasin Laitíneoir. 'Lapis' ⁊ 'petra' ⁊ 'scropula' lasin Laítineoir, 'lia' ⁊ 'ail' ⁊ 'carrac' lasin nGoedel. 'Cloch' lasin nGoedel, ni fil a ⟨ḟ⟩recra lasin Laitineoir. 'Aqua' lasin Laitineoir, 'uisce' lasin nGoedel. 'Línd' lasin nGoedel, ni fil a ⟨ḟ⟩recra lasin Laitineoir ⁊ rl.

Ro laithea iarum a fedha *for* leath aile co bail cach dib *for* leath o 'lailiu. Ni fil leathguta and am*al* ní fil la Grecu *acht* mutí uli. Ca*ch* duil dona raba ainmnigud isna berlaibh ailib ar-rícta ainmnigithi doib (.i. ⟨i⟩isin Goedelg), ut 'grus' ⁊ 'cloch' ⁊ 'lind'.

Is ed tosach in libair an*n*so iar Fení*us* ⁊ iar nGoediul ⁊ iar nIar m*a*c Nema ⁊ is i*n* Aichia ar-richt {isi*n*} i *n*-aimsir i tangadar m*a*c Israel [a hE]gipt ⁊ iar tidnac*ul* Recta do Maisi ⁊ iar foglaím do Cai Cai*n*brethach oca, co*n*id iar si*n* ar-ríchta na h-aipgit*ri* i *n*-oentabaill am*al* as-be*r*t:

'Cadiat ⟨a⟩ípgit*ri* na t*ri* primberla' ⁊ rl.

Cetheora randa na fodailtea o⟨con Tur⟩ .i. da comarlíd *sechtmogat* ⁊ da deíscipul *sechtmogat* ⁊ da berla *sechtmogat* ⁊ da cenel *sechtmogat*. Se primthoesig lasi *n*dernad .i. Eber m*a*c Sale ⁊ Grecíus m*a*c Gomeoir o tat Grec ⁊ Latín m*a*c Puín o taít Latíndai, Riafeth Scot o tait Scoit ⁊ Nemruadh m*a*c Cuís, m*e*ic Cai*m*, m*e*ic Noe. Fení*us* F*a*rsaid tra m*a*c Eogaín, m*e*ic Gluín⟨ḟ⟩ind, m*e*ic Laimfind, m*e*ic Etheoír, m*e*ic Thau, m*e*ic Buídhb, m*e*ic {h}ṡein Íair, m*e*ic Iartecht, m*e*ic Aboíth, m*e*ic Ara, m*e*ic Sru, m*e*ic Esru, m*e*ic Bath, m*e*ic Riafaith, m*e*ic Gomeoír, m*e*ic Iafeth, m*e*ic Noe. Partholon m*a*c Sairn, m*e*ic Sera, m*e*ic Sru, cetna fer ro gab Eiri*n*d iar nDili*n*d. Nemeadh m*a*c Agnoma*n*, m*e*ic Paín, m*e*ic Sera, m*e*ic Sru, m*e*ic Esru ⁊ rl.

diphthongs (those are the supplementary letters), rather than to have a single group of five represent all of these.

'*What was widest . . .*'[8]

i.e. the Latinist has *galmarium* and *glinula* and *glamulum* or *galinulum* (corresponding to the words for) 'cheese' [*gruth*] and 'pressed curd' [*fáiscre*] and 'curdled milk' [*gruthrach*] in Irish.[9] However, the Gael has 'cheese' [*grus*], and the Latinist does not have an equivalent for this. The Latinist has *lapis* and *petra* and *scropula* (corresponding to the words for) 'stone' [*lia*] and 'boulder' [*ail*] and 'rock' [*carrac*] which the Gael has. The Gael's 'stone' [*cloch*] has no equivalent for the Latinist. The Latinist's *aqua* (corresponds to the word for) 'water' [*uisce*] for the Gael. The Gael's 'sea' [*linn*] has no equivalent for the Latinist, and so on.[10]

Its vowel letters [*feda*] were placed apart, so that each of them [vowels and consonants] is separate from the other. There are no semivowels, as the Greeks have nothing but mutes alone. Names were found (that is, in Irish) for every thing that did not have a name in the other languages, such as 'cheese' [*grus*] and 'stone' [*cloch*] and 'sea' [*linn*].

This is the beginning of the book according to Fénius and Goídel and Iar son of Nema and it is in Asia that it was invented, in the time when the sons of Israel came from Egypt and after the Law had been given to Moses and after Cai Caínbrethach had studied with him, so that after that the alphabets were invented on one tablet, as he said:

'*What are the alphabets of the three chief languages . . .*'.

Four divisions were dispersed at the Tower, i.e. 72 counsellors, 72 disciples, 72 languages and 72 peoples. Six principal chieftains by whom it [the Tower] was made: Eber son of Saile; Grecus son of Gomer, from whom the Greeks descend; and Latinus son of Faunus from whom the Latins descend; Riabad Scot from whom the *Scoit* [i.e. Gaelic Irish] descend; and Nimrod son of Cush, son of Ham, son of Noah. Fénius Farsaid was the son of Eogan, son of Glunfind son of Lamfind son of Etheoir, son of Tau, son of Bodb. The latter was the son of Iar son of Iartecht, son of Abodh, son of Arah, son of Sru, son of Esru, son of Boath, son of Riafath, son of Gomer, son of Japheth, son of Noah. Partholon son of Sarn, son of Sera, son of Sru, the first man to rule Ireland after the Flood. Nemed son of Agnomen, son of Pan, son of Sera, son of Sru, son of Esru and so on.

Ceist: Cadeat aipgit*ri* na *tri primberla* et*er* ai*n*mnígthi ⁊ carectaírí? Ni ansae. Aipgítír ⟨Ebraide⟩ cet*us*: aleph, beth, gemel, deleth, he, uau, ut, ai*n*, heth, teh, ioth, caph, lamiach, me*m*, nun, phameth, am, phe, sade, caph, re, sin, thau.

Aipgítír Grecda: alpha, beta, ga*m*ma, della, e, erisinon, zeta, eta, theta, iota, kapa, luta, mon, noi, csi, o, phi, copi, ro, sima, thau, phi, c<h>i, psi, oo, ennacosse.

Aipgitír Laitín: a, b, c, d, e, f, g, h, i, k, l, m, n, o, p, q, r, s, t, u, x, y, z, ⁊.
⁊ is e ín fer cetna t*ra* Feníus Fa*r*said ar-raníc na h-ai⟨p⟩*gitri* adub*ra*mar ⁊ Bethe-Luis-Ni*n* índ Ogaim ⁊ is airi as certiu an denach ar ís fo deoid ar-rícht ín Bethe-Luis-Ní*n* ind O*gaim*, ut: ⟩

Question: What are the alphabets of the three chief languages, both names and characters? Not difficult. (The Hebrew) alphabet first: *alef, bet, gimel, dalet, he, waw, zayin, chet, tet, yod, kaf, lamed, mem, nun, samech, ayin, pe, tsadi, qof, resh, shin, tav.*[11]

The Greek alphabet: *alpha, beta, gamma, delta, e(psilon), episemon,*[12] *zeta, eta, theta, iota, kappa, lambda, mu, nu, xi, o(micron), pi, kofi,*[13] *rho, sigma, tau, (upsilon), phi, psi, o(mega), ennacose.*[14]

The Latin alphabet: 'a,' 'b,' 'c,' 'd,' 'e,' 'f,' 'g,' 'h,' 'i,' 'k,' 'l,' 'm,' 'n,' 'o,' 'p,' 'q,' 'r,' 's,' 't,' 'u,' 'x,' y,' 'z,' '⁊'[15] – and it is the same man, namely Fénius Farsaid, who invented the alphabets we have mentioned, as well as the Beithe-Luis-Nin of the Ogam, and the latter is the more precise because the Beithe-Luis-Nin of the Ogam was invented last, thus:

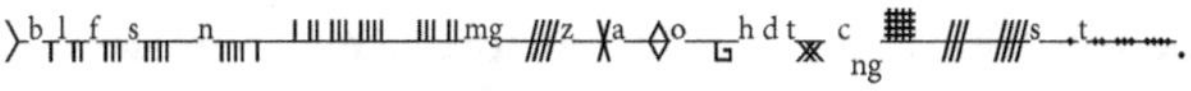

Essay: The Tower of Babel and the early Irish grammarians

Auraicept na nÉces 'The Scholars' Primer' is the earliest preserved grammatical description of any Western European non-classical language. The first edition and translation of the text was published in 1917 by George Calder, while the so-called 'canonical part' of the text was edited and translated by Ahlqvist (1983), who dates this part to *c.* 700. The evidence supporting such an early date is dubious, however. Its rhetoric gives insight into the ways in which Irish was promoted as a vehicle for intellectual discourse. *Auraicept na nÉces* is exceptional for extending the Babel narrative in the Pentateuch (Genesis 11.1–9) with an account of the origin of the Irish language. We are told that Irish is made up of the 'finest parts' of all the 72 tongues that were scattered around the world after the dispersal at the Tower of Babel and that it is therefore richer in expression and more euphonious than both Greek and Latin.[16]

This extension of the biblical aetiology of the diversity of human speech enhances the prominence of the Irish language, not only in relation to the other vernaculars, but also in relation to the three sacred languages: Hebrew, Greek and Latin. This is further reinforced by an imaginative and sometimes tendentious reading of mainstay Latin authorities, such as Donatus, Priscian and Isidore. We also find material that may derive from the common source of a particular set of three ninth-century Insular commentaries based on Donatus (Poppe 2002; Holtz 1973).

Alcuin of York's *Interrogationes et responsiones in Genesin* 'Questions and Answers on Genesis' (*PL* vol. 100), from the last decade of the eighth century, offers a key to understanding the logic of the passage in *Auraicept na nÉces* edited and translated above (Engesland 2021: 477–8). Alcuin's was one of the most popular biblical commentaries of the early Middle Ages and was also abridged and translated into Old English by Ælfric of Eynsham, the author of the first vernacular Latin grammar in Europe (Zupitza 1880).[17] By comparing the phrase *in virga ferrea* 'with a rod of iron' (the Douay-Rheims wording) in the Latin and Greek translations of the Psalms, he notes that the word *sidera* exists in both languages, but with different meanings:

> If God rested from all his works on the seventh day, from where did the diversity
> of the languages suddenly appear? It is not believed that the Creator created
> anything new in this division of languages [*linguarum*], but that the modes and
> forms of expression [*dicendi modos*] were divided into various kinds of speech
> [*loquelarum*]. For this reason we find the same syllables and letters of the same

value, combined in different ways in the various languages of the nations. Often also the same nouns or verbs have one meaning in one language and another meaning in another (language). When we say in the psalm [Psalm 2.9]: 'with a rod of iron [*in virga ferrea*]', we have ἐν ῥάβδῳ σιδηρᾷ [*en rhabdōi sidērāi*] in Greek. Latin *sidera* does not mean 'iron', but 'stars'.[18]

In another passage, Alcuin comments on the vanity that led mankind to construct a tower with its top in the sky, and states that 'Pride, then, caused the diversity of languages (the humility of Christ has unified the diversity of languages) and the Church has put together that which the Tower had separated'.[19] In the passage from *Auraicept na nÉces*, on the other hand, the pieces separated in the land of Shinar are put together by Fénius Farsaid and his scholars.[20] The new language is then given grammatical rules[21] – a precondition for an analysis in keeping with that of the Latin treatises. The peerless vocabulary of Irish is illustrated in very practical terms by an eclectic comparison of lexical items in Irish and Latin.

The profusion of sounds resulting from the confluence of linguistic forms further necessitated the fabrication of a new alphabet for the accurate reduction of the new language to writing. The letter was the fundamental unit of late antique and medieval linguistic analysis, and the comparison between the native Irish alphabet Ogam and the Latin alphabet informs a great deal of *Auraicept na nÉces* beyond what is included here (see Calder 1917 and Ahlqvist 1983). Particular attention is devoted to the so-called 'supplementary characters', which entered the Ogam inventory as a distinct group after the decline of the use of Ogam as a monumental script in the seventh century.[22] In the prefatory discussion of the text (*accessus*) towards the end of the extract we get an alternative account which seems to suggest that Cai Caínbrethach extracted the alphabets from Moses' tablets, thus connecting God's own writing not only with the script of the three sacred languages but also with that of Irish.

The lists of the names of the letters of the Hebrew, Greek and Latin alphabets that end the section quoted above derive from a range of sources that probably went through the prism of Hrabanus Maurus' *De inventione litterarum* ('The Invention of Letters') from the ninth century (edition and analysis in Derolez 1954). The Greek letters were used mainly for computistical purposes in the early medieval period and were transmitted in influential works such as Bede's *De temporum ratione* ('On the Reckoning of Time') from 725 (Jones 1975–80: vol. 2), and Isidore's *Etymologies* (Lindsay 1911) from the early seventh century. The alphabet lists are more complete in other manuscript copies of *Auraicept na nÉces* and include the shapes of the letters as well as an interpretation of their names.[23] The interpretations of the Hebrew letter names go back to Eusebius through Jerome and are not found in the common handbooks mentioned above.[24] The Hebrew letters, letter names and interpretations were frequently transmitted in commented versions of the Psalter.

Notes

1 I am grateful to Isabelle Torrance, Michael Clarke, Erich Poppe and Máire Ní Mhaonaigh for valuable comments on earlier drafts of this chapter. In the notes below, M indicates the Book of Uí Mhaine version of the text; B is the Book of Ballymote, Y is the Yellow Book of Lecan. For full details see Engesland 2020.

2 This enables us to get around some of the problems that of the approach followed in Ahlqvist's 1983 edition. It also guarantees the presence of this passage in the archetype, which can be dated to the eleventh century, roughly three centuries before the earliest preserved manuscript copies. See discussions in Calder 1917: xxvi; Thurneysen 1928a: 285; Ahlqvist 1983: 33; Hayden 2013: 162–4; and Engesland 2020: 151–5. See Hayden 2013: 160–5 for an analysis of the rhetorical *circumstantiae* that introduce the text reproduced here.

3 This passage on the origin of the Irish language at the Tower of Babel may be compared to the text in Calder's 1917 edition of B 1034–1134 (cf. also Y 3989–4228).

4 The Ogam symbols can be represented in the text only approximately. For the second and longer series, see the manuscript image in Fig. 7.

5 This is a quotation from the preceding paragraph. The quotation is followed by commentary.

6 The observation that neither Irish nor Greek has semivowels is based on one of the definitions of semivowels that we find in Priscian (*GL* 2: 8) in a citation from Servius' commentary on Donatus (*GL* 4: 476–7). Following this definition, all acrophonic letter names (such as the Greek letters γάμμα, δέλτα, θῆτα or the Ogam letters *beithe, luis, nin*) must be mutes (*mūtae*).

7 See note 4.

8 See note 4, but note that 'what was widest' has been lost in the preceding passage in the text of M.

9 Note here the phrase *lasin nGoedelg* 'according to the Irish language', instead of *lasin nGoedel* 'according to the Gael/Irishman', which is common in this passage.

10 See Hayden 2013: 166 n.101 with references on the terminology in this paragraph. See also Milani 1978 on the (poorly attested) Latin words.

11 The letter-names have been standardized in this translation. See my discussion of the alphabet tables with comparison between the manuscript copies of *Auraicept na nÉces*, Engesland 2020: 186–226 (tables reproduced at 306–20).

12 The Greek letters were frequently transmitted with their numerical value in the Middle Ages. The letter *digamma* was referred to in the Byzantine period with the name *(vau) episemon* (βαῦ ἐπίσημον). The sound /w/ denoted by the letter was lost at various times in the Greek dialects, but the letter remained in use with its numeric value '6'.

13 See note 11. The letter *koppa/qoppa* (*kofi* M) denoted the numeral '90'.

14 See note 11. The last item in this list, *ennacose* (from a Greek form such as ἐνακόσια/ἐννιακόσια) denotes '900'.

15 This symbol is the Tironian *et*, frequently employed in Irish manuscripts as an abbreviation for *ocus* 'and'.

16 The idea that Irish had been assembled from the 72 post-Babel languages had wider currency in Irish literature. Another version of the story is found in the pseudohistorical *Lebor Gabála Érenn* 'The Book of Invasions of Ireland' (Macalister 1938–56). The idea further entered Geoffrey Keating's *Foras Feasa ar Éirinn* 'Foundation of Knowledge on Ireland', completed in 1634 (Comyn and Dinneen 1902–14). The first of the *Irish Grammatical Tracts* (Mac Cárthaigh 2014) also draws on *Auraicept na nÉces*.

17 The passage cited from Alcuin here is found in the commentary on Genesis by his student Hrabanus Maurus (*PL* vol. 107: cols 530–1), in the commentary by Angelomus of Luxeuil (*PL* vol. 115: cols 167–8), and in later commentaries, such as one version of the later collection of biblical commentaries known as the *Glossa ordinaria* (*PL* vol. 113: col. 115).

18 *PL* vol. 100: col. 543. Translation reproduced from Engesland 2021: 477.

19 *PL* vol. 100: col. 533. Author's translation.

20 See Carey 1990 for a discussion of Fénius Farsaid and his genealogy.

21 The non-classical languages were frequently held to lack grammatical rules in the Middle Ages. Otfrid of Weissenburg and Dante Alighieri are two prominent exponents of this idea. Otfrid's *Evangelienbuch* is edited by Erdmann 1973, see also Hartmann 2005–14; Dante's *De vulgari eloquentia* is edited by Tavoni 2015.

22 These additional letters are attested in manuscripts from the eighth century onwards, first in Bern, Burgerbibliothek MS 207, from a Continental monastery with Irish connections. See McManus 1991 for a full discussion.

23 On these tables, see note 10 above, and see also Hayden 2016.

24 See Berschin 1980 and Thiel 1973 on the knowledge of Greek and Hebrew respectively in Western Europe in the Middle Ages.

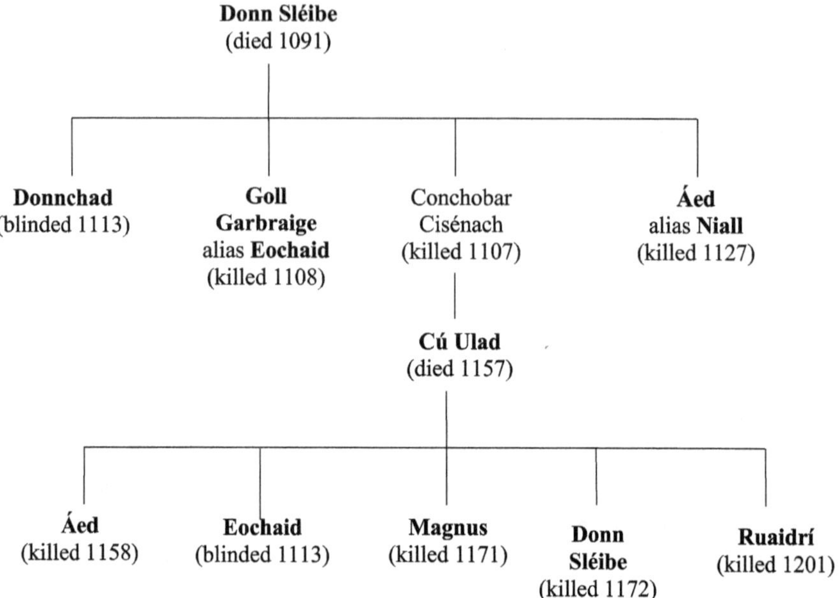

Figure 8 A section of the lineage of Dál Fiatach, with Kings of Ulster in **bold type** (based on Byrne 1964).

24

Clann Ollaman uaisle Emna 'The nobles of Emain Macha are Ollam's descendants'

Michael Clarke

The text is adapted from the edition of Byrne 1964 with a new translation.[1]

Text: Two extracts on ancient and modern Kings of Ulster

1.   Clann Ollaman uaisle Emna,
        Ulltaig Sléibe lethain Liac,
    cined Ír ro-fhial na réimenn:
        Tro-fhian fhír na hÉirenn iat.

2.   Is don Chúiced Dál finn Fiatach,
        na fir ó Éiremón oll,
    maicne do shíl Fiachna Fairrge
        co llín sciath, co ngairge nglonn.

    Comoirrdeirc Asia re hUlltaib
        im écht, im allaid, im uaill;
    Priaim ainm Conchobair Codail
        borrfadaig im Thoraig thuaid.

4.   Coimfhedma Treóil is Cú Chulainn
        im chomlonn, im ré is im rath:
    Fergus Énias re luad loingse,
        glé-dias buan nar choimse i cath.

5.   Alexandair Naíse nertmar,
        rena néim Troí ocus Táin;
    Echtair mar Chonall cert Cernach
        nert ro-garb re hernach n-áig.

6.   Cosmail gach áen-fher d' iath Emna
        d' fhir ar Tróe muirnig na máer;
    ropo datta a n-áirem uile,
        gach sáir-fher don chuire cháem.

7.   Inneósat d' airdrígaib Ulad
        iar nÍsa oirdnide uag,
    co mbet i llaídib i llebraib
        ac daínib ar selbaib suad.

8.   Eól dam ainm gach fhir 's a oidid
        iar n-eólchaib gach monair maith:
    a ed re ro-áirem ríme
        is comáirem ríge raith.

9.   Do chreit Muiredach mál Macha
        do mac Muire na cét clann;
    réim in airdríg ó Thuinn Tuaige
        fairbríg re muirn uaille ann.

Translation

The nobles of Emain Macha are Ollam's descendants;
the Ulstermen of broad Slieve League,[2]
the full-generous race of Ír in their ranks,
they are Ireland's genuine Trojan warband.

The bright Dál Fiatach belong to the Fifth,[3]
the men descended from great Éremón,
manhood of the seed of Fiachna of the Sea,[4]
with many shields, with boldness of deeds.

Asia (Minor) is as renowned as the Ulstermen
for valour, for glory, for pride;
Priam is the name of Conchobar of Codal,[5]
the ebullient one, round Tory[6] in the north.

Equal in force are Troilus and Cú Chulainn,
for combat, for lifespan, for fortune;
Aeneas is Fergus for the tale of exile,
a bright pair, enduring, not moderate in battle.

Strong Naoise is Alexander,[7]
for whose beauty were (the wars of) Troy and the Táin:
Hector is like goodly Conall Cernach,
a full-fierce strength against the weaponry of battle.

Each man of Emain's land is the likeness
of a man in spirited Troy of the masters;
it would be pleasant to recount them all,
each free man of the fine host.

I will tell of the great kings of the Ulaid
since Jesus the anointed and pure,
so that it will be among the poems that people hold
in books, in the possession of sages.

Known to me is the name of each man and his death
according to those who are learned in every effort,
his time according to the long count of its reckoning
and the calculation of his powerful kingship.

Muiredach, prince of Macha, believed
in Mary's son of the hundred lineages;
the rule of the high king, (extending) from Tonn Tuaige,[8]
was excessive with the ebullience of his pride.

10. Cúic bliadna fichet fat ríge,
     rath Muiredaig fa blad buan,
     gurbo marb rí Cille Comgaill;
     nírbo time i ndograinn duad.

11. A choimlín eile i nAird Ulad
     Eocho mac Muiredaig mir:
     rena éc rí blasda Bennchair
     ropo gasda ar serrchaib sin.

12. A cúic fo chúic Cairell calma
     do chlainn Muiredaig, minn sluaig,
     marb in fer do mudaig Manainn
     do chumaid ac Arainn uair.

13– 64. *[The lives, deaths and counts of regnal years of the kings continue through
     a further 52 quatrains, which are here omitted.]*

65. Ro maídset sluag Eógain Ailig
     ainécht ar Donn Sléibe i sír:
     fiche ropo becht do bliadnaib
     co cert i rriaglaib in ríg.

66. Mac Duinn Shléibe a trí tenna,
     truag lem gan a beith trí secht;
     a cúic fós cor dallad Donnchad,
     rop allad a borrfad becht.

67. Goll Garbraige sebuc Sabaill,
     secht mbliadna ós Tuaig na treb;
     Ua Mathgamna láech lán Line,
     ro thráeth in bán bile Breg.

68. Lámfhata Macha ro mudaig
     mac Duinn Shléibe, nirt na náem:
     a deich is áen-bliadain brugad
     ós cáemriagail Ulad Áed.

69. Ua Mathgamna finn re fichit
     fuair 'sa cúic Garrchú mar grís:
     i cath uas millte na Mullach
     cinnte bas dubach don dís.

70. Trí bliadna glóir Gilla Comgaill,
     cróda a ríge tuillmech thuaid,
     cor thuit i cath ar leirg Lugmaid
     brath dá fheirg i n-urbaid fhuair.

Twenty-five years was the length of his reign,
Muiredach's good fortune was a glory forever,
till the king of Comgall's Church[9] died;
it was not cowardice under the harshness of affliction.

For another equal length in Ards of Ulster[10]
fierce Eochaid son of Muiredach (was king):
before his death, sweet king of Bangor,
that one was a swift (rider) on colts.

Five times five years valiant Cairell (was king),
of Muiredach's stock, diadem of a host:
the man who ravaged the Isle of Man
died of grief on chill Arran.

[...]

The host of Eóghan of Ailech[11] boasted
for long of their ill deed against Donn Sléibe;
twenty was the exact number of years
rightly in the measure of the king.

Donn Sléibe's son (had) his three firm (years),
my sorrow that it was not three times seven:
five again till Donnchadh was blinded,[12]
his stiff ebullience was renowned.

Goll Garbraige the hawk of Saul[13]
(had) seven years over Tuag of the tribes;[14]
the fine Ua Mathgamna,[15] complete hero of Line,
overcame the white one, tree of Brega.

The long-armed one of Macha[16] overcame
Donn Sléibe's son by saints' strength:
for eleven years of hospitality
Áed was over the fair rule of the Ulstermen.

Fair Garrchú Ua Mathgamna got the span of twenty
and five years in his ardour;
in the destructive battle of the Mullaigh
it is certain that grief came to the pair.[17]

Three years of the glory of Gilla Comgaill,[18]
valiant was his worthy kingship in the north
till he fell in battle on the slope of Louth;
betrayal from his anger did he take in destruction.

71. Lán-rí a cúic fo chúic Cú Ulad,
    iarmua Echach fhír gan fhell;
ro chaith re n-éc Corp in Choimded
    gan bét olc, gan choinnmed cell.

72. Tres na haidche ó Chenél Chonaill,
    do claidbed ann Áed na n-ech;
bliadain rí Ulad in échta,
    clí curad créchta na crech.

73. Seisser ar trí fhichit finn-fher
    fuarus co hEochaid in áig;
anois is rí Echaid adma,
    clí re clethaib garba gáid.

74. Gur togba Éirenn ua hArdgail,
    Eochaid Locha Cuan na clann;
láech cáid co tairbeirt nár tubad,
    is airrdeirc báid Ulad ann.

75. Tairngertaid Locha Cuan cloidmig,
    comrád ban, báire gach baird,
sochar Dúin Celtchair gan chréidim,
    súil re hEchtair d' Éirinn aird.

76. Ro múch cath Airgiallach Emna,
    ro airg sluag Érna na n-ech;
re hindshamail léime Loga
    a déine im Choba na crech.

77. In muir co Hí lán do longaib,
    lebar tar Glenn Rige a ruaic,
saidbir 'na thír blicht iar mbolc-bráen,
    at-chíd 'na chirt folt-cháem Fuait.

78. Láech laimthenach airthir Éirenn,
    innsaigthech Alban na n-iath,
tairm mar chlised Brátha buidnig
    brised Átha cloidmig Cliath.

79. Sirtheóir Éirenn d' Inber Scéne
    ar slicht mac Míled, dar lim,
ro-sia ler comrumach cliarach,
    fer forburach fianach finn.

80. Coiméirgit Ulaid is Eochaid
    d' argain Gáedel, do guin Gall:
atáit fa buaid aíbe uile
    sluaig a daíne, cuire a clann.

Clann Ollaman.

Full king for five times five years was Cú Ulad,
great-grandson of Eochaid,[19] who was true without deceit;
he received before death the Body of the Lord
without deed of evil, without occupation of monasteries.[20]

An attack at night by the Kindred of Conall,
there Áed of the horses was pierced by a sword;
for a year the king of the Ulaid of the valorous deed
was the support of heroes of wounding amid plunder.[21]

Six and thrice twenty fair men
I found as far as Eochaid the warlike:
now Eochaid the skilful is king,
a prop against peril with harsh spears.

May Ardgal's descendant[22] be Ireland's choice,
Eochaid of Loch Cuan[23] of the lineages:
the pure conquering warrior unvanquished,
glorious is the Ulstermen's love for him.

The prophesied one of Loch Cuan of the swords,
talk of women, topic of every poet,
Dún Celtchair's[24] good fortune undiminished,
hope of a Hector for lofty Ireland.

The man of Emain has extinguished the Airgiallan army
and has plundered the host of Erne of the steeds;
in the likeness of the leap of Lugh[25]
is his nimbleness around Coba[26] of plunder.

The sea to Iona is full of warships,
swift is his onrush across Glenree,[27]
rich in his land is milk after dewy drops:
these things Fuait's[28] fair-haired one sees in his rightful country.

The audacious warrior of the east of Ireland,
attacker of Scotland of the plains,
a tumult like the springing of the peoples' Doomsday
is the overthrow of Dublin of the swords.

Marauder of Ireland from Inber Scéne
in the path (so it seems) of the sons of Míl,
he will reach the sea triumphant, with his retinue,
a prosperous man, with his warband, fair.

The Ulaid and Eochaid will arise
to slaughter Irishmen, to attack foreigners:
all are under the gift of beauty,
the hosts of his people, the company of their offspring.

Ollam's descendants.

Essay: The glories of a royal lineage

This poem, brilliantly edited by F. J. Byrne (1964),[29] is a witness to the ideology and mythology of kingship as constructed in Irish chronological verse from the early eleventh century onward (Smith 2002 is the fundamental study). By the 1160s, when it was composed, claims to the over-kingship of Ulster and the population-name of *Ulaid* had long been contested among the various lineages who competed for regional pre-eminence in the province known as *an Cóiced*, the 'Fifth' par excellence (as here in line 5).[30] Ownership of the title of *rí Ulad* 'king of Ulaid' represented the status of heir, in bloodline or in spirit, to the original, heroic Ulaid, who were coeval with the Roman emperor Augustus and were famed as the warrior élite of Conchobhar's court at Emain Macha, enshrined in *Táin Bó Cúailnge* and the other narratives of the Ulster Cycle. Emain Macha's associations with the glorious past remained potent, although the descendants of the original Ulaid had long ceased to occupy the site and it was probably little more than the grassy mound that it remains today. For the poet, the realm of the Ulaid stretches across the full expanse of Ulster, from Emain Macha itself in the south-east as far as the great cliffs of Slieve League in the north-west (1.4) and Tory Island in the northern ocean (3.4). In fact, long beforehand these territories had come to be dominated by other peoples – most obviously the Uí Néill, whom our poem conspicuously avoids mentioning – while the Ulaid proper had shrunk to become a petty people of the eastern and south-eastern parts of Ulster.

The genealogical tract *Senchas Síl hÍr* 'The Lore of the Seed of Ír'[31] includes information closely matched in the opening of our poem, and it may even have been a direct source (Byrne 1964: 58, 81–2). Here the ancestry of the chief lineages of Ulster is traced back to two of the sons of Míl, the leaders of the original occupation of Ireland by the ancestors of the Gaelic Irish. One of these lineages, the Dál nAraide, is descended from Ír son of Míl, while their rivals the Dál Fiatach are traced to Ír's brother Éremón: hence these ancient and noble ancestors are invoked in the opening lines of our poem. The mention of 'Ollam' in the first line gains weight from the information in *Senchas Síl hÍr* that the name of this king, Ollam Fótla of the Dál nAraide, provides one of the etymologies of the very name of the Ulaid, *Ulaid Olleith ó Ollaman* (O'Brien 1962: 270.1451).

The assertion that these Ulstermen are the 'true Trojans' of Ireland, the authentic claimants to that name, depends on onomastic learning of a different kind. Unlike so many of the nations of medieval Europe, the Goídil never claimed that they were genealogically descended from the men of Troy (Clarke 2015). This, then, is a metaphorical expression. It resembles one seen in *Cogadh*

Gáedhel re Gallaibh 'The War of the Irish against the Foreigners' in an extended prose panegyric of the Dál gCais, the heroic defenders of Ireland against the Danes, when they are named as *Frainc na Fodla fondairdi*, 'the Franks of high-surfaced Ireland'.[32] But there is etymological subtlety here too. The fixed count of syllables in this metre guarantees that the word translated as 'Trojan-warband' must be read as *Tro-fhian*, and the lenited *f*, spelt *fh*, is pronounced silent and in effect signals no more than a hiatus between vowels. This prompts a pronunciation that matches one of the correct ancient pronunciations of Latin *Troiani*, while also identifying the second element of the word with Irish *fían*, 'warband', which in this period must have signalled a reference to the Fianna of Fionn mac Cumhaill, the classic example of the heroic and patriotic warband in existing Gaelic tradition (Clarke 2014a: 97–8; Darwin 2021: 206–7). Crucially, the spelling also gives a clue to the intertextual background to the poem, because the same strange and learned spelling is attested in the 'Recension 3' branch of the transmission of *Togail Troí*, the prose saga of the Trojan War (see Chs 6 and 9 in this volume).

In the quatrains that come next, the series of parallels between the two peoples seems at first to reflect first-hand knowledge of classical Latin sources, most obviously Virgil's *Aeneid* and its commentary tradition. This would be sufficient to explain the potent (though conventional) match between Hector and Conall Cernach as prime warriors, and between Priam and Conchobhar as kings. But as we continue, we must look further to recover the poet's logic. Paris the abductor of Helen, and Deirdre's lover Naoise, son of Uisnech, were protagonists in the sexual politics that caused their wars, and both were responsible for abductions (albeit of different kinds). Fergus and Aeneas both went into exile, but one was involved in violent strife for the kingship while the other fled from his defeated homeland to found another city. Above all, the parallel between Cú Chulainn and Troilus seems at first sight superficial. The Cú Chulainn of *Táin Bó Cúailnge* 'The Cattle-Raid of Cooley' is the Hound, the preternaturally valiant defender of his stricken people at the ford on the border of their land, but Vergil's Troilus is remembered for one line only, as the hapless boy mowed down and killed by the raging Achilles in his chariot (Virgil, *Aeneid* 1.474).

The problems of the more surprising correspondences melt away if we think not in terms of Latin-to-Irish correspondences but of a series of textual linkages between the Ulster Cycle and the Middle Irish saga of the Trojan War, *Togail Troí*. Here, of course, the roles of Priam, Alexander/Paris and Hector are largely unchanged from the classical sources, but Aeneas and Troilus are different. In *Togail Troí*, as in the source text of Dares Phrygius, Aeneas is foremost among the traitors who open the gates of Troy to the invading Greeks in return for safe passage (*TTr-H* 1799–1840, Stokes 1884: 56–7, 127–8). In the Ulster Cycle, similarly, Fergus mac Róich turns to violence against Conchobhar in the conflict that erupts over Deirdre, and ravages Ulster before going into exile to the court of Ailill and Medb – so that in *Táin Bó Cúailnge* itself he guides the Connachta to the place where they will attack the Ulaid (on Fergus see Ó hUiginn 1993). When Troilus and Cú Chulainn are paired, we find still better clues to uncovering the poet's relationship with his sources. Cú Chulainn, the Hound of Ulster, is the boy hero who in *Táin Bó Cúailnge* stands in defence of his people when they are struck down by debility as the host of the Connachta approach. In *Togail Troí*, similarly, Troilus is a young boy who arises to be the champion of his people in battle after Hector has been killed (*TTr-H* 1351–1570, Stokes 1884: 43–9, 111–19). Each is the great hope of his people, each will die young in battle. So stated, this would be as true of the base text in Dares Phrygius as it is of the Middle Irish rendering in *Togail Troí*. The parallel becomes more potent, however, if we posit that the poet has been engaging directly with the Irish rather than the Latin, which he perhaps did not know directly at all (see Clarke 2009: 247–50). The key passage appears in a section of the first recension of *Togail Troí*, studied by Miles earlier in this volume (Ch. 7). The clue is in the phrasing of the passage describing the battle-fury of Troilus, which is a radical creation of the Irish author(s) with no model in the Latin:

> . . . Ros-lín bruth ⁊ ferg, ⁊ ata-racht an lon láich asa éton combó comfhota frisin sróin, ⁊ do-dechatar a dí shúil asa chind combat sithithir artemh fria chenn anechtair. Ropo cumma a fholt ⁊ cróebrad scíad. (*TTr-H* 1473–6, adapted from Stokes 1884: 46–7)

> Fury and anger filled him, and the warrior's moon [*lon láich*] rose from his forehead until it was as long as his nose, and his two eyes went out from his head until they were a hand's breadth beyond his head in front. His hair was like the branches of a hawthorn.

Again following Miles in Ch.7 (see also Miles 2011: 95–144 *passim*), this description unmistakeably resembles the imagery of the *ríastrad* ('warp-spasm') of Cú Chulainn:[33]

> His hair curled about his head like branches of red hawthorn used to re-fence a gap in a hedge. . . . The warrior's moon rose from his forehead, as long and thick as a hero's fist and it was as long as his nose, and he was filled with rage . . .
>
>   *TBC 1* 2268–273, adapted from the translation of O'Rahilly 1976a: 187

Although it is impossible to tell whether this or a different version of the *ríastrad* motivates the author of *Togail Troí*, the correspondences leave no doubt that the poet has recognized and exploited the intertextual similarity between Cú Chulainn's battle-rage and that of the Middle Irish Troilus. There is, so far as I know, no passage in any of the Latin Troy texts that would serve to motivate this connection of ideas. Our poet is working from a bookshelf of Irish and classical learning that is framed by the Middle Irish canon of texts.

We can now reconstruct the poet's procedures with confidence. Beginning from the need to assert the antiquity and heroic credentials of the over-kingship of Ulster, he used *Senchas síl hÍr* or a related document to work together names and tokens that linked Ulster to the foundations of Goidelic Ireland, and that identified contemporary Ulster with the traditions of the heroic Ulaid of Emain Macha. Taking *Táin Bó Cúailnge* alongside *Togail Troí*, he established a set of close parallelisms between the two narratives, including the equations between Conall Cernach and Hector and between Cú Chulainn and Achilles. On that basis, returning to the genealogical tract, he versified the succession of holders of the high-kingship of Ulster, from the first Christian king, Muiredach at the Conversion in the fifth century CE, down to his own time in the mid-twelfth century. This sequence of names, deeds and deaths makes up quatrains 7–72, most of which have been omitted from our printed selection for reasons of space.

This sequence of kings culminates in Eochaid of the Dál Fiatach, and the wording from quatrain 73 onward confirms that he is king of Ulster at the time of composition. For a short space of time in the years 1159–65, the men of Ulster under Eochaid played a prominent part in the internecine struggles of the island, first joining Muirchertach Ua Lochlainn on his raiding expeditions, then turning against him to engage in hostile campaigns of their own (Byrne 1964: 93–4). Eochaid was seized and deposed, then restored to his kingship, then treacherously blinded and overthrown by Muirchertach himself. The composition of our poem clearly precedes these disasters, and its closing verses are full of hope for Eochaid's future glories. Royal names are apt to be freighted with political meaning, and it is significant (see Figure 8 for the family tree) that Eochaid's grandfather (albeit no king himself) was called Conchobhar Cisénach, and that in the next generation his father was Cú Ulad, Hound of the Ulstermen. The invocation of the tradition of Cú Chulainn is obvious, and chimes further with the claim (alluded to in quatrains 38, 47) that the Dál Fiatach lineage descends from Conall Cernach son of Conchobhar. Thus the vaunt that 'Ireland hopes for you as its Hector' (quatrain 75d) picks up on the parallelism between Troy and Ulster that began the poem, and combines it with claims about the Ulaid bloodline to forge a political prophecy. King Eochaid will lead a new generation of heroes of the Ulaid into victory.

Extravagant as this is, it fits the realities of that brief moment around 1165. It must be noted, however, that this political configuration can only be reconstructed by inference, and is possible today only by working through the painstaking reconstruction worked out by Byrne from scattered clues in annals and genealogies. In the poem's surviving manuscripts, the earliest of which dates from around two centuries after its composition, this original context has been lost, and the poem is preserved simply as part of a larger body of traditional knowledge about the history of Irish kingships. In this way the persuasive urgency of the closing quatrains was lost, and the comparisons between legendary Troy and equally legendary Emain Macha in the opening movement may have come to seem like no more than a display of bookish erudition. In its own time it was politically and persuasively alive, even if the hopes that it expresses soon came to nothing in the real world of Ulster.

Notes

1 I am grateful to the Editor of *Studia Hibernica* for confirming permission to quote at length from the edition of Byrne 1964.
2 Mountains on the western coast of Co. Donegal.
3 i.e. the province of Ulster.
4 Ancestor of the Dál Fiatach and other lineages.
5 Possibly an Ulster place-name, or a metonymic name for Ireland as a whole.
6 The remote Tory Island, off the north-western corner of Co. Donegal.
7 Forms based on *Alexandros* are as common in Gaelic reception as those based on *Paris*.
8 At the mouth of the Bann at Ballintoy, Co. Antrim.
9 The monastery of Bangor, Co. Down.
10 The area of Co. Down in which Bangor is situated.
11 The 'host of Ailech' are the forces of Domnall mac Lochlainn, who defeated Donn Sléibe in 1091.
12 Blinding means the cancellation of the victim's kingship. Cf. Bartlett 2020: 249–51.
13 A placename in Co. Down. Byrne in his commentary suggests that he may have been fostered there.
14 Tonn Tuaige, as in quatrain 9 above.
15 A rival claimant to the kingship, from a different lineage.

16 Áed died fighting another claimant to the kingship of Ulster, hence his rival is identified with (Emain) Macha.

17 This refers to the battle of 1127 in which both claimants to the throne were killed.

18 Another member of a different lineage.

19 The father of Donn Sléibe.

20 Monasteries might be requisitioned in time of war to serve as soldiers' quarters.

21 The translation of this line is doubtful.

22 Ardgal, killed 970, is an earlier king of Ulster of the Dál Fiatach.

23 Loch Cuan is identified with Strangford Lough, the long sea-loch on the Irish Sea coast.

24 The ancient fort at Downpatrick, Co. Down.

25 Byrne suggests that this refers to the proverbial nimbleness of Lugh, hero of the Tuatha Dé, who boasts in a fourteenth-century poem that he can 'leap on a bubble without bursting it' (Bergin 1913, at quatrain 38).

26 Mag Coba, the Plain of Coba, is in Co. Armagh and is here associated with Emain Macha.

27 Another area of the hinterland of Emain Macha.

28 The name Fuait refers to the area of the Fews mountains, also in Co. Armagh.

29 Byrne's edition and rich commentary are fundamental to my presentation here. For discussions of the allusions to the Trojan War see Ó hUiginn 1992: 37–41; Poppe 1995: 28–30; Clarke 2009; Miles 2011: 49–50, 156; O'Connor 2014b: 11–12.

30 See Ó Corráin 1988: 14–15; Byrne 1973: 106–12, with Byrne 1964: 81–2.

31 The tract is preserved in Oxford, Bodleian Library, MS Rawlinson B502 and numerous later manuscripts. See O'Brien 1962: 269–87; Dobbs 1921–3, with translation.

32 Todd 1867: 160; cf. *imairchor Briain hi Frangcoibh* 'the conduct of Brian among the Franks' in a poem cited elsewhere in the same text (Todd 1867: 208). For heroic metaphor in *Cogadh Gáedhel re Gallaibh* see Ch. 25 in this volume.

33 On the *ríastrad* of Cú Chulainn and the amiguity between heroism and madness see O'Connor 2016, with Henry 1982.

25

Cogadh Gáedhel re Gallaibh
'The War of the Irish against the Foreigners'

Máire Ní Mhaonaigh

The following excerpts are transcribed from Dublin, TCD MS 1319 (referred to below as D), a composite manuscript of varying dates. Punctuation is editorial; macrons (ā, ē, etc) have been inserted to indicate long vowels not marked by the scribe. Square brackets indicate editorial insertions; round brackets indicate letters that may be superfluous. Italics are used for unambiguous expansions of compendia, lenition marks etc; <u>underlining</u> is used for expansions of suspension strokes where this involves editorial interpretation. Notes give occasional variant readings from a later seventeenth-century manuscript written by Mícheál Ó Cléirigh (Brussels, KBR, The Royal Library of Belgium, MS 2569–2572, fols 103–35, referred to below as B), where these aid interpretation. In the translation, I have attempted to convey something of the style as well as the meaning of the narrative. References are also provided to the nineteenth-century published edition and translation of the text by James Henthorn Todd (1867).

Text extracts

Murchad's presentation as battle leader (cf. Todd 1867: 166–7, §95)

Tuccad im*morro* tosa*ch* cat*h*a B*r*iai*n* ⁊ mat*h*i Ē*r*end *ar*c[h]ena du dāmraid dēin, díulai*ng* re*m*rāti, du*n* gam[a]ndraid glai*n*gasta, geta[1] galaig, gnímaig, *g*argbeōda .i. do Dāl Cais curat(h)a, *com*rumaig ⁊ do C[h]la*n*naib Luigdea*ch* *ar*c[h]ena. Baī rompu side i*n* He*ch*toir i*n*tamlaigte*ch* ilbuada*ch* na hĀdamclai*n*ni ilcenēalaichi allatai .i. M*ur*c*h*ad m*a*c B*r*iain, eō Rossa rīg(d)raidi Ē*r*end, cend gaili ⁊ gascid ⁊ gnímrada, enig ⁊ engnuma ⁊ aebda*ch*ta fe*ar* talma*n* re rē ocus re remis; dāig ní á*r*mit sen*ch*aidi[2] Goedel co mbeth do*n* Āda*m*claind re rē fēi*n* oe*n*duni no *ch*ongbad sciat*h* *com*restail imbualta dō.

Murchad's place in a chronology of heroes (cf. Todd 1867: 186–7, §107)[3]

I*m*t[h]ūsa im*morro* M*ur*c*h*aid mic B*r*iai*n* in rīgmīlid, ro gab side a dā claidiu*m* crōda, *com*nerta .i. claidiu*m* i*n*a deis ⁊ claid*ium* i*n*a clē, u*a*ir is(s) ē si*n* duni dēdena*ch* riba *com*deis i*m*bualta da deis ⁊ da clí baí i *n*Ērind. Is ē du*n*i dēdenach i rrabi i*n* fīrgaisced i *n*Ērind ē. Is ē tuc a b*r*ēt[h]ir fīrlaīg na*ch* bērad oent*r*aig tei(gh)chid resi*n* ciniud doe*n*na uli *ar* coma sa bit*h* *ach*t mi*n*bad ci*n*nti leis ca*n* éc t*r*e bithu. Is ē du*n*i dēdena*ch* i rrabi comlond cét i *n*Ērind é. Is ē du*n*i dēden*ach* ro m*ar*b cét i n-oenlō é. Is ē coscēim dēd[e]nach ruc i*n* fīrgaisced i *n*Ērind é. Dāig is ed i*n*nisit sen*ch*aidi na nGoedel: mōrfesiur amail M*ur*c*h*ad comlond M*e*ic Samā[i]*n* ⁊ vii a*m*ail M*a*c Sa[máin] comlond Luga Lāga ⁊ vii a*m*ail Lu*g*a Lá*g*a comlo*n*d Conaill Cernaig ⁊ vii amail Con*all* C*e*rnach comlo*n*d Loga Lāmafata m*e*ic Et[h]le*n*n ⁊ vii a*m*ail Lu*g* Lá*m*fata comlo*n*d Hechtor m*e*ic P*r*iaim. ⁊ *con*id iat si*n* uideda ⁊ imt[h]e*ch*ta in p[h]*r*īmgaiscid ō t*h*ús i*n* domain, ⁊ gunach beit*h* i*n* p*r*īmgaisced reim Hechtor,[4] u*a*ir naīdiu é conici sin ⁊ nír i*n*engnuma é ro hōcci ⁊ conā beit*h* iar M*ur*c*h*ad, u*a*ir senōir c*r*it*h*ach, crīndīblidi é ō [s]hin amach. ⁊ cosmaill*ius* aīsi duneta tomtenaigit amlaid si*n* don gaisced ⁊ do*n* domu*n* *ar* n-i*n*tamlugud i*n*tliuch*t*a.

Translations

Murchad's presentation as battle leader

Leading Brian's battalion, as well as the nobles of Ireland, was the aforementioned invincible, impetuous host, the pure, precipitous, prepared, valorous, vital, vibrant company, namely valiant, victorious Dál Cais, also known as Clanna Luigdeach.[9] At their head was the incomparable, ever-triumphant Hector of the marvellous, many-nationed descendants of Adam, that is Brian's son, Murchad, the Yew of Ross of Ireland's rulers;[10] surpassing the valour, weaponry and vitality, the honour, ingenuity and artistry of the men of the world in his time and in his day. For Irish chroniclers record that there was no one among Adam's descendants in his time who could uphold a shield when engaging and exchanging blows with him.

Murchad's place in a chronology of heroes

Concerning the royal warrior, Murchad son of Brian: he seized his two fierce, forceful swords, one in his right hand and the other in his left, since he was the last person in Ireland who was equally expert in smiting with his right and with his left. He was the last person in Ireland who had true valour. It was he who gave his true champion's word that he would not take a single step in retreat from all of the human race for any reason whatsoever, unless he were certain that he would never die.[11] He was the last person in Ireland who was a match for a hundred; he was the last person in Ireland who killed a hundred in a single day. His was the last step that true valour took in Ireland. For this is what the chroniclers of the Irish relate: seven like Murchad were the equivalent of Mac Samáin; seven like Mac Samáin were the equivalent of Lug Lága; seven like Lug Lága were the equivalent of Conall Cernach; seven like Conall Cernach were the equivalent of Lug Lámfhata son of Ethliu; seven like Lug Lámfhata were the equivalent of Hector son of Priam. So these are the measurements and progressions of pre-eminent heroism from the beginning of the world. There was no pre-eminent heroism before Hector, for it [i.e. the world] was a child up to then and it was not capable of prowess because of its youth. And there has not been since Murchad, for it has been a decrepit, decaying elder since that time. And in this way, heroism and the world is compared with the ages of man, according to comparison of meaning.

Murchad as Hector, Samson, Hercules and Lug Lámfhata (cf. Todd 1867: 186–9, §107 continued)

Rob ē sin int Ec[h]toir intamlaigtech na Ērend ilbuadaigi *ar* credium ⁊ *ar* gail ⁊ *ar* gaisced, *ar* eneach ⁊ *ar* engnum. Rob ē sin in Samson suairc, soc[h]omaind, sēg(d)aind sōerbēsach na nEbraidi im sochur ocus *im* saíri a at[h]arda ⁊ a c[h]eneōil re rē fēn ⁊ re amsir. Rob ē sin int E[r]coil tothac[h]tach tānasi ro scris ocus ro dēlāris piasta ⁊ torathru a hĒrind, ro sir lacha ⁊ linti ⁊ uamanna na Fōtla fondardi *ar* nach rabi dūn *nó* digenn isin domun. Rob ē in Lug Lāmata comc[h]osmail ro ling cach doc[h]air ⁊ ro lomair cach trēnc[h]end, ro scris ⁊ ro marb gullu ocus allamarthu a hĒrind. Ocus rob ē *in* comla catha ⁊ in cliath ugra ⁊ *in* dos dīten ⁊ *in* tor brūti bidbad a atharda ⁊ a c[h]eneōil re rē ⁊ re remis.

Murchad active in battle (cf. Todd 1867: 188–91, §108)

Ōt-connaic *in* rīgmīlid romōr rochalma sin ⁊ *in* cur crōda comnart in [n-i]mesargain ⁊ frithōlum tucsat danair ⁊ anmargaigh allmarda fri Dāl Cais, is amail baīs *nó* bithanim do-roinnestair dō-som sein, comardud gall friu, ⁊ ro gab ferg dīchra dímōr é ⁊ bruth borrfadach adbulmōr, ro gab mēt menman ⁊ aicnid. At-racht ēn gaili ⁊ gaiscid ind co mbí *ar* luamain ōs hinib ⁊ ōs anāil et ruc taichim trēn, tricc, tairbtech, tinnesnach fo cath na n-anmargach, amail dam dian, denmnetach, dāsachtach arna drochgabāil, *nó* amail lēomon lond, letartach, lūthmar, lānchalma, todūscithir ⁊ crátir ima culēnaib, *nó* mar borbruathur dianbunni dīlend brisseas ⁊ brécas cach ní cosa ricc. ⁊ ruc berind[5] curad ⁊ lāt[h]air míled dar cath na n-amarcach. Forglit a escarit da hēis .i. senchaidi gall ⁊ Lagen cor thuit .l. do deis ⁊ .l. da c[h]lí don ruat[h]ur sin ⁊ nír aitheraig bēim riam[6] can lēod cuirp ⁊ cendmullaig ⁊ cnām maroen dīb. Cid trā *acht* ro siacht [t]resin cath siar co ba trī mar sin.

Murchad's fighting followers (cf. Todd 1867: 188–91, §108 continued)

Ro lenait é *immorro* dāmraid dian, díulaing, dīrecra Clainni Lugdeach ⁊ gamandraid glangasta, gērata, galac[h], gnímach, gar[g]bēoda a theglach badēin

Murchad as Hector, Samson, Hercules and Lug Lámfhata

He was the metaphorical Hector of ever-victorious Ireland, in religion, in valour and in warlike feats, in dignity and dexterity. He was the agreeable, affable, intelligent, accomplished Samson of the Hebrews, for promoting the privileges and prosperity of his patrimony and kin, in his own day and time. He was the second substantial Hercules, who destroyed and drove serpents and monsters out of Ireland, who traversed the lakes and pools and caves of the noble Isle, whom no fortress or fastness in the world could resist. He was the equivalent of Lug Lámfhata, who surmounted every obstacle and cut off every powerful head, and exterminated and expelled foreigners and enemies from Ireland. And he was the shelter against strife, the bulwark against battle, as well as the defending tree and the fortress for the destruction of the foes of his patrimony and kin in his own day and time.

Murchad active in battle

When that very great, valiant royal warrior, that spirited, strong hero saw the attack and affliction that enemies and ferocious foreigners inflicted upon Dál Cais, it was like death itself or a deathly blemish to him that foreigners should rise up against them. An intense, immense anger emerged in him and a gargantuan rising rage, as well as great resolve and courage. A bird of valour and valiance arose in him and fluttered over his essence and breath. He made a brave, bullish, urgent, immediate charge at the foreigners' battalion, like an active, impetuous, incensed ox, having been badly caught, or like a vehement, violent, vigorous, valiant lioness who is roused and persecuted about her cubs, or like the rough rush of a rapid flood-torrent that damages and destroys everything in its path. And he forged a warrior's breach and a soldier's space right through the battalion of the foreigners. His enemies – the chroniclers of the foreigners and the Leinstermen – attest that fifty fell by his right hand and fifty by his left in that onset. He never repeated a blow without mutilating torso, top and bones of every one of them. And indeed he proceeded through the battalion three times like that.

Murchad's fighting followers (cf. Todd 1867: 188–91, §108 continued)

He was followed by an invincible, unparalleled, impetuous host of Clann Luigdeach, the pure, precipitous, valiant, valorous, vital, vibrant heroes of his

.i. vii fic*h*it m*a*c ríg bāt*ar* i*n*a *t*hegluc*h* ⁊ [fer]⁷ t*r*īc[h]a cē*t* i*n* fer ba lugu dūc*h*us díb sin. Ro lenait⁸ é co hāit[h], at*h*lu*m*, imētru*m* co *m*benad bond f*r*i bond ⁊ cend f*r*i cend ⁊ cnes f*r*i cnes da ēis cac*h* co*n*air 'ma rāncat*ar*. ⁊ ris do samailset si*n* daíni Āt*h*a Cli*ath* bātar f*o*rsna scemlib ic(c)a fēgad, co*n*árba lia leo serrt*h*laigi eta*r*(u)ūas ō mōrmet*h*il ic buai*n* goirt corci, cid dā cat*h* *n*ó t*r*ī do g*r*eistea faí, oldas folt ōs gaīt*h* uat*h*ib *ar*na let*r*ad do *t*huagaib t*r*oma, taīdlec*h*aib ⁊ do c[h]laidbib lai*n*nerda lasa*n*na. Co*n*id *air*sin as-bert m*a*c A*m*laíb baí *ar* scemled a grianān fēi*n* aca fēgad: 'Is mait*h* benait na gaill i*n* gort', *ar*se, 'is imda serrtlaigi leccait uat*h*ib'. 'A*r* dered laí is tēcasta', *ar* i*n*gen B*r*iain .i. be*n* [meic] A*m*laíb.

own household, that is twenty-seven kings' sons from his household and the man of the smallest patrimony among them controlled a cantred. They followed him actively, agilely, expeditiously, so that it was heel to heel, head to head and body to body following him everywhere they went. And it is this to which the people of Áth Cliath [Dublin] who were on the ramparts looking at them likened it: they thought that sheaves cast aloft by a great party reaping a field of oats would not be more numerous, even if two or three battalions were at it, than was their hair flying with the wind as they were being hacked with heavy, illustrious axes and gleaming, glistening swords. Then Amlaíb's son who was on the rampart of his own chamber looking at them said: 'the foreigners reap the field well', he said, 'numerous are the sheaves let loose by them'. 'At the end of the day all will be clear', said Brian's daughter, the wife of Amlaíb's son.[12]

Essay: Ireland's Hector: The literary portrayal of Murchad, son of Brian Boru

Cogadh Gáedhel re Gallaibh, 'The War of the Irish (*Gaídil*) against the Foreigners (*Gaill*)', is a twelfth-century literary composition describing Viking attacks on Ireland and resistance to them at the hands of a single dynasty, variously known as Dál Cais or Uí Briain after their eponymous ancestor Brian Boru (Bórama), with whose death at the battle of Clontarf in 1014 CE, and its immediate aftermath, the story ends. Brian was eighty-eight at the time (Todd 1867: 204–5) and in that final battle, his son, Murchad, is presented as the premier hero. The text excerpts focus on his portrayal.

The conflict at Clontarf marks the noble end-point of what is depicted as Brian's lengthy, illustrious career in the narrative. Composed at the behest of his great-great-grandson, Muirchertach, seeking to bolster his own considerable ambition with reference to his ancestor's glorious deeds, the text is in large part a biography of Brian (Ní Mhaonaigh 1995). It culminates in a remarkable obituary in which he is elevated 'as one of the three best people ever born in Ireland' and equated with a pair of classical heroes, Octavian/Augustus Caesar and Alexander the Great, as well as with a trio of biblical greats, Solomon, David and Moses (Todd 1867: 202–7; Ní Mhaonaigh 2017a: 187). In being linked with Octavian and Alexander, both associated with the transfer of power into a Christian era, Brian's successful and continuous rule is being underlined. His embodiment as both 'the Solomon of the Irish' and 'the David of Ireland' further emphasizes his prosperous kingship, the equivalence with Moses, the pious lawgiver, providing additional divine justification (Ní Mhaonaigh 2017a: 175–8, 181–5). In being aligned with these pivotal biblical and classical figures, therefore, Brian's remarkable stature and his triumphant leadership are consciously cast in terms of the grand narrative of world historiography.

The text suggests that at the time of the battle of Clontarf, succession was being passed to Murchad, who is presented in the *Cogadh* as the military commander and active leader during the encounter (Todd 1867: 166–7, 186–91, 192–5). Moreover, the younger man's actions frame this battle-portion of the narrative. A verbal altercation between Murchad and the king of Leinster is depicted as the ultimate catalyst for the onslaught at Clontarf, and Murchad acts as his father's right-hand man from the start, attacking Leinster in the lead up to the battle (Todd 1867: 142–51). Viking attempts to plea-bargain with Brian the night before the conflict gets underway were motivated by their fear of Murchad's valour in particular, it is claimed (Todd 1867: 156–7). Leading Brian's battalion during the encounter, as is described in the first passage above, he excels other earthly men of his day in 'valour, weaponry and vitality, honour, ingenuity and artistry'. The authority of Irish chroniclers (*senchaidi Goedel*) is invoked in relating that none of Adam's descendants could withstand him in mutual exchange of blows. And as his father takes his place – in death at least – in a roll-call of exceptional figures, including Alexander the Great, Murchad is the 'incomparable, ever-triumphant Hector', embodying the Trojan warrior in the conflict at Clontarf (Todd 1867: 166–7; Ní Mhaonaigh 2014: 142–3). This and the other excerpts above are drawn from the final section of the narrative and focus on Murchad's extended and elaborate portrayal in the text. The passages selected provide some insight into the literary depiction of premier heroes and the influence of classical literature on that presentation, as well as illuminating how battles are delineated. They also contextualize the remarkable comparison of Murchad with Hector, a text and translation of which is included above.[13] The other material concerning Murchad in the *Cogadh* informs, but is also informed by, the learned, classicizing purple passage situating Murchad in heroic space and time.

The earliest manuscript in which the narrative is found is the late twelfth-century Book of Leinster (Dublin, TCD MS 1339), in which is also preserved a version of the Irish adaptation of the Troy tale, *Togail Troí* (see Ch. 8). Only the first one-seventh or so of *Cogadh Gáedhel re Gallaibh* is extant in the manuscript, since it breaks off at that point, long before the account of the final battle at Clontarf. Nonetheless, the two later manuscripts drawn on in the excerpts, Dublin, TCD MS 1319 (D) and Brussels, KBR, the Royal Library of Belgium MS 2569–2572 (B), indicate considerable interest in the text in the decades after its composition, suggesting rewriting for different purposes at various points in the twelfth century (Ní Mhaonaigh 1992; Casey 2020). Evidence for engagement with contemporary scholastic thinking and an interest in rhetorical interpretation of this time is also provided in the extant copies, underlined by a meta-literary comment only contained in the earlier of that pair of manuscripts. This is embedded in the comparison between Murchad and a litany of heroes, rising through pre-eminent, prehistoric Irish champions, such as Conall Cernach and Lug Lámfhata, to Hector son of Priam himself, with whom heroism is said to have commenced. The B version of the text written by the seventeenth-century scribe, Mícheál Ó Cléirigh, ends with reference to Hector, but the earlier, perhaps fourteenth-century, copy D continues with an explanation of why Hector marks the commencement of valour – because before Hector the world was but a child and so not capable of prowess. According to this account, Murchad marks the culmination of courage, as the world 'is a decrepit, decaying elder' since his time;

'and in this way heroism and the world were deemed to be the analogy of human life, according to comparison of meaning (*intamlugud intliuchta*)', the latter phrase echoing Latin terminology of rhetorical figures (Clarke and Ní Mhaonaigh 2020: 481–2, 485–7). Murchad's synchronization with Hector – found elsewhere in the text as well (in the first passage above) – was accorded augmented meaning in this way.

The synthetic equation of Murchad and a catalogue of heroes, culminating in Hector, as well as the synchronization of his father Brian with classical and biblical figures noted above, reveal the author of the *Cogadh* – and at least one reviser of the text – to have applied the same syncretistic approach in his writing of history as such scholars as the compiler of the *Annals of Tigernach* and Gilla Cóemáin (see Chs 3 and 4). In its alignment of local and global heroes, and the underlying implied equation between the encounters at Troy and Clontarf, the narrative exhibits classicizing influence of a kind that refers to concepts familiar from international Latinate learning of the period (Ní Mhaonaigh 2014: 161; see Clarke 2009, Ní Mhaonaigh 2015). But in its detailed depictions of military formations, fighting, battle-observation, by way of example, the *Cogadh* also sets up other resonances. Specific parallels have been drawn with *Togail Troí*, both Recension 1, and the version sharing the pages of the Book of Leinster with the Clontarf account (Myrick 1993: 141–57; Miles 2011: 142–3; Ní Mhaonaigh 2014: 158–60; Clarke and Ní Mhaonaigh 2020: 482–3). Echoing passages have also been highlighted in the *Cogadh* and another battle-tale preserved in the Book of Leinster, *Cath Ruis na Ríg* 'The Battle of Rosnaree' (Mac Gearailt 1988 and 1999). *In Cath Catharda* 'The Civil War [of the Romans]' also reverberates with similar tones (Mac Gearailt 2022: 54–63; see Chs 14, 15 and 16 in this volume). Thus, in both structure and content, the *Cogadh* reveals classicizing influence of various kinds, as the selected excerpts show.

The third excerpt above, for example, depicts Murchad not only as Hector, but also as Hercules. In so doing, the author of the *Cogadh* may have had the account of 'the heroic deeds (*gnímrada*) of Hercules' in the Book of Leinster version of *Togail Troí* in mind. As 'the second substantial Hercules', Murchad destroys serpents and monsters, traversing waters and lakes, just as Hercules sought out and slew Hydra in her lake-cave. These exploits of Hercules are not so described in the Latin source from which the Irish Troy tale was adapted, Dares Phrygius' *De Excidio Troiae Historia*, and are an innovation in the developing text of *Togail Troí*, first witnessed in the Book of Leinster copy of Recension 2 (Ní Mhaonaigh 2014: 156–7). But the tenor of the *gnímrada* of Hercules is universally heroic and cast in descriptive, dramatic language common in numerous tales, so that direct dependency on any given text is difficult to prove. The fact that echoes of *Togail Troí* are found in the passage immediately following, however, makes it more likely that the comparison between Murchad and Hercules was also informed by a Troy narrative in Irish rather than one in Latin.

In the last excerpt above, when Murchad is described as entering battle like 'a lioness who is roused and persecuted about her cubs' and 'an active, impetuous, incestuous ox', a further classical echo is evoked, because identical similes are applied in the same sequence to Achilles in *Togail Troí* (*TTr* 1 727–9, Stokes 1884: 24) and also appear in *Togail na Tebe* (lines 4017–19, Calder 1922: 258–9). Both Murchad and Achilles resemble a roaring deluge in their military prowess, with Achilles 'levelling tree and tree-slope before it', while like 'the rough rush of a rapid flood-torrent', Murchad 'damages and destroys everything in his path' (Miles 2011: 133–4; Ní Mhaonaigh 2014: 158–60; Clarke 2014c: 127–8). The exploits of the Irish leader are authenticated by the chroniclers of the enemy army, who – observing the battle, it is implied – 'attest that fifty fell by his right hand and fifty by his left in that onset'. In never needing to perform more than one blow, Murchad resembles Hector in *Togail Troí* (Ní Mhaonaigh 2014: 159). Similarly in the last excerpt above, when it is noted that those observing the conflict 'thought that sheaves cast aloft by a great party reaping a field of oats would not be more numerous' than they, the author uses a formula also applied to the carnage caused by Hector's sword in *Togail Troí* (Miles 2011: 135–6, 142–3; Ní Mhaonaigh 2014: 158). Literary influence from one text to another seems the most likely explanation for such resonances in these instances. Since they occur within a relatively confined passage of the *Cogadh* above (Miles 2011: 142) and form part of a longer section in which Murchad son of Brian is being deliberately presented in classical mould, it is clear that the author is informed by specific sources, among them *Togail Troí*, in creating his extended image of the battle-hero at Clontarf.

This learned classicism is dressed in the descriptive rhetorical style seen across a wide range of Middle Irish narratives of war (*catha*); alongside the *Cogadh* and *Togail Troí* these include *Cath Ruis na Ríg* (Hogan 1892), *In Cath Catharda* (Stokes 1909), and others. The narrative's regular use of synonyms, frequently alliterating and often in rhythmical runs of twos and threes is typical. The host (*dámrad*) is invincible and impetuous (*dian, díulaing*) and the synonymous *gamanrad* 'heroic company' is *glaingasta, geta, galaig, gnímaig, gargbeóda* 'pure, precipitous, prepared, valorous, vital, vibrant' (the first excerpt above). Very many such phrases appear across numerous texts, including Murchad as *in dos díten* 'the shelter against strife' (the third passage above), refusing to take *oentraig tei(gh)chid* 'a single step in retreat' (the second passage above), both of which also occur in *Cath Ruis na Ríg* (Hogan 1892: 42.17 and 44.7). Such correspondences can indicate textual dependency; in portraying Murchad as Hector in particular, the *Cogadh* author was drawing on specific classical knowledge to create very purposefully a special kind of hero. But the learned and literary milieu in which he was writing was one in which a generically honed style and approach to writing battle-narratives had become established. This literary development came in response to cultural changes, and was indicative of a well-connected, highly specialized learned class, serving the needs of a political elite. The *Cogadh* is a master example of this approach, as illustrated in the excerpts, not least in its deployment of synthesizing world knowledge, alongside classicizing character description, and bombastic battle descriptions of exceptional complexity and skill.

Notes

1 *glain gasta geta*] Note that *goinglésta gasta* is the reading of MS B. D's *geta* is otherwise unattested. The sense of B's *glésta* is therefore followed here, translating with the adjective 'prepared'. In a parallel passage (Todd 1867: 190, see the final excerpt here), both manuscripts have *gérata* 'valiant' in this position.

2 I have chosen to translate *senchaid* as 'chronicler', since throughout the narrative it refers to those responsible for creating a record of important events.

3 This passage is discussed in detail in Ní Mhaonaigh 2014 and Clarke and Ní Mhaonaigh 2020. Text and translation are not given in their entirety in those earlier publications, and so are provided here.

4 B ends this section here.

5 For *berind,* B has *bern.* B has standard orthography, so the reading here may preserve a phonetic spelling.

6 *riam*] B adds as follows:

> do neoch *acht* ænbeim ⁊ nír gab*h* sciat*h* no lúir*ech* no catbair f*ri* beim dib*h.*

This translates as 'on anyone, except for a single blow, and shield, breastplate or helmet did not protect against any blow.' These words may have been inadvertently omitted in the earlier manuscript, since the sense of only having to inflict one blow makes better sense.

7 This is supplied from B.

8 *ro lenait*] B reads *ro lensattar*; the active form seen in B makes better sense in the context and is translated here.

9 Both Cas and Lugaid Menn appear as ancestor figures in the genealogies of the O'Briens, so that they were known most frequently as Dál Cais, 'the seed of Cas', but also as Clann or Clanna Luigdeach 'the descendants of Lugaid'. The term Uí Briain (O'Briens), 'descendants of Brian' only emerged as the fame of Brian Boru (who died in 1014) grew.

10 *Eo Rossa* 'the Yew of Ross', was one of five famous trees of Ireland, on which see, for example, Stokes 1894–5: 1895.277–8; Gwynn 1903–35: 3. 148–9.

11 Todd 1867: 187 translates this 'that he might die of his wounds', without the negative; the sense might be that Murchad would not retreat unless he were certain of everlasting fame.

12 Amlaíb's son was the king of Dublin at the time of the battle of Clontarf, Sitric Silkenbeard; he was married to Sláine, daughter of Brian Boru.

13 For detailed discussion of this passage, see Ní Mhaonaigh 2014 and Clarke and Ní Mhaonaigh 2020.

26

Lebor Gabála Érenn 'The Book of Invasions of Ireland'

John Carey

The text is based on a transcription from the third-recension copy of Lebor Gabála Érenn *in Dublin, Royal Irish Academy MS 23 P 2 ('The Great Book of Lecan', also known simply as 'The Book of Lecan'), fol. 277ra 19–b 14. The edition is semi-diplomatic. All abbreviations have been silently expanded except in cases where the horizontal suspension stroke is used for something other than* n.

The translation is based on the text as edited here, but I have adopted readings from the copy on fol. 193va 7–37 where these improve the sense. All such cases are noted. Instead of paragraphs 7 and 8, the copy on fol. 193v concludes at lines 34–7 with a brief paragraph peculiar to itself; I have provided this as well.

Text: A tract on Nemed's ancestry and descendants

1. Is examail fo·gabar in genelach-sa Parrthalon ⁊ Nemid .i. da m*eic* Agnoimean m*eic* Sdairn m*eic* Thæid m*eic* Beoein m*eic* Mair m*eic* Airrthecht m*eic* Iathacht m*eic* Iathfeth m*eic* Næi m*eic* Laimiach.

2. Sil mBeothaich m*eic* Iardanainis. Sil Semiainis m*eic* Sdairnainis. Sil Fergusa Leithderg m*eic* Nemid is ead fil i Mainn Conain.

3. Is airi ad·bearar Fir Bolc friu uair do·b*er*dis uir leo a hEr*inn* da reic re Grecaib ar or ⁊ ar airgead do thuigiudug na cathrach. Uair do badar naithreacha nemnecha nemi ⁊ piasta urchoidecha isna cathrachaib-sin la *Grécu* ⁊ is e-sin bunad firindi in adbair fa n-abar Fir Bolc riu ⁊ no theiddis cusin cendaigecht-sin soir ⁊ anoir cacha bliadna ⁊ Fir Domnann o domaintoirnem na huiri isna bolcaib ⁊ Gaileoin ona tachailt. Ocus is do sil Nemid doib dib linaib.

4. Ad·bearaid aroile Tuatha De Danann comad do sil Beothaich m*eic* Iardanainis doib .i. do m*uintir* Nemid don lucht do·chuadar soir do chuindgid na hingine. Ar gabus tair ⁊ do·ronsad feis mair thair co tangadar iarum cind re maire a n-ui ⁊ a n-iarmui. La med a n-eolais d*ano* do·lodar can noithi cen eathra co ndeisidar for Sleib Conm*a*icne Rein i Condachtaib.

5. At·beraid aroile comad deamna grada ecsamla *Túatha Dé Danann* ⁊ combad iad-siden do·deachadar do nim ar æn risin loinges do·deachaid Luitcifear cona deamnaib do nibh. Ar·fæmad chuirp ærda umpu do millead ⁊ d'aslach for sil nAdaim. Is he les fris' tucadar æs in iarmorachta-sin i ndiaid demain ⁊ a muintiri.

6. Tiagaid thra in lucht-sin i sidaib. Ocus tiagaid fo muirib. Ocus tiagaid[1] i conrechtaib. Ocus tiagaid co hamaide. Ocus tiagait co tuaithciṅgtha. Is as-sin is bunadus doib uili .i. m*uinter* deamain.

7. Ni ruca genelach na ndaine-sea for cula nocho ro·ḟeasidar fir in domain olchena. Ocus do·ræbadar in sluag-sa uili la firindi mac Milead ⁊ la tairchedal chreidme Cr*íst*.

8. Acht ata isin Libar de Subt*er*nis: As·beartadar aroile comad ḟileada do Grecaib *Túatha Dé Danann* co n-imad a cumachta co n-imthigdis for murib cen leasdru

Translation

1. This genealogy of Partholón and Nemed is found to be different: they are the two sons of Agnoman son of Starn son of Táet son of Beoén son of Már son of Airthecht son of Íathacht son of Japheth son of Noah son of Lamech.

2. The race of Bethach son of Iardanainis. The race of Semiainis son of Starnainis. The race of Fergus Lethderg son of Nemed: it is that which was in Mainn Conáin.

3. This is why they are called Fir Bolg ['Men of Bags']: because they used to bring the soil of Ireland with them [in bags][2] to sell to the Greeks for gold and silver, for the establishing of their cities. For there were venomous poisonous snakes and injurious beasts in those cities among the Greeks; and that is the true basis of the reason why they are called Fir Bolg. And they used to go to and from the east every year to conduct that business. And they are of the race of Nemed.[3]

4. Some say of the Túatha Dé Danann that they are of the race of Bethach son of Iardanainis; that is, of the household of Nemed, the company that went into the east in search of the maiden. For they were held[4] in the east, and they held a great wedding feast there; so that, at the end of a long time thereafter, their grandsons and great-grandsons came [back]. So great was their knowledge, then, that they went without ships, without vessels, until they alighted upon Slíab Conmaicne Réin in Connacht.

5. Others say that the Túatha Dé Danann are demons of a special kind, and that they came from heaven together with the exile from heaven of Lucifer with his demons. They put on bodies of air, to ruin and tempt the race of Adam: that is the reason for which that rearguard went,[5] following the Devil and his household.

6. That company goes, then, into the hollow hills, and they go beneath the seas, and they go in wolf-shapes, and they go to witches, and they go to those who walk contrary to the direction of the sun. They all have the same[6] origin: the Devil's household.[7]

7. The genealogy of those folk cannot be taken back;[8] nor[9] can the men of the rest of the world know it. And this entire host perished through the righteousness of the sons of Míl, and the prophecy of the faith of Christ.

8. But [this] is in the *Liber de Subternis* ['Book Concerning the Underground Ones']: 'Some say that the Túatha Dé Danann were poets of the Greeks, with such abundance of power that they used to travel upon the seas without vessels,

i ndiaid inna deasorbiba in bithfaithi. Robdar tuatha rig ⁊ cenela. It e a n-anmanna na coimthech cona Tuathaib Dea .i. Dealbæth ⁊ Ealathan ⁊ Breas las' roferad cath Bresi .i. cath Muigi Turead fri Fomorchaib ⁊ Dagda ⁊ Lug Lamfota foden.

Conclusion of the text on fol. 193va 34–7

Ata fis ⁊ eacna leo co n-adradis ⁊ ro chachnadar brichta goband ⁊ druad ⁊ leigi ⁊ luamnachta ⁊ deogbairi ⁊ airidechta. Is uaidib atait adraithi i nEri. Finit.

according to the fair ease (?)[10] of the eternal prophet. They were tribes of kings, and peoples. These are the names of the strangers (?) among[11] the Túatha Dé: Delbáeth, and Elatha, and Bres (by whom was waged the battle of Bres; that is, the battle of Mag Tuired against the Fomoraig), and Dagda, and Lug Lámfota himself.'

Conclusion of the text on fol. 193va 34–7

They have knowledge and wisdom, so that they used to be worshipped; and they recited the spells of blacksmiths and druids and physicians, and of steering, and of cupbearers, and of chariotry. And so it is from them that there are adorations [of idols?] in Ireland. *Finit.*

Essay: The Christian problem of the pagan gods

The schema of Irish 'pseudohistory' or 'synthetic history' undertook to situate Ireland and its people within the larger context of Christian sacred history. It drew for information on the Bible, and on such patristic writers as Augustine, Orosius and Isidore, while also incorporating lore of native origin. Additionally, to establish a bridge between these heterogeneous bodies of doctrine, Irish scholars would have been obliged to resort to invention. Figures such as the early settler Partholón (from *Bartholomaeus*), or the Gaelic ancestor Míl Espáine (from Latin *miles Hispaniae* or 'soldier of Spain'), with non-Irish names but no basis in Latin historiography, appear to reflect fabrication of this kind. There is evidence that the schema thus created was already in existence, perhaps only in a rudimentary state, in the eighth and perhaps even the seventh century; and its exposition by various scholar-poets shows that it had attained a highly developed form by the beginning of the second millennium. Several of their compositions, and further material, provided the basis for the massive work known as *Lebor Gabála Érenn* ('The Book of Invasions of Ireland'), first composed in the course of the eleventh century. This was a work of enormous popularity and influence. It exists in a multitude of copies, dating from the twelfth century to the eighteenth, and its doctrines have been invoked by innumerable poets, historians and others.[12]

It would however be a mistake to imagine that the *Lebor Gabála* imposed a monolithic or 'canonical' doctrine of the Irish past on the tradition as a whole. Indeed, it is not really even a single work itself. The medieval copies alone fall into four 'recensions', and within each of these groupings there is extensive variation between the individual manuscripts. So great is this diversity that it has not yet proved possible to produce a satisfactory critical edition of the whole, nor even of one of the recensions. And there is abundant evidence that, throughout the period of the literary predominance of the *Lebor Gabála*, ideas at variance with those of any of its versions continued to flourish. The tract translated here is one specimen of such heterodoxy.

The text is found in the copy of the 'third recension' or 'Recension C' of the *Lebor Gabála* in the manuscript known as the Great Book of Lecan (Dublin, RIA MS 23 P 2; catalogue number 535), at the end of one of its sections (on fol. 277r). The manuscript was compiled and largely written by the scholar Giolla Íosa Mór Mac Firbhisigh early in the fifteenth century. This placement, and the circumstance that it is introduced as providing an alternative account ('This genealogy of Partholón and Nemed is found to be different'), point to its being an originally autonomous piece that has been inserted here by a compiler. This view is confirmed by the fact that another copy is found earlier in the manuscript (on fol. 193v), this time as a free-standing item. Although the two copies are both the work of the main scribe of the manuscript, Giolla Íosa, and correspond to one another quite closely on the whole, it is evident that neither is dependent on the other.

That our tract originated independently of Recension C is also evident from the circumstance that its language appears to be significantly earlier – a fact of which I have not taken proper account when I have mentioned it in previous publications (Carey 1999: 18–19; Carey 2015b: 57–8). As emerges particularly clearly from a comparison of the two copies, nothing in our tract rules out a date of composition in the later tenth century; I certainly see no reason to put it later than the first half of the eleventh. Verbal echoes in Recension B of the *Lebor Gabála*, moreover, point to its having been known to that recension's author, perhaps around the beginning of the twelfth century.

The tract deals, in a series of disconnected sections, with the four peoples who occupied Ireland between the time of the Flood and the coming of the Gaels: the followers of Partholón, the followers of Nemed, the Fir Bolg,[13] and the Túatha Dé Danann. While interesting and unusual statements are found throughout, I shall in what follows be concerned only with the most extensive section, which discusses the Túatha Dé Danann.

The Túatha Dé Danann ('Tribes of the Goddess Danann') or Túatha Dé ('Tribes of the Gods') were the divinities of the pagan Irish, as these were remembered by their medieval descendants. How were they to be accounted for in Christian terms? The standard Christian view of pagan gods and goddesses, found in such writers as Augustine, Sulpicius Severus and Isidore, was that they were either demons, or remarkable humans who had lived long ago (the theory called 'euhemerism'). The latter position is best suited to legendary history, and it is that which we find in paragraph 4 of our tract.

Paragraph 4 agrees with the lore found elsewhere in the *Lebor Gabála* tradition in stating that the Túatha Dé were descended from Bethach, that their knowledge allowed them to travel without ships, and that they alighted on Slíab Conmaicne Réin in Connacht. But they are there said to have departed from Ireland as fugitives after a disastrous battle, and thereafter to have studied magic in 'the northern islands of the world'. I know of no other source for the quest for an unnamed maiden in the east, and the wedding celebrations which detained them there for generations. An entire saga concerning their origins appears to have disappeared, leaving no other trace. The main thrust of the paragraph, in any case, is to assert that the Túatha Dé Danann were of human ancestry, even though possessed of supernatural powers.

This is directly contradicted by the assertions of the next three paragraphs, according to which the Túatha Dé Danann are demons. But they are said to be demons 'of a special kind': connected to 'Lucifer with his demons', but by the same token not identical with them. The same distinction, whatever its basis may be, appears in the statement that they are an *íarmóracht* – a word that can mean 'persecution', or 'following', but here seemingly used in the sense of 'rearguard' – for 'the Devil and his household'. The wording recalls that of the ninth-century tale *Scél Tuáin meic Cairill* 'The Tale of Tuán mac Cairill', which says of the *Túatha Dé ocus Andé* ('Tribes of Gods and Un-gods') that the learned do not know their origin, 'but they thought it likely that they are some of the exiles who came from heaven' (*loinges do·dechaid de nim*): the phrase, indeed, is shared by the two texts (Carey 1984: 102, line 58). This position that the Túatha Dé Danann are demons, but somehow not quite like other demons, contrasts with other sources in which it is held that, if not human, they were demons pure and simple. Whatever the differences may be, they share the mission 'to ruin and tempt the race of Adam'.

The statement that the Túatha Dé assume (note the present tense) bodies of air is in line with the view of such writers as Augustine, Isidore of Seville, and the seventh-century Irish author of the treatise *De ordine creaturarum* 'On the Order of Creation' that demons are embodied in this way.[14] That the bodies of the Túatha Dé might be illusory is hinted at in the thirteenth-century tale *Acallam na Senórach*, 'The Colloquy of the Ancients'; and in the even later *Eachtra Thaidhg mheic Céin* 'The Adventure of Tadhg mac Céin' their bodies are described as being weightless, and perhaps composed of air.[15]

Paragraph 6, again in the present tense, speaks of further activities of the Túatha Dé. That they go into the *síde*, or hollow hills, and beneath the seas, is not surprising, as the medieval literature and later folklore both portray supernatural folk as dwelling in such places. More surprising is the statement that 'they go in wolf-shapes', as werewolves are generally regarded as being mortal humans, albeit extraordinary ones. Female werewolves belonging to the Túatha Dé do figure in *Acallam na Senórach*, however (Stokes 1900a: 214–16). The statement that the Túatha Dé visit witches, and 'those who walk withershins' (presumably for the purpose of casting curses) looks like an allusion to contemporary beliefs concerning black magic. In one glossary, the people of the *síde* themselves are said to be the folk who turn withershins (*O'Davoren's Glossary*, Stokes 1904b: 482 §1600). Elements in our passage recall the glosses to a list of exceptional categories of women in the Old Irish law tract *Bretha Crólige* 'Judgments on Sick-Maintenance'. Two of these, occurring together in the list, are the female werewolf, and the half-witted vagrant woman who is visited by the *síd*-people (Binchy 1938: 26–7 §32). It has been argued that the original meaning of *ammait*, the word for 'witch' in our text, was also 'feeble-minded woman'.

Paragraph 7 continues with the argument that the Túatha Dé are not human, claiming that they have no reliable genealogies. Here they are assigned firmly to the past, having 'perished' with the coming of the Gaels to Ireland, and with the prospect of the coming of Christianity.

Finally, paragraph 8 reasserts the euhemeristic position, invoking the authority of an otherwise unknown work called *Liber de Subternis* ('Book Concerning the Underground Ones'). Here it is stated that the Túatha Dé Danann were Greek *filid*, or scholar-poets, whose magical powers enabled them to travel on the sea without ships; and there is an enigmatic allusion to an 'eternal prophet'. Five *coimthig* of the Túatha Dé are listed: the context would suggest that this term should mean something like 'leaders', but in fact it appears to mean 'strangers'. There is accordingly much here to engage our curiosity. Also interesting, and significant, is the fact that these few concluding sentences exhibit a couple of linguistic features which distinguish them from the language of the rest of our tract. This can be taken to confirm that *Liber de Subternis*, whatever its nature, was indeed a separate work.

Our tract is only about 370 words long, but it bears witness to a rich and varied body of speculation concerning the earliest inhabitants of Ireland and their connections to Greece, independent of, and very likely older than, the *Lebor Gabála* itself.

Notes

1　*tiagaid tiagaid* in the manuscript: the dittography occurs across a column break.
2　The phrase *i mbolcaib* supplied from fol. 193v.
3　This sentence from fol. 193v is substituted for the last two sentences in the paragraph on f. 277r, as the latter appear to represent interpolation and to yield less satisfactory sense.
4　Reading *gabtha* with fol. 193v.
5　Reading *tudchadar* with fol. 193v.
6　Reading *inand* with fol. 193v.
7　Following this point there is no corresponding text in the copy on fol. 193v.

8   Reading *rucar* for MS *ruca*.

9   Reading *nach* for MS *nocho*.

10 Reading *deas-soirbi* for MS *deasorbiba*; but the meaning of the entire phrase is
    uncertain.

11 Reading *ocna* for MS *cona*.

12 The only edition, seriously flawed, is Macalister 1938–56. For discussion of the text,
    see e.g. Carey 1994b, Scowcroft 1987, Scowcroft 1988, Carey 2005, Scowcroft 2009,
    Clarke 2015.

13 That the Irish soil which the Fir Bolg are said to have brought to Greece was used for
    protection against poisonous reptiles shows that Ireland's freedom from snakes was
    not always, or indeed originally, attributed to Saint Patrick. This quality could be held
    to be inherent, as in Bede's *Ecclesiastical History* I.1 (Colgrave and Mynors 1969:
    18–21) and 'Recension M' of *Lebor Gabála* (Macalister 1938–56: 1.164–5), or
    attributed to a blessing by Moses, as in *Lebor Gabála*'s 'Recension B' (Macalister
    1938–56: 2.34–5). The story of Patrick expelling snakes from Ireland is first attested
    in sources of the twelfth century.

14 Thus Augustine, *De Genesi ad litteram* 11.19.3 (*PL* 122: col. 437B); Isidore, *De
    differentiis* II.xiv.42 (*PL* 83: col. 76BC); *Liber de Ordine Creaturarum*, Díaz y Díaz
    1972: 142–4.

15 Discussion in Carey 2014: 85 n. 40; Carey 2015b: 62.

27

Dindshenchas Érenn 'Knowledge of Ireland's Notable Places': The River Boyne

Máire Ní Mhaonaigh

The text is from the edition of Gwynn 1903–35: 3.27–9. The translation has been adapted in places.[1]

Text: The names of the Boyne, from the *Dindshenchas* poem known as *Boand I*

Síd Nechtain sund forsin tṡléibh,
lecht mic Labrada láin-géir,
assa silenn in sruth slán
dianid ainm Bóand bith-lán.

Cóic anmand déc, demne drend,
forsin tsruth-sin adrímem,
ótá Síd Nechtain asmaig
co rosaig pardus Adaim.
[…]

Banna ó Loch Echach cen ail,
Drumchla Dílenn co h-Albain;
Lunnand hí i n-Albain cen ail
nosturrand iarna tucsain.

Sabrann dar tír Saxan slán,
Tibir i ráth na Román,
Sruth n-Iordanen iarsain sair,
ocus Sruth n-Eufrait adbail.

Sruth Tigir i pardus búan,
fota sair síst fri himlúad,
ó phardus darís ille
co srothaib na síde-se.

Translation

Síd Nechtain is here on the mountain,
the grave of the very keen son of Labraid,
from which flows the perfect river
whose name is Boand ever-full.

Fifteen names (certainty of disputes)
are on this stream we reckon,
from *Síd Nechtain* away
until it reaches the Paradise of Adam.
[…]

The *Bann* is her name from faultless Lough Neagh:
Drumchla Dílenn [The Surface of the Ocean] as far as Scotland:
The *Lunan* she is in blameless Scotland –
the name denotes her according to its meaning.

The *Severn* she is called through the land of the sound Saxons;
the *Tiber* in the Romans' enclosure,
the *River Jordan* thereafter in the east
and the vast *River Euphrates*.

The *River Tigris* in enduring Paradise,
for a long time, she wanders in the east,
from Paradise back again to here
to the streams of this *síd*.

Essay: Framing space, creating place

Medieval Irish versions of the events of classical antiquity transported contemporary audiences to unaccustomed physical space. Troy and Thebes, the wanderings and homecomings of Aeneas and Odysseus, the empire of journeys in the Alexander legend, were plotted on the maps of extrinsic story-worlds. Connecting with the heroes and events of these far-flung geographies engendered a sense of cultural familiarity, so that the warriors of Ulster could be conceived of as the Trojan band (*Tro-fhian*) of Ireland (Byrne 1964: 61, 76; Ch. 24, this volume). The origins of the Gaels themselves lay in remote, biblically-inspired places. In the ninth-century poem *Can a mbunadus na nGáedel* 'Whence the origin of the Irish?' ascribed to the cleric, Máel Muru of Fahan, Co. Donegal (Todd 1848: 232–3, cf. Carey 2015a), as well as in *Lebor Gabála Érenn* 'The Book of Invasions of Ireland' (on which see Ch. 26 in this volume), their ancestors are said to have wandered in Egypt and Scythia before taking Ireland from Spain. In the well-known extract cited above, the River Boyne forms a global waterway, flowing from its source at Nechtan's otherworld mound, Síd Nechtain in Co. Kildare, encompassing other great rivers of the world, including the Severn, the Tiber and the Jordan 'until it reaches the Paradise of Adam' (Gwynn 1903–35: 3.28–9). Becoming one both in name and essence with biblically-inspired conduits such as the Euphrates and Tiger, it meanders back again 'to the streams of this *síd*'. In this way does the Boyne too become a connecting node and an integral part of Paradise on earth (see Muhr 1999: 198–9; Theuerkauf 2017: 62, 67–77).

As this example illustrates, both spatially and conceptually, Ireland's peoples and places were made part of, and also represented a Christian worldview. The learned milieu in which the Irish antiquity-sagas were adapted and developed shaped and framed origin-narratives of various kinds. Its influence is evident in the synchronizing history in *Lebor Gabála Érenn*, and in the concept of parallel languages underlying *Auraicept na nÉces* 'The Scholars' Primer' (on which see Ch. 23, above). *Dindshenchas Érenn*[2] represents another cultural construct informed by the same approach, and directly linked to the tradition of *Lebor Gabála*, as the extracts on the Theban origin of Tara in the next chapter (Ch. 28) will show.

Dindshenchas Érenn is a topography of Ireland, comprising historical knowledge (*senchas*) concerning Ireland's prominent places (*dinda*, singular form *dind*). It is a lengthy and sophisticated composition in prose and verse, dealing with over two hundred places and natural features. Narratives relating the origins of particular places form thematic clusters in the late twelfth-century manuscript, Dublin, Trinity College, MS 1339, the 'Book of

Leinster' (see McCay 2020). A number of the poems collected therein are ascribed to earlier authors and much of the material is tenth- or eleventh-century, and thus Middle Irish in date, but Old Irish *dindshenchas* texts are also preserved (Theuerkauf 2023: 48–67). Much of this material, alongside other chronologically diverse narratives, form part of a unified creation accorded the title *Dindshenchas Érenn* (or variants of that) in later manuscripts (Theuerkauf 2023: 8–15). Its unity is underlined in an introduction (*acessus*) witnessed in some manuscript copies (Stokes 1892: 469; Stokes 1894–95: 1894.277–9). This situates its production in a specific place (*locus*) and time (*tempus*), at an assembly hosted by the sixth-century king of Tara, Diarmait mac Cerbaill. Moreover, it accords authority to the entire compilation by means of a *causa scribendi* linking it with the distinguished sage of Ireland (*ardsenóir Érenn*), Fintan mac Bóchra (cf. Ch. 1). It is implied that the 'truthful accounts of the notable places of Ireland' (*senchasa fíra dind nÉrenn*) this antediluvian figure of extraordinary longevity relates under compulsion, form the basis for the origin-narratives that follow. The poem on the locations of Tara which is next recounted is put into Fintan's mouth (*co n-epert* 'and he said'), while other items in the corpus are also attributed to him.

The language of this short explanatory preface suggests it could have been written in the Middle Irish period. In addition, it is resonant of another text composed about this time, *Suidigud Tellaig Temrach* 'The Establishment of Tara's Dominion' (discussed in Ch. 29; traditional title 'The Settling of the Manor of Tara'), in which Fintan, by virtue of his great age, can provide essential knowledge on the extent of Tara's lands. The sage's preservation of *senchas* in *Suidigud* has legal and political significance, and Fintan's specific type of wisdom, concerned with boundaries and places, makes him an especially appropriate authority for the type of information about places that is provided in *Dindshenchas Érenn*. According to the *Suidigud* narrative, Fintan's own knowledge had been augmented and interpreted by a figure of extraordinary proportions, Trefhuilngid Tre-eochair, who had come to Ireland on the day of the Crucifixion and was, in Fintan's words 'an angel of God or God himself' (*ba haingel Dé héside, nó fa Día féisin*: Best 1910, 152–3, §31; and see Ch. 29 below, pp.372–3). Trefhuilngid's amplification of Fintan's expertise involved assigning different branches of knowledge to each of the four cardinal directions in the island of Ireland, ranging from learning, fundamental principles and teaching (*a fis, a forus, a foirceatol*) to renown, great fame and prosperity (*a clothaigi, a rroblad, a rathmaire*) (Best 1910: 146–9, §§24, 28). It was this sanctioned arrangement that he entrusted to Fintan, along with berries from a golden multi-coloured branch of Lebanese wood that he held (*cróeb órda illdathach do fhid Lebáin*) and from which he derived sustenance (Best 1910: 140–3, §§13, 19, pp.372–5 below). From these grew Ireland's five famous trees whose longevity is linked with that of Fintan himself (Best 1910: 150–1, §29). It is significant that some versions of *Dindshenchas Érenn* close with an account of one of the trees in question, the Tree of Tortu (*Bile Tortan*) which also refers to another two, the Tree of Ross and the Tree of Mugna (Gwynn 1903–35: 4. 240–7; see also Ch. 29 below, pp.372–3). Thus, the authority of Fintan allowed the compendium of knowledge about places that is *Dindshenchas Érenn* to be positioned with reference to an established scheme of Ireland's pseudohistory.

This scheme also underlies the *Lebor Gabála*, whose elaborate account of Ireland's settlement and history itself incorporates some of Fintan's poems from the *Suidigud* (see Best 1910: 122). It is therefore not surprising that connections to the *Lebor Gabála* permeate *Dindshenchas Érenn* with considerable overlap in terms of characters and events. Moreover, there is what may be an explicit cross-reference to the *Lebor Gabála* under a Latin title in the *dindshenchas* of Sliab Betha 'Bith's mountain', named after Noah's son, Bith, father of Cessair. According to *Lebor Gabála* it was Cessair, a grand-daughter of Noah, who led the first group of settlers to Ireland; in the text on Sliab Betha, it is said that Bith and Cessair came to Ireland to avoid the Flood, *ut dicitur in Capturis Hiberniae*, 'as is claimed in the *Takings of Ireland*' (Stokes 1894–95: 1895. 155). Bith's association with the naming of Sliab Betha, his place of burial, is recounted in broadly similar terms in various versions of the *Lebor Gabála* (Macalister 1938–56: 2.182–3, §170). Cessair is also a pivotal figure in the introduction to *Dindshenchas Érenn*: Fintan's accurate account commences with her, since she was the first settler (*is í cétna ro gab Ére*: Stokes 1892: 469; Stokes 1894–95: 1894.277, 279). In another link with the *Lebor Gabála*, Cessair is said in some *Dindshenchas* versions to be 'of the Greeks of Scythia' (*do Grécaib Sgiethia*, Stokes 1892: 469). Both histories are interlinked learned accounts emanating from the same intellectual context which also produced the Irish World Chronicle as well (see Ní Mhaonaigh 2023; cf. Ch. 3 in this volume). Read alongside these overarching origin-narratives, *Dindshenchas Érenn* highlights a concrete and physical aspect of universal knowledge, that of universal place. Together this material facilitates an understanding of the past that is intricately detailed and causally integrated.

Dindshenchas Érenn is thus representative of a shared approach to historiographical learning. It is informed by sources drawn on by other contemporary scholars, such as the writings of the historian Orosius, who flourished in the early 400s, and the seventh-century bishop of Seville, Isidore. For Orosius, by way of example, space was an important ordering element. His *Historiae adversus Paganos*, 'Histories against the Pagans', written a few years before his death in 420, include a detailed geographical introduction, extending from India to Spain, from Africa to that most northerly location *ultima Thule* ('farthest Thule'). Place, as well as happenings, provides his universal history with structure and meaning. The same principle is reflected in the overarching concept structuring *Dindshenchas Érenn*. Central to the corpus also is Isidore's guiding maxim, to name is to explain (*Etymologies* 1.29.2). In essence, *dindshenchas* is history organized around accounts of how places were named.

Dindshenchas accounts for the naming of physical features through a record of human activity, making the names embody and define a precise relationship between people and particular locations. And as a result, out of undefined space, culturally significant place was formed. In this way, *Dindshenchas Érenn* constitutes a monumental literary construction relating how people shaped and forged the landscape across territories and down through time. It forms a memorial to human endeavour in its history of people's interactions with their surroundings. An enveloping universal aetiology influenced the way in which authors and audiences constructed meaning out of the learning (*senchas*) pertaining to each notable place (*dind*).

In *Dindshenchas Érenn*, therefore, the topography of Ireland is clarified onomastically with reference to the interaction of human beings with the natural world. Human agency and imagination combine to create a cultural construct in which physical features are categorized and an overarching landscape is shaped. That landscape in turn bears witness to the narratives that accord it meaning, giving it historical depth. Out of literary representations order is created across space but also down through time. The intellectual context in which the landscape-history that is *Dindshenchas Érenn* was shaped, also provided a frame for other kinds of history writing. The varied and complex ways in which the multifarious strands of Ireland's history were presented were informed by the same scholarly milieu. The organization of the past represented in interrelated compendia of knowledge, such as the *Lebor Gabála*, the Irish World Chronicle and *Dindshenchas Érenn* reflect wider European currents flowing together with other streams of Ireland's tradition, as the Boyne, the Severn, the Tiber, Tigris and Euphrates are said to become one in the *dindshenchas* story of how the Boyne got its name.

Notes

1   This chapter is informed by ongoing research which forms part of the Leverhulme Trust-funded project 'Mapping the Medieval Mind: Ireland's Literary Landscapes in a Global Space', University of Cambridge 2022–5. I am grateful to my colleagues on that project, Dr David McCay and Dr Marie-Luise Theuerkauf, for stimulating discussion.
2   The spellings *Érend* and *Érenn* are interchangeable for the genitive of *Ériu* 'Ireland'; for the title of the corpus under discussion, the latter has been used throughout this book for consistency.

28

Dindshenchas Érenn 'Knowledge of Ireland's Notable Places': The Theban Origins of Tara

Marie-Luise Theuerkauf[1]

Texts are based on the editions of O'Daly, Gwynn and Stokes as indicated below, with translations revised by the author.

Text: Four sources on the origins of the name of Tara

Dublin, National Library of Ireland MS G 7, col. 11 lines 1–14

This passage survives only in a single late manuscript with peculiar spelling, which bears the title Codex Hibernicus *in golden lettering on its spine. It also contains a cluster of texts from the lost eighth-century compilation* Cín Dromma Snechta *'The Book of Druim Snechta', such as* Compert Conchobair *'The Conception of Conchbar',* Tucait Baile Mongáin *'The Occasion of Mongán's Frenzy', the short version of* Togail Bruidne Da Derga *'The Destruction of Da Derga's Hostel', and* Immacaldam in druad Brain ⁊ in banfatho Febuil *'The Conversation of Bran's wizard and Febul's prophetess'. Our passage forms the prose introduction to a poem of twelve quatrains (ll. 15–33), beginning* Ind filid ra fetatar *'The poets have discovered'.*[2]

[M]ac Miled Espaine .i. hÉrimhon *nomine* di-pert mnuí di Teipip .i. ciuitas Tebi nomine de qua fuit mulior. Gaipis eulchairi ind mbein i ndÉri ⁊ in indmaille im Tepiss .i. ciuitas ho da-deochith hÉrimhón i ndhÉri[nn] ⁊ is-pert in pen no regath hi fridisi di Tepiss. Is-pert Eirimón frie erna teissiuth ⁊ di-gell-siði aurd pad caímum no peth hi ndÉre noo déniuth dun doip and ⁊ no béradh sen don dún .i. laste conac[ha] gebad eolchaire and. Is nde for-fueoratar Temraig. To-gníthi trí muir leutha inna hoċtar. Is nde ra hainmnightie Temir .i. Tebe-mur hoc di *Tebis muri .i. mulieris uel similitudine murorum* conit Temir tra a mberla rustac.

Translations

A son of Míl Espáine [lit. 'Míl of Spain'], by the name of Érimon, took a wife from among the Thebans, that is, the city of Thebes, from which [*or* from whose name] came the woman. Homesickness seized the woman in Ireland, and a longing for Thebes, that is the city from which Érimón had come to Ireland. And the woman said that she was going to go back to Thebes. Érimón told her not to go, and he promised [her] the loveliest hill in Ireland, that she could choose a *dún* ['fort'] for them there and that he would put an incantation on the *dún*, namely *'laste'* ['blazing'],[3] so that longing for home would not come upon her. As a result, they seized Tara. Three walls were made by them on its upper rampart. From that was Temair [i.e. Tara] named, namely *Tebe-mur* ('Theban-wall'), this is from *Tebis muri* ('Walls of Thebes'), that is from the woman or from the resemblance of walls; so that Temair then is its name in common speech.

Sanas Cormaic 'Cormac's Glossary' s.v. *temair*

This passage is from the late Old Irish etymological and lexical compendium Sanas Cormaic *(literally 'Cormac's Whisper'), commonly known as* Cormac's Glossary. *It is ascribed to the ninth-century bishop and king of Cashel Cormac mac Cuillenáin (d. 908* CE*), to whom further texts have also been attributed.* Sanas Cormaic *is an alphabetized glossary replete with Isidorean etymology, derived mostly from Latin, Greek, and Irish, but also Hebrew, Norse, Old English and Pictish. It contains explanations of common nouns, personal names and place names.*[4]

Temair .i. te-mur .i. mur Tea ingine Luigdech maic Ithæ. Temair .i. Grec ro truailled and .i. *teomoro* id est *conspicio*. Temair didiu cech locc as mbi aurgnam déicsi iter mag ⁊ tech, ut dicitur temair na tuaithe ⁊ temair in tige.

Temair [i.e. Tara], that is, *te-mur*, namely the *múr* ('rampart') of Tea, the daughter of Lugaid son of Íth. Temair, that is, Greek was corrupted there, namely *teomoro*, that is *conspicio. Temair*, then, is every place from which the view is most excellent between plain and house, *as is said* 'temair* of the land and *temair* of the house'.

Quatrains from *Ní cheil maissi dona mnáib* 'It hides not the glory due to women'

This is a series of extracts from the poem 'Temair II' on the history of the women of Tara, by Cináed úa hArtacáin (died 975 CE), following the edition by Gwynn 1903–35: 1.6–13.

1. Ní cheil maissi dona mnáib
Temair cen taissi ar tócbail,
fúair ingen Lugdach 'na láim
tulmag bad líach do lotbáig.
[…]
4. Ro boí ic Érimón umal
ben i nglémedón gemel,
ruc úad cach roga romer
at-nóimed cech ní at-bered.
[…]
6. Ingen Foraind co lín argg
Tephi rolaind lúaded leirg,
ro chum cathraig croda in chuird
dia luirg ros torna is dia deilg.

7. Do-rat ainm dia cathraig caím
in ben co n-aíb rathmair ríg,
Múr Tephi fris' toirged dáil
as'n-oirged cen gráin cech ngním.

10. At-chúala i nEspáin uillig
ingin lescbáin láechbuillig
cin ó Bachtir mac Buírig
dos-fuc Camsón cáemchuingid.

11. Tephi a hainm ó cech gérad
mairg fors' mélad a múrad
ráth sescat traiged tólach
leo do-rónad dia rúnad.

Tara free from weakness does not hide
the glory due to women for its building;
the daughter of Lugaid obtained in her possession
a high plain which it would be grievous to destroy.

Humble Éremón had
a wife in the very midst of imprisonment;
she got from him every wild desire,
he would consent to everything she spoke of.

The daughter of Pharaoh, with many champions
Tephi the bright, who used to traverse the slope
framed a stronghold, a fierce occupation
with her staff she traced it, and with her brooch.

The king's wife, gracious and lovely
gave a name to her fair stronghold,
the Rampart of Tephi, from which she would grant a meeting
from which she executed every deed without loathing.

I have heard in many-cornered Spain
of a maiden fair and indolent, heroic in fight,
offspring of Bachtir son of Buirech,
Camson the fair champion took her to wife.

Tephi she was called by every champion,
woe to him on whom her burial should be inflicted,
an abundant rath of sixty feet
was built by them to conceal her.

18. Temair tuathi ocus tigi

cen luathi cen láechmiri

máthair anai cech ḟini

co nos bráthaig báethbini.

Excerpts from the prose *Dindshenchas* of Tara
(Stokes 1894–95: 1894.277–9)

§1 Temair didiu, ol Amorgein, múr Tea ingine Luigdech meic Itha dia luidh co Geidhe nOllgothach. [...]

§2 Nó Temair .i. Teipe múr .i. múr Teiphis ingine Bachtir rí Espainía is hí bai ac [C]anthon mac [C]aithmend rí Breatan conid ro marb occo si ⁊ do-radudh hEithiurún idhal na mBretan fria taisecc go mba béo nó marb. Ruccad sidhe iarum iarna bás co hEspain co ndernadh múr impe and .i. Teipe múr. At-connairc Tea didiu ben Eirimoin in sin .i. múr Tephis. Luid-sidein co hEirind le fear ⁊ do-beredh dí cach tulach toghadh in Eirinn conid le iarum conarnecht múr amail múr Tephis conid inde ro hadhnacht. Unde Temair dicitur.

[...]

§4 Vel ita: Temair a uerbo graeco *temorio* quod latine interpretatur conspicio. Huius oppidi quod Temoriam uocamus nomen esse deriuatum autores affirmant; omnisque locus conspicuus et eminens, siue in campo [glossing *túath*], siue in domo [glossing *tige*], siue in quocumque loco sit, uocabulo quo dicitur Temair nominari potest. Sic in prouerbio scotico reperitur, ut dicitur *temair na tuaithi* et *temair in tigi*, quam sententiam in suo *Silentio* [i.e. *Sanas*] Cormaccus de hoc nomine disputando possuit. Hoc igitur oppidum multorum sibi commune uindicat, nunc cunctis enim Hibernensibus oppidis excellens congruenter eorum commune uocabulum possidet, quippe cum huius rector usque hodie totius insolae Scotorum monarchiam sortitur.

Temair of the land and of the house

without haste, without heroes' frenzy

was mother to the prosperity of every family

until a foolish crime doomed her.

Translation slightly adapted from Stokes

§1 Temair [i.e. Tara] then, said Amorgein, is the *múr* ('rampart') of Tea, daughter of Lugaid son of Íth when she went with [i.e. married] Géde the Loud-Voiced [...]

§2 Or Temair, that is *Teipe-múr*, that is the rampart of Tephe, daughter of Bachter king of Spain. It is she who lived with Canthon son of Cathmenn king of Britain, until she died with him, and Eithiurún, the idol of the Britons, had been given as security for her return (to Spain) whether alive or dead. So after her death she was brought to Spain, and there a rampart was built around her, namely, *Teipe-múr*. Now Tea, Éremón's wife, saw that, namely, the rampart of Tephis. She went to Ireland with her husband, and every hill she would choose in Erin was given to her, and afterwards she designed [on the hill of Tara] a rampart like the rampart of Tephis, and therein she was buried. Hence it is called Temair.

[...]

§4 Or thus: Temair is from the Greek word *temorio* which is translated into Latin as *conspicio*. Authorities affirm that the name of this stronghold which we call *Temoria* is derived [from it]. And every conspicuous and eminent place, whether on a plain or in the house, or wherever it may be, can be called by this word 'temair'. Thus it is found in the Irish[5] saying, as is said *temair na tuaithi* 'temair of the land' and *temair in tigi* 'temair of the house', an opinion concerning this debatable name which Cormac, cited in his *Silence* [i.e. *Sanas*]. This *oppidum*, then, claims for itself what is common to many, since surpassing all Irish *oppida* it now appropriately possesses their common name, since naturally even today its ruler obtains the sovereignty of the entire island of Ireland.

Essay: Three accounts of the origins of Tara

The heroes of classical antiquity, such as Hercules, Alexander, Aeneas or Troilus, whom we encounter in their Irish guises elsewhere in this volume, make no appearance in the *Dindshenchas*. But the places and civilizations from which they hail play a significant role in several origin legends of important Irish localities. The *Dindshenchas* in its fully-fledged prosimetrical form follows in the conceptual footsteps of *Lebor Gabála Érenn* 'The Book of Invasions of Ireland' – the historiographical framework charting the history of Irish civilization within biblically-based world chronology (see Ch. 26). In this scheme, Ireland had no truly indigenous population as such, but was conquered and inhabited by six waves of foreign settlers, hailing from such places as Greece, Scythia, Egypt and Spain. These peoples – the entourage of Noah's granddaughter Cessair, the people of Parthalón, of Nemed, the Fir Bolg, the Túatha Dé Danann and finally the Sons of Míl Espáine (i.e. the Gaels) – all left their imprint on the Irish landscape.

While topographical history (broadly speaking) is not exclusively a learned phenomenon and forms part of oral tradition, in Ireland as elsewhere, the sort of written place-name histories we find in the *Dindshenchas* were certainly intended for a sophisticated literate audience. Their clerical authors were masters of both the biblical and pagan classical past, and were versed in the writings of late antique authors such as Servius and Orosius. The place where these intellectual efforts appear to be most concentrated is the Neolithic site and ancient royal stronghold at Tara (Irish *Temair*) in Co. Meath. Although it had been abandoned long before our earliest written records, Tara continued to exert immense symbolic power over the Irish imagination for centuries to come. While officially uninhabited, political dominion of the site and surrounding area usually bolstered a dynasty's claim to power over the entire island, even if this goal was never truly achieved militarily. In the late Middle Irish *Dindshenchas* collections, which survive as a continuous tract in manuscripts from the fourteenth century onwards, four poems and various associated prose passages dealing with the origin of Tara survive.[6] They were probably compiled from earlier independent and divergent traditions, and later consolidated into a continuous account. The extracts presented above illustrate this process of textual harmonization.

In the first passage, Érimón son of Míl Espáine chooses for wife a woman personifying the city of Thebes, and brings her with him to Ireland. The name which she herself has taken from the city of Thebes, she subsequently lends to the new foundation, named *Tebe-múr* 'Rampart of Tebi/Thebes'. The figure of Érimón is well established in Irish tradition.[7] According to the *Lebor Gabála* tradition, he is one of the Milesians, the sons of Míl Espáine, that is, the final wave of settlers who came to Ireland from Spain.[8] These 'Milesians' are none other than the Gaels, from whom most historical Irish kings descend.

Érimón's wife Tebe, on the other hand, is an outlier to Irish tradition.[9] And yet, a woman symbolizing the city of Thebes whose name subsequently becomes synonymous with the centre of Irish kingship *par excellence*, appears to be more than the fortuitous result of Isidorean word-play. If Thebes was chosen as the birthplace of Irish sovereignty, classical accounts of the origin of Thebes must have resonated with elements in Irish legendary history.[10] The etymologizing of Irish *Temair* as *Tebe-múr* 'rampart of Tebi/ Thebes' calls to mind the foundation myth of Boeotian Thebes. According to Homer (*Odyssey* 11.5), Zethus and Amphion, Zeus's sons by Antiope, were responsible for building the fortifications of 'seven-gated' Thebes;[11] Hyginus informs us that this was done at the behest of Apollo (*Fabulae* 9); and Apollodorus relates that Zethus married a woman called Thebe after whom the city is named (*Library* 3.5.6). While these particular sources may not have been in circulation in medieval Ireland, the foundation of Thebes is mentioned in several late antique and medieval sources which were likely available in Irish intellectual circles, notably Lactantius Placidus' commentary on Statius *Thebaid* and, of course, Isidore's *Etymologies*.[12]

Though Amphion and Zethus may be credited with the construction of the fortifying walls, the foundation of the city itself goes back to the Phoenician prince Cadmus, and there is reason to believe that it is indeed in Cadmus' footsteps that Érimón is supposed to step here. Isidore states that Cadmus founded not only Boeotian Thebes, but also the Egyptian city on the Nile bearing the same name (*Etymologies* 15.1.35).[13] Although our first passage does not make clear which of the two is being alluded to, the emphasis on the *múr*, the 'rampart' or 'wall' of Tara would suggest that the Irish stronghold is supposed to represent Boeotian rather than Phoenician Thebes, especially in view of the assault on the walls of Thebes which is the subject of Statius' *Thebaid* (later rendered into the Middle Irish as *Togail na Tebe*, on which see Ch. 11).

Sanas Cormaic (passage 2) etymologizes *Temair* as *Tea-múr* 'rampart of Tea', rather than 'rampart of Tebi'. In this text, as well as in the wider *Lebor Gabála* tradition, Tea is the daughter of Lugaid son of Íth and the wife of Érimón.[14] As is common in the glossary tradition, Cormac includes a Greek origin for *Temair* as well, stating that the name is derived from a Greek word *teomoro*, which translates as Latin *conspicio*.[15]

While *Sanas Cormaic* makes no reference to Tebe, this origin story seems not to have been entirely lost. One of the *Dindshenchas* poems, of which excerpts are given in passage 3, focuses on the women who, *mutatis mutandis*, have lent their name to the royal site of Tara. The poem, attributed to Cináed úa hArtacáin (died 975 CE), is a versified account of the various etymologies of the name, combining eponymy and Isidorean etymology in the same vein as *Sanas Cormaic*.[16] But Cináed evidently knew more than one origin for the name Tara, and he introduces another woman, Tephi (= Tebe?) as the daughter of Pharaoh (quatrain 6). If Tephi is a reflex of the Tebi we have encountered in our first passage, then her pedigree has shifted considerably. In the *Lebor Gabála* tradition, it was Scota (a name which is the Latin equivalent of *Ériu*) who was the daughter of Pharaoh; she was either the wife of Míl Espáine and therefore Érimón's mother, or (as Máel Muru Othna's poem *Can a mbunadas na nGáedel* 'Whence the origin of the Irish?' describes it), she was the wife of Niul son of Fénius Farsaid and mother of Goídel Glas, the eponymous ancestor of the Goídil – that is, the Gaelic Irish.

In addition to this, Cináed introduces a second Tephi, the daughter of Bachtir, the king of Spain. In her now Spanish incarnation, Tephi is abducted by Camsón, the king of Britain, and apparently becomes his wife and queen. Upon her death, her body is returned to Spain, and a rampart is built which is called *Tephe-múr*. It is Tephi's Spanish incarnation which we find in our fourth passage in the prose *dindshenchas* of Tara. In this passage, the Spanish *Tephi-múr* is then spotted by Tea, wife of Érimón (in agreement with *Sanas Cormaic* and with *Lebor Gabála Érenn* more broadly). After coming to Ireland with her husband, Tea designs her own *Tephi-múr* and calls it *Tea-múr*. This detail is not given in Cináed's poem and it appears that the prose seeks to harmonize different traditions, effectively creating two Taras: *Tephi-múr*, the sepulchral monument dedicated to Tephi, and *Tea-múr*, Tea's Hibernian *simulacrum* of the Spanish monument.

The ninth-century Theban origin of Tara, if we follow the argument advanced here, did not disappear without a trace, but was displaced and modified before finding a new home in Spain. Wonderfully learned and Isidorean as it might appear, Tara's Theban origin could not be accommodated within the *Lebor Gabála* paradigm; it could only survive vestigially. What we may see in Cináed's poem, therefore, is evidence that the poet attempted to do justice to both the Theban origin and the (probably more dominant) *Lebor Gabála* tradition, by connecting the idea of an Egyptian Thebes with that of Scota daughter of Pharaoh. It is possible that the Spanish *Teiphi* was his own innovation, and that, when *Dindshenchas Érenn* was compiled (likely at a later stage than the earliest version of the *Lebor Gabála*) the Spanish connection was retained, since the Sons of Míl come to Ireland from Spain.

The Theban origin of Tara is demonstrably an outlier to the wider topographical tradition about the royal site. Its later development is, however, instructive in demonstrating how the work of the medieval Irish syncretistic historians was exerting its own pressures on *dindshenchas* as a tradition. It was no doubt under the influence of *Lebor Gabála Érenn*, and strictly within its temporal paradigm, that the branch of traditional learning known as *dindshenchas* evolved to produce the corpus of prose and poetry which was anthologized under that name in our manuscripts.

Notes

1   The research on which this chapter is based has been generously funded by the Leverhulme Trust as part of the 'Mapping the Medieval Mind' project (2020–5), based at the University of Cambridge. My thanks to Mariamne Briggs, the editors and an anonymous reader for feedback.

2   The prose and poem, evidently taken to be a textual unit, were edited and translated in O'Daly 1960. The translation above has been slightly adapted from O'Daly's text.

3   Presumably for *lasta*, as in *eDIL* s.v. *lasta* 'alight, flaming', verbal adjective from *lasaid* 'takes fire, blazes'.

4   For the text see Arbuthnot, Moran and Russell 2016, last accessed for this paper in January 2023.

5   The word *scotico* refers here to the Irish language.

6   See the editions and translations in Gwynn 1903–35 and Stokes 1892, 1894–5.

7   The earliest reference to him appears in a text dated to the seventh century, see Carey 1994b: 12 n.16.

8   By '*Lebor Gabála* tradition' I here refer to the various versions of the prosimetric tracts which survive from the Middle Irish period onwards, as well as their earlier textual forebears such as *Historia Brittonum* and Máel Muru Othna's poem *Can a mbunadas na Gáedel* 'Whence is the origin of the Irish?'. On the history of this tradition, see Carey's Ch. 26 in the present book, with further references.

9   Perhaps to be pronounced *Tébe*? The prose does not allow us to test for vowel quantity.

10 A parallel, though likely later, tradition is no doubt the deliberate casting of famous characters from the Ulster Cycle as Trojan kings and heroes, and the comparison of their stronghold Emain Macha (Navan Fort, Co. Armagh) to the citadel of Ilium. See Ch. 24.

11 We may note that another *Dindshenchas* poem, penned by the poet of our third passage, counts the doors of the stronghold of Temair as *dá shecht* 'two times seven' (see Gwynn 1903–35: 1.32, line 64).

12 For the circulation of Lactantius among the Irish, see Miles 2011: 90.

13 Note especially *Etymologies* 15.1.35, which makes clear the relationship between the two Thebes: 'Cadmus founded Egyptian Thebes, which is held to be quite famous among Egyptian cities for the number of its gates [...] The Egyptian region Thebaica is named after it. There is a Thebes in Boeotia and a Thebes in Egypt, but both were established by one founder' (tr. Barney et al. 2006). See also *Etymologies* 14.4.11 (Cadmus follows a cow and founds Boeotian Thebes); 15.1.29; 15.1.46.

14 The earliest reference to Tea as the wife of Érimon appears again to be in Máel Muru's poem *Can a mbunadas na nGáedel* 'Whence is the origin of the Irish? (see Todd 1848: 244–5, with Carey 2015a). Her husband Érimón was also her great-uncle: Míl Espáine was the son of Bile son of Bregon. Íth, who was the first Milesian to see Ireland from Spain, was Bile's brother. When his father was killed by the then occupants of Ireland, the Túatha Dé Danann, it was Íth's son Lugaid, Tea's father, who mustered the first armed expedition to Ireland in order to avenge his father. Míl followed and brought Tea with him.

15 On the meaning of the Greek word see Marie-Luise Theuerkauf, 'The Irish Jerusalem: Etymological Politics and the Study of Greek in Medieval Ireland', forthcoming.

16 That Cináed likely used *Sanas Cormaic* as a source is shown by quatrain 18, where he employs Cormac's phrase *temair na túaithe ocus temair na tige* 'temair of the land and *temair* of the house', as in the last extract above.

29

Suidiugud Tellaig Temra 'The Establishment of Tara's Dominion'[1]

Daniel James Watson

This narrative was edited and translated into English by Best 1910 on the basis of the version of the text found in 'Yellow Book of Lecan', Dublin, TCD MS 1318 (formerly H.2.16), p.105, col. 740, line 1 – p. 109, col. 749, line 19, with readings from the version found in the 'Book of Lismore', fols 132 ra1–134 rb 35. The semi-diplomatic edition of the Yellow Book of Lecan text offered here is based on Best 1910. Most of the punctuation and capitalization has been introduced by the editor, and minor adjustments have been imposed for clarity.

Text extracts

Fintan on the source of his ancient lore

13. 'Maith sin, a Findtain', ar siad. 'Is ferrdi dūn do thīachtain do thurim sheanchasa hErend'. 'Am mebrach-sa ēm', ollse, 'i sreathaib senchusa h*Erend* indus ro·bas indte cosin n-uair-se ⁊ indus bether indti bēos co brāth'. 'Ceist', ar siad, 'canas ro·thucais-seo sin, ⁊ cid as neasom diar cobair-ne den tṡenchas sin immonī im·rāidim im sui*diugu*d tellaich Themrach?'. 'Nī ansa', ar Fintan, 'indisfet-sa dūibse collēc nī de*side*'.

14. Bāmar-ni feachtus i mmōrdāil fer nĒreand sun*d* im Chonaing Begeclach im rīg nErend. Lāa n-an*d* dūin isin dāil sin iarum, con·acamar in scālfer mōr caīn *c*umachtach chucaind anīar la fuinead ṅgrēne. Don·bert ingantas mōr mēd a delba. Comard fri fid māel a dā gūaland, ecnach nem ⁊ grīan fo gabal ara fot ⁊ ara chāime. Fīal ētrocht glainidi imme amal ētach līnda līghda. Dā māelasa imma chosaib ⁊ nī feas cīa luib dia ra·badar. Moṅg legta ōrbuidi fochas fair co clār a dā leas. Taibli lecda inna lāim cli. Crōeb co trī toirthib ina lāim deis; ittē trī toraid ro·bādar fuirre: cnōe ⁊ ubla ⁊ dercain i cētemun sin, ⁊ ba hanabaid cech torad dīb. Do·chechaing sechond iarum morthimchell na hairechtai ⁊ a crōeb ōrda illdathach do ḟid Lebāin ria ais. Con·ēbairt fer ūaindi fris. 'Tadall lat', arse, 'coro·aicilli in rīg .i. Conaing mBececlach'. Fris·rogart-*s*om con·ērbairt. 'Cid is ailicc dūib hūam?', arse. 'Co·fesamar ūait', arsiat, 'can do·deachaid ⁊ cid thēge ⁊ caidi th'ainm ⁊ caidi do slon*d*u*d*'.

15. 'Do·dechaid-sa ēm', arse, 'ō fuined ⁊ tēgim do thurgbāill, ⁊ isē m'ainm Trēḟuilngid Treëochair'. 'Cid diatā duit-seo int ainm hī sein?', arsiat. 'Nī ansa', arse. 'Dāig is mē immo·foilnge turcbāil ṅgrēine ⁊ a fuiniud'. '⁊ cid dod·tuc dond fuiniud mas oc turcbāil bī?' 'Nī ansa', arse. 'Fer im·rinodair .i. ro·crochad le hlūdaidib indiu. Ro·chechaing iarum tairsiu tarēis in gnīma, ⁊ nī·rothaitne friu. Et is*ed* dom·fuc-sa co fuiniud, dia ḟis cid ro·bāi grīan. Conid an*d*sin ro·foillsiged dam. ⁊ ō ro·fetar cindus tīri darsi fuiniud co rochtus iarum Inis nGlūairi iar

Translations by the author

Fintan on the source of his ancient lore

13. 'That is good, Fintan', they said. 'We are better off for your coming to tell the ancient history of Ireland'. 'I am indeed familiar', he said, 'with the ordering [i.e. the sequential patterns] of Ireland's ancient history: how it has been up to this time, and how it will yet be until the Judgement'. 'A question', they said, 'where is it that you have got this from? And also, what aspect of the lore is the most indispensable for helping us concerning what we reflect upon: the establishment of Tara's Dominion?' 'That is not difficult', said Fintan, 'I will tell you something about it presently'.

14. 'We were once in a great assembly of the men of Ireland here, round about Conaing Bececlach, that is, round about the king of Ireland. Then one day, when we were in that assembly, we saw a gigantic man – fair, invested with power – come towards us from the west at the setting of the sun. The magnitude of his form gave us cause for great wonder. As high as a tree, the crest of his shoulders; the firmament and the sun, visible between his thighs: such was his extent, and such was his beauty. A shining crystal veil was about him, as a garment of bright linen. Two sandals were upon his feet, and the material of which they were made is not known. Golden, flowing, curly, hair was upon him, down to the level of his thigh. Stone tablets were in his left hand. A branch with three fruits was in his right hand. These are the three fruits which were upon it: nuts, apples, and acorns of May-time, and each of these fruits was unripe. He advanced past us then, in a great circuit of the assembly, with his golden many-coloured branch of Lebanon-wood upon his back.[3] One of our men spoke to him: 'Come here', he said, 'and speak to the king' (that is, to Conaing Bececlach). He replied, and said 'What is it that you desire of me?' 'That we might learn from you', they said, 'where you have come from, where you are going, and what your name and your lineage are.'

15. 'I have, in fact, come', he said, 'from the sunset, and I am going to the sunrise, and my name is Trefhuilngid Tre-eochair'. 'For what reason do you have this name?', they said. 'That is not difficult', he said, 'Because I am the one who causes the rising of the sun and its setting'. 'And what brought you to the sunset, if you are always at the sunrise?' 'That is not difficult', he said. 'A man who has been everywhere pierced, that is, he who was crucified by the Jews today.[4] Thereafter,

nIrrus Domnand ⁊ nī·fūair tīr ō sein sīar. Ar is*ed* sin tairrsech darsa fuinean*n* grīan am*ail* isē tarsech darsa turcbāill Par̄dus Ādaiṁ.

Trefhuilngid as the ultimate historical authority

20. Anais iarum oċaib .xl. lāa ⁊ aidchi, co ro·tinōlta fir hĒr*enn* dō frisin rē sin co Teṁraiġ. ⁊ con·ḟaca uili ind oenḃaili conid iarum ro·róidh-sem riu. 'Cad iat libse', arse, 'ailgi comgni fer nĒreand i rrīgthich Themra. Taisfenaid dūn'. 'Nī·rabadar ēm', arsiaḋ, 'seanchaidi farrsaidi oconne frisin lāmmais ailgi choimgni co tānoc-sa chucund'. 'Robar·bia-si ōn hūaimse', arse, 'rodo·suidiġiub-sa dūib sreith seanchusa ⁊ ailgi chomgni tellaich Temrach fēsin co ceithri hardaib hEren*n* imbi. Ar is mesea in fīada fīrēolach foillsiges cech n-ainfis do chāch'.

Fintan as the oldest historian in Ireland

22. [. . .] 'is rimsa', ar Fintan, 'ro·hērbad ar eisnēis ⁊ a acallaim fīad int ṡlūag, ar is misi seanchaidh bad siniu fūair ara chind i n-hĒr*ind*. Ar bā-ṡa i Tul Tuindi fri rē inna dīlen*n*. ⁊ ro·bo m'ōenur inti iar ṅdīlind co cean*n* dā blī*adna* ar mīle eret ro·būi Ēriu fās. ⁊ ro·bā-sa iarsin i comaimisir re cech ndīne rus·gab ō sin cosin lā-sa i tānic Trēḟuilngid dond oirecht-sa Conaing Bececl*aig*. Conid ō sin rofiarfaid Trēḟui*lngid* dīmsa tria ḟis imchomairc.

the sun advanced[5] past them on account of that deed, and it did not shine upon them. And that is what brought me to its setting, namely, to find out what was wrong with it. So that is how it was revealed to me. And inasmuch as I discovered what kind of lands they were over which it sets, I came then to Inis Gluairi, on the farther side of Irrus Domnann, and did not find any land from there westwards. For that is the threshold over which the sun sets, just as the Paradise of Adam is the threshold over which it rises.'

Trefhuilngid as the ultimate historical authority

20. He remained, then, with them for forty days and nights, until the men of Ireland had been mustered there before him at that time at Tara. And so, when he saw everyone in the one place, he spoke to them. 'What' he says 'foundations of the historical knowledge of the men of Ireland, do you have in the royal house of Tara? Show them to us.' 'Honestly, there have not been', they said, 'reliable historians among us, to whom we might entrust the foundations of historical knowledge, until you came to us.' 'You will have that from me', he said. 'I will establish for you the ordering of ancient history, and of the foundations of historical knowledge, those of the dominion of Tara itself, together with the four quarters of Ireland around it. For I myself am the truly learned witness who reveals to everyone all that is unknown.'

Fintan as the oldest historian in Ireland

22. […] 'And it was to me', said Fintan, 'that it was committed, to explain and discuss before the assembly, seeing as I was the oldest historian that he found there before him in Ireland. For I was in Tul Tuinde at the time of the Flood. And I was alone there after the Flood, until the end of two years, plus a thousand, during which time Ireland was uninhabited. And after that I was contemporaneous with every generation that held it: from that time, to the very day on which Trefhuilngid came to this assembly of Conaing Bececlach. So it is on account of this that I was the one who Trefulilngid questioned, using his expertise in the art of enquiry.'

Fintan's mission to Ireland

29. Fācbais iarum Trēfuil*ng*id Treëochair firu hĒrend fon n-ordug*u*d sin co brāth, ⁊ fācbais nī do chōeraib inna crōibi bāi inna lāim oc Fintan m*a*c Bōchra. Conas·rola-*si*de isna hinadaib in robo dōig leiṡ a nn-ās i n-hĒr*ind*, ⁊ itē craind ro·fāsait isna cōeraib sin: Bili Tortan, ⁊ Eō Rosa, Eō Mugna ⁊ Crōeb Daithi ⁊ Bili hUissn*ig*. Ocus airis[2] Fintan ic sloind seanchassa do ḟeraib hĒr*enn* co mbo hē ba hiarlathi dona bilib, ⁊ co ra crīnsad ria lind. Ō ro·airig iarum Fintan a sentaiṫ fēn ⁊ sentaith na mbilid is and do·rōne in lāid. . .

Fintan's final judgement

31. Do·rōne iarum in lāid sin, ⁊ ro·airis re sloind senchasa do ḟeraib hĒrind bēos connice in inbaid sin tānic fo gair*m* Diarmata m*ei*c Cerbaill ⁊ Fland Foebla m*ei*c Scandlāin ⁊ Chindḟāelad m*ei*c Aililla, ⁊ fer nĒren*n* ar chena do brith breithi dōib im sui*di*ug*u*d tell*aig* Themra. Acus asī breth ruc dōib: 'A bith am*ai*l dos·airnicmair', ar Findtan. 'Nī·thargom tara n-ordug*u*d fo·rḟācaib Trēfuil*ng*id Treëoch*a*r remum. Ar ba haingel Dē hēs*ide*, *nō* fa Dīa fēisin'.

32. Tāngadar iarsein mathi hĒren*n* am*ai*l ro·rāidsem do tidnocol Fintain co hUisneach. Conid and ro·chelebair cach dīb di arailiu i mmulluch Usnig. Ocus ro·suigid ina fīadnaisi lia cloichi cōic druimneach i fīrmullach Uisnig. Ocus do·be*r*t drumain de fri cech cōiced i[si]n n-hĒrind, ar is amlaid atā Temair ⁊ hUisnech i n-hĒrind am*ai*l bit a di ārai*nd* a mmīl indile. Ocus co·tōraind forrach and .i. *ir*rondus cach cōiced dīb i n-hUisnech. ⁊ do·roindi Fintan in lāid so iar cōrug*u*d ind lia . . .

Fintan's mission to Ireland

29. So Trefhuilngid Tre-eochair left the men of Ireland under that dispensation until the Judgement, and he left some of the berries on the branch that was in his hand with Fintan mac Bochra. Thus he set them in the places in Ireland where he thought it was most likely that they would grow. And these are the trees that grew by those berries: the Venerable Tree of Tortu, and the Mighty Tree of Ross, the Mighty Tree of Mugna, the Great Tree of Daithi, and the Venerable Tree of Uisneach. And Fintan remained, telling the ancient histories to the men of Ireland, until he was the survivor of those venerable trees, and until they had, in his time, all withered away. So when Fintan had perceived his own old age, and the old age of those venerable trees, he composed a poem ...

Fintan's final judgement

31. So he composed this poem, and remained to tell the ancient histories to the men of Ireland, even up to the time when he came at the summons of Diarmait mac Cerbaill, and of Flann Febla, mac Scanlan, and Cennfaelad mac Ailill (and the men of Ireland besides), to pronounce judgement for them concerning the establishment of Tara's dominion. And this is the judgement that he gave: 'Let it be as we have found it', said Fintan, 'we shall not go against the dispensation that Trefhuilngid Tre-eochair has left to us. For he was an angel of God, or he was God himself'.

32. After that, the nobles of Ireland came, as we mentioned before, to accompany Fintan to Uisneach. So it is there, at the crown of Uisneach, that each of them took leave of the other. And he established, in their presence, on the very crown of Uisneach, a stone pillar of five ridges. And he assigned a ridge of it to each province in Ireland. For it is thus that Tara and Uisneach are in Ireland: as two kidneys are in an ox.[6] So he marked out a measurement of the land there, that is, the apportionment of each province by means of the corresponding portions at Uisneach. And he composed this poem, after setting up the stone ...

Essay: Ireland as successor to the empire of the Romans

Suidiugud Tellaig Temra is a narrative in alternating prose and verse of 487 lines (in the Yellow Book of Lecan's version of the text) telling of the circumstances that putatively led to the final reestablishment of Ireland's ancient political order. By its own account, this occurred during the reign of Diarmait mac Cerbaill, which, as the Annals have it, ran from 544 to 565 CE. It says that when Diarmait was king, the nobles of Ireland would not come to the 'Feast of Tara' (*feis Temra*) until the extent of the land that belonged to the royal dominion of Tara – and thus of the land belonging to the provinces of Ireland in distinction from Tara – had been determined for all time (§3).[7] The problem is solved by Fintan mac Bóchra, the most ancient person in Ireland. The significance of his extreme old age is, in part, that it allowed him to remember what the political order in Ireland was like from the most ancient times. But most importantly, it meant that he was alive at the time of Christ's Passion, when one Trefhuilngid (who, Fintan says, 'was an angel of God', or else, 'God himself'[8]) came to Ireland and divinely re-established its political partitioning, together with its history as a whole, then entrusting to Fintan the responsibility of passing this knowledge to future generations (§§14ff.). This made him uniquely qualified to confirm that the contemporary political partitioning of Ireland was just. For he alone could verify its fidelity to Trefhuilngid's divine clarification of Ireland's ancient political order.

It is not currently possible to be more specific about the date of the text than to say that its language is Middle Irish, this being as far as its only editor took the matter (Best 1910: 121). It has been suggested, in passing (McCone 1990: 75; Carey 1994b: 18), that it belongs to the tenth or eleventh century. Short of a systematic study of the language, its thematic parallels with other Middle Irish works –'The Wooing of Ailbe',[9] *Dindshenchas Érenn* (see above, Chs 27–8),[10] 'The Colloquy between Fintan and the Hawk of Achill'[11] – seem to be the principal, if inconclusive, evidence.[12] However, the character of its implicit reception of Orosius' *Histories against the Pagans* may provide further guidance.[13] For insofar as it is influenced by Orosius, this is Orosius conciliated with the relevant elements of Augustine's *City of God*.[14] And the form of the implied conciliation closely resembles positions more explicitly held by Hugh of St Victor and Otto of Freising.[15] This suggests dependence on one or both of these authorities, and thus implies a composition date towards the end of the Middle Irish period, in the twelfth century. The selections provided here are those that best illustrate the text's creative reception of Orosius, and its remarkable implications.

The *Suidiugud* is a work fundamentally concerned with a vision of empire. The political order that serves as the story's primary focus is ruled over by a king (*ríg*), but not in a restrictive sense of the word (§14). He is the kind of king who is presented as ruling over all the other kings on the island of Ireland (§2), i.e. as an emperor in all but name. In this, our text belongs with the other Irish examples identified by Boyle (2021: 124–33) of a preoccupation with the theme of empire that 'emerged over the course of the eleventh century and was well-established by the twelfth' (133). For our purposes, the most important feature of its own vision of an Irish empire is the way in which it adapts and transforms Orosius' idea of *translatio imperii*, the 'translation of empire'.

The simplest and most universal form of this idea is that, from the first emergence of Babylon, only one empire has dominated the world at any given time, but that this prime empire sometimes moves from one polity to another. Orosius was not the first to conceive of such an idea. Nevertheless, his conception of it had a broad influence on medieval explorations of this theme.[16] A major factor in making this influence discernible is that Orosius' historiography provided a framework for understanding the process of the translation of empire as one of rising achievement,[17] in contrast to the systematic decline that St. Jerome notably attributed to the same process.[18]

The Holy Roman Empire and its Frankish precursors are the best-known examples of polities that were interpreted as inheriting imperial power in this way.[19] However, medieval applications of this concept are far more diverse. Aside from eleventh- and twelfth-century Ireland, Lombardy, Iberia and Wessex[20] are also among the medieval polities that were in some way imagined to be the most recent instances of empire's ongoing translation (DiTommaso 2021: 227). There are generally two ways in which this 'translation' was presented. Either the polity in question was conceived of as the latest configuration of the Roman Empire,[21] or as a successor to the Roman Empire (and thus to all earthly empires),[22] which, as such, presaged or inaugurated Christ's eschatological kingdom. Our text is an example of the latter.

The political order described here has, in some sense, existed from the most ancient times, and Fintan mac Bóchra is old enough to be able to know this first-hand. It is, however, Trefhuilngid's confirmation (and extension) of what Fintan knew by experience that is the decisive factor in Fintan's authority. When he makes his judgement on the ideal nature of this order, in the time of Diarmait mac Cerbaill, the rationale he offers is that he does not wish to contradict the angelic (or else, absolutely divine) authority of Trefhuilngid (§31). It is of fundamental significance here that this occurs at the time of Christ's crucifixion.

As the one who causes the rising and setting of the sun, Trefhuilngid has come to Ireland, as to the place where the sun sets, to see what might be wrong with it, since it leaped past Judaea on that day without shining on it (§15). In this way, the divine revelation of the political order of Ireland is a direct result of the central event of Christian history. It is the kind of polity that emerges, and presumably could only emerge, as a result of the Passion.

This bears closely on the parallels with biblical history that are often made in texts which discuss the translation of empires. The emergence of the Babylonian Empire and the life of Abraham were commonly understood to be contemporaneous (and thus mutually illuminating) realities, as were the liberation of the Jewish people from exile in Babylon, and the liberation of Rome from the Tarquins. This receives particular emphasis in Augustine's *City of God*, following him in Bede's *De Temporum Ratione* (*On the Reckoning of Time*), and – perhaps most significantly for our text – in Otto of Freising's *History of the Two Cities*.[23] In any event, to claim that the initial establishment of the Irish political order is contemporaneous with the Passion of Christ (and resultant from it) is to make a bold argument about the eschatological significance of that order. In effect, it is a claim that just as Christ is superior to the earlier realities that pointed to him, so the Irish political order is (or will be) in some way superior to its Babylonian and Roman precursors,[24] thus providing a striking parallel to the insistence on the superiority of the Irish language over its Latin, Greek and Hebrew precursors that we find in *Auraicept na nÉces* 'The Scholars' Primer' (on which see Ch. 23).

In this way, an Orosian historiographical framework is further developed by assimilating materials to it from other historiographers who do not, like him, find an increasing grandeur in the succession of empires. Put more broadly, it is a striking example of the kind of synchronism between the figures of the Irish past and those of the classical world that proliferated at this time, as we have seen throughout this book. And we find another example of just such an extension of Orosius in the emphasis on the location of Ireland in the distant west, in conjunction with the establishment of its imperial order. Trefhuilngid informs those gathered at Tara that, in his search to find out what was wrong with the sun, he found no lands west of Inis Gluairi, an island just of the coast of modern-day Co. Mayo. He found that this island was the threshold over which the sun set, just as the 'Paradise of Adam' (*pardhus Ádhaim*) was the threshold over which it rose. This comparison of Ireland with the 'Paradise of Adam' is further emphasized by the implications of the golden branch that Trefhuilngid carries. The 'Land of Promise' (*tír tarngire* / *terra repromissionis*), from which such branches generally come in other medieval Irish narratives, is the equivalent of Eden, or Eden itself (Watson 2020: 39–41). Hence it seems clear that, in the context of *Suidiugud Tellaig Temra*, Trefhuilngid has brought it to Ireland from the place he has identified as its eastern counterpart, Eden, the 'Paradise of Adam'.[25]

The crucial detail here is that he gives this branch to Fintan, and that this seems to be inseparable from also giving divine political knowledge to him. Fintan plants berries of this branch wherever he thinks they might grow, and relates the revelation of Ireland's political order while the resulting trees flourish, until they finally die (§29). The subsequent erection of the stone pillar of five ridges on the hill of Uisneach acts as a replacement both for himself and the trees: a summary of the revelation that he received from Trefhuilngid that will ensure its continuity until the end of the world (§32). The message here seems to be that Ireland's character as the western counterpart to the eastern paradise of Eden makes it the intrinsically ideal place for the character of that lost Paradise to be realized politically in the mortal world, but that such a thing could only ever take place following the Passion of Christ.

For Orosius, the translation of empire follows the points of the compass, so that once it has reached Rome, in the West, there is effectively no place left for another empire to emerge before the end of the world. However, for Augustine, empire does not follow the points of the compass, but moves from East to West.[26] It is for this reason that Hugh of St Victor and Otto of Freising argued, in the first half of the twelfth century, that the end of the world was near. Since the divinely-ordained sequence of empires had reached the 'world's end' (*finis mundi*), its intrinsic westward movement evidently had nowhere else to go. Yet aspiring polities to the west of the Holy Roman Empire might well protest that the translation of empires had yet to reach its furthest possible western extent.[27] And it is just such a protest that we observe here. The most fundamental reason that history unfolds from East to West is that it is only in the uttermost West that what was first lost in the uttermost East can be regained. The end is a return to the beginning. In this, our text can be said to complete the story told by Hugh of St Victor. For of the other authors discussed here, he is unique in beginning the account of the westward movement of empires, not with Babylon, but with Paradise.

In *Suidiugud Tellaig Temra* we see the result of its author's search for ancient authorities that could help to identify Ireland's role in world history. The importance of Orosius and Augustine was not the fact that they were late antique citizens of the Roman Empire, but the authority that their respective accounts of history were understood to have. Yet the result of turning to these authorities is that ideas about the role of the Roman Empire in history, many of them inherited or derived from foundational classical authors, became fundamental to how the author of *Suidiugud Tellaig Temra* conceived of Ireland. Moreover, there is no reason to suppose that the classical reception represented, even by this one theme, was limited to the mediation of the authorities we have discussed to this point. We have, for example, seen that a return to Paradise is understood to be implicit in the transference of empire from Rome to Tara. From one perspective, this is clearly a biblical motif: the Paradise in question is that of Genesis 2–3. Nevertheless, the motif has another antecedent in Virgil's fourth *Eclogue*,[28] where he marks the return of the Hesiodic Golden Age, the 'reign of Saturn' (*saturnia regna*), in the empire of Augustus (see esp. *Eclogues* 4.6). For the moment, it must remain a matter of debate whether the return of the Golden Age from Virgil is also at work in the return of the biblical paradise in the *Suidiugud*'s Irish empire. But it certainly must have seemed so to Virgil's Irish readers.

Notes

1 Following Best's edition (1910), *Suidiugud Tellaig Temra* has usually been translated as 'The Settling of the Manor of Tara'. However, since the verbal noun *suidiugud*, and other forms of the verb *suidigidir*, are variously used to describe Trefhuilngid's and Fintan's re-founding of Ireland's history (§20) and its internal geographical borders (§13 and 31), together with their erection of the stone symbolizing these borders (§32), and since *manor* is potentially misleading, it seems advisable to switch to this new title.

2 Above *airis*, *is* appears as a superscript.

3 Given the context, this seems to involve an allusion to Christ bearing the cross. But if so, it is a victorious bearing of the cross that is evoked, rather than one in which his victory is not yet visible, such as we would expect to find in later medieval devotion. On the image of Christ bearing the cross in later medieval art, as contrasted with earlier interpretations of this image, see Schiller 1972: 78–82.

4 *Suidiugud Tellaig Temra* seems to be unique in taking the reign of Conaing Bececlach to overlap with Christ's Passion. Notable here are the synchronisms beginning *Adam primus pater fuit*, 'Synchronisms B' in the Book of Ballymote (fol. 6r–7r, at 6v, column b, lines 10–13: see Mac Carthy 1892: 300–1) and the king-list in Recension 3 of *Lebor Gabála Érenn* (Macalister 1938–56: 5.258, para. 544). The former regards him as the contemporary of the fifth-century Persian emperors, Xerxes II, Sogdianus and Darius II; the latter similarly regards him as the contemporary of Darius II. For further references to primary sources, see Best 1910: 167 n. 15. My thanks to Erich Poppe for advising me on this.

5   Note that the verb used to describe the sun's movement past the people of Judaea here (*do-cing*), is the same as was used to Trefhuilngid's movement past the men of Ireland a little earlier.

6   *dam indile*, common as 'head of cattle'.

7   All section references to *Suidiugud Tellaig Temra* are those of Best's 1910 edition and translation.

8   Trefhuilngid also appears in the prose of *Dindshenchas Érenn*, in the section on Mag Munga (see also Ch. 27). In this context, Stokes suggested that the name Trefhuilngid means 'Upholder' (see *eDIL* s.v. *fo-loing*) and represents an alternative name for God or Christ (Stokes 1894–95: 1894.419–20). The ambiguity regarding Trefhuilngid's relative divinity is also a feature of 'The Colloquy of Fintan and the Hawk of Achill' §§72–7 (Meyer 1907: 34, see also Runge 2020). My thanks to Erich Poppe for kindly advising me on this issue.

9   *Tochmarc Ailbe*, Thurneysen 1920/1, Ní Dhonnchadha 2002b.

10 Note esp. the poem *Temair I*, lines 41–4 (Gwynn 1903–35: 1.4–5).

11 No conventional Irish title for this work currently exists. For the most recent edition and translation, see Runge 2020, comparing Meyer 1907, Hull 1932: 392ff.

12 My thanks to John Carey for kindly advising me on this.

13 Notably Orosius 2.1.4–5 and 7.2.1–16.

14 *City of God* 18.2 (Dombart and Kalb 1955: 593; Bettenson 2003: 762–5).

15 *De Archa Noe* 4.9 = 677D, lines 22–9 (Sicard 2001: 111–12; Squire 1962: 147–8); Otto of Freising, *Chronica sive historia de duabus civitatibus* 'Chronicles, or History of the Two Cities' 5 [prologue] (Mierow 2002: 322–3, sim. Lammers 2011: 227).

16 e.g. Le Goff 1988: 171; Akbari 2009: 35–6; Rubenstein 2019: 127.

17 My own contention is that Rufinus' Latin version of Eusebius' *History of the Church* (*Historia Ecclesiastica*) would most likely have played an important role in supporting such an interpretation of Orosius' account of the translation of empire, given that its triumphalism is far less subtle than that of Orosius. See Watson 2019: 195–209.

18 *Commentarii in Danielem* 3.1.2.31–40.

19 e.g. Ermoldus Nigellus, *Carmen in honorem Ludovici Christianissimi Caesaris Augusti* 4; Adso Dervenensis, *De ortu et tempore Antichristi*, lines 100–14.

20 For Wessex, see Leneghan 2015.

21 For a seminal example, see the eighth-century Latin version of Pseudo-Methodius *Revelationes* by Peter the Monk, *Sermo de regnum Gentium et in Novissimis Temporibus Certa Demonstratio*, §14.

22 While this is arguably already implicit in Eusebius' various depictions of Constantine, the earliest explicit example known to me after is found in Notker Balbulus of St Gall's *Gesta Karoli Magni Imperatoris* I.1.

23 This is present, but not emphasized, at Orosius 1.1.5, 2.2.10, and in Jerome's *Chronicle*. This emphasis comes from Augustine, *City of God* 16.17, 18.26, and passes

from him to Bede's *On the Reckoning of Time*, where they are found together at *Anno Mundi* (year since Creation) 2023 and 3423 respectively (Wallis 1999: 165, 182). See also Otto of Friesing, *Chronica* 2.15–16 (Mierow 2002: 170).

24 Similar claims by other polities include Notker Balbulus of St Gall, *Gesta Karoli Magni imperatoris* I.1. See also Lambert of Saint-Omer's *Florida*, Guibert of Nogent's *Dei Gesta* and Peter the Venerable's *In laudem sepulchri Domini*, as discussed by Rubenstein 2019: 31–5.

25 One wonders if this is meant to evoke the 'golden bough' (*aureus ramus*) of Virgil's *Aeneid*, see *Aeneid* 6.136–41, 185–8, 201–11.

26 *City of God* 16.17, 18.2.

27 As did the early modern Spain of Ferdinand and Isabella (Bartosik-Vélez 2009).

28 For the reception of the *Eclogues* in early medieval Ireland, see Miles 2011: 28–32, 45–6, esp. 155–6, incl. n.34.

30

Scéla na Esérgi 'Treatise on the Resurrection'

Elizabeth Boyle

The text is adapted from Best and Bergin 1929: 84–5, with contractions silently expanded, incorporating some readings from Stokes 1904a.

Text: An eschatological treatise

Cestnaigther dano do forcraid na foltni ⁊ a n-ingen, cía ord bias forru isind esérgi. Érnid Augustin in fer naem in cesta-sin, ⁊ is i a thomtiu, forcraid na foltni ⁊ na n-ingen con-nách intib féin nammá comthóither tháll isind esergi, acht i n-aicned in chuirp hi coitchiunn. Úair ni de fat na foltni .i. dia forcraid, acht día n-árim nammá cumniges Ísu isin t-shoscelu, in tan aithnes aní-seo día apstalaib, co n-abbair: Foltni for cind-si, ar Isu fria apstalu, atát i n-árim chinti ⁊ i n-aichnius demin icon Chomdid, ⁊ mértait ule duib-se aci thall isind esergi.

Nó dano maso intib fein nammá comthothir forcraid na foltni ⁊ na n-ingen, amail is chetfaid do fairind – ar iss ed as chosmail forcraid cech baill do thinól ⁊ do thimarcain ind féin corop isin bull-sa fein fo-gaba ciped do phéin nó do fochraic dliges tria chomchétfaid ⁊ comopred in baill sin – is ed as chretithe co n-dluthfa ⁊ co timaircfea thall in Comdiu isind esergi tria elathain di-asneti ind ecnai díadai curpu trúalnidi na n-dóeni i sémi ⁊ i fáelli ind folaid nemthrualnidi ⁊ a n-aicnid spirtállai, iarna terbud ⁊ iarna n-deligud o cech elniud, iar n-desmirecht sin ⁊ int samail inna tinni dogníter do dlúthad ⁊ timarcain tria eladain ind ecnai dóennai i sémi ⁊ i foilli a cuirp dilis iar n-díchur cech élniuda ⁊ cech slaidrid úadib.

Nó dano is tomtiu and co cruthaigfea in Comdiu andall curpu na esergi dind adbur toltanaigfes dó, cip é méit nó luget i m-bé in t-adbar sin .i. do neoch ro thirúarthestar din churp doenna isin duine ar cind báis, amail cumthaiges innossa inna curpu móra dena sílaib dereolaib ⁊ dano amail ro chumtaig thall i céttustin na n-dúl na curpu dermara den dligud nemaicside ⁊ den dligud nemchorptha ro techtsat co h-inchlithe intib na dúli dia ro tusmidea na cuirp sin.

[…]

Ar fomtin didu ⁊ ar imgabáil remshlatratad .i. demnigthea neich na dlegar do demnigud, acht is coir do bith i cumtabairt ata in brechtrad tomten-sa. Uair cidat demni ⁊ cidat falsi araile di ruinib na esergi – ar is todochaide n-airchend ind

Translation by the author

It is asked, moreover, regarding excess of hair and nails: what arrangement will there be for them in the resurrection? Augustine, the holy man, solved this question, and this is his opinion: regarding the excess of hair and nails, they will not be returned as themselves alone in the resurrection there, but into the nature of the body in general. For it is not the length of their hairs, i.e. of their excess, but their number alone that Jesus recalls in the Gospel when he commends this to the apostles, when he says: 'The hairs on your head', says Jesus to his apostles, 'are of fixed number, and in the certain knowledge of the Lord, and they will all remain for you there with Him in the resurrection'.

Or, alternatively, if the excess of hair and nails are returned only as themselves, as is the interpretation of some (for it is likely that the excess of every appendage will be collected and compacted into itself, in order that in this appendage itself one will get whatever of pain or reward is due, through the agreement and co-operation of that appendage), it is to be believed that there in the resurrection, through the ineffable art of divine intelligence, the Lord will compress and compact the corrupt bodies of the people into their rarefied and subtle incorruptible substance and spiritual essence, after removing and separating every defilement, following that example, and metaphor, of ingots which are compressed and compacted, through the art of human intelligence, into their proper rarefied and subtle mass, after every defilement and dross has been removed from them.

Or, alternatively, there is an opinion that there the Lord will shape the bodies of the resurrection from the material that will please him, whatever the magnitude or smallness of that material may be, i.e. from whatever remained of the human body in the person before death, just as he fashions now the great bodies from the lowly seeds; and, moreover, as, in the primal creation of the elements, he fashioned there the vast bodies from the invisible idea and from the incorporeal idea, which they possessed, hidden within the elements from which he generated those bodies.

[…]

For the sake of caution, then, and for the sake of avoiding premature boldness, i.e. of affirming that which it is not right to affirm, but is fittingly in doubt, there is this variety of opinion. For although some of the mysteries of the resurrection

esergi fein iar forcetul ind apstail ⁊ na screptra archena – araide atat ruini díb
indemni ⁊ anfalsi. Conid trebairiu ⁊ conid ecnaidiu a m-bith í n-dóchus ⁊ i
tomtin andás i n-demnigud tria shlatrataid.

Atresat tra na h-uli dáini thall i n-deilb ⁊ i n-écosc ecsamail .i. na fir i n-ecosc
ferda ⁊ na mná i n-ecosc banda. Uair airm i n-apair in t-apstal na ule dóeni do
esergi i fer forbthe, ainm fir dorat and-sin forsin duine coitchenn eter firu ⁊ mná.
Uair dígebthair thall a lochta ⁊ a n-anmi ar a corpaib na n- dáeni, cométfaider
immorro intib rudilse a n-delbe ⁊ a n-ecosca dílis.

are indisputable and manifest (for the resurrection itself is certain to come, according to the teaching of the apostle, and of the Scriptures besides), others of the mysteries are questionable and obscure, so that it is more secure, and wiser, that they be hoped for and thought rather than boldly affirmed.

Everyone will arise there, then, in a different form and appearance, i.e. the men with a male appearance, and the women with a female appearance, because wherever the apostle says that everyone will arise as a perfect 'man', there he has given the name 'man' to people collectively, both men and women; although their faults and blemishes will be take away from people's bodies, their inherent form and proper appearance will be preserved.

Essay: Neoplatonic theology in medieval Ireland?

Scéla na Esérgi is a Middle Irish treatise (probably composed in the eleventh century) on the general resurrection of mankind at the end of time. It survives in just one manuscript, namely *Lebor na hUidre* 'The Book of the Dun Cow' (Dublin, Royal Irish Academy, MS 23 E 25), fols 33v–35r, according to the modern foliation).[1] The text is in the hand known as 'H', the last of the three scribes to have worked on the manuscript, who was probably active at some point in the early twelfth century (on the manuscript's contents, scribes and the linguistic dating of its texts see the essays in Ó hUiginn 2015; on 'H' cf. in this volume Ch. 3, p.37). The first part of the treatise is concerned with the materiality of resurrection, and exceptional cases in particular: the disabled, stillborn babies, those whose corpses were dismembered and spread over a wide area, and so on. The text discusses the practicalities of how such people will be gathered and resurrected, as well as their appearance and age at resurrection. As such, the text participates in a tradition that was common across early Christendom, since these types of questions were crucial for understanding the mechanics of the *eschaton* – that is, the end of the world and final judgement of mankind. Although eschatological texts can (and *Scéla na Esérgi* does) engage in quite abstract theological speculation, one can also see how, in societies with high infant mortality rates, or where people may have lost limbs through warfare, such questions would have an important resonance. If someone had lost their leg in battle, would they be resurrected with the limb restored? If a baby died before baptism, would it still participate in the moment of universal judgement?

In the case of *Scéla na Esérgi*, it displays a particular debt to the thought of Augustine of Hippo (especially his *De Civitate Dei* 'The City of God' and *De Genesi ad litteram* 'Literal Commentary on Genesis'), although it also proffers alternative authoritative explanations for some problems where there is no generally accepted solution. Indeed, the way in which the author moves from topic to topic, and offers contrary interpretations from various sources, seems to suggest that he may have been working from a *florilegium* made up of excerpts of eschatological teachings, perhaps something like Julian of Toledo's seventh-century *Prognosticon futuri saeculi* 'Prophecy of the Future Age' (although there is no definitive evidence for the presence of that text, or any other specifically eschatological *florilegia*, in early medieval Ireland).

I have argued (Boyle 2009: 216–18) that *Scéla na Esérgi* had a strong preference for Neoplatonic conceptions of the eschaton and its eternal aftermath, and that even the structure of the text itself moves in a kind of Neoplatonic ascent from consideration of the material (the matter of resurrected humans) to the form (the nature of those ideal humans in heaven) to the experience of the divine. I suggested that 'the text moves from purification (in the removal of bodily imperfections that will occur at the resurrection) to illumination (in heaven) to union (with other righteous souls and ultimately with God)' (2009: 218). Thus, after its consideration of the physicality of the resurrected body, the text proceeds to consider what will happen to those resurrected bodies and their souls if, at the final judgement, they are permitted to enter heaven. How will people communicate with each other? What will it be like to exist in the presence of God?

Some of the text's indebtedness to classical and late antique conceptions of reality and the divine can be seen in its understanding of how the elect will experience God in heaven. The author offers the ubiquitous trope that the heavenly community will spend their time in praise of God, but his elaboration of this is filled with Neoplatonic terminology rendered into Middle Irish:

> Ni ó briathraib immorro nó ó gothaib corpdaib sechtair dogénat na nóim in molad-sa for Dia, acht o theorfegad spirtalla ⁊ o scrútan inmedónach a ndligid ⁊ a n-intliuchta.

> It is not through speech, however, or through corporeal, external voices that the holy will make this praise of God, but through spiritual contemplative vision, and by internal investigation of their form and their intellect (Boyle 2009: 221).

Much of the significance of *Scéla na Esérgi*, I have argued, is in this use of the vernacular to express complex Neoplatonic concepts in Irish. These include *dliged*, which is used in this text as equivalent to *ratio* in the sense of 'ontological necessity'; *folud*, used as equivalent to *substantia* 'substance'; and the compound *teorfegad*, not attested elsewhere, which is a glossing calque comprised of *teoir* (equivalent to Latin *theoria*) and *fégad* 'looking at, beholding'. Irish *teoir* is found in other texts in reference to *meditatio theorica* 'sacred contemplation', but the use in *Scéla na Esérgi* of *teorfegad* clearly indicates that the author wanted to draw out the visual sense of *theoria* as opposed to its other meanings, such as 'theory' or 'idea'. The author qualifies *teorfegad* with the adjective *spirtalla* ('spiritual'), showing that the concept he is expressing here is 'contemplative vision, one's sight being fixed on God' (Boyle 2009: 222).

The author of *Scéla na Esérgi* offers 'proofs' of the resurrection for those who may be sceptical. However, his proofs are in fact examples of the cyclical nature of the cosmos: the rising and setting of constellations; the renewal of grass and herbs each year. In this way, he links the microcosmic and the macrocosmic, and alludes to Gregory of Nyssa's view that man is 'a little world in himself [containing] all the elements which go to complete the universe' (cited in Boyle 2009: 225). If plants can be renewed each year, and if stars can continue in their cosmic cycles, then surely so can humans re-emerge from death in order to face judgement.

Although *Scéla na Esérgi* attempts to articulate the heavenly community's experience of the divine, it never seeks to articulate the divine itself. That remains ineffable. Instead, the author brings his audience directly to its antithesis. The experience of those in hell is presented as an absence of intellect, a lack of knowledge. The souls of the damned will not radiate with intellect or the illumination of understanding. The author writes of the 'dark stain (or "shadow") of their ignorance' (*temel dorchaide a n-aneólais*), explicitly contrasting the bright intellectual experience of the elect with the unlit ignorance of the damned. The final part of the text is hortatory and urges its audience to arise in repentance. It speaks of a metaphorical 'first resurrection' now – a resurrection into good Christian living, the rejection of sin and the embrace of virtue – in order to ensure admittance to heaven at the final, universal resurrection. This hortatory ending to the text, along with its opening which begins 'Let everyone keep in mind that judgement will come' (*Tabrad cách dia airi co ticfa brath*), has led some scholars to refer to *Scéla na Esérgi* as a homily. Indeed, the name 'H' was given to its scribe precisely because he was regarded as having added homilies to *Lebor na hUidre*. However, *Scéla na Esérgi* does not conform to a traditional homiletic structure, and it is perhaps best to refer to it as a 'treatise', since its intended audience and precise purpose is unclear. It is a sophisticated text, articulating highly complex ideas, and yet its composition in the vernacular broadens its potential audience beyond a highly-educated Latinate one. It is perhaps best to remain open-minded about the potential purpose(s) and audience(s) of the text. It has been noted that its themes and ideas have resonances with other literary narratives and sagas in the same manuscript (Carey 2002b; McKenna 2011) and, as a result of the scholarly and historiographically-inclined tendencies of 'H', it is possible that its function within *Lebor na hUidre* is not the same as its original intended purpose (Boyle 2015).

The extract of the text presented here is from the section on the material of the resurrected body, and it is chosen because it offers a representative example of the author's discursive and scholastic approach. The section deals with the problem of the totality of hair and nails that a person produces in a lifetime. The quantity of hair that is cut; the length of fingernails and toenails that have been trimmed – what happens to this corporeal material at the resurrection? The author begins with Augustine's solution, which is that their totality will be returned, not necessarily specifically as hair matter or nail matter, but 'into the nature of the body in general' (*i n-aicned in chuirp hi coitchiunn*). But he then offers an alternative explanation: that, since whatever of reward or punishment is due to the particular part of the body that has done good or committed sin (e.g. a hand that has killed someone should be punished in hell *as a hand*), then hair must be resurrected as hair, and nails as nails. This could be achieved, he suggests, 'through the ineffable art of divine intelligence' (*tria elathain di-asneti ind ecnai díadai*), which would have the power to 'compress and compact the corrupt bodies of the people into their rarefied and subtle incorruptible substance and spiritual essence' (*co n-dluthfa ⁊ co timarcain . . . curpu trúalnidi na n-dóeni i sémi ⁊ i fáelli ind folaid nemthrualnidi ⁊ a n-aicnid spirtállai*). With this example he uses the analogy of ingots, which can be purified 'through the art of human intelligence' (*tria eladain ind ecnai dóenni*), which is clearly being compared to – though it is lesser than – the divine intelligence mentioned above.

Our author then offers a third alternative: that it is entirely up to God how he chooses to 'shape the bodies of the resurrection from the material that will please him' (*co cruthaigfea . . . curpu na esergi dind adbur toltanaigfes dó*). This arbitrary approach, the author asserts, is in accordance with divine creation, whether microcosmic or macrocosmic:

> . . . amail cumthaiges innossa inna curpu móra dena sílaib dereolaib ⁊ dano amail ro chumtaig thall i céttustin na n-dúl na curpu dermara den dligud nemaicside ⁊ den dligud nemchorptha ro techtsat . . .

> . . . just as he fashions now the great bodies from the lowly seeds; and, moreover, as, in the primal creation of the elements, he fashioned there the vast bodies from the invisible idea and from the incorporeal idea, which they possessed . . .'

God's limitless power means that he alone can determine how the totality of hair and nails produced in a human lifetime will be resurrected. After presenting these possibilities, the author comes down on the side of caution. He suggests that there are some aspects of the eschaton that remain uncertain. Rather than asserting confidently things which are unknown, it is 'more secure, and wiser, that they be hoped for and thought rather than boldly affirmed' (*. . . trebairiu ⁊ conid ecnaidiu a m-bith í n-dóchus ⁊ i tomtin andás i n-demnigud tria shlatrataid*).

The final paragraph included here relates to gender, and the question of whether resurrected bodies will present as 'male' or 'female', or whether they will be resurrected as genderless beings. The author affirms (again following Augustine) that there will be gender differentiation between the resurrected bodies, and that when it is stated that 'man' will arise in perfect form at the final judgement, the word 'man' should be understood to refer to 'people collectively, both men and women' (*duine coitchenn eter firu ⁊ mná*). Although people's supposed 'faults' will be removed and their 'deficiencies' restored, the author is confident that, at the end of time, humankind will rise from its tombs and places of death, gendered, at the age of thirty, in the ideal 'form' of a human, without disability and without blemish, but with the ontologically necessary appearance to stand as people before their divine judge.

Scéla na Esérgi is a theologically, philosophically and linguistically important text, which would repay further study. It sits within a broader, established Christian tradition of eschatological enquiry, but its strong Neoplatonic leanings situate it particularly within a strand of Christian thought whose most obvious debt is to Augustine of Hippo but which also spins out to other major thinkers of the classical and late antique world, such as Gregory the Great and pseudo-Dionysius.

Note

1 A new complete translation is a desideratum. The best available edition and translation is Stokes 1904a, but his accompanying notes are idiosyncratic to say the least. For discussion of the context in which Stokes' edition and translation were produced – and some possible explanation for its unusual nature – see Boyle 2013.

Part Seven

Epilogue

31

Classical Reception and Medieval Irish Texts[1]

Isabelle Torrance

The medieval period, however we define it as a span of time, has tended to be seriously underrepresented in the avalanche of 'companion' volumes on the reception of classical authors and classical genres published in recent years, alongside further 'companions' to individual classical authors or works containing discussions of their reception, and guides to or studies of classical reception itself. Where the medieval period *is* discussed, there is habitually little mention of Irish sources, and none at all on the works in Middle Irish that dominate this book.[2] There are a number of reasons for the dearth of medieval material in classical reception publications. The field of Classical Reception Studies has developed, to a large extent, as a response to the increasing democratization of classical culture in the modern world, and through a rising appreciation for diverse kinds of engagements with classical culture which do not necessarily entail training in the classical languages (Hardwick 2003; Hardwick and Harrison 2013; Hardwick 2024). This kind of democratic engagement without scholarly training conspicuously fails to map on to what we know of the learned medieval experience of classical sources. Where philology and expertise in classical Latin were crucial to the production of medieval Irish versions of Graeco-Roman texts, Classical Reception Studies validates access to the classical world through translations and a variety of popular media (such as art, film, music). A presumption in contemporary scholarship of a separation or even opposition between classical pagan antiquity (which is remote from us) and faith-based Christianity (which is familiar) further obscures what can be gained by reading medieval Irish texts as case studies in classical reception. So what does it mean to discuss medieval Irish texts within the framework of a Classical Reception Series? In this short essay, I first discuss the concept of 'reception' in examining medieval Irish literature before returning to what we mean by 'classical'. In conclusion, I offer some brief observations on what these works meant for nineteenth- and twentieth-century Ireland, when the study of the texts presented in this volume began.

A recent volume, edited by Rita Copeland, the first in the monumental *Oxford History of Classical Reception in English Literature*, and a rare exception to general trends in focusing on the medieval period, may provide us with a comparative starting point for our discussion. 'To study classical reception in the English Middle Ages is to encounter the pervasive presence of the ancient past in medieval thought' (Copeland 2016b: 1). From this definition, we might extrapolate that 'classical reception' is, self-evidently, the study of how classical literature (in this case) has been 'received' by intellectuals in subsequent historical periods. At the same time, however, we might benefit from going beyond Copeland's definition to consider how 'Classical Reception Studies' as a research area tends to focus on democratic, popular, and anti-elitist engagements with the classical world. Not to be confused with the German *Rezeptionsgeschichte* 'reception history', akin to the 'classical tradition' model which places a high value on education in the classical languages for accessing classical culture (Hardwick 2003: 2–3), Classical Reception Studies offers an alternative theoretical framework for plotting tradition and continuity without necessarily requiring study of an original *Ur*-text in its original language. A playwright like Marina Carr, for example, who reworks Graeco-Roman literature in many of her dramas but has no training in Greek or Latin, reads many translations and considers numerous mediations on her subject in preparing her own texts.[3] The relationship between a new work and its classical source remains important for Classical Reception Studies, where more traditional language-based reception also continues to be a significant part of the discipline. More salient, however, than access through language are the cultural contexts that shape new works (related to the 'cultural turn' in translation studies discussed below), and the reminder that all receptions, even linguistic ones, are ultimately mediated.

In medieval Irish texts, mediation comes through commentaries, such as Servius' commentary on Virgil's *Aeneid*, through scholia/glosses and mythographic compilations (cf. Ch. 16 in this volume), and through the continuing intensely close study and extension of the information provided by late antique authors. Learnedness is a quality repeatedly accorded to the authors discussed in this book, who were highly educated and writing for educated elites, and who may have formed very small and isolated textual communities within the much broader world of the monastic *literati* and their successors in the world of Irish-language learning. As O'Connor (Ch. 2) reminds us, moreover, members of the medieval Gaelic speech-community 'saw themselves as conquering colonists', so that the 'decolonizing' potential of classical reception is not relevant in the medieval period, although, I will suggest below that it became significant, partly through medieval texts, in more recent Irish history. There is no doubt that the texts in this volume would have circulated within elite circles during periods when literacy levels were low by Early Modern and later standards, at least among the laity. At the same time, however, certain works presented here such as the *Merugud Uilixis* 'The Wandering of Ulysses', *Sgél in Mínaduir* 'The Story of the Minotaur', and even *Fingal Chlainne Tantail* 'The Kin-Slaying of the Family of Tantalus', display elements akin to those familiar from folktale genres which might imply a more supple and syncretistic approach on the part of the authors, combining lore from different areas for their own creative purposes.[4] Narratives elucidating place-names and their origins, some of them even linking Ireland with ancient Greece, such as the *dindshenchas* of Tara discussed by Theuerkauf (Ch. 28), also suggest the possibility of wider local awareness of Graeco-Roman antiquity beyond the written texts, existing in tandem with a learned literary project designed to link the Irish past to world history. In a different context (of performance), and commenting on more recent centuries, Lorna Hardwick (2024: forthcoming) reminds us that 'rigid polarization between 'popular culture' and 'elite culture' is misleading'. Although we cannot reconstitute with any certainty how well-known any of the texts within this volume would have been outside educated circles, one wonders, for instance, about medieval Irish song. Medieval Irish texts often refer to the phenomenon of public singing in secular contexts (Kelly 2021), but it remains difficult to explicate the relationship between such references and the textual reality of the written texts that survive. For example, the tenth-century heroic narrative *Cath Almaine* 'The Battle of Allen', set in the early eighth century, describes an episode where the king, Fergal mac Maíle-dúin, asks his champion Donn Bó, to provide musical entertainment (*airfited*) at the feast on the eve of battle. The latter passes on the task to the 'royal jester' or 'royal poet' (*ríg-drúth*, an ambiguous word), who obeys with a recitation of the great battles of the people of Leinster in earlier, legendary ages of their history (*Cath Almaine* 57–71, Ó Riain 1978: 5, Stokes 1903: 50–1, cf. Radner 1978: 70–1).[5] Is this a glimpse of a lived reality of traditional performance, or is the whole scene the repetition of a literary trope? If such recitation were performed or even imagined, might it have featured allusions to Greek and Roman myths, heroes, and history, in line with the poems presented in this anthology and as a precursor to these same motifs in Irish-language song of later centuries? Even if the events themselves were for the elite, these upper classes would have been served and attended by plentiful numbers of less exalted persons, who would thus also have had access to the performances.

Produced between the twelfth and seventeenth centuries, numerous 'apologues' (*apalóga*), or prose summaries of stories and exempla that appear in bardic poems, contain explanations of learned allusions, which included eulogizing comparisons between patrons and heroes from classical antiquity. Katharine Simms (2013: 140–1) notes forty-four examples of apologues based on 'tales originating in classical Greece or Rome, even where these have been mediated through English and French retellings or translations', with the earliest example dating to *c.* 1165. Building on the work of Ó Caithnia (1984: 123–35), who lists thirty-six apologues based on Greek and Latin literature from 1200 to 1650, Simms supports Ó Caithnia's conclusions that the bardic poets seem to have accessed Graeco-Roman topics primarily through the Middle Irish adaptations (Simms 2013: 141; Ó Caithnia 1984: 123, 126, 133). At the same time, however, most of the classical material in the apologues dates from the sixteenth and seventeenth centuries, when we see a surge in classical references in the exile poetry produced following the 'Flight of the Earls' in 1607 (Darwin 2024a). Cathal Ó Háinle (2015) discusses a cluster of mid-seventeenth-century apologues referencing the Roman civil war between Caesar and Pompey, also showing that the information is demonstrably derived, in several cases at least, from the Irish version of Lucan's *Civil War* (*In Cath Catharda*). The early modern apologues are thus examples of the mediated reception of Graeco-Roman literature through Middle Irish sources.

Learned allusions to Graeco-Roman mythology are also known to feature in the early seventeenth-century compilation of poems or 'lays' on the traditions of the Fianna, *Duanaire Finn* (MacNeill and Murphy 1908–53). Gregory Darwin (2024b: forthcoming) observes that later eighteenth- and nineteenth-century Irish poetry with classical references was often set to music so that although the poets were 'highly-educated *literati*, no doubt, a small minority in the Irish-speaking world, these poems had a much broader audience: in the absence of significant print culture in Irish, poetry was typically performed publicly, often set to music, and transmitted both via manuscript culture and orally'. At a time when the Gaelic aristocracy was becoming vestigial to social reality on the island, these performances must have had a significant non-elite Irish-speaking audience.

We cannot, of course, necessarily infer anything about medieval Ireland from later periods, and any oral access to classical sources cannot be retrieved. Nevertheless, it is helpful to be reminded that, even within a hierarchical society of learning, there are spaces for those without access to elite educational culture to encounter tales from Greece and Rome in oral and performance contexts. As Peadar Mac Gabhann observes in his discussion of Flann Mainistrech, the poem contains a reference to the enumeration *fíad cach slúag* 'in the presence of all peoples' at public assemblies of *flaithe na Rómán* 'the sovereigns of the Romans'. 'Is this an allusion,' wonders Mac Gabhann, 'to a similar custom of reciting the histories of the kings at public assemblies in Ireland?' (Ch. 5, p.74). If so, such recitation might have involved lists of Irish kings alongside or enmeshed with outward-looking references to non-Irish kingships. Even if, moreover, as Erich Poppe mentions (Ch. 13), prose is the preferred medium for narrative in this period of Irish textual culture, the metrical regularity of syllabic verse, both in strictly chronological poetry like that of Flann Mainistrech and Gilla Cóemáin, as well as in narrative works such as 'Jason went in his ample ship', suggests, as Michael Clarke proposes (Ch. 6), the possibility of a mnemonic function, enabling this lore to be memorized (and thus disseminated) more easily and effectively.

It is, in any case, beyond doubt that medieval Irish engagements with classical literature all bear the hallmarks of substantive cultural transformation for a contemporary Irish audience as evidenced throughout this collection. A remarkable instance of figured language from *Togail Troí* 'The Siege of Troy' (*TTr-LL* 32783–6 in Best et al.) illustrates such transformation while alluding to the jarring contrast between different grades of medieval society. Immediately prior to Hector and Achilles meeting in battle, the author underlines the heroes' awareness of the gravity of their encounter: 'they knew it would not be the teasing of little boys about playing-poles, nor that of a peasant [*athig*, gen. of *aithech*, 'rent-payer', 'peasant', *eDIL* s.v.] with his mate seeking to be spared, nor that of a loving couple about the arrangement of one side of their bed, nor that of family friends about two cups of ale...' (translation from Stokes 1881: 117).[6] If we focus too narrowly on sources and education, although these are also important, we risk missing the very vitality and cultural significance of classical antiquity reimagined in new ways.

Much nineteenth- and twentieth-century scholarship on the classical tradition has been skewed in this vein. Thus, as I have discussed elsewhere, in his extraordinarily rich survey *Ireland and the Classical Tradition*, W. B. Stanford (1976b: 87) concluded rather negatively that in Irish-language versions of classical narratives, including the medieval antiquity-sagas, 'conventional categories are broken down and new modes, *sometimes monstrous or barbaric by conventional standards*, come to birth' (emphasis added). The concept of 'conventional categories' and 'conventional standards', which must be adhered to in order to avoid 'monstrosity' or 'barbarism' is an unfortunate byproduct of the rigid 'classical tradition' approach. In Stanford's case, the language used regrettably perpetuates the crypto-colonial notion of an acceptable stylistic norm against which the Irish example is viewed as barbaric, in spite of Stanford's own efforts to push forward his view of the Irish achievement as both scholarly and creative. Ultimately the weight of the classical tradition, with all its implications, is too heavy a burden for the Irish case. The framework of Classical Reception Studies, on the other hand, frees us from the kind of constraints that assume a singular normative view of classicism and allows us to focus on the cultural processes that shape responses to classical material.[7] This collection has sought to highlight how medieval Irish authors made sense of Graeco-Roman antiquity for their audiences. All of the texts excerpted and discussed in this anthology were composed in the Irish vernacular, with *The Annals of Tigernach* incorporating Latin as well in a bilingual creation. The range and number of these works is quite simply remarkable and they deserve further scholarly attention, which we hope this collection will generate. Even within the large industry of scholarship on the medieval reception of Alexander the Great, the lengthy Irish saga on the topic, *Scéla Alaxandair*, seems to be essentially unknown, to give just one striking example (cf. Ch. 21). Including also the earliest vernacular version of the Trojan War story in Europe (cf. Ch. 6), the medieval Irish corpus is radically different from contemporary medieval literature in Middle English, for instance, where 'authors whose works express an immediate connection with classical sources are few' (Copeland 2016b: 1). And while medieval Irish was a learned and scholarly language, elitist one might argue, the very process of creating texts for an Irish audience in the Irish language generated with it remarkable cultural shifts in the representation of Graeco-Roman material, even in the case of texts that have been called 'translations' of Roman works. The Middle Irish versions of Virgil's *Aeneid*, Lucan's *Civil War*, Statius' *Thebaid* and *The History of the Destruction of Troy*, supposedly written by Dares Phrygius, are 'translations' not in the strict sense of 'faithfulness' to the text of the originals (although they are at times very close to these). Rather they are 'translations' as conceived by theorists who initiated 'the cultural turn' in translation studies, where translation 'is always doubly contextualized since the text has a position in two cultures' (Bassnett 2014: 30; cf. Bassnett and Lefèvre 1990) and where translations should 'be considered as texts in their own right as well as reflections or refractions of their sources' (Morini 2008: 37). Certain parts of these 'translations' might be called 'adaptations', where adaptation theory has tended to focus on what is changed and on the form or medium in which the new work appears (Hutcheon 2012). The Middle Irish works often expand upon the original to give additional mythological information, for example, and they are written in highly ornamented prose rather than the verse forms of Virgil, Lucan and Statius or the unadorned prose of Dares Phrygius. There is also the possibility for a 'mutually enhancing relationship between translation and adaptation' where the symbiosis of both produces a translation-as-adaptation (Hardwick 2021). The latter concept seems particularly appropriate to understanding the Middle Irish versions of the Latin works, so skillfully relocated into an Irish cultural and linguistic landscape while staying relatively close in many ways to their sources.

We have thus far been discussing 'reception' as a lens through which to examine our corpus, and we must now return to the term 'classical'. What does 'classical' mean in relation to medieval Irish texts? The term itself did not exist, and *antiqui* 'the ancients' was the generic expression used to reference classical authors. Our title *Classical Antiquity and Medieval Ireland* is a nod in this direction. Nevertheless, the concept of 'antiquity' for medieval authors and audiences was much more porous than 'classical antiquity' is for us today with its rather strict evocation of the Graeco-Roman and mostly pagan world (cf. Copeland 2016b: 3). One aim of this anthology has been to contextualize for our readers how the world of ancient Greek and Roman gods, heroes and history was entirely enmeshed for medieval Irish thinkers within a synchronistic world history, including biblical history, which was of crucial importance. Events we would consider mythological were treated in the same manner as occurrences we would deem historical. Pagan classical literature and Christian literature did not operate on separate planes. The extraordinary influence of the late antique Christian authorities Orosius, Eusebius-Jerome, and Isidore of Seville on medieval Irish synchronism and on points of information relating to pagan Graeco-Roman antiquity has been made abundantly clear throughout this volume and they appear in almost every chapter. Much of what we see in Irish sources concerns an attempt to place Ireland as a central force on the international stage of ancient cultures. The earliest example of this is the description of the formation of the Irish language, discussed by Engesland (Ch. 23), where the superlative status of Irish potentially extends to putting it on a par with Greek, Latin and Hebrew, the three sacred languages. Most remarkable, however, is the much later tale of *How Samson Slew the Gesteda*, which places the biblical Samson *en route* to Troy in a narrative that casts him very closely as a Hercules figure (Ch. 17). We see here just how deeply interconnected with the biblical past Graeco-Roman antiquity was for medieval Irish authors. Samson is associated with the Trojan War and imagined on an adventure that echoes Hercules' experiences with Busiris in Egypt. 'Classical antiquity' in relation to medieval Ireland, then, describes a fusion of mythography and history alongside a deep connection between classical and Christian learning.

As observed above, we have very limited insight, unfortunately, into the wider reception of our texts within the medieval period. We do know that some became extremely popular. *Lebor Gabála Erenn* 'The Book of Invasions of Ireland', arguably *the* foundational text of Irish historiography, which contains much classical material, was, as John Carey observes 'a work of enormous popularity and influence' existing 'in a multitude of copies from the 12th to the 18th centuries' which inspired 'innumerable poets, historians and others' (Ch. 26, p. 340; see also Blanco Ríos 2024). Moving forward further into the nineteenth and early twentieth centuries, scholarly and popular interest in medieval Irish texts gained significant momentum during the period of the Irish Revival when many of the texts presented in this volume were being edited and translated. The names George Calder, Whitley Stokes and Kuno Meyer have all appeared many times within these pages. This 'rediscovery' of the medieval Irish classical material, along with new channels of accessibility through translations, generated a new wave of reception in a profoundly political climate. Although the Revivalists were interested above all in works that would enable the reconstruction of a purely indigenous tradition looking back to a Celtic past with its own authentic mythology, our collection has shown that the separation of Celtic and classical is artificial for the medieval period. Moreover, the classically-inflected Irish texts were proof of a deeply embedded ownership of Graeco-Roman antiquity at a time when Ireland was still part of an empire in which classical education was an imperial tool (cf. Goff 2005; Bradley 2010; Vasunia 2013: 193–238; Kiberd 2020). Notably, the Fir Bolg, the mysterious ancestral race said to have come to Ireland from Greece who appear in *Lebor Gabála Erenn* and elsewhere (e.g. in Gilla Cóemáin's poem of historical synchronisms quoted in Ch. 4), were co-opted in various ways within revivalist debates on identity politics as discussed by Arabella Currie (2020). The monumental forts on the Aran Islands reputedly built by the Fir Bolg encouraged comparisons to the archaeology of the Graeco-Roman past in the decades following the remarkable discovery of the site of ancient Troy in the 1870s. At the same time, the Fir Bolg could become enshrined in an atemporal primitivism associated with island life and island writing, as a kind unspoiled '*Ur*-culture'. Irish historian and politician Eoin Mac Néill rejected as colonialist those readings of the Fir Bolg in which they were abject and downtrodden; John Millington Synge, on the other hand, resisted their atemporality in an apparently deliberate evasion. His unpublished notes and drafts contain numerous musings on the Fir Bolg, while his published works bear virtually no trace of them. In another example, Edith Hall has identified Kuno Meyer as a figure parodied in the 'Cyclops' episode of James Joyce's *Ulysses*, arguing that Joyce cannot have failed to have been influenced by Meyer's 1886 translation of *Merugud Uilixis* which Meyer entitled 'The Irish Odyssey' (Hall 2020: 206–16).[8]

In the years after the publication of *Ulysses* and the creation of the Irish Free State, Greek and Latin literature was being translated into the Irish language as part of a government scheme to expand the availability of works of world literature for Irish readers (see Ní Mhurchú 2020). A bitter debate would develop, however, concerning the value of such translations as pitted against the value of 'original' Gaelic literature championed by 'nativists'. Nativists, led by Daniel Corkery, would win the public debate against progressives, essentially halting the work of important figures like Pádraig de Brún (Kiberd 2020: 38–41; Ní Mhurchú 2020: 89). Several decades later, the developing conflict in Northern Ireland would generate a whole new wave of classical reception in Ireland and it is perhaps telling that Ireland is the case study for the cultural politics of translation in Lorna Hardwick's study of translation and classical reception (Hardwick 2000: 79–95). In the early twentieth century, however, nativists such as Daniel Corkery were arguing, as Kiberd summarizes, that 'the only viable models must be from within a national tradition', even if, as Kiberd argues, 'refusal of any meaningful comparison between literatures leaves each one helplessly marooned within its own space, submitting a literature only to a local franchise' (Kiberd 2020: 40–1).

One deep irony, of course, in the furious clash over appropriate literature, was the fact that, as this volume has shown, so much indigenous medieval Gaelic literature is indebted to and influenced by the authors of classical antiquity.[9] That point was not lost on the mid-twentieth-century modernist author Flann O'Brien (Brian O'Nolan), who brought the issue to an extraordinarily wide readership through his humorously pointed 'Cruiskeen Lawn' columns, which he published several days a week in *The Irish Times* under the pseudonym Myles na gCopaleen for twenty-six years from 1940 until his death in 1966. In these columns, as Cillian O'Hogan has shown, 'Myles' uses English, Irish, Greek and Latin, sometimes critiquing Greek and Latin to the advantage of Irish. This makes essentially the same point, in accessible form, as the densely grammatical arguments of 'The Scholars' Primer', the earliest text in our volume. In a public arena, 'Myles' consistently references classical and medieval culture, code-switching between Latin and Irish, and often taking on the persona of a medieval scribe. He consistently downplays the English language to suggest that Irish, Greek and Latin are intrinsically connected European cousins (O'Hogan 2020). In their longevity, popularity and reach, the *Cruiskeen Lawn* columns are a modern testament to the importance of medieval texts for classical reception in Ireland.

Notes

1   I am indebted to the generosity of Michael Clarke, Erich Poppe and Ralph O'Connor for their expert feedback and suggested improvements on earlier drafts of this chapter.

2   For the Western or Latin Middle Ages, direct acquaintance with pre-Christian Greek authors was minimal. In contrast, a varied curriculum of classical Latin authors was studied and in many cases rendered into the vernacular languages. These included, as identified by Copeland 2016b: 4, 18–19n.9: Virgil's *Aeneid*; Lucan's *Civil War*; Statius' *Thebaid*; Ovid's *Heroides, Ars Amatoria* and *Metamorphoses*; the histories of Sallust; Caesar's *On the Gallic War*; the *Lives* of Suetonius; sections of Livy's history of ancient Rome *Ab urbe condita* (*From the founding of the city*); Quintus Curtius' *Histories of Alexander the Great*; Vegetius' *Epitome of Military Science*; the collection of historical anecdotes preserved in the work of Valerius Maximus; Cicero's *On Friendship, On Old Age, On Invention* (a handbook on oratory) and the *Rhetoric for Herennius* attributed to Cicero; Seneca's *Moralia*. As we have seen in this volume, Virgil's *Aeneid*, Lucan's *Civil War*, and Statius' *Thebaid* are direct inspirations for medieval Irish vernacular works (see Chs 11, 13, 14, 15, 16), and sources for the life of Alexander the Great have also been discussed (Ch. 21). Another crucial prose text is the Second-Sophistic style *History of the Destruction of Troy*, supposedly by Dares Phrygius (see Chs 6–10 in this volume); Clark (2020: 77–168) discusses its influence on medieval Europe without more than the briefest mention of Ireland.

3   Carr's *Phaedra Backwards*, for instance, was inspired by an extraordinary range of classical and contemporary literature and art; see Torrance 2022: 231–4 with n.5, 242.

4   See Chs 18 and 20, and note Motif K2111 'Potiphar's Wife' in Ch. 19.

5   I am grateful to Michael Clarke for suggesting this example.

6   I am grateful to Mariamne Briggs for bringing this passage to my attention.

7   The discussion of Stanford is taken from Torrance and O'Rourke 2020: 16.

8   Stanford (1970: 35) comments that the *Merugud* 'anticipates the freedom of treatment that is to be found in James Joyce's *Ulysses*'.

9   As O'Connor mentions at the beginning of this book (Ch. 2, p.15), this opposition has a reflex within the discipline of Celtic Studies, where since the 1980s the terms

'nativist' and 'revisionist' have been customized for the purposes of a debate, often urgent and polemical, about the essential character of medieval Irish literature (McCone 1990 remains the foundational 'revisionist' manifesto). The texts gathered in this volume, and their interpretation, may have parts to play in the ongoing resolution of that debate – but a full discussion lies beyond the scope of the present book.

Table of the Principal Manuscript Sources for the Texts Excerpted in the Anthology[1]

Michael Clarke

Manuscript	Date	Texts excerpted here	Chapter
Dublin, Royal Irish Academy MS 23 E 25, *Lebor na hUidre*, The Book of the Dun Cow	*c.* 1100	*Scéla na Esérgi*	30
Oxford, Bodleian Library MS Rawlinson B502, first part (= fols 1–12)[2]	*c.* 1110	*Annals of Tigernach*, First Fragment	3
Dublin, Trinity College MS 1339, *Lebor na Nuachongbála*, 'The Book of Leinster'[3]	*c.* 1160	*Annálad anall uile* *Togail Troí* Rec. 2 *Cogadh Gáedhel re Gallaibh* (fragmentary) *Dindshenchas* poem: *Boand I* *Dindshenchas* poem: *Temair II*	4 8 25 27 28
Dublin, Royal Irish Academy MS D.ii.1, The Book of Uí Mhaine	*c.* 1400	*Annálad anall uile* *Flaithius Rómán ríge glonn* *Auraicept na nÉces* *Clann Ollaman uaisle Emna* *Dindshenchas* poem: *Boand I*	4 5 23 24 27
Dublin, Royal Irish Academy MS 23 P 2, The (Great) Book of Lecan[4]	*c.* 1410	*Flaithius Rómán ríge glonn* (two copies) *Auraicept na nÉces* *Lebor Gabála* tract on the kin of Nemed	5 23 26
Oxford, Bodleian Library MS Rawlinson B512	*c.* 1500	*Annálad anall uile*	4
Dublin, Royal Irish Academy MS D.iv.3	*c.* 1540?	*Flaithius Rómán ríge glonn*	5
Edinburgh, National Library of Scotland MS 72.i.19	*c.* 1400?	*Luid Iasón ina luing lóir*	6
Dublin, Trinity College MS 1319 (composite MS)[5]	*c.* 1400?	*Togail Troí* Rec. 1 *Cogadh Gáedhel re Gallaibh*	7 25

Manuscript	Date	Text	
Dublin, Royal Irish Academy MS D.iv.2, The Book of Kilcormac	c. 1450?	Togail Troí Rec. 3	9
		Don Tres Troí	10
		Riss in Mundtuirc	12
		In Cath Catharda	14–16
		How Samson Slew the Gesteda	17
		Merugud Uilixis	18
		Fingal Chlainne Tanntail	19
		Sgél in Mínaduir	20
Dublin, King's Inns MS 12 + 13[6]	c. 1490	Togail Troí Rec. 3	9
		Don Tres Troí	10
		Imtheachta Aeniasa	13
		Merugud Uilixis	18
		Fingal Chlainne Tanntail	19
London, British Library MS Egerton 1781	c. 1485	Togail na Tebe	11
Edinburgh, National Library of Scotland MS 72.i.8[7]	c. 1400?	Togail na Tebe	11
		Togail Troí Rec. 3 (shortened)	9
Dublin, Royal Irish Academy MS 23 P 12, The Book of Ballymote	c. 1390	Togail Troí Rec. 2/3	8, 9
		Imtheachta Aeniasa	13
		Merugud Uilixis	18
		Scéla Alaxandair	21
		Auraicept na nÉces	23
		Clann Ollaman uaisle Emna	24
		Dindshenchas poem: Boand I	27
		Dindshenchas poem: Temair II	28
Dublin, Trinity College MS 1298[8]	c. 1490	Stair Ercuil ocus a bás	22
		In Cath Catharda	14–16
		Togail na Tebe	11
Dublin, Trinity College MS 1318, The Yellow Book of Lecan, section 16[9]	1391–92	Auraicept na nÉces	23
		Suidiugud Tellaig Temra	29

Notes

1 Manuscripts are included in this table only if they have been used by our contributors as a source for at least one of the texts studied in this volume.

2 The main body of MS Rawlinson B502 (from folio 13 onward) was originally a distinct manuscript of similar or slightly later date.

3 The name is customary, but it is generally regarded as unhistorical when applied to this manuscript.

4 The Book of Lecan proper is often called the *Great* Book of Lecan to distinguish it from the *Yellow* Book of Lecan.

5 This manuscript is made up of many fragments bound together in modern times. Our two texts are separate in origin.

6 A single manuscript was divided into two parts in modern times.

7 It is not clear how early these copies of the two sagas were bound together as one.

8 Another composite manuscript combining parts of separate origins (Briggs 2018: 53–5). See also above, Ch. 1: 10–11.

9 See Ó Corráin 2017: 2.1078–80 for the section divisions in this composite manuscript. Once again, our two texts are separate in origin.

Bibliography

A Note on Finding the Medieval Irish Sources

For tracing the sources and publication history of any Irish text, up-to-date bibliographical guides can be found on the CODECS database of the A.G. van Hamel Foundation for Celtic Studies (https://codecs.vanhamel.nl/Home), and the Bibliography of Irish Linguistics and Literature project of the Dublin Institute for Advanced Studies (https://bill.celt.dias.ie/). Ó Corráin 2017 has exhaustive listings of publications up to about 2016, and includes valuable brief commentary by the compiler.

For an up-to-date survey of Old and Middle Irish literature, see Ní Mhaonaigh 2006a. For mythological narratives concerned with the past of Ireland itself, Carey's survey treatment (2018) is an excellent starting-point: see also Williams 2015. Many of the principal texts of this kind are available in good translations in Gantz 1981 and Koch and Carey 2003. Explicitly Christian material, including speculative theology, is gathered in authoritative translations in Carey 2002a, and in parallel-text format in Carey et al. 2014.

For the earliest surviving remains in the Old Irish language, mostly glosses to Latin works, the essential reference source remains Stokes and Strachan 1901–03, with facing translations. For *Táin Bó Cúailnge*, the authoritative editions are those of Recension 1 in O'Rahilly 1976a, and of the Book of Leinster version in O'Rahilly 1967. The many recent translations available (e.g. Carson 2008) should always be compared closely with O'Rahilly. For going further into the literature, the best starting-point will be the Irish Texts Society's series of editions with facing translations (see https://irishtextssociety.org/publications.htm), and the continuing series of editions published by the Dublin Institute for Advanced Studies.

For less widely-known Irish texts, including most of those gathered in this volume, we very often rely on editions published over a century ago, many of them in such journals as *Revue Celtique*, *Ériu*, and *Zeitschrift für celtische Philologie*, or in the monumental collection *Irische Texte* (Stokes and Windisch 1880–1909) and the Todd Lecture Series of the Royal Irish Academy. Where the passage of time means that such sources are out of copyright, they are nearly always available from scanned copies of the original printed volumes, freely available from Internet Archive (https://archive.org/). The Celtic Digital Initiative database (https://www.ucc.ie/en/smg/cdi/), from University College Cork, is often invaluable for locating such items in the Internet Archive, and offers other resources as well.

More even than in other branches of philology, the vital step in this field is to focus on the physical reality of the manuscripts. The available and projected volumes in the *Codices*

Hibernenses Eximii series (e.g. Ó hUiginn 2015, 2018a) provide invaluable aid here. More generally, the increasing availability of digitized images of the manuscripts is revolutionizing the field. Many are available from the websites of the individual libraries and from national repositories on the Continent. However, the principal resource for manuscripts held in Ireland itself, alongside a selection of those held abroad, is the Irish Script on Screen repository managed by the Dublin Institute for Advanced Studies (https://www.isos.dias.ie/). This resource, in tandem with the regularly updated resources of *eDIL*, creates unending opportunities for engaging with this challenging literature.

Referencing System for the Principal Greek and Latin Texts

Aeschylus	Sommerstein 2008
Apollodorus, *Library of Greek Mythology*	Frazer 1921
Augustine, *City of God*	Dombart and Kalb 1955, tr. Bettenson 2003
Bede, *De Temporibus/On Times*	Jones 1975–80. 3: 579–611, tr. Kendall and Wallis 2010
Bede, *De Temporum Ratione/On the Reckoning of Time*	Jones 1975–80. 2, tr. Wallis 1999
Bede, *Chronica maiora*	Jones 1975–80.2: 461–544, tr. Wallis 1999: 157–239
Brevis Expositio on Virgil's *Georgics*	Thilo and Hagen 1881–1902: 3.191–320
Dares Phrygius, *De Excidio Troiae/ History of the Destruction of Troy*	Meister 1873; tr. Frazer 1966, Lelli 2016
Diodorus Siculus, *Library of History*	Oldfather 1933–1967
Euripides	Kovacs 1994–2008
Eusebius-Jerome, *Chronicle*	Schöne 1900, Helm 1913
Excidium Troie	Bate 1986
Explanatio in Bocolica on Virgil's *Eclogues*	Thilo and Hagen 1881–1902: 3.1–189
Homer, *Iliad* and *Odyssey*	Murray 1919–1925
Hyginus, *Fabulae*	Marshall 2002, tr. Smith and Trzaskoma 2007
Isidore, *Etymologies*	Lindsay 1911, tr. Barney et al. 2006
Isidore, *Chronica maiora*	Mommsen 1894
Lactantius Placidus, *Commentaries on Statius*	Jahnke 1898, Sweeney 1987

Lucan, *De Bello Civili/Civil War/Pharsalia*	Duff 1928
Orosius, *Historiae adversus Paganos/Histories against the Pagans*	Arnaud-Lindet 1990–91, tr. Fear 2010
Ovid, *Fasti*	Frazer and Goold 1989
Ovid, *Metamorphoses*	Miller 1977–84
Scholia Bernensia on Virgil	Hagen 1867
Servius, Commentaries on Virgil	Thilo and Hagen 1881–1902, vols 1–2, 3.2
Sophocles	Lloyd-Jones 1994–96
Seneca, tragedies of	Fitch 2002–04
Statius, *Achilleid* and *Thebaid*	Shackleton Bailey 2003
Varro, *De Lingua Latina/On the Latin Language*	Kent 1951
Vatican Mythographers, First and Second	Kulcsár 1987, tr. Pepin 2008
Virgil, *Eclogues, Georgics, Aeneid*	Fairclough 1999–2000

Abbreviations Used

AAbr	Year since the birth of Abraham
AM	*Anno Mundi*, year since Creation
ATU	Aarne-Thompson-Uther classification of folktales: see Uther 2004
BB	The Book of Ballymote: Dublin, Royal Irish Academy MS 23 P 12
Aen.	Virgil, *Aeneid*
ATig	*Annals of Tigernach*, first fragment (in Oxford, Bodleian Library MS Rawlinson B502): Stokes 1895
CCath	*In Cath Catharda*: Stokes 1909
CGreG	*Cogadh Gaedhel re Gallaibh*: Todd 1867
eDIL	*Electronic Dictionary of the Irish Language*, based on the *Contributions to a Dictionary of the Irish Language* (Dublin: Royal Irish Academy, 1913–76) (www.dil.ie 2019). Last accessed for this volume on 1 May 2023
fol.	folio
GL	*Grammatici Latini*: Keil 1855–80
IA	*Imtheachta Aeniasa*: Calder 1907

LGÉ	*Lebor Gabála Érenn*, 'The Book of Invasions of Ireland': Macalister 1938–56
LL	The 'Book of Leinster': Dublin, TCD MS 1339: Best et al. 1954–83
LU	*Lebor na hUidre*, The Book of the Dun Cow: Dublin, Royal Irish Academy MS 23 E 5: Best and Bergin 1929
MS	manuscript
MVI, MVII	The First and Second Vatican Mythographers: Kulcsár 1987, Pepin 2008
PL	J.-P. Migne (ed.), *Patrologiae cursus completus, series Latina*, 217 vols, Paris (usually known as *Patrologia Latina*)
RIA	Royal Irish Academy
TBC 1	*Táin Bó Cúailnge Recension I*: O'Rahilly 1976a
TBC-LL	*Táin Bó Cúalnge from the Book of Leinster*: O'Rahilly 1967
TCD	Trinity College Dublin
TTeb	*Togail na Tebe*: Calder 1922
TTr-H	*Togail Troí* Recension 1 from Dublin, TCD MS 1319 (formerly H.2.17): Stokes 1884
TTr-LL	*Togail Troí* from the Book of Leinster: Best et al. 1954–83, 1063–1117; Stokes 1881
TTr Rec. 3	*Togail Troí* Recension 3: Ó hAodha 1979, Clarke 2014a

References List

Aeschbach, Marc (1987), *Raoul Lefèvre: Le Recoeil des Histoires de Troyes*, Frankfurt: Peter Lang.

Ahl, Frederick (1989), 'Uilix Mac Leirtis: the Classical Hero in Irish Metamorphosis', in Rosanna Warren (ed.), *The Art of Translation: Voices from the Field*, 173–98. Boston: Northeastern University Press.

Ahlqvist, A. (1983), *The Early Irish Linguist: An Edition of the Canonical Part of the Auraicept na nÉces*, Commentationes Humanarum Litterarum 73, Helsinki.

Akbari, Suzanne Conklin (2009), *Idols in the East: European Representations of Islam and the Orient, 1100–1450*, Ithaca: Cornell University Press.

Anderson, Harald (Revised edition, 2009), *The Manuscripts of Statius*, 3 vols, Arlington, Virginia: Harald Anderson.

Anderson, O. O. (1909), 'Ranna an Aeir', *Revue Celtique*, 30: 404–17.

Arbuthnot, Sharon (2007), *Cóir Anmann: A Late Middle Irish Treatise on Personal Names*, 2 vols, Irish Texts Society Vols 59–60, London: Irish Texts Society.

Arbuthnot, Sharon, Pádraig Moran, and Paul Russell (2016), *Early Irish Glossaries Database*, Department of Anglo-Saxon, Norse and Celtic, Cambridge, available online at https://www.asnc.cam.ac.uk/irishglossaries/texts.php?versionID=9&readingID=18213#18213. Last consulted for this volume November 2022.

Arnaud-Lindet, Marie-Pierre (1990–1), *Orose, Histoires contre les païens*, 3 vols, Paris: Les Belles Lettres.

Bampi, Massimiliano (2017), 'Translating and Rewriting in the Middle Ages: a Philological Approach', in Harry Lönnroth (ed.), *Philology Matters! Essays on the Art of Reading Slowly*, 164–81, Leiden: Brill.

Bampi, Massimiliano (2022), 'The Cultural and Ideological Function of Charlemagne', in Helen Fulton and Sif Rikhardsdottir (eds), *Charlemagne in the Norse and Celtic Worlds*, 31–49, Cambridge: Boydell & Brewer.

Bantinaki, Katerina (2020), 'The Literary Translator as Author: a Philosophical Assessment of the Idea', *Translation Studies*, 13: 306–17.

Barney, Stephen, W. J. Lewis, J. A. Beach and Oliver Berghof (2006), *The* Etymologies *of Isidore of Seville*, Cambridge: Cambridge University Press.

Bartlett, Robert (2020), *Blood Royal: Dynastic Politics in Medieval Europe*, Cambridge: Cambridge University Press.

Bartosik-Vélez, Elise (2009), '*Translatio imperii*: Virgil and Peter Martyr's Columbus', *Comparative Literature Studies*, 46.4: 559–88.

Bassnett, Susan (2014), *Translation*, Abingdon: Routledge.

Bassnett, Susan and Lefevre, Andre (1990) (eds), *Translation, History and Culture*, London: Pinter Publishers.

Baswell, Christopher (1995), *Virgil in Medieval England: Figuring the Aeneid from the Twelfth Century to Chaucer*, Cambridge: Cambridge University Press.

Bate, Alan Keith (1986), *Excidium Troie*, Frankfurt: Peter Lang.

Bately, Janet (1961), 'King Alfred and the Latin MSS. of Orosius' History', *Classica et Mediaevaliai*, 22: 69–105.

Bately, Janet (1980), *The Old English Orosius*, Early English Texts Society, supplementary series, 6, Oxford: Oxford University Press.

Battles, Dominique (2004), *The Medieval Tradition of Thebes: History and Narrative in the Old French Roman de Thèbes, Boccaccio, Chaucer, and Lydgate*, New York: Routledge.

Bergin, Osborn J. (1913), 'A Poem by Godfraidh Fionn Ó Dálaigh', in *Essays and Studies Presented to Sir William Ridgeway*, 323–32, Cambridge: Cambridge University Press.

Bergin, Osborn J. (1923), Review of George Calder, *Togail na Tebe: The Thebaid of Statius, the Irish Text, Studies: An Irish Quarterly Review*, 12.46: 320–2.

Bernard, J. H. and Atkinson, Robert (1898–1902), *The Irish Liber Hymnorum*, 2 vols, London.

Berschin, Walter (1980), *Griechisch-lateinisches Mittelalter: Von Hieronymus zu Nikolaus von Kues*, Bern: Francke.

Best, Richard Irvine (1910), 'The Settling of the Manor of Tara', *Ériu*, 4: 121–72.

Best, Richard Irvine (1914), 'Palaeographical notes I. The Rawlinson B 502 Tigernach', *Ériu*, 7: 114–20.

Best, Richard Irvine and Osborn J. Bergin (1929), *Lebor na hUidre: The Book of the Dun Cow*, Dublin: Royal Irish Academy.

Best, Richard Irvine, Osborn J. Bergin, M. A. O'Brien and Anne O'Sullivan (1954–83), *The Book of Leinster, formerly Leabhar na Nuachongbála*, 6 vols, Dublin: Dublin Institute for Advanced Studies.

Bettenson, Henry (2003), *St Augustine: Concerning the City of God against the Pagans*, 3rd edition, London: Penguin.

Bieler, Ludwig (1979), *The Patrician Texts in the Book of Armagh*, Scriptores Latini Hiberniae 10, Dublin: Dublin Institute for Advanced Studies.

Binchy, D. A. (1938), '*Bretha Crólige*', *Ériu*, 12: 1–77.

Binchy, D. A. (1978), *Corpus Iuris Hibernici*, 6 vols, Dublin: Dublin Institute for Advanced Studies.

Bischoff, Bernhard (1990), *Latin Paleography: Antiquity and the Middle Ages*, translated by Dáibhí Ó Cróinín and David Ganz, Cambridge: Cambridge University Press.

Blanco Ríos, Paula (2024, forthcoming), 'Late Antique Historiography and the Irish Migrations in *Lebor Gabála Érenn* (*Book of Invasions*)', in Isabelle Torrance (ed.), *Irish Migrations and Classical Antiquity*, London: Bloomsbury.

Boer, W. Walther (1973), *Epistola Alexandri ad Aristotelem*, Meisenheim am Glan: Hain.

Bondarenko, Grigory (2012), 'Fintan mac Bóchra: Irish Synthetic History Revisited', in Maxim Fomin, Václav Blažek and Piotr Stalmaszczyk (eds), *Transforming Traditions, Studies in Archaeology, Comparative Linguistics and Narrative: Proceedings of the Fifth International Colloquium of Societas Celto-Slavica, held at Příbram, 26–29 July 2010*, 129–47, Łódź: Łódź University Press.

Borsje, Jacqueline (1999), 'Omens, Ordeals and Oracles: on Demons and Weapons in Early Irish Texts', *Peritia*, 13: 224–48.

Boyle, Elizabeth (2009), 'Neoplatonic Thought in Medieval Ireland: The Evidence of *Scéla na esérgi*', *Medium Ævum*, 78: 216–30.

Boyle, Elizabeth (2013), 'Resurrection: The Study of Medieval Irish Eschatology in the Nineteenth Century', in P. Lyons, W. Maley and J. Miller (eds), *Romantic Ireland From Tone to Gonne: Fresh Perspectives on Nineteenth-Century Ireland*, 52–63, Newcastle: Cambridge Scholars Press.

Boyle, Elizabeth (2014), 'On the Wonders of Ireland: Translation and Adaptation', in Elizabeth Boyle and Deborah Hayden (eds), *Authorities and Adaptations: The Reworking and Transmission of Textual Sources in Medieval Ireland*, 233–61, Dublin: Dublin Institute for Advanced Studies.

Boyle, Elizabeth (2015), 'Eschatological Themes in *Lebor na hUidre*', in Rúairí Ó hUiginn (ed.), *Lebor na hUidre*, Codices Hibernenses Eximii I, 115–30, Dublin: Royal Irish Academy.

Boyle, Elizabeth (2021), *History and Salvation in Medieval Ireland*, Studies in Early Medieval Britain and Ireland, London: Routledge.

Boyle, Elizabeth and Deborah Hayden (2014) (eds), *Authorities and Adaptations: The Reworking and Transmission of Textual Sources in Medieval Ireland*, Dublin: Dublin Institute for Advanced Studies.

Bradley, Mark (2010) (ed.), *Classics and Imperialism in the British Empire*, Oxford: Oxford University Press.

Breathnach, Séamus (1952), Togail Troí *curtha in eagar as B.B.*, MA diss., University College Galway.

Breatnach, Liam (1987), *Uraicecht na Ríar: The Poetic Grades in Early Irish Law*, Early Irish Law Series 2, Dublin: Dublin Institute for Advanced Studies.

Breatnach, Liam (1994), 'An Mheán-Ghaeilge', in Kim McCone, Damian MacManus, Cathal Ó Háinle, Nicholas Williams and Liam Breatnach (eds), *Stair na Gaeilge*, 221–334. Maynooth: Roinn na Sean-Ghaeilge, Coláiste Phádraig.

Breatnach, Liam (2005), *A Companion to the Corpus Iuris Hibernici*, Early Irish Law Series 5, Dublin: Dublin Institute for Advanced Studies.

Briggs, Mariamne (2018), *The Middle Irish Translation of Statius's Thebaid: A Study in Reception*, PhD diss., University of Edinburgh. Available online at http://hdl.handle.net/1842/35733.

Briggs, Mariamne (2019), 'Removing the Muses: Responses to Statian Subjectivity in the Middle Irish *Thebaid*', in Aisling Byrne and Victoria Flood (eds), *Crossing Borders in the Insular Middle Ages*, 179–202, Turnhout: Brepols.

Briggs, Mariamne (2024), 'What's in a Tale Title? *Togail na Tebe* as an Editorial Construction', *Studia Hibernica* 50, forthcoming.

Brown, Virginia (1976), 'Gaius Julius Caesar', in F. Edward Cranz and Paul Oskar Kristeller (eds), *Catalogus Translationum et commentariorum: Medieval and Renaissance Latin Translations and Commentaries*, vol. 3, 87–139, Washington, DC: Catholic University of America Press.

Bruggisser, Philippe (2002), 'Clin d'œil latin: *Latiaris* avant, chez et après Symmaque', in Jean-Michel Carrié and Rita Lizzi Testa (eds), *Humana sapit: Études d'Antiquité Tardive offertes à Lellia Cracco Ruggini*, 97–110, Turnhout: Brepols.

Burgess, Glyn and Douglas N. Kelly (2017), *The Roman de Troie by Benoît de Sainte-Maure*, Cambridge: Brewer.

Burgess, R.W. (2002), 'Jerome Explained: an Introduction to his *Chronicle* and a Guide to its Use', *Ancient History Bulletin*, 16: 1–32.

Burgess, R.W. and M. Kulikowski (2013), *Mosaics of Time: The Latin Chronicle Tradition from the First Century BC to the Sixth Century AD, Volume 1: A Historical Introduction to the Chronicle Genre from its Origins to the High Middle Ages*, Turnhout: Brepols.

Burnyeat, Abigail (2013), 'The *Táin*-complex in MS Egerton 1782', in Gregory Toner and Séamus Mac Mathúna (eds), *Ulidia III: Proceedings of the Third International Conference on the Ulster Cycle of Tales*, 287–97, Berlin: Curach Bhán.

Busby, Keith (2017), *French in Medieval Ireland, Ireland in Medieval French: The Paradox of Two Worlds*, Medieval Texts and Cultures of Northern Europe 27, Turnhout: Brepols.

Byrne, Aisling (2013), 'The Earls of Kildare and their Books at the End of the Middle Ages', *The Library* 14.2: 129–53.

Byrne, Aisling (2016), 'Cultural Intersections in Trinity College Dublin MS 1298', in Axel Harlos and Neele Harlos (eds), *Adapting Texts and Styles in a Celtic Context, Interdisiplinary Perspectives on Processes of Literary Transfer in the Middle Ages: Studies in Honour of Erich Poppe*, Studien und Texte zur Keltologie 13, 289–304, Münster: Nodus.

Byrne, Aisling and Victoria Flood (2019) (eds), *Crossing Borders in the Insular Middle Ages*, Medieval Texts and Cultures of Northern Europe 30, Turnhout: Brepols.

Byrne, Francis John (1964), '*Clann Ollaman uaisle Emna*', *Studia Hibernica*, 4: 54–94.

Byrne, Francis John (1973), *Irish Kings and High-Kings*, London: Batsford.

Byrne, Mary E. (1927), 'The Parricides of the Children of Tantalus', *Revue Celtique*, 44: 14–33.

Calder, George (1907), *Imtheachta Aeniasa: The Irish Aeneid*, Irish Texts Society Vol. 6, London: Irish Texts Society.

Calder, George (1917), *Auraicept na nÉces: The Scholars' Primer*, Edinburgh: John Grant.

Calder, George (1922), *Togail na Tebe: The Thebaid of Statius, the Irish Text*, Cambridge: Cambridge University Press.

Carey, John (1984), 'Scél Tuáin meic Chairill', *Ériu*, 35: 93–111.

Carey, John (1990), 'The Ancestry of Fénius Farsaid', *Celtica*, 21: 104–12.

Carey, John (1994a), 'An Edition of the Pseudo-Historical Prologue to the *Senchas Már*', *Ériu*, 45: 1–32.

Carey, John (1994b), *The Irish National Origin-Legend: Synthetic Pseudo-History*, Quiggin Memorial Lecture 1, Cambridge: Department of Anglo-Saxon, Norse and Celtic.

Carey, John (1999), *A Single Ray of the Sun: Religious Speculation in Early Ireland, Three Essays*, Aberystwyth: Celtic Studies Publications.

Carey, John (2002a), *King of Mysteries: Early Irish Religious Writings*, revised edition, Dublin: Four Courts Press.

Carey, John (2002b), 'Werewolves in Medieval Ireland', *Cambrian Medieval Celtic Studies*, 44: 37–72.

Carey, John (2005), '*Lebor Gabála* and the Legendary History of Ireland', in Helen Fulton (ed.), *Medieval Celtic Literature and Society*, 32–48, Dublin: Four Courts Press.

Carey, John (2010), 'Donn, Amairgen, Íth and the Prehistory of Irish Pseudohistory', *Journal of Indo-European Studies*, 38: 319–42.

Carey, John (2014), '*Acallam na Senórach*: a Conversation between Worlds', in Aidan Doyle and Kevin Murray (eds), *In Dialogue with the Acallam*, 76–89, Dublin: Four Courts Press.

Carey, John (2015a), 'In Search of Mael Muru Othna', in Emer Purcell, Paul MacCotter, Julianne Nyhan, and John Sheehan (eds), *Clerics, Kings and Vikings: Essays on Medieval Ireland in Honour of Donnchadh Ó Corráin*, 429–39, Dublin: Four Courts Press.

Carey, John (2015b), 'The Old Gods of Ireland in the Later Middle Ages', in Alexandra Bergholm and Katja Ritari (eds), *Understanding Celtic Religion: Revisiting the Pagan Past*, 51–68, Cardiff: University of Wales Press.

Carey, John (2018), *The Mythological Cycle of Medieval Irish Literature*, Cork Studies in Celtic Literatures 3, Cork: CSCL Publications.

Carey, John, Emma Nic Cárthaigh and Caitríona Ó Dochartaigh (2014) (eds), *The End and Beyond: Medieval Irish Eschatology*, 2 vols, Aberystwyth: Celtic Studies Publications.

Cary, George (1956), *The Medieval Alexander*, Cambridge: Cambridge University Press.

Carson, Ciarán (2008), *The Táin: Translated from the Old Irish Epic Táin Bó Cúailnge*, London: Penguin.

Casey, Denis (2020), '"A Man of No Mean Standing": the Career and Legacy of Donnchad mac Briain (d. 1064)', *Peritia*, 31: 29–57.

Cavajoni, G. A. (1979–90), *Supplementum adnotationum super Lucanum*, 3 vols, Milano: Cisalpino-Goliardica.

Charles-Edwards, Thomas M. (2000), *Early Christian Ireland*, Cambridge: Cambridge University Press.

Cizek, Alexandru (2015), '*Historia de Preliis J²*, au plus tard début de XIIe siècle', in Catherine Gaullier-Bougassas (ed.), *La Fascination pour Alexandre le Grand dans les littératures européennes (Xe-XVIe Siècle)*, vol. 4, 35–42, Turnhout: Brepols.

Clancy, Thomas Owen (2008), 'Before the Ballad: Gaelic Narrative Verse before 1200', *Scottish Gaelic Studies*, 24: 115–36.

Clark, Frederic N. (2020), *The First Pagan Historian: The Fortunes of a Fraud from Antiquity to the Enlightenment*, New York: Oxford University Press.

Clarke, Michael (2006), 'Achilles, Byrhtnoth, Cú Chulainn: from Homer to the Medieval North', in M. J. Clarke, B. G. F. Currie and R. O. A. M. Lyne (eds), *Epic Interactions: Essays on Homer, Virgil and the Epic Tradition Presented to Jasper Griffin by his Pupils*, 243–71, Oxford: Oxford University Press.

Clarke, Michael (2009), 'An Irish Achilles and a Greek Cú Chulainn', in Ruairí Ó hUiginn and Brian Ó Catháin (eds), *Ulidia II: Proceedings of the Second International Conference on the Ulster Cycle of Tales*, 238–51, Maynooth: An Sagart.

Clarke, Michael (2014a), 'The Extended Prologue of *Togail Troí*: From Adam to the Wars of Troy', *Ériu*, 64: 23–106.

Clarke, Michael (2014b), 'Demonology, Allegory and Translation: the Furies and the Morrígan', in Ralph O'Connor (ed.), *Classical Literature and Learning in Medieval Irish Narrative*, 101–22, Cambridge: D. S. Brewer.

Clarke, Michael (2014c), 'Reconstructing the Medieval Irish Bookshelf: a Case Study of *Fingal Rónáin* and the Horse-Eared Kings', in Ralph O'Connor (ed.), *Classical Literature and Learning in Medieval Irish Narrative*, 123–39, Cambridge: D. S. Brewer.

Clarke, Michael (2015), 'The *Leabhar Gabhála* and Carolingian Origin Legends', in Pádraic Moran and Immo Warntjes (eds), *Early Medieval Ireland and Europe, Chronology, Contacts, Scholarship: A Festschrift for Dáibhí Ó Cróinín*, 440–80, Turnhout: Brepols.

Clarke, Michael (2016), 'International Influences on the Later Medieval Development of *Togail Troí*', in Axel Harlos and Neele Harlos (eds), *Adapting Texts and Styles in a*

Celtic Context, Interdisciplinary Perspectives on Processes of Literary Transfer in the Middle Ages: Studies in Honour of Erich Poppe, Studien und Texte zur Keltologie 13, 75–102, Münster: Nodus.

Clarke, Michael (2019), *Achilles Beside Gilgamesh: Mortality and Wisdom in Early Epic Poetry*, Cambridge: Cambridge University Press.

Clarke, Michael (2020), 'A Latin Source for *Merugud Uilix*, the Medieval Irish Narrative of Ulysses', *Ériu*, 70: 95–118.

Clarke, Michael (2021), 'The Choice of Achilles and the Choice of Cú Chulainn: Intertextuality and the Manuscripts', *North American Journal of Celtic Studies*, 5: 1–29.

Clarke, Michael (2022a), 'The Manuscripts of the Irish *Liber Hymnorum*, a Bilingual Anthology of Sacred Verse', in Michael Clarke and Máire Ní Mhaonaigh (eds), *Medieval Multilingual Manuscripts: Case Studies from Ireland to Japan*, 119–50, Berlin: De Gruyter.

Clarke, Michael (2022b), '*Énchennach*: a Study in the Terminology of Shape-changing', *Celtica*, 33: 35–58.

Clarke, Michael (2022c), 'Translation and Creativity in the Antiquity Sagas: the Arming of Julius Caesar in *In Cath Catharda*', in Ken Ó Donnchú (ed.), *Tintúd-Aistriú: Papers on Translation in Irish Tradition*, 22–49, Cork: Cló Torna.

Clarke, Michael (2023), 'The "Poems on World-Kingship" in the Book of Uí Mhaine', in Elizabeth Boyle and Ruairí Ó hUiginn (eds), *Book of Uí Mhaine*, Codices Hibernenses Eximii 3, 79–110, Dublin: Royal Irish Academy.

Clarke, Michael and Máire Ní Mhaonaigh (2020), 'The Ages of the World and the Ages of Man: Irish and European Learning in the Twelfth Century', *Speculum*, 95.2: 467–99.

Clogan, Paul M. (1968), *The Medieval Achilleid of Statius*, Leiden: Brill.

Colgrave, Bertram and R. A. B. Mynors (1969), *Bede's Ecclesiastical History of the English People*, Oxford: Oxford University Press.

Comyn, David, and Patrick S. Dinneen (1902–14), *Foras feasa ar Éirinn: The History of Ireland by* Geoffrey Keating, Irish Texts Society Vols 4, 8, 9, 15, London: Irish Texts Society.

Constans, Léopold (1904–12), *Le Roman de Troie par Benoît de Sainte-Maure*, 6 vols, Paris.

Copeland, Rita (2016a) (ed.), *The Oxford History of Classical Reception in English Literature Volume I: 800–1558*, Oxford: Oxford University Press.

Copeland, Rita (2016b), 'Introduction: England and the Classics from the Early Middle Ages to Early Humanism', in Rita Copeland (ed.), *The Oxford History of Classical Reception in English Literature Volume I: 800–1558*, 1–20, Oxford: Oxford University Press.

Crampton, Robert (2010), *Fingal Chlainne Tanntail: Text and Context*, PhD diss., University of Cambridge. Available online at https://doi.org/10.17863/CAM.93012

Crampton, Robert (2014), 'The Uses of Exaggeration in *Merugud Uilixis Meic Leirtis* and *Fingal Chlainne Tanntail*', in Ralph O'Connor (ed.), *Classical Literature and Learning in Medieval Irish Narrative*, 58–82, Cambridge: D. S. Brewer.

Cronin, Michael (1996), *Translating Ireland: Translation, Languages, Culture*, Cork: Cork University Press.

Cullhed, Anders (2017), *The Shadow of Creusa: Negotiating Fictionality in Late Antique Latin Literature*, translated by Andrew Knight, Berlin: De Gruyter.

Currie, Arabella (2020), 'Abjection and the Irish-Greek Fir Bolg in Aran Island Writing', in Isabelle Torrance and Donncha O'Rourke (eds), *Classics and Irish Politics, 1916–2016*, 173–192, Oxford: Oxford University Press.

Darwin, Gregory (2021), 'On Greek and Latin Names in Early Modern Irish Syllabic Verse', *Celtica*, 33: 195–247.

Darwin, Gregory (2024a, forthcoming), '*Tiocfa Séasair clann Cholla*: Exiles and Homecomings in Early Modern Gaelic Political Poetry', in Isabelle Torrance (ed.), *Irish Migrations and Classical Antiquity*, London: Bloomsbury.

Darwin, Gregory (2024b, forthcoming), '*Ór na Gréige is stór na hÉigipt*: Classical Antiquity in Irish-language Popular Poetry of the Eighteenth and Nineteenth Century', in Christian Thrue Djurslev, Jens A. Krasilnikoff and Vinnie Nørskov (eds), *Popular Receptions of Classical Antiquity*, Aarhus: Aarhus University Press.

De Bernardo Stempel, Patrizia (2006), 'Phaedra und Hippolytus in irischem Gewand: Die mittelalterliche *Fingal Rónáin*, "Der Verwandtenmord des Rōnān", als Theaterstück', in B. Bosold-DasGupta et al. (eds), *Festschrift anlässlich des 60. Geburtstages von Klaus Ley*, 237–66, Berlin: Weidler Buchverlag.

De Bernardo Stempel, Patrizia (2016), 'The Reassessment of *Fingal Rónáin*: Theatrical Plot and Classical Origins', *Cambrian Medieval Celtic Studies*, 72: 33–71.

De Melo, Wolfgang (2019), *Varro: De lingua Latina: Introduction, Text, Translation, and Commentary*, Oxford: Oxford University Press.

Derolez, René (1954), *Runica Manuscripta: The English Tradition*, Rijksuniversiteit te Gent. Werken uitgegeven door de Faculteit van de Wijsbegeerte en Letteren 118, Brugge: De Tempel.

Díaz y Díaz, Manuel C. (1972), *Liber de Ordine Creaturarum: un anónimo irlandés del siglo VII*, Santiago de Compostela: University of Santiago de Compostela.

DiTommaso, Lorenzo (2021), 'The Four Kingdoms of Daniel in Early Medieval Apocalyptic Tradition', in Andrew B. Perrin, Loren T. Stuckenbruck, Shelby Bennett, and Mathew Hama (eds), *Four Kingdom Motifs Before and Beyond the Book of Daniel*, 205–50, Leiden: Brill.

Dobbs, Margaret E. (1921–3), 'The History of the Descendants of Ír', *Zeitschrift für celtische Philologie*, 13 (1921): 308–59, 14 (1923): 421–2.

Dobbs, Margaret (1921–4), 'The Pedigree and Family of Flann Mainistrech', *Journal of the County of Louth Archaeological Society*, 5: 149–53.

Dombart, Bernhard and Alphonse Kalb (1955), *Sancti Augustini De civitate Dei*, 2 vols, Corpus Christianorum Series Latina 47–8, Turnhout: Brepols.

Dominik, William J., Carole E. Newlands, and Kyle Gervais (2015) (eds), *Brill's Companion to Statius*, Leiden: Brill.

Dooley, Ann and Harry Roe (1999), *Tales of the Elders of Ireland: A New Translation of Acallam na Senórach*, Oxford: Oxford University Press.

Duff, J. D. (1928), *Lucan: The Civil War*, Loeb Classical Library, Cambridge, Mass.: Harvard University Press.

Dumville, David N. (1977), 'Ulster Heroes in the Early Irish Annals: a Caveat', *Éigse*, 17: 47–54.

Duncan, Elizabeth (2012), '*Leabhar na hUidre* and a Copy of Boethius' *De re arithmetica*: a Palaeographical Note', *Ériu*, 22: 1–32.

Edwards, Nancy and Máire Ní Mhaonaigh (2017), 'Transforming Landscapes of Belief in the Early Medieval World and Beyond: an Introduction', in Nancy Edwards, Máire Ní Mhaonaigh and Roy Flechner (eds), *Transforming Landscapes of Belief in the Early Medieval Insular World and Beyond: Converting the Isles II*, Cultural Encounters in Late Antiquity and the Middle Ages 23, 1–20, Turnhout: Brepols.

Edwards, Robert R. (2015), 'Medieval Statius: Belatedness and Authority', in William J. Dominik, Carole E. Newlands and Kyle Gervais (eds), *Brill's Companion to Statius*, 497–511, Leiden: Brill.

Ehrmantraut, Brigid (2022), 'A Wrong Turn on the Way to Troy: Samson and the Classical Tradition in Medieval Ireland', *Celtica*, 34: 39–59.

Ehrmantraut, Brigid (forthcoming), *The Reception of Classical Mythology in Medieval Ireland*, Studies in Celtic History, Cambridge: D. S. Brewer.

Ekrem, Inge, Peter Fisher, and Lars Boje Mortensen (2003), *Historia Norvegie*, Copenhagen: Museum Tusculanum Press.

Ellis, Roger (2019), 'Translation', in Peter Brown (ed.), *A New Companion to Chaucer*, 487–99, Oxford: Wiley.

Endt, Johannes (1909), *Adnotationes super Lucanum*, Bibliotheca Scriptorum Graecorum et Romanorum Teubneriana, Stuttgart: Teubner.

Engesland, Nicolai Egjar (2020), *Auraicept na nÉces: A Diachronic Study with an Edition from The Book of Uí Mhaine*, PhD diss., University of Oslo.

Engesland, Nicolai Egjar (2021), 'The Intellectual Background of the Earliest Irish Grammar', *Journal of Medieval History*, 47.4–5: 472–84.

Erdmann, Oskar (1973), *Otfrids 'Evangelienbuch'*, 6th edn, Tübingen: Niemeyer.

Fairclough, H. Rushton (1999–2000), *Virgil: Eclogues, Georgics, Aeneid*, 2 vols, revised by G.P. Goold, Loeb Classical Library, Cambridge, Mass.: Harvard University Press.

Fear, Andrew T. (2010), *Orosius: Seven Books of History against the Pagans*, Translated Texts for Historians 54, Liverpool: Liverpool University Press.

Fitch, J. D. (2002–4), *Seneca: Tragedies*, 2 vols, Loeb Classical Library, Cambridge, Mass.: Harvard University Press.

Flanagan, Marie Therese (2010), *The Transformation of the Irish Church in the Twelfth Century*, Studies in Celtic History 29, Woodbridge: Boydell.

Flanagan, Marie Therese (2013), 'Jocelin of Furness and the Cult of St Patrick in Twelfth-century Ulster', in Clare Downham (ed.), *Jocelin of Furness: Proceedings of the 2011 Conference*, 45–66, Donington: Shaun Tyas.

Flutre, L.-F. and K. Sneyders de Vogel (1937–8), *Li Fet des Romains*, 2 vols, Paris.

Forster, Edward Seymour (1984), *Florus: Epitome of Roman History*, 2nd edn, Loeb Classical Library, Cambridge, Mass.: Harvard University Press.

Fotheringham, J. K. (1925), *Eusebii Pamphilii Chronici Canones latine vertit, adauxit, et ad sua tempora produxit S. Eusebius Hieronymus*, Oxford: Oxford University Press.

Fowler, H. W. and F. G. Fowler (1906), *The King's English*, Oxford: Oxford University Press.

Frazer, James (1921), *Apollodorus: The Library*, 2 vols, Loeb Classical Library, Cambridge, Mass.: Harvard University Press.

Frazer, James and G. P. Goold (1989), *Ovid: Fasti*, revised edition, Loeb Classical Library, Cambridge, Mass.: Harvard University Press.

Frazer, R. M. (1966), *The Trojan War: The Chronicles of Dictys of Crete and Dares the Phrygian*, Bloomington: Indiana University Press.

Freeman, A. Martin (1924–7), 'The Annals in Cotton MS Titus A. XXV', *Revue Celtique*, 41 (1924): 301–30, 42 (1925): 283–305, 43 (1926): 358–84, 44 (1927): 336–61.

Freeman, Philip (2001), *Ireland and the Classical World*, Austin: University of Texas Press.

Gabriele, Mathew (2012), 'The Last Carolingian Exegete: Pope Urban II, the Weight of Tradition, and Christian Reconquest', *Church History*, 81.4: 796–814.

Gantz, Jeffrey (1981), *Early Irish Myths and Sagas*, Harmonsworth: Penguin.

Gaullier-Bougassas, Catherine (2015) (ed.), *La Fascination pour Alexandre le Grand dans les littératures européennes (Xe-XVIe siècle)*, 4 vols, Turnhout: Brepols.

Glennon, William F. X. (1996–7), 'The Similes in the Book of Leinster *Táin Bó Cúailnge*', *Proceedings of the Harvard Celtic Colloquium*, 16/17: 206–22.

Glorie, F. (1964), *S. Hieronymi Presbyteri Commentariorum in Danielem Libri III*, Corpus Christianorum Series Latina, 75A, Turnhout: Brepols.

Godden, Malcom (2012), 'Literacy in Anglo-Saxon England', in Richard Gameson (ed.), *The Cambridge History of the Book in Britain, Vol. 1: c. 400–1100*, 580–90, Cambridge: Cambridge University Press.

Goez, Werner (1958), *Translatio Imperii: Ein Beitrag zur Geschichte des Geschichtsdenkens und der politischen Theorien im Mittelalter und in der frühen Neuzeit*, Tübingen: J. C. B. Mohr.

Goff, Barbara (2005), *Classics and Colonialism*, London: Bristol Classical Press.

Gotoff, Harold C. (1971), *The Transmission of the Text of Lucan in the Ninth Century*, Cambridge, Mass.: Harvard University Press.

Grafton, Anthony and Megan Williams (2006), *Christianity and the Transformation of the Book: Origen, Eusebius and the Library of Caesera*, Cambridge, Mass: Belknap Press.

Gray, Elizabeth (1983), *Cath Maige Tuired: The Second Battle of Mag Tuired*, Irish Texts Society Vol. 52, London: Irish Texts Society.

Greene, David (n.d.), *Saltair na Rann*, typescript available online at https://www.dias.ie/celt/celt-publications-2/celt-saltair-na-rann/. Last consulted for this volume December 2022.

Greene, David (1955), *Fingal Rónáin and Other Stories*, Medieval and Modern Irish Series, 16, Dublin: Dublin Institute for Advanced Studies.

Greene, David, Fergus Kelly and Brian O. Murdoch (1976), *The Irish Adam and Eve Story from Saltair na Rann*, 2 vols, Dublin: Dublin Institute for Advanced Studies.

Gropper, Stefanie: *See Würth, Stefanie*

Gummere, R. M. (1917–25), *Seneca ad Lucilium Epistulae Morales*, 3 vols, London.

Gwynn, Edward J. (1903–35), *The Metrical Dindshenchas*, Todd Lecture Series 8-12, Dublin: Royal Irish Academy.

Hagen, Hermann (1867), *Scholia Bernensia ad Vergili Bucolica atque Georgica*, Jahrbücher für classische Philologie 4. suppl., Leipzig: Teubner.

Hall, Edith (2020), 'Sinn Féin and *Ulysses*: Between Professor Robert Mitchell Henry and James Joyce', in Isabelle Torrance and Donncha O'Rourke (eds), *Classics and Irish Politics, 1916-2016*, 193–217, Oxford: Oxford University Press.

Hardwick, Lorna (2000), *Translating Words, Translating Cultures*. London: Bloomsbury.

Hardwick, Lorna (2003), *Reception Studies*, Cambridge: Cambridge University Press.

Hardwick, Lorna (2021), 'Translation and/as Adaptation', in Vayos Liapis and Avra Sidiropoulou (eds), *Adapting Greek Tragedy: Contemporary Contexts for Ancient Texts*, 110–30, Cambridge: Cambridge University Press.

Hardwick, Lorna (2024), 'What's Behind the Label?', in Christian Thrue Djurslev, Jens A. Krasilnikoff and Vinnie Nørskov (eds), *Popular Receptions of Classical Antiquity*, Aarhus: Aarhus University Press, forthcoming.

Hardwick, Lorna and Stephen Harrison (2013) (eds), *Classics in the Modern World. A Democratic Turn?* Oxford: Oxford University Press.

Harlos, Axel and Neele Harlos (2016) (eds), *Adapting Texts and Styles in a Celtic Context, Interdisiplinary Perspectives on Processes of Literary Transfer in the Middle Ages: Studies in Honour of Erich Poppe*, Studien und Texte zur Keltologie 13, Münster: Nodus.

Harrington, Jesse (2024, forthcoming), 'S. Stefano al Monte Celio, Donnchad mac Briain, and Papal Legates in Ireland, 1064–1203', *Irish Historical Studies*.

Harris, John R. (1998), *Adaptations of Roman Epic in Medieval Ireland: Three Studies in the Interplay of Erudition and Oral Tradition*, Lewiston: Edwin Mellen Press.

Hartmann, Heiko (2005–14), *Otfrid von Weissenburg, Evangelienbuch aus dem Althochdeutschen übertragen*, 2 vols, Herne: Verlag für Wissenschaft und Kunst.

Hawkes, Greta (2014), *Rationalising Myth in Antiquity*, Oxford: Oxford University Press.

Hayden, Deborah (2013), 'Two Fragments of *Auraicept na nÉces* in the Irish Franciscan Archive: Context and Content', in Anders Ahlqvis and Pamela O'Neill (eds), *Celts and their Cultures at Home and Abroad: A Festschrift for Malcolm Broun*, 91–124, Sydney Series in Celtic Studies 15, Sydney: Celtic Studies Foundation, University of Sydney.

Hayden, Deborah (2016), 'Cryptography and the Alphabet in the "Book of Ádhamh Ó Cianáin"', in Deborah Hayden and Paul Russell (eds), *Grammatica, Gramadach and Gramadeg: Vernacular Grammar and Grammarians in Medieval Ireland and Wales*, 35–64, Studies in the History of the Language Sciences 125, Amsterdam: John Benjamins.

Haynes, Justin (2021), *The Medieval Classic: Twelfth-Century Latin Epic and the Virgilian Commentary Tradition*, Oxford: Oxford University Press.

Helm, Rudolf (1913), *Eusebius Werke. Siebenter Band. Die Chronik des Hieronymus: Hieronymi Chronicon*. Erster Teil. Text, Leipzig: J. C. Hinrichs.

Henderson, George (1899), *Fled Bricrend: The Feast of Bricriu*, Irish Texts Society Vol. 2, London: Irish Texts Society.

Henry, P. L. (1982), 'Furor heroicus', *Zeitschrift für celtische Philologie*, 39: 235–42.

Herbert, Máire (2001), 'Crossing Historical and Literary Boundaries: Irish Written Culture around the Year 1000', *Cambrian Medieval Celtic Studies*, 53/4: 87–101.

Heslin, Peter J. (2005), *The Transvestite Achilles: Gender and Genre in Statius' Achilleid*, Cambridge: Cambridge University Press.

Hilka, Alfons (1976–7), *Historia Alexandri Magni (Historia de Preliis) Rezension J² (Orosius-Rezension)*, 2 vols, Meisenheim am Glan: Hain.

Hillers, Barbara (1996), '*In fer fíamach fírglic*: Ulysses in Medieval Irish Literature', *Proceedings of the Harvard Celtic Colloquium*, 16: 15–38.

Hillers, Barbara (1997), *The Medieval Irish Odyssey: Merugud Uilixis meic Leirtis* (Harvard University dissertation), UMI, Ann Arbor, Michigan.

Hillers, Barbara (1999a), 'Ulysses and the Judge of Truth: Sources and Meanings in the Irish Odyssey', *Peritia*, 13: 194–223.

Hillers, Barbara (1999b), '*Sgél in Mínaduir*: Dädalus und der Minotaurus in Irland', in Erich Poppe and Hildegard L. C. Tristram (eds), *Übersetzung, Adaptation und Akkulturation im insularen Mittelalter*, 131–44, Münster: Nodus.

Hillers, Barbara (2014), 'The Medieval Irish *Wanderings of Ulysses* between Literacy and Orality', in Ralph O'Connor (ed.), *Classical Literature and Learning in Medieval Irish Narrative*, 83–97, Cambridge: D. S. Brewer.

Hillers, Barbara (forthcoming), *The Medieval Irish Odyssey*, Aberystwyth: Celtic Studies Publications.

Hofman, Rijcklof (1988), 'Some New Facts concerning the Knowledge of Vergil in Early Medieval Ireland', *Études Celtiques*, 25: 189–212.

Hogan, Edmund (1892), *Cath Ruis na Ríg for Bóinn*, Todd Lecture Series, 4, Dublin: Royal Irish Academy.

Holtz, Louis (1973), 'Sur trois commentaires irlandais de l'*Art majeur* de Donat au IXe siècle', *Revue d'histoire des textes*, 2: 45–72.

Hull, Eleanor (1932), 'The Hawk of Achill or the Legend of the Oldest Animals', *Folklore* 43.4: 376–409.

Hull, Vernam (1949), *Longes macc nUislenn: The Exile of the Sons of Uisliu*, New York: Modern Language Association of America.

Hutcheon, Linda (2012), *A Theory of Adaptation*, 2nd edn, London: Routledge.

Ingledew, Francis (1994), 'The Book of Troy and the Genealogical Construction of History: the Case of Geoffrey of Monmouth's *Historia regum Britannie*', *Speculum* 69.3: 665–704.

Irvine, Martin (1994), *The Making of Textual Culture: 'Grammatica' and Literary Theory 350-1100*, Cambridge Studies in Medieval Literature 19, Cambridge: Cambridge University Press.

Jackson, Kenneth Hurlstone (1938), *Cath Maighe Léna*, Medieval and Modern Irish Series, 9, Dublin: Dublin Institute for Advanced Studies.

Jackson, Kenneth Hurlstone (1990), *Aislinge Meic Con Glinne*, Dublin: Dublin Institute for Advanced Studies.

Jaeger, C. Stephen (1994), *The Envy of Angels: Cathedral Schools and Social Ideas in Medieval Europe, 950-1200*, Philadelphia: University of Pennsylvania Press.

Jahnke, R. (1898), *Lactantii Placidi qui dicitur commentarii in Statii Thebaida et commentarius in Achilleida* (= P. Paninius Statius, Vol. 3), Bibliotheca Scriptorum Graecorum et Romanorum Teubneriana, Leipzig: Teubner.

Johnston, Elva (2013), *Literacy and Identity in Early Medieval Ireland*, Studies in Celtic History 33, Woodbridge: Boydell.

Jones, Charles W. (1975–80), *Beda Venerabilis: Opera didascalica*, 3 vols, Corpus Christianorum Series Latina 123A–123C, Turnhout: Brepols.

Karst, Joseph (1911), *Eusebius Werke. Fünfter Band. Die Chronik aus dem Armenischen Übersetzt mit Textkritischem Commentar*, Leipzig: J. C. Hinrichs.

Keil, Heinrich (1855–80), *Grammatici Latini*, 8 vols, Bibliotheca Scriptorum Graecorum et Romanorum Teubneriana, Leipzig: Teubner.

Kelly, Fergus (1988), *A Guide to Early Irish Law*, Early Irish Law Series 3, Dublin: Dublin Institute for Advanced Studies.

Kelly, Fergus (2021), 'Vocal Music in Medieval Ireland: the Textual and Linguistic Evidence', in Conor Caldwell, Moyra Haslett and Lillis Ó Laoire (eds), *The Oxford Handbook of Irish Song 1100-1850*, Oxford: Oxford University Press.

Kendall, Charles B. and Faith Wallis (2010), *Bede: On the Nature of Things* and *On Times*, Translated Texts for Historians 56, Liverpool: Liverpool University Press.

Kent, Roland G. (1951), *Varro: On the Latin Language*, Loeb Classical Library, Cambridge, Mass.: Harvard University Press.

Kershner, Stephen (2019), 'Statius' Dynamic Absence in the Narrative Frame of the Middle Irish *Togail na Tebe*', in Joseph Nagy and Charles MacQuarrie (eds), *The Medieval Cultures of the Irish Sea and the North Sea: Manannán and His Neighbors*, The Early Medieval North Atlantic 7, 99-122, Amsterdam: Amsterdam University Press.

Kiberd, Declan (2020), 'The Use and Abuse of Classics: Thoughts on Empire, Epic, and Language', in Isabelle Torrance and Donncha O'Rourke (eds), *Classics and Irish Politics, 1916-2016*, 27-42, Oxford: Oxford University Press.

Kimpton, Bettina (2009), *The Death of Cú Chulainn: A Critical Edition of the Earliest Version of Brislech Mór Maige Muirthemni*, Maynooth Medieval Irish Texts 6, Maynooth: School of Celtic Studies, National University of Ireland, Maynooth.

Kinsella, Thomas (1970), *The Táin*, Oxford: Oxford University Press.

Knott, Eleanor (1936), *Togail Bruidne Da Derga*, Medieval and Modern Irish Series, 8, Dublin: Dublin Institute for Advanced Studies.

Knott, Eleanor (1957), *An Introduction to Irish Syllabic Poetry of the Period 1200–1600*, 2nd edn, Dublin: Dublin Institute for Advanced Studies.

Kobus, Isabel (1995), 'Imtheachta Aeniasa: "Aeneis"-Rezeption im irischen Mittelalter', *Zeitschrift für Celtische Philologie*, 47: 76–86.

Koch, John T. and John Carey (2003), *The Celtic Heroic Age: Literary Sources for Ancient Celtic Europe and Early Ireland and Wales*, 4th edn, Aberystwyth: Celtic Studies Publications.

Kovacs, David (1994–2008), *Euripides*, 8 vols, Loeb Classical Library, Cambridge, Mass.: Harvard University Press.

Kulcsár, Peter (1987), *Mythographi Vaticani I et II*, Corpus Christianorum Series Latina 91C, Turnhout: Brepols.

La Bua, Giuseppe (2018), 'Late Ciceronian Scholarship and Virgilian Exegesis: Servius and Ps.-Asconius', *Classical Quarterly*, 68: 667–80.

Lambert, Pierre-Yves (1986), 'Les Gloses celtiques aux commentaires de Vergile', *Études Celtiques*, 23: 81–128.

Lammers, Walther (2011), *Otto Bischof von Friesing: Chronik oder Die Geschichte der zwei Staaten*, Berlin: Wissenschaftliche Buchgesellschaft.

Le Goff, Jacques (1988), *Medieval Civilization 400–1500*, Translated by Julia Barrow, Oxford: Blackwell.

LeBlanc, Julie (2019), 'Heroic Traditions in Dialogue: the *Imtheachta Aeniasa*', in Aisling Byrne and Victoria Flood (eds), *Crossing Borders in the Insular Middle Ages*, 203–25, Turnhout: Brepols.

Lehmacher, Gustav (1921), 'Goedel Glass', *Zeitschrift für Celtische Philologie*, 13: 151–63.

Lelli, Emanuele (2016), *Ditti di Creta, L'Altra Iliade, con la Storia della Distruzione di Troia di Darete Frigio e i testi bizantini sulla Guerra Troiana*, Milano: Bompiani.

Leneghan, Francis (2015), '*Translatio Imperii*: the Old English Orosius and the Rise of Wessex', *Anglia* 133.4: 656–705.

Lewis, Barry (2022), 'Irish and Welsh', in Mark Chinca and Christopher Young (eds), *Literary Beginnings in the European Middle Ages*, 45–68, Cambridge: Cambridge University Press.

Lindsay, W. M. (1911), *Isidori Hispalensis episcopi etymologiarum sive originum libri XX*, 2 vols, Scriptorum Classicorum Bibliotheca Oxoniensis, Oxford: Oxford University Press.

Lloyd-Jones, Hugh (1994–6), *Sophocles*, Loeb Classical Library, Cambridge, Mass.: Harvard University Press.

Louis-Jensen, Jonna (1963), *Trójumanna saga*, Editiones Arnamagnaeanae A8, Copenhagen: Munksgaard.

Mac Airt, Seán (1944), *The Annals of Inisfallen (MS Rawlinson B.503)*, Dublin: Dublin Institute for Advanced Studies.

Mac Airt, Seán (1953–9), 'Middle-Irish Poems on World-kingship', *Études Celtiques*, 6 (1953–4): 255–80, 7 (1955): 18–45, 8 (1959): 98–119, 284–97.

Mac Airt, Seán and Gearóid Mac Niocaill (1983), *The Annals of Ulster*, Dublin: Dublin Institute for Advanced Studies.

Macalister, R. A. S. (1938–56), *Lebor Gabála Érenn: The Book of the Taking of Ireland*, Irish Texts Society Vols 34, 35, 39, 41, 44, London: Irish Texts Society.

Mackinnon, Donald (1912), *A Descriptive Catalogue of Gaelic Manuscripts in the Advocates' Library, Edinburgh, and Elsewhere in Scotland*, Edinburgh: Brown.

Mac an Aircinn, Caolán (2019), 'How to Use Giant Sheep to Prove that the Gods Are Dead', *Classics Ireland*, 26: 1–24.

Mac Cana, Proinsias (1980), *The Learned Tales of Medieval Ireland*, Dublin: Dublin Institute for Advanced Studies.

Mac Cárthaigh, Eoin (2014), *The Art of Bardic Poetry: A New Edition of Irish Grammatical Tracts I*, Dublin: Dublin Institute for Advanced Studies.

Mac Carthy, Bartholomew (1892), *The Codex Palatino-Vaticanus No. 830: Texts, Translations and Indices*, Todd Lecture Series 3, Dublin: Royal Irish Academy.

Mac Eoin, Gearóid (1960), 'Das Verbalsystem von *Togail Troí*', *Zeitschrift für Celtische Philologie*, 28: 73–223.

Mac Eoin, Gearóid (1961), 'Dán ar chogadh na Traoi', *Studia Hibernica*, 1: 1–28.

Mac Eoin, Gearóid (1967), 'Ein Text von *Togail Troí*', *Zeitschrift für celtische Philologie*, 30: 42–70.

Mac Eoin, Gearóid (2006), 'The Greek Background to *Stair Ercuil ocus a Bás*', in Kevin Murray (ed.), *Translations from Classical Literature: Imtheachta Aenasa and Stair Ercuil ocus a Bás*, Irish Texts Society Subsidiary Series 17, 20–36, London: Irish Texts Society.

Mac Eoin, Gearóid (2012), 'Early Irish Narrative Verse', in Bo Almqvist, Liam Mac Mathúna, Seamus Mac Mathúna, Seosamh Watson and Criostóir Mac Carthaigh (eds), *Atlantic Currents: Essays on Lore, Literature and Language in Honour of Séamus Ó Catháin*, 303–21, Dublin: UCD Press.

Mac Gabhann, Peadar: *See Smith, Peter J.*

Mac Gearailt, Uáitéar (1988), 'On Textual Correspondences in Early Irish Heroic Tales', in Gordon W. MacLennan (ed.), *Proceedings of the First North American Congress of Celtic Studies*, 343–55, Ottawa: University of Ottawa Press.

Mac Gearailt, Uáitéar (1996), 'Change and Innovation in Eleventh-century Prose Narrative in Irish', in Hildegard L. C. Tristram (ed.), *(Re)Oralisierung*, 443–93, Tübingen: Narr.

Mac Gearailt, Uáitéar (1999), '*Togail Troí*: ein Vorbild für spätmittelirische *catha*', in Hildegard L. C. Tristram and E. Poppe (eds), *Übersetzung, Adaptation und Akkulturation im insularen Mittelalter*, 123–39. Münster: Nodus.

Mac Gearailt, Uáitéar (2000/1), '*Togail Troí*: an Example of Translating and Editing in Medieval Ireland', *Studia Hibernica*, 31: 71–86.

Mac Gearailt, Uáitéar (2006/7), 'The Making of *Fingal Rónáin*', *Studia Hibernica*, 34: 63–84.

Mac Gearailt, Uáitéar (2016), 'Issues in the Transmission of Middle and Early Modern Irish Translation Prose: *Togail Troí* and *Scéla Alaxandair*', in Axel Harlos and Neele

Harlos (eds), *Adapting Texts and Styles in a Celtic Context, Interdisiplinary Perspectives on Processes of Literary Transfer in the Middle Ages: Studies in Honour of Erich Poppe*, Studien und Texte zur Keltologie 13, 103–34, Münster: Nodus.

Mac Gearailt, Uáitéar (2018), 'Translations of Latin Works in the Book of Ballymote', in Ruairí Ó hUiginn (ed.), *Book of Ballymote*, Codices Hibernenses Eximii II, 101–54, Dublin: Royal Irish Academy.

Mac Gearailt, Uáitéar (2022), '*In Cath Catharda*: Translation in Transition in Late Middle Irish and Early Modern Irish', in Ken Ó Donnchú (ed.), *Tintúd-Aistriú: Papers on Translation in Irish Tradition*, 50–119, Cork: Cló Torna.

Mac Neill, J. (= Eoin Mac Neill) (1910), 'An Irish Historical Tract Dated AD 721', *Proceedings of the Royal Irish Academy*, 28C: 123–48.

Mac Neill, Eoin (1914), 'The Authorship and Structure of the "Annals of Tigernach"', *Ériu*, 7: 30–113.

Mac Neill, Eoin and Gerard Murphy (1908–53), *Duanaire Finn: The Book of the Lays of Fionn*, Irish Texts Society Vols 7, 28, 43, London: Irish Texts Society.

Marstrander, Carl (1911), 'How Samson Slew the Gesteda', *Ériu*, 5: 145–59.

Marti, Berthe M. (1958), *Arnulfi Aurelianensis Glosule super Lucanum*, Papers and Monographs of the American Academy in Rome, 18, Rome: American Academy.

Mathis, Kate (2011), 'Gaelic *gemina opera*: the Verse and Prose Texts of *Saltair na Rann* and *Scél Saltrach na Rann*', *Scottish Gaelic Studies*, 28: 1–20.

McCarthy, Daniel P. (2008), *The Irish Annals: Their Genesis, Evolution and History*, Dublin: Four Courts Press.

McCay, David (2020), *The Dindshenchas in the Book of Leinster*. Unpublished PhD dissertation, University of Cambridge.

McCone, Kim (1990), *Pagan Past and Christian Present in Early Irish Literature*, Maynooth Monographs 3, Maynooth: An Sagart.

McCone, Kim (2005), *A First Old Irish Grammar and Reader*, Maynooth Medieval Irish Texts 3, Maynooth: School of Celtic Studies, National University of Ireland, Maynooth.

McGinty, Gerald (2000), *Pauca Problesmata de Enigmatibus ex Tomis Canonicis*, Corpus Christianorum, Continuatio Mediaevalis 83, Turnhout: Brepols.

McKenna, Catherine (2011), 'Angels and Demons in the Pages of *Lebor na hUidre*', in Joseph F. Eska (ed.), *Narrative in Celtic Tradition: Essays in Honor of Edgar M. Slotkin*, Celtic Studies Association of North America Yearbook 8–9, 157–80, New York: Colgate University Press.

McManus, Damian (1991), *A Guide to Ogam*, Maynooth Monographs 4, Maynooth: An Sagart.

Meister, F. (1873), *Daretis Phrygii De Excidio Troiae Historia*, Biblioteca Scriptorum Graecorum et Romanorum Teubneriana, Leipzig: Teubner.

Merkle, Stefan (1996), 'The truth and nothing but the truth: Dares and Dictys', in Garrett Schmeling (ed.), *The Novel in the Ancient World*, 563–80, Leiden: Brill.

Meyer, Kuno (1884), *Eine irische Version der Alexandersage*, PhD diss., University of Leipzig.

Meyer, Kuno (1886), *Merugud Uilix Maicc Leirtis: The Irish Odyssey*, London: David Nutt.

Meyer, Kuno (1887), 'Die Geschichte von Philipp und Alexander von Macedonien', in Whitley Stokes and Ernst Windisch, *Irische Texte mit Wörterbuch*, Vol 2: 1–108, Leipzig: Hirzel.

Meyer, Kuno (1903), 'Mitteilungen aus irischen Handschriften: *Sgél in Mhínaduir*', *Zeitschrift für Celtische Philologie*, 4: 238–40.

Meyer, Kuno (1907), 'The Colloquy between Fintan and the Hawk of Achill', in Osborn Bergin, Richard Irvine Best, Kuno Meyer and J. G. O'Keeffe (eds), *Anecdota from Irish Manuscripts I*, 24–39. Halle: M. Niemeyer.

Meyer, Kuno (1913), 'The Laud Synchronisms', *Zeitschrift für Celtische Philologie*, 9: 471–85.

Meyer, Kuno and Alfred Nutt (1895–97), *The Voyage of Bran Son of Febal to the Land of the Living*, 2 vols, London: David Nutt.

Meyer, Robert T. (1949), 'The Sources of the Middle Irish Alexander', *Modern Philology*, 47.1: 1–7.

Meyer, Robert T. (1952), 'The Middle Irish *Odyssey*: Folktale, Fiction, or Saga?', *Modern Philology*, 50: 73–8.

Meyer, Robert T. (1958), *Merugud Uilix Maic Leirtis*, Medieval and Modern Irish Series 17, Dublin: Dublin Institute for Advanced Studies.

Meyer, Robert T. (1962), 'The Middle-Irish Version of the *Thebaid* of Statius', *Papers of the Michigan Academy of Science, Arts, and Letters*, 47: 687–99.

Meyer, Robert T. (1967), 'The T.C.D. Fragments of the *Togail na Tebe*', *Trivium*, 2: 121–32.

Mierow, Charles Christopher (2002), *'The Two Cities': A Chronicle of Universal History to the Year 1146 A.D., by Otto, Bishop of Freising*, New York: Columbia University Press.

Milani, Celestina (1978), 'Anglico-Celtica', *Rendiconti dell'Istituto Lombardo*, Classe di lettere e scienze morali e storiche 112, 286–96, Milano: Istituto Lombardo.

Miles, Brent (2007), '*Riss in muindtuirc*: the Tale of Harmonia's Necklace and the Study of the Theban Cycle in Medieval Ireland', *Ériu*, 57: 67–112.

Miles, Brent (2011), *Heroic Saga and Classical Epic in Medieval Ireland*, Studies in Celtic History 30, Cambridge: D. S. Brewer.

Miles, Brent (2014), 'The *Sermo ad reges* from the Leabhar Breac and Hiberno-Latin Tradition', in Elizabeth Boyle and Deborah Hayden (eds), *Authorities and Adaptations: The Reworking and Transmission of Textual Sources in Medieval Ireland*, 141–58, Dublin: Dublin Institute for Advanced Studies.

Miles, Brent (2020), *Don Tres Troí: The Middle Irish History of the Third Troy*, Irish Texts Society Vol. 68, London: Irish Texts Society.

Miller, Frank Justus (1977–84), *Ovid: Metamorphoses*, revised by G. P. Goold, 2 vols, Loeb Classical Library, Cambridge, Mass.: Harvard University Press.

Minnis, A. and I. Johnson (2005) (eds), *The Cambridge History of Literary Criticism, Vol. 2: The Middle Ages*, Cambridge: Cambridge University Press.

Mommsen, Theodor (1894), 'Isidori iunioris episcopi Hispalensis chronica maiora', *Monumenta Germaniae Historica Chronica Minora II*: 391–488, Berlin: Weidmann.

Mommsen, Theodor (1898), 'Historia Brittonum cum additamentis Nennii', *Monumenta Germaniae Historica Chronica Minora III*: 111–222, Berlin: Weidmann.

Moran, Pádraic (2012), 'Greek in Early Medieval Ireland', in Alex Mullen and Patrick James (eds), *Multilingualism in the Greco-Roman Worlds*, 172–92, Cambridge: Cambridge University Press.

Moran, Pádraic (2015), 'Language Interaction in the St Gall Priscian Glosses', *Peritia*, 26: 113–42.

Moran, Pádraic (2019), *De origine Scoticae linguae/ O'Mulconry's Glossary: An Early Irish Linguistic Tract*, Corpus Christianorum, Lexica Latina Medii Aevi 7, Turnhout: Brepols.

Moran, Pádraic and John Whitman (2022), 'Glossing and Reading in Western Europe and East Asia: a Comparative Case Study', *Speculum*, 97.1: 112–39.

Morini, Massimiliano (2008), 'Outlining a New Linguistic Theory of Translation', *Target* 20.1: 29–51.

Mortensen, Lars Boje (1990), 'Orosius and Justinus in One Volume: Post-Conquest Books Across the Channel', *Cahiers de l'Institut du moyen-âge grec et latin*, 60: 389–99.

Mortensen, Lars Boje (1999–2000), 'The Diffusion of Roman Histories in the Middle Ages: a List of Orosius, Eutropius, Paulus Diaconus, and Landolfus Sagax Manuscripts', *Filologia Mediolatina* 6–7: 101–200.

Mortensen, Lars Boje (2018), 'Latin as Vernacular: Critical Mass and the "Librarization" of New Book Languages', in Norbert Kössinger, Elke Krotz, Stephan Müller and Pavlína Rychterová (eds), *Anfangsgeschichten/Origin Stories: The Rise of Vernacular Literacy in a Comparative Perspective*, 71–90, Paderborn: Fink.

Moss, Rachel (2014) (ed.), *The Art and Architecture of Ireland, Volume 1: Medieval*, Dublin: Royal Irish Academy.

Muhr, Kay (1999), 'Water Imagery in Early Irish', *Celtica*, 23: 193–210.

Mullally, Evelyn (2002), *The Deeds of the Normans in Ireland, La geste des engleis en Yrlande: A New Edition of the Chronicle Formerly Known as The Song of Dermot and the Earl*, Dublin: Four Courts Press.

Müller-Lisowski, K. (1921), 'Stair Nuadat Find Femin', *Zeitschrift für Celtische Philologie*, 13: 195–250.

Munk Olsen, Birger (2009), *L'Étude des auteurs classiques latins aux XIe et XIIe siècles. Tome IV, 1re partie: La Réception de la littérature classique manuscrits et textes*, Paris: CNRS.

Murphy, Gerald (1956), *Early Irish Lyrics*, Oxford: Oxford: Oxford University Press.

Murphy, Gerald (1961), *Early Irish Metrics*, Dublin: Dublin Institute for Advanced Studies.

Murray, A. T. (1919–25), *Homer*, 4 vols, Loeb Classical Library, Cambridge, Mass.: Harvard University Press.

Murray, Kevin (2017), *The Early Finn Cycle*, Dublin: Four Courts Press.

Mynors, R. A. B., et al. (1991) (eds), *Registrum Anglie de Libris Doctorum et Auctorum Veterum*, London: British Library.

Myrick, Leslie Diane (1993), *From The De Excidio Troiae Historia to the Togail Troí: Literary-Cultural Synthesis in a Medieval Irish Adaptation of Dares' Troy Tale*, Heidelberg: Winter.

Nagashima, Maio (2019), 'Lucan's Simile in *In Cath Catharda* 567–70 and the Meaning of the Middle Irish Hapax *uchtcrand*', *Philologica*, 14: 71–9.

Nagashima, Maio (2021), '*Uair innister isna sdairib*: authorities of Histories in *In Cath Catharda* and the Scholarly Milieu of Its Adaptation', *Celtic Forum (Japan Society for Celtic Studies)*, 24: 5–16.

Nagy, Joseph Falaky (1997), *Conversing with Angels and Ancients: Literary Myths of Medieval Ireland*, Ithaca: Cornell.

Nagy, Joseph Falaky, and MacQuarrie, Charles W. (2019) (eds), *The Medieval Cultures of the Irish Sea and the North Sea: Manannán and His Neighbors*, The Early Medieval North Atlantic 7, Amsterdam: Amsterdam University Press.

Nettlau, W. (1889), 'On some Irish Translations from Medieval European Literature', *Revue Celtique*, 10, 179–83.

Ní Dhonnchadha, Máirín (2002a), 'Gormlaith and her Sisters, *c*. 750–1800', in Angela Bourke et al. (eds), *The Field Day Anthology of Irish Writing, Vol. IV: Irish Women's Writing and Traditions*, 166–249, Cork: Cork University Press.

Ní Dhonnchadha, Máirín (2002b), '*Tochmarc Ailbe*', in Angela Bourke et al. (eds), *The Field Day Anthology of Irish Writing, Vol. IV: Irish Women's Writing and Traditions*, 206–10, Cork: Cork University Press.

Ní Mhaonaigh, Máire (1992), 'Bréifne Bias in *Cogad Gáedel re Gallaib*', *Ériu*, 43: 135–58.

Ní Mhaonaigh, Máire (1995), 'The Date of *Cogad Gáedel re Gallaib*', *Peritia*, 9: 354–77.

Ní Mhaonaigh, Máire (2001), 'The Outward Look: Britain and Beyond in Medieval Irish Literature', in Peter Linehan and Janet L. Nelson (eds), *The Medieval World*, 105–23, London: Routledge.

Ní Mhaonaigh, Máire (2006a), 'The Literature of Medieval Ireland, 800–1200: from the Vikings to the Normans', in Margaret Kelleher and Philip O'Leary (eds), *The Cambridge History of Irish Literature I: to 1890*, 32–73, Cambridge: Cambridge University Press.

Ní Mhaonaigh, Máire (2006b), 'Classical Compositions in Medieval Ireland: the Literary Context', in Kevin Murray (ed.), *Translations from Classical Literature:* Imtheachta Aeniasa *and* Stair Ercuil ocus a Bás, Irish Texts Society Subsidiary Series 17, 1–19, London: Irish Texts Society.

Ní Mhaonaigh, Máire (2011), 'Cormac mac Cuilennáin: King, Bishop and "Wondrous Sage"', *Zeitschrift für Celtische Philologie* 58: 108–28.

Ní Mhaonaigh, Máire (2014), 'The Metaphorical Hector': the Literary Portrayal of Murchad mac Bríain', in Ralph O'Connor (ed.), *Classical Literature and Learning in Medieval Irish Narrative*, 140–61, Studies in Celtic History 34, Cambridge: D. S. Brewer.

Ní Mhaonaigh, Máire (2015), 'The Hectors of Ireland and the Western World', in John Carey, Kevin Murray, and Caitríona Ó Dochartaigh (eds), *Sacred Histories: A Festschrift for Máire Herbert*, 258–68, Dublin: Four Courts Press.

Ní Mhaonaigh, Máire (2017a), 'Glorious by Association: the Obituary of Brian Boru', in *Medieval Dublin XVI: Proceedings of Clontarf 1014–2014, National Conference Marking the Millennium of the Battle of Clontarf*, 170–87, Dublin: Four Courts Press.

Ní Mhaonaigh, Máire (2017b), 'The Peripheral Centre: Writing History on the Western 'Fringe', *Interfaces: A Journal of Medieval European Literature* 4: 59–84, available online at https://riviste.unimi.it/interfaces/article/view/9469. Last accessed for this volume 11 January 2023.

Ní Mhaonaigh, Máire (2018), 'Universal History and the Book of Ballymote', in Ruairí Ó hUiginn (ed.), *Book of Ballymote*, 33–50, Codices Hibernenses Eximii II, Dublin: Royal Irish Academy.

Ní Mhaonaigh, Máire (2020), 'Medieval Irish Battle Narratives and the Construction of the Past', in Rory Naismith, Máire Ní Mhaonaigh and Elizabeth Ashman Rowe (eds), *Writing Battles: New Perspectives on Warfare and Memory in Medieval Europe*, 131–46, London: Bloomsbury.

Ní Mhaonaigh, Máire (2022), 'International Vernacularisation, *c.* 1390 CE: the "Book of Ballymote"', in Michael Clarke and Máire Ní Mhaonaigh (eds), *Medieval Multilingual Manuscripts: Case Studies from Ireland to Japan*, 209–29, Berlin: De Gruyter.

Ní Mhaonaigh, Máire (2023), 'Irish World Annals and Universal Chronicling: Medieval Irish Scholars and their "Global Turn"', *Proceedings of the Harvard Celtic Colloquium*, 40: 1–31.

Ní Mheallaigh, Karen (2008), 'Pseudo-documentarism and the Limits of Ancient Fiction', *American Journal of Philology*, 129: 403–31.

Ní Mhurchú, Síle (2020), 'Translating into Irish from Greek and Latin in the Early Years of the Irish State', in Isabelle Torrance and Donncha O'Rourke (eds), *Classics and Irish Politics, 1916–2016*, 83–99, Oxford: Oxford University Press.

Nichols, Kenneth (2003), *Gaelic and Gaelicised Ireland in the Middle Ages*, 2nd edn, Dublin: Four Courts Press.

Nótári, Tamás (2011), '*Translatio imperii*: Thoughts on Continuity of Empires in European Political Traditions', *Acta Juridica Hungarica* 52.2: 146–56.

Ó Caithnia, Liam P. (1984), *Apalóga na bhFilí 1200–1650*, Dublin: Clóchomhar.

Ó Cathasaigh, Tomás (2014), *Coire Sois, The Cauldron of Knowledge: A Companion to Early Irish Saga*, edited by Matthieu Boyd, Notre Dame: Notre Dame University Press.

Ó Corráin, Donnchadh (1988), *Ireland Before the Normans*, 2nd edn, Dublin: Gill and Macmillan.

Ó Corráin, Donnchadh (2011–12), 'What Happened to Ireland's Medieval Manuscripts?', *Peritia*, 22–3: 191–223.

Ó Corráin, Donnchadh (2017), *Clavis Litterarum Hibernensium: Medieval Irish Books and Texts (c. 400–c, 1600)*, Corpus Christianorum: Claves, 3 vols, Turnhout: Brepols.

Ó Cróinín, Dáibhí (1983), *The Irish Sex Aetates Mundi*, Dublin: Dublin Institute for Advanced Studies.

Ó Cróinín, Dáibhí (2005), 'Ireland, 400–800', in Dáibhí Ó Cróinín (ed.), *A New History of Ireland, I: Prehistoric and Early Ireland*, 182–234, Oxford: Oxford University Press

Ó Cuív, Brian (2001–3), *Catalogue of Irish Language Manuscripts in the Bodleian Library at Oxford and Oxford College Libraries*, 2 vols, Dublin: Dublin Institute for Advanced Studies.

Ó Háinle, Cathal (2015), 'Three Apologues and *In Cath Catharda*', *Ériu*, 65: 87–126.

Ó hAodha, Donnchadh (1979), 'The Irish Version of Statius' *Achilleid*', *Proceedings of the Royal Irish Academy* 79 C 4: 83–137.

Ó hUiginn, Ruairí (1992), 'The Background and Development of *Táin Bó Cúailnge*', in James P. Mallory (ed.), *Aspects of the Táin*, 29–68, Belfast: December Publications.

Ó hUiginn, Ruairí (1993), 'Fergus, Russ, and Rudraige: a Brief Biography of Fergus mac Róich', *Emania* 11: 31–40.

Ó hUiginn, Ruairí, (2015) (ed.), *Lebor na hUidre*, Codices Hibernenses Eximii I, Dublin: Royal Irish Academy.

Ó hUiginn, Ruairí, (2018a) (ed.), *Book of Ballymote*, Codices Hibernenses Eximii II, Dublin: Royal Irish Academy.

Ó hUiginn, Ruairí (2018b), 'The Book of Ballymote: Scholars, Sources and Patrons', in Ruairí Ó hUiginn (ed.), *Book of Ballymote*, Codices Hibernenses Eximii II, 191–208, Dublin: Royal Irish Academy.

Ó Macháin, Pádraig (1986), 'Ar bhás Chuinn Chéadchathaigh', *Éigse*, 21: 53–65.

Ó Macháin, Pádraig (2018), 'The Book of Ballymote and the Irish Book', in Ruairí Ó hUiginn (ed.), *Book of Ballymote*, Codices Hibernenses Eximii II, 221–50, Dublin: Royal Irish Academy.

Ó Muraíle, Nollaig (2005), 'The Learned Family of Ó Cianáin/Keenan', *Clogher Record*, 18.3: 387–436.

Ó Néill, Pádraig (1997), 'An Irishman at Chartres in the Twelfth Century: the Evidence of Oxford, Bodleian Library, MS Auct. F.III.15', *Ériu*, 48: 1–35.

Ó Néill, Pádraig (1999), 'The Latin Colophon to the *Táin Bó Cúailnge* in the Book of Leinster: a Critical View of Old Irish Literature', *Celtica*, 23: 269–75.

Ó Néill, Pádraig (2005), 'Irish Glosses in a Twelfth-century Copy of Boethius's *Consolatio Philosophiae*', *Ériu*, 55: 1–17.

Ó Raithbheartaigh, Toirdhealbhach (1932), *Genealogical Tracts*, Vol. 1, Dublin: Irish Manuscripts Commission.

Ó Riain, Pádraig (1978), *Cath Almaine*, Medieval and Modern Irish Series 25, Dublin: Dublin Institute for Advanced Studies.

O'Brien, M. A. (1955), 'A Middle-Irish Poem on the Christian Kings of Leinster', *Ériu*, 17: 35–51.

O'Brien, M. A. (1962), *Corpus Genealogiarum Hiberniae*, Dublin: Dublin Institute for Advanced Studies.

O'Connor, Frank (1967), *The Backward Look: A Survey of Irish Literature*, London: Macmillan.

O'Connor, Ralph (2013), *The Destruction of Da Derga's Hostel: Kingship and Narrative Artistry in a Mediaeval Irish Saga*, Oxford: Oxford University Press.

O'Connor, Ralph (2014a) (ed.), *Classical Literature and Learning in Medieval Irish Narrative*, Studies in Celtic History 34, Cambridge: D. S. Brewer.

O'Connor, Ralph (2014b), 'Irish Narrative Literature and the Classical Tradition, 900–1300', in Ralph O'Connor (ed.), *Classical Literature and Learning in Medieval Irish Narrative*, 1–22, Studies in Celtic History 34, Cambridge: D. S. Brewer.

O'Connor, Ralph (2014c), 'Was Classical *imitatio* a Necessary Precondition for the Writing of Large-scale Native Irish sagas? Reflections on *Táin Bó Cuailnge* and the "Watchman Device"', in Ralph O'Connor (ed.), *Classical Literature and Learning in Medieval Irish Narrative*, 165–95, Studies in Celtic History 34, Cambridge: D. S. Brewer.

O'Connor, Ralph (2016), 'Monsters of the Tribe: Berserk Fury, Shapeshifting and Social Dysfunction in *Táin Bó Cúailnge*, *Egils saga* and *Hrólfs saga kraka*', in Jan Erik Rekdal and Charles Doherty (eds), *Kings and Warriors in Early North-West Europe*, 180–236, Dublin: Four Courts Press.

O'Connor, Ralph (2022), '*Scélśenchus* Revisited: Historical Function and Literary Artistry in the Gaelic Kings' Sagas', in Kevin Murray (ed.), *Revisiting the Cycles of the Kings*, 1–24, Cork Studies in Celtic Lireratures 6, Cork: CSCL Publications.

O'Connor, Ralph (2023), *The Music of What Happens: Narrative Terminology and the Gaelic and Norse-Icelandic Saga*, E. C. Quiggin Memorial Lectures, 23, Cambridge: Department of Anglo-Saxon, Norse and Celtic, University of Cambridge.

O'Connor, Ralph (2024, forthcoming), 'The Semantics of *scél* and the Truth of Stories in Mediaeval Gaelic Culture', in Alice Taylor-Griffiths and Seosamh Mac Cárthaigh (eds), *Storytelling in Gaelic Literature from 700 AD to the Present*, Studies in Celtic History, Cambridge: D. S. Brewer.

O'Daly, Máirín (1960), 'On the Origin of Tara', *Celtica*, 5: 186–91.

O'Daly, Máirín (1975), *Cath Maige Mucrama*, Irish Texts Society Vol. 50, London: Irish Texts Society.

O'Grady, Standish Hayes (1892), *Silva Gadelica: A Selection of Tales in Irish*, London: Williams and Norgate.

O'Grady, Standish Hayes (1929), *Caithréim Thoirdhealbhaigh: The Triumphs of Turlough*, Irish Texts Society Vols 1–2, London: Irish Texts Society.

O'Hara, James J. (1997), 'Virgil's Style', in Charles Martindale (ed.), *The Cambridge Companion to Virgil*, 241–58, Cambridge: Cambridge University Press.

O'Hogan, Cillian (2014), 'Reading Lucan with Scholia in Medieval Ireland: *In Cath Catharda* and its Sources', *Cambrian Medieval Celtic Studies*, 68: 21–50.

O'Hogan, Cillian (2020), 'Classics, Medievalism, and Cultural Politics in Myles na gCopaleen's *Cruiskeen Lawn* Columns', in Isabelle Torrance and Donncha O'Rourke (eds), *Classics and Irish Politics, 1916–2016*, 156–70, Oxford: Oxford University Press.

O'Keeffe, J. G. (1913), *Buile Shuibhne: The Frenzy of Suibhne*, Irish Texts Society Vol. 12, London: Irish Texts Society.

O'Rahilly, Cecile (1967), *Táin Bó Cúalnge from the Book of Leinster*, Dublin: Dublin Institute for Advanced Studies.

O'Rahilly, Cecile (1976a), *Táin Bó Cúailnge: Recension I*, Dublin: Dublin Institute for Advanced Studies.

O'Rahilly, Cecile (1976b), 'Cathcharpat serda', *Celtica*, 11: 194–202.

O'Rahilly, Thomas F. (1957), *Early Irish History and Mythology*, Dublin: Dublin Institute for Advanced Studies.

O'Sullivan, Sinéad (2016), 'Servius in the Carolingian Age: a Case Study of London, British Library, Harley 2782', *Journal of Medieval Latin*, 26: 77–123.

O'Sullivan, Sinéad (2018), 'Glossing Vergil and Pagan Learning in the Carolingian Age', *Speculum*, 93: 132–65.

O'Sullivan, Sinéad (2021), 'The Practice of "Alignment" in Medieval Ireland', in Scott Bruce (ed.), *Litterarum Dulces Fructus: Studies in Honour of Michael Herren*, 355–84, Instrumenta Patristica et Mediaevalia 85, Turnhout: Brepols.

Oldfather, C. H. (1933–67), *Diodorus of Sicily*, 12 vols, Loeb Classical Library, Cambridge, Mass.: Harvard University Press.

Oschema, Klaus (2017), 'An Irish Making of Europe (Early and High Middle Ages)', in Wolfram R. Keller and Dagmar Schlüter (eds), *'A Fantastic and Abstruse Latinity?' Hiberno-Continental Cultural and Literary Interactions in the Middle Ages*, 12–30, Münster: Nodus.

Oskamp, H. A. (1972), 'The First Twelve Folia of Rawlinson B 502', *Ériu*, 23: 56–72.

Otis, Brooks (1963), *Virgil: A Study in Civilized Poetry*, Oxford: Oxford University Press.

Palandri, Andrea (2018), *A Study of the Irish Adaptation of Marco Polo's* Travels *from the Book of Lismore*, PhD diss., University College Cork.

Palandri, Andrea (2019), 'The Irish Adaptation of Marco Polo's Travels: Mapping the Route to Ireland', *Ériu*, 69: 127–54.

Pavlyshyn, Marko (1985), 'The Rhetoric and Politics of Kotliarevsky's *Eneida*', *Journal of Ukrainian Studies*, 10.1: 9–24.

Pepin, Ronald E. (2008), *The Vatican Mythographers*, New York: Fordham University Press.

Peters, Erik (1967), 'Die Irische Alexandersage', *Zeitschrift für celtische Philologie*, 30: 71–264.

Pichette, Jean-Pierre (1991), *L'Observance des conseils du maître*, Folklore Fellows Communications 250, Helsinki: Academia Scientiarum Fennica.

Pinkernell, G. (1971), *Raoul LeFevre: L'Histoire de Jason*, Frankfurt: Athenäum.

Poppe, Erich (1992), 'The Early Modern Irish Version of Beves of Hamtoun', *Cambridge Medieval Celtic Studies*, 23: 77–98.

Poppe, Erich (1995), *A New Introduction to Imtheachta Aeniasa, The Irish Aeneid: The Classical Epic from an Irish Perspective*, Irish Texts Society Subsidiary Series 3, London: Irish Texts Society.

Poppe, Erich (1997), '*Stair Nuadat Find Femin*: eine irische Romanze?', *Zeitschrift für celtische Philologie*, 49/50: 749–59.

Poppe, Erich (2002), 'The Latin Quotations in *Auraicept na nÉces*: Microtexts and their Transmission', in Próinséas Ní Chatháin and Michael Richter (eds), *Ireland and Europe in the Early Middle Ages: Texts and Transmission/ Irland und Europa im früheren Mittelalter: Texte und Überlieferung*, 296–312, Dublin: Four Courts.

Poppe, Erich (2004a), '*Imtheachta Aeniasa*: Virgil's *Aeneid* in Medieval Ireland', *Classics Ireland* 11: 74–94.

Poppe, Erich (2004b), 'A Virgilian Model for *lúirech thredúalach*?', *Ériu*, 54: 171–7.

Poppe, Erich (2005), 'Narrative Structure of Medieval Irish Adaptations: the Case of *Guy* and *Beues*', in Helen Fulton (ed.), *Medieval Celtic Literature and Society*, 205–29, Dublin: Four Courts.

Poppe, Erich (2006), '*Stair Ercuil ocus a Bás*: Rewriting Hercules in Ireland', in K. Murray (ed.), *Translations from Classical Literature*: Imtheachta Aenasa *and* Stair Ercuil ocus a Bás, 37–68, Irish Texts Society Subsidiary Series 17, London: Irish Texts Society.

Poppe, Erich (2008), *Of Cycles and Other Critical Matters: Some Issues in Medieval Irish Literary History and Criticism*, Quiggin Memorial Lecture 9, Cambridge: Department of Anglo-Saxon, Norse and Celtic.

Poppe, Erich (2009), 'The Matter of Troy and Insular Versions of Dares's *De Excidio Troiae Historia*: an Exercise in Historical Typology', *Beiträge zur Geschichte der Sprachwissenschaft* 19: 253–98.

Poppe, Erich (2014a), 'Narrative History and Cultural Memory in Medieval Ireland: Some Preliminary Thoughts', in Jan Erik Rekdal and Erich Poppe (eds), *Medieval Irish Perspectives on Cultural Memory*, 135–76, Münster: Nodus.

Poppe, Erich (2014b), '*Imtheachta Aeniasa* and Its Place in Medieval Irish Textual History', in Ralph O'Connor (ed.), *Classical Literature and Learning in Medieval Irish Narrative*, 25–39, Studies in Celtic History 34, Cambridge: D. S. Brewer.

Poppe, Erich (2015), 'Scholia: a Medieval Learned Background to *In Cath Catharda*', in Guillaume Oudaer, Gaël Hily, and Herve Le Bihan (eds), *Mélanges en l'honneur de Pierre-Yves Lambert*, 431–9, Rennes: Tir.

Poppe, Erich (2016a), 'Lucan's *Bellum Civile* in Ireland: Structure and Sources', *Studia Hibernica*, 42: 97–120.

Poppe, Erich (2016b), 'The Epic Styles of *In Cath Catharda*: *imitatio, amplificatio*, and *aemulatio*', in Axel Harlos and Neele Harlos (eds), *Adapting Texts and Styles in a Celtic Context, Interdisciplinary Perspectives on Processes of Literary Transfer in the Middle Ages: Studies in Honour of Erich Poppe*, Studien und Texte zur Keltologie 13, 1–20, Münster: Nodus.

Poppe, Erich (2023), '*Imtheachta Aeniasa*'s *lúirecha* Re-visited', *Ériu*, 73: 89–96.

Poppe, Erich and Dagmar Schlüter (2011), 'Greece, Ireland, Ulster, and Troy: of Hybrid Origins and Heroes', in Wendy Marie Hoofnagle and Wolfram R. Keller (eds), *Other Nations: The Hybridization of Insular Mythology and Identity*, 127–43, Heidelberg: Winter.

Punzi, Arianna (1990), 'I volgarizzamenti della *Tebaide* nella cultura romanza ed in quella irlandese', *Cultura Neolatina* 1: 7–43.

Quin, Gordon (1939), *Stair Ercuil ocus a Bás: The Life and Death of Hercules*, Irish Texts Society Vol. 38, Dublin: Irish Texts Society.

Raby, F. J. E. (1934), *A History of Secular Latin Poetry in the Middle Ages*, Vol. 1, Oxford: Oxford University Press.

Rackham, H., D. E. Eichholz and W. H. S. Jones (1938–62), *Pliny: Natural History*, 10 vols, Loeb Classical Library, Cambridge, Mass.: Harvard University Press.

Radner, Joan (1978), *Fragmentary Annals of Ireland*, Dublin: Dublin Institute for Advanced Studies.

Radner, Joan (1982), 'Fury Destroys the World: Historical Strategy in Ireland's Ulster Cycle', *Mankind Quarterly*, 23.1: 41–60.

Robinson, F. (1908), 'The Irish Lives of Guy of Warwick and Bevis of Hampton', *Zeitschrift für celtische Philologie*, 6: 9–180, 273–338.

Roche, Paul (2009), *Lucan: De Bello Ciuili Book 1*, Oxford: Oxford University Press.

Roelofs, M. F. and P. R. J. Groos (2007), *Van Μέγας Ἀλέξανδρος tot Alaxandar Mór*, PhD diss., University of Utrecht.

Ross, Bianca (1989), *Bildungsidol, Ritter, Held: Herkules bei William Caxton und Uilliam Mac an Lega*, Heidelberg: Winter.

Ross, Bianca (1995–7), 'The Transformation of Non-Irish Narratives into an Irish Context: Uilliam Mac an Lega's Early Modern Irish Adaptation of the Story of Hercules', *Studia Hibernica*, 29: 185–93.

Ross, D. J. A. (1963), *Alexander Historiatus: A Guide to Medieval Illustrated Alexander Literature*, London: Warburg Institute.

Rubenstein, Jay (2019), *Nebuchadnezzar's Dream: The Crusades, Apocalyptic Prophecy and the End of History*, Oxford: Oxford University Press.

Rudolph, Conrad (2014), *The Mystic Ark: Hugh of Saint Victor, Art, and Thought in the Twelfth Century*, Cambridge: Cambridge University Press.

Runge, Roan M. (2020), *The Colloquy of Fintan and the Hawk of Achill*, online edition available at https://www.ambf.co.uk/fintan. Last accessed for this volume 30 December 2022.

Sanford, Eva Matthews (1934), 'The Manuscripts of Lucan: *accessus* and *marginalia*', *Speculum* 9: 278–95.

Sayers, William (1996), 'Homeric Echoes in *Táin Bó Cúailnge*?', *Emania* 14: 65–73.

Scaffai, M. (1997), *Ilias Latina: Introduzione, edizione critica, tradiuzione italiana e commento*, 2nd edn, Bologna: Patròn.

Schiller, Gertrud (1972), *Iconography of Christian Art: Vol. 2*, Translated by Jane Seligman, London: Lund Humphries.

Schlüter, Dagmar (2010), *History or Fable? The Book of Leinster as a Document of Cultural Memory in Twelfth-Century Ireland*, Münster: Nodus.

Schmidt, Jürgen (2009), 'Zu Réidig dam a Dé do nim/ co hémidh a n-indisin', in Gisbert Hemprich (ed.), *Festgabe für Hildegard L. C. Tristram*, 211–87, Berlin: Curach Bhán.

Schmidt, Karl Horst (1960–1), 'Boí rí amrae for Laignib, Mac Dathó a ainm', *Zeitschrift für celtische Philologie*, 28: 224–34.

Schmidt, Moritz (1866), 'Ein Scholion zum Statius', *Philologus*, 23: 541–7.

Schöne, Alfred (1900), *Die Weltchronik des Eusebius in ihrer Bearbeitung durch Hieronymus*, Berlin: Weidmannsche Buchandlung.

Scowcroft, R. Mark (1987), '*Leabhar Gabhála* Part I: the Growth of the Text', *Ériu*, 38: 81–140.

Scowcroft, R. Mark (1988), '*Leabhar Gabhála* Part II: the Growth of the Tradition', *Ériu*, 39: 1–66.

Scowcroft, R. Mark (2009), 'Medieval Recensions of the *Lebor Gabála*', in John Carey (ed.), *Lebor Gabála Érenn: Textual History and Pseudohistory*, 1–20, Irish Texts Society Subsidiary Series 20, London: Irish Texts Society.

Sfyroeras, Pavlos (2014), 'Like Purple on Ivory: a Homeric Simile in Statius' *Achilleid*', in Antony Augoustakis (ed.), *Flavian Poetry and its Greek Past*, 235–48, Leiden: Brill.

Shackleton Bailey, David Roy (2003), *Statius: Thebaid and Achilleid*, 2 vols, Loeb Classical Library, Cambridge, Mass.: Harvard University Press.

Sharpe, Richard (2010), 'Books from Ireland, Fifth to Ninth Centuries', *Peritia*, 21: 1–55.

Shimahara, Sumi (2008), 'Daniel et les visions politiques à l'époque Carolingienne', *Études Médiévales*, 55: 19–31.

Sicard, Patrice (2001), *Hugo de Santo Victore opera: De archa Noe. Libellus de formatione*, Corpus Christianorum Continuatio Mediaevalis 176, Turnhout: Brepols.

Simms, Katharine (2013), 'Foreign Apologues in Bardic Poetry', in Seán Duffy and Susan Foran (eds), *The English Isles: Cultural Transmission and Political Conflict in Britain and Ireland 1150–1500*, 139–50, Dublin: Four Courts Press.

Sims-Williams, Patrick and Erich Poppe (2005), 'Medieval Irish Literary Theory and Criticism', in A. Minnis and I. Johnson (eds), *The Cambridge History of Literary Criticism, Vol 2: The Middle Ages*, 289–309, Cambridge: Cambridge University Press.

Slotkin, Edgar M. (1978–9), 'Medieval Irish Scribes and Fixed Texts', *Éigse*, 17: 437–50.

Smith, Peter (2002), 'Early Irish Historical Verse: the Evolution of a Genre', in Próinséas Ní Chatháin and Michael Richter (eds), *Ireland and Europe in the Early Middle Ages: Texts and Transmission/ Irland und Europa im früheren Mittelalter: Texte und Überlieferung*, 326–41, Dublin: Four Courts Press.

Smith, Peter J. (2007), *Three Historical Poems Ascribed to Gilla Cóemáin: A Critical Edition of the Work of an Eleventh-Century Irish Scholar*, Münster: Nodus.

Smith, Peter J. (2015), 'An Edition of *Tigernmas mac Follaig aird*', in Emer Purcell, Paul MacCotter, Julianne Nyhan, and John Sheehan (eds), *Clerics, Kings and Vikings: Essays on Medieval Ireland in Honour of Donnchadh Ó Corráin*, 458–76, Dublin: Four Courts Press.

Smith, Peter J. (2016), 'Eochaid Úa Flainn's *Éitset áes ecna aíbind* and Medieval Irish Poetics', in Axel Harlos and Neele Harlos (eds), *Adapting Texts and Styles in a Celtic Context, Interdisciplinary Perspectives on Processes of Literary Transfer in the Middle*

Ages: Studies in Honour of Erich Poppe, Studien und Texte zur Keltologie 13, 21–52, Münster: Nodus.

Smith, R. Scott and Stephen M. Trzaskoma (2007), *Apollodorus' Library and Hyginus' Fabulae: Two Handbooks of Greek Mythology*, Indianapolis: Hackett.

Solomon, Jon (2007), 'The Vacillations of the Trojan Myth: Popularization and Classicization, Variation and Codification', *International Journal of the Classical Tradition*, 14: 482–534.

Sommer, O. (1894), *The Recuyell of the Historyes of Troye, written in French by Raoul Lefevre, Translated and printed by William Caxton (about A.D. 1474)*, London: David Nutt.

Sommerfelt, Alf (1915–23), 'Le Système verbal dans *In Cath Catharda*', *Revue Celtique*, 36 (1915–16): 23–62; 38 (1920–1): 295–357; 40 (1923): 157–69.

Sommerstein, Anthony H. (2008), *Aeschylus*, 3 vols, Loeb Classical Library, Cambridge, Mass.: Harvard University Press.

Spiegel, Gabrielle (2002), 'Historical Thought in Medieval Europe', in Lloyd Kramer and Sarah Maza (eds), *A Companion to Western Historical Thought*, 78–97, Malden, Mass. Blackwell.

Squire, Aelred, O.P. (1962), *Hugh of Saint Victor: Selected Spiritual Writings*, London: Faber and Faber.

Stanford, William Bedell (1968), *The Ulysses Theme: A Study in the Adaptability of a Traditional Hero*, Ann Arbor, Mich.: University of Michigan Press.

Stanford, William Bedell (1970), 'Towards a History of Classical Influences in Ireland', *Proceedings of the Royal Irish Academy*, 70 C 3: 13–91.

Stanford, William Bedell (1976a), 'Monsters and Odyssean Echoes in the Early Hiberno-Latin and Irish Hymns,' in J. J. O'Meara and Bernd Nauman (eds), *Latin Script and Letters A. D. 400–900: Festschrift Presented to Ludwig Bieler on the Occasion of his 70th Birthday*, 113–20, Leiden: E. J. Brill.

Stanford, William Bedell (1976b), *Ireland and the Classical Tradition*. Dublin: Allen Figgis.

Stansbury, Mark (2016), 'Irish Biblical Exegesis', in Roy Flechner and Sven Meeder (eds), *The Irish in Early Medieval Europe: Identity, Culture and Religion*, 116–30, London: Palgrave Macmillan.

Steinmann, Marc (2012), *Alexander der Große und die 'nackten Weisen' Indiens*, Berlin: Frank und Timme.

Stern, Joseph (1996), *Palaephatus: On Unbelievable Tales*, Wauconda, Illinois: Bolchazy-Carducci.

Stifter, David (2006), *Sengoidelc: Old Irish for Beginners*, New York: Syracuse University Press.

Stifter, David (2009), 'Early Irish', in Martin J. Ball and Nicole Müller (eds), *The Celtic Languages*, 2nd edn, 55–116, London: Routledge.

Stohlmann, J. (1968), *Anonymi historia Daretis Frigii*, Untersuchungen und kritische Ausgabe, Mittellateinisches Jahrbuch, Beiheft 1, Wuppertal: Henn.

Stokes, Whitley (1881), *Togail Troí: The Destruction of Troy from the Facsimile of the Book of Leinster*, Calcutta.

Stokes, Whitley (1884), 'The Destruction of Troy, aus H.2.17', in Whitley Stokes and Ernst Windisch, *Irische Texte mit Wörterbuch*, Vol 2.1: 1–141, Leipzig: Hirzel.

Stokes, Whitley (1892), 'The Bodleian *Dinnshenchas*', *Folk-Lore*, 3: 467–516.

Stokes, Whitley (1894–95), 'The Prose Tales in the Rennes Dindshenchas', *Revue Celtique*, 15 (1894): 272–336, 418–84; 16 (1895): 31–83, 135–67, 269–312, 468.

Stokes, Whitley (1895), 'The Annals of Tigernach: the Fragment in Rawlinson B.502', *Revue Celtique*, 16: 374–419.

Stokes, Whitley (1896a), 'The Annals of Tigernach. Second Fragment. A.D. 143–A.D. 361 (Rawl. B. 488, Fo. 4ᵃ 2.)', *Revue Celtique*, 17: 6–33.

Stokes, Whitley (1896b), 'The Annals of Tigernach. Third Fragment. A.D. 489–766. Rawl. B. 482, ff. 7ᵃ 1–14ᵇ 2', *Revue Celtique*, 17: 119–263.

Stokes, Whitley (1900a), 'Acallam na Senórach', in Whitley Stokes and Ernst Windisch, *Irische Texte mit Wörterbuch*, Vol. 4: 1–438, Leipzig: Hirzel.

Stokes, Whitley (1900b), 'O'Mulconry's Glossary', *Archiv für celtische Lexikographie*, 1: 232–324, 473–81, 629.

Stokes, Whitley (1903), 'The Battle of Allen', *Revue Celtique*, 24: 41–70, 466.

Stokes, Whitley (1904a), 'Tidings of the Resurrection', *Revue Celtique*, 25: 234–59.

Stokes, Whitley (1904b), 'O'Davoren's Glossary', *Archiv für celtische Lexikographie*, 2: 197–504.

Stokes, Whitley (1909), 'In Cath Catharda: the Civil War of the Romans', in Whitley Stokes and Ernst Windisch, *Irische Texte mit Wörterbuch*, Vol. 4.2, Leipzig: Hirzel.

Stokes, Whitley and John Strachan (1901–3), *Thesaurus Palaeohibernicus*, 2 vols, Cambridge: Cambridge University Press.

Stone, Brian (2022), *The Rhetorical Arts in Late Antique and Early Medieval Ireland*, Amsterdam: Amsterdam University Press.

Stokes, Whitley and Ernst Windisch (1880–1909), *Irische Texte mit Wörterbuch*, 4 vols forming 6 parts in all, Leipzig: Halle.

Stone, Charles Russell (2013), *From Tyrant to Philosopher-King: A Literary History of Alexander the Great in Medieval and Early Modern England*, Turnhout: Brepols.

Stoneman, Richard (2008), *Alexander the Great: A Life in Legend*, New Haven, Conn.: Yale University Press.

Sweeney, Robert Dale (1997), *Lactantii Placidi in Statii Thebaida Commentum Volumen I, Anonymi in Statii Achilleida Commentum, Fulgentii ut fingitur Planciadis super Thebaiden Commentariolum*, Biblioteca Scriptorum Graecorum et Romanorum Teubneriana, Stuttgart: Teubner.

Szerwiniack, Olivier (2018), 'Le Mythe de Troie en Irlande au Moyen Âge: *Togail Troí* et ses recensions', *Troianalexandrina*, 18: 101–25.

Taranu, Catalin, and Ralph O'Connor (2022), 'Introduction: *Vera Lex Historiae*?', in Catalin Taranu and Michael J. Kelly (eds), *Vera Lex Historiae? Constructions of Truth in Medieval Historical Narrative*, 35–74, New York: Gracchi.

Tavoni, Mirko (2011), 'De vulgari eloquentia', in Marco Santagata (ed.), *Dante Alighieri. Opere*, Vol. 1, 1067–1547, Milan: Mondadori.

Teeuwen, Mariken (2003), *The Vocabulary of Intellectual Life in the Middle Ages*, Turnhout: Brepols.

Theuerkauf, Marie-Luise (2017), 'The Death of Boand and the Recensions of *Dindshenchas Érenn*', *Ériu*, 67: 49–97.

Theuerkauf, Marie-Luise (2023), *Dindshenchas Érenn*, Cork Studies in Celtic Literatures 7, Cork: CSCL Publications.

Thiel, Matthias (1973), *Grundlagen und Gestalt der Hebräischkenntnisse des frühen Mittelalters*, Spoleto: Centro Italiano di Studi sull'Alto Medioevo.

Thilo, G. and H. Hagen (1881–1902), *Servii Grammatici qui feruntur in Vergilii carmina commentarii*, 3 vols forming 4 parts in all, Leipzig: Teubner.

Þorbjörg Helgadóttir (2010), *Rómverja saga*, 2 vols, Reykjavík: Stofnun Árna Magnússonar.

Thurneysen, Rudolf (1915), 'Flann Manistrechs Gedicht: *Rédig dam, a Dé do nim, co hémig a n-innisin*', *Zeitschrift für Celtische Philologie*, 10: 269–73.

Thurneysen, Rudolf (1920/1), '*Tochmarc Ailbe* (Das Werben um Ailbe)', *Zeitschrift für Celtische Philologie*, 13: 251–82.

Thurneysen, Rudolf (1928a), '*Auraicept na n-éces*', *Zeitschrift für Celtische Philologie*, 17: 277–303.

Thurneysen, Rudolf (1928b), 'Review of *Togail na Tebe: The Thebaid of Statius, the Irish Text* ed. and trans. by George Calder', *Zeitschrift für Celtische Philologie*, 17: 420–21.

Thurneysen, Rudolf (1935), *Scéla Mucce Meic Dathó*, Medieval and Modern Irish Series 6, Dublin: Dublin Institute for Advanced Studies.

Thurneysen, Rudolf (1975), *A Grammar of Old Irish with Supplement*, translated by D. A. Binchy and O. Bergin, with Supplement, Dublin: Dublin Institute for Advanced Studies.

Todd, James Henthorn (1848), *Leabhar Breathnach annso sis: The Irish Version of the Historia Britonum of Nennius*, Dublin: Irish Archaeological Society.

Todd, James Henthorn (1867), *Cogadh Gaedhel re Gallaibh: The War of the Gaedhil with the Gaill, or the Invasions of Ireland by the Danes and Other Norsemen*, Rolls Series 48, London: Longmans.

Toner, G. (2000), 'The Ulster Cycle: Historiography or Fiction?', *Cambrian Medieval Celtic Studies*, 40: 1–20.

Toner, Gregory (2005), 'Authority, Verse and the Transmission of *senchas*', *Ériu*, 55: 59–84.

Torrance, Isabelle (2022), 'Rewriting *Hippolytus*: Hybridity, Posthumanism, and Social Politics in Marina Carr's *Phaedra Backwards*', *Arethusa* 55: 229–44.

Torrance, Isabelle, and Donncha O'Rourke (2020), 'Classics and Irish Politics: Introduction' in Isabelle Torrance and Donncha O'Rourke (eds), *Classics and Irish Politics, 1916–2016*, 1–23, Oxford: Oxford University Press.

Tosi, Renzo (2014), 'The History of Corpora Scholiastica: a Series of Unfortunate Events', *Trends in Classics*, 6: 15–23.

Tristram, Hildegard L. C. (1985), *Sex Aetates Mundi, Die Weltzeitalter bei den Angelsachsen und den Iren: Untersuchungen und Texte*, Heidelberg: Winter.

Tristram, Hildegard L.C. (1989), 'Der insulare Alexander', in Willi Erzgräber (ed.), *Kontinuität und Transformation der Antike im Mittelalter*, 129–55, Sigmaringen: Thorbecke.

Tristram, Hildegard L.C. (1990), 'More Talk of Alexander', *Celtica*, 21: 658–63.

Tristram, Hildegard L. C. (1995), 'The "Cattle-Raid of Cuailnge" in Tension and Transition between the Oral and the Written: Classical Subtexts and Narrative Heritage', in Doris Edel (ed.), *Cultural Identity and Cultural Integration: Ireland and Europe in the Early Middle Ages*, 61–81, Dublin: Four Courts Press.

Tristram, Hildegard L. C. (1997), 'Latin Learning in the *Táin Bó Cuailnge*', *Zeitschrift für celtische Philologie*, 50: 847–77.

Tyler, Elizabeth (2012), 'Trojans in Anglo-Saxon England: Precedent without Descent', *Review of English Studies*, 64. 263: 1–20.

Usener, Hermann (1869), *M. Annaei Lucani Commenta Bernensia*, Leipzig: Teubner.

Uther, Hans-Jörg (2004), *The Types of International Folktales: A Classification and Bibliography*, 3 vols, Folklore Fellows Communications, 133–6, Helsinki: Academia Scientiarum Fennica.

Van Hamel, A. G. (1915), 'On *Lebor Gabála*', *Zeitschrift für celtische Philologie*, 10: 97–197.

Van Hamel, A. G. (1932), *Lebor Bretnach: The Irish Version of the Historia Britonum Ascribed to Nennius*, Dublin: The Stationery Office.

Van Hamel, A. G. (1933), *Compert Con Culainn and Other Stories*, Mediaeval and Modern Irish Series 3, Dublin: Dublin Institute for Advanced Studies.

Vasunia, Phiroze (2013), *The Classics and Colonial India*, Oxford: Oxford University Press.

Wadden, Patrick (2016a), 'The Frankish Table of Nations in Insular Historiography', *Cambrian Medieval Celtic Studies*, 72: 1–31.

Wadden, Patrick (2016b), 'The Pseudo-historical Origins of the *Senchas Már* and Royal Legislation in Early Ireland', *Peritia*, 27: 141–58.

Wallis, Faith (1999), *Bede: The Reckoning of Time*, Translated Texts for Historians 29, Liverpool: Liverpool University Press.

Warntjes, Immo (2011), 'Irische Komputistik zwischen Isidor von Sevilla und Beda Venerabilis: Ursprung, karolingische Rezeption und generelle Forschungsperspektiven', *Viator*, 42: 1–32.

Watson, J. Carmichael (1941), *Mesca Ulad*, Medieval and Modern Irish Series 13, Dublin: Dublin Institute for Advanced Studies.

Watson, Daniel (2019), *Philosophy in Early Medieval Ireland: Nature, Hierarchy and Inspiration*, PhD diss., Maynooth University.

Watson, Daniel (2020), 'The Mortal and Divine Histories of Mongán mac Fiachna in *Cín Dromma Snechtai*', *Celtica*, 32: 27–75.

Werner, Shirley (1994), 'On the History of the *Commenta Bernensia* and the *Adnotationes Super Lucanum*', *Harvard Studies in Classical Philology*, 96: 343–68.

Werner, Shirley (1998), *The Transmission and Scholia to Lucan's Bellum Civile*,
    Münsteraner Beiträge zur klassischen Philologie 5, Hamburg: Lit.
Williams, Mark (2015), *Ireland's Immortals: A History of the Gods of Irish Myth*,
    Princeton: Princeton University Press.
Windisch, Ernst (1905), *Die altirische Heldensage Táin Bó Cúalnge nach dem Buch von
    Leinster*, Leipzig: Hirzel.
Woods, Marjorie Currie (2019), *Weeping for Dido: The Classics in the Medieval
    Classroom*, Princeton: Princeton University Press.
Würth, Stefanie (1998), *Der 'Antikenroman' in der isländischen Literatur des Mittelalters:
    Eine Untersuchung zur Übersetzung und Rezeption lateinischer Literatur im Norden*,
    Basel: Helbing und Lichtenhahn.
Würth, Stefanie (2006), 'The Common Transmission of *Trójumanna saga* and *Breta
    sögur*', in A. N. Doane and Kirsten Wolf (eds), *Beatus Vir: Studies in Early English and
    Norse Manuscripts in Memory of Phillip Pulsiano*, 297–327, Tempe, Arizona: ACMRS.
Ziolkowski, Jan M. and M. C. J. Putnam (2008) (eds), *The Virgilian Tradition: The First
    Fifteen Hundred Years*, New Haven, Conn.: Yale University Press.
Zupitza, Julius (1880), *Ælfrics Grammatik und Glossar*, Berlin: Weidmannsche
    Buchhandlung.
Zuwiyya, David (2011) (ed.), *A Companion to Alexander Literature in the Middle Ages*,
    Leiden: Brill.

Index

www.ingramcontent.com/pod-product-compliance
Lightning Source LLC
Chambersburg PA
CBHW060302100726
47907CB00002B/245